AUTOCOURSE

CART™

WORLD SERIES

1997-98

HAZLETON PUBLISHING

Race Car.

Your Car.

Same Tough, Beautiful Paint.

Every race car in the PPG CART World Series wears a tough, urethane paint finish supplied by PPG, the world leader in automotive finishes. PPG finishes are also found on the best of today's new cars, minivans and trucks. So if your car ever needs repainting, insist on a PPG finish. It's available at your nearest PPG certified collision repair shop.

The world leader in automotive finishes.

foreword

by Alex Zanardi • 1997 PPG Cup champion

I'm very pleased to have the chance to write the Foreword for the *Autocourse CART Yearbook*. It is traditional for the champion driver to contribute a few words and, since they asked me, that means I won the PPG Cup!

All the fans and supporters of our sport know that the CART series is extremely competitive, and since Reynard joined the series in 1994 it has been tougher than ever. By supplying their customers with a very competitive car they have obliged other manufacturers to improve their product, raising the overall level of competition.

In such a close-fought series, all the members of the Target/Chip Ganassi Racing team can be very proud of our achievement of winning two titles in a row – and with different drivers.

Michael C. Brown

So I wish to congratulate and thank Chip Ganassi, Tom Anderson and Mike Hull for the brilliant job they have done in managing the team, Michael Knight, who, while you're reading this book, is sure to be on the phone organizing my future PR commitments, my engineer Mo Nunn, a legend at the track and a friend to me away from it, Rob Hill and all my boys, who not only gave me a super-reliable car but always made me feel like I would have been their pick even if they had had the choice of a million drivers. Great job, guys!

I must also thank our technical partners, Reynard, Honda and Firestone. It was Rick Gorne and Adrian Reynard who recommended me to Chip. They believed in me when others did not, so I'm happy to have helped win Reynard another Constructors Championship. The Honda engines gave us not only power but fantastic reliability while the Firestone tires were great and definitely played a big part in our success.

Last but not least, I want to thank a special friend, 'Jee-mee' Vasser. He had some bad luck this year, but he has always had a sincere smile for me and there is nobody easier than him to get on well with.

So you! . . . Yes, you, Chip Ganassi! You are very lucky to have two fantastic boys like Jimmy and me, and between us I hope we'll have the opportunity to write for the *Autocourse CART Yearbook* again next year.

Congratulations are in

order for Alex Zanardi, Gil

de Ferran and Jimmy Vasser.

Literally. The Honda trio

finished one, two, three in the

race for the 1997 PPG Cup Driver's Championship.

Zanardi, the newly crowned PPG Cup king with

195 points, continued his PPG CART World Series

record run for consecutive poles from last year. With

poles at Miami and Australia, he established a new

record at six. Not to mention capturing two more later

in the season, which is when he really started to heat

up. In all, Zanardi captured five wins to take the crown

from reigning champion and Target/Chip Ganassi

teammate, Jimmy Vasser.

Vasser, by the way, was no

slouch, finishing third in the

PPG Cup race with 144 points.

Jimmy won big at Laguna

Seca and collected second-place trips to the podium in

Vancouver and Fontana, as well as two third-place finishes. Mr. Consistency also used his Honda power to its utmost, finishing third in miles completed.

Not to be outdone, Gil de Ferran and his Valvoline/ Cummins Special kept things in the Honda family by completing the second-most miles. Gil and his team-mates at Walker Racing also finished second overall in the race for the PPG Cup crown, and gave Zanardi one

heck of a run for his money with 162 points. De Ferran raced to the podium seven times, finish-ing second twice, and garnering five third-place trophies.

At Honda, we've always said our toughest com-petition is ourselves. We just didn't think these guys would take us so literally. Congratulations to all our drivers and teams. The race for the 1997 PPG Cup was very competitive to say the least. Just about any Honda-powered driver could have taken it.

HONDA

STREETS AHEAD

HOW intense was the competition in the 1997 PPG CART World Series? Consider this: Seven of the 17 races, which averaged 231.927 miles in length, were decided by less than one second. Only two events saw the top finishers separated by more than five seconds. (And to answer any skeptics, just one, at Nazareth, finished under caution. In fact, the average length of uninterrupted green-flag racing prior to the checkered flag was 32 laps.)

The statistics do not lie. The 1997

PPG Cup season featured some sensational racing action from beginning to end. There were myriad highlights, of which the most widely publicized was a spectacular battle to the finish line at Portland International Raceway in June, when Mark Blundell embellished the memory of his maiden CART victory – and the first for the PacWest Racing Group – by speeding beneath CART Starter Jim Swintal's twin checkered flags a scant 0.027 seconds in front of Gil de Ferran. The margin equated to less than the length of his

Reynard's nosecone. It was the closest finish in CART history, eclipsing the 0.043s differential between Al Unser Jr. and Scott Goodyear at Indianapolis in 1992. Bear in mind, too, that Raul Boesel crossed the line an almost identical distance behind de Ferran in third place!

A total of 16 drivers earned at least one podium finish, and no fewer than a dozen claimed the honor either of a pole or a race victory (or both). Blundell, PacWest teammate Mauricio Gugelmin and Greg Moore all visited

Victory Lane for the first time in their CART careers.

As further proof of the burgeoning quality of the competition, exactly half of the 28 drivers who assembled for the final round at California Speedway had previously garnered a CART victory. And of the top 20 PPG Cup point scorers, only four (Blundell, Ribeiro, Salles and, ironically, Zanardi) could not boast a major championship title prior to the beginning of the season. Now make that three. Arguably, no other series can boast such strength in

CART goes from strength to strength, drawing bigger and bigger crowds with close and exciting racing at venues ranging from street circuits like Toronto *(left)* to the magnificent California Speedway at Fontana *(bottom right)*. Adrian Reynard *(below left)* was the big winner in 1997. His chassis proved superior to all challengers and is currently the car to beat.

depth. By comparison, while Formula 1 may remain at the pinnacle of the sport in terms of technological advancement, only seven current F1 drivers have tasted the spoils of victory at the ultimate level.

The competitiveness of the PPG Cup series is equally intense from the point of view of the engine manufacturers, chassis constructors and tire suppliers. Prior to the 1997 season, CART, as part of its on-going bid to minimize the escalation in speeds, mandated a reduction in manifold boost pressure of the 2.65-liter turbocharged motors from 45 inches of mercury to 40 inches on all circuits. (For the previous two years, the cutback had been in effect merely for the superspeedway events at Michigan.) The changes initially resulted in the loss of perhaps 100 horsepower, although constant development soon saw most of that deficit recouped. Even so, by popular opinion, there was little to choose between the Ford/Cosworth, Honda and Mercedes-Benz powerplants. Once again, the facts supported that assertion: in 11 of the 17 races, all three engines led at one stage or another.

Ford/Cosworth's XD displayed the most substantial improvement by comparison with 1996, both in outright horsepower and reliability. Ilmor

In Memoriam

Mike Byrne, 51, congenial and well-respected hospitality specialist for Davis Racing (and previously with Jim Hall Racing), lost his battle with cancer on September 26, 1997. Compounding the loss, his wife of a mere two weeks, Judy, 43, also died just three days later.

James P. Chapman, named by *Indy Car Racing Magazine* as the sport's 'Most Influential Man of the 1980s,' died following a lengthy illness on October 10, 1996. Chapman, 80, was the prototypical public relations practitioner. Born in Charleston, S.C., Chapman began his career as a journalist, became a close friend and confidant of baseball legend Babe Ruth, and founded his own public relations business in 1950. He directed PPG Industries' involvement with the CART series from 1981 to 1992 and played an influential role in the sport's enormous growth during that time-frame.

Gino Gagliano, 40, who entered the PPG CART World Series under his Nu-Tech Motorsports banner in 1990 and later was involved in a partnership with Dale Coyne, died in an industrial accident in his hometown of Detroit on October 28, 1996.

Eddie Kuzma, a legendary self-taught engineer who built a string of highly

successful front-engined Indy car 'roadsters' in the 1950s, died at the age of 85. Many of the top names in the sport won races in Kuzma-built cars, including Mario Andretti, Jimmy Bryan, Duane Carter, A.J. Foyt, Troy Ruttman and Eddie Sachs.

Troy Ruttman passed away on May 19, 1997 after a lengthy illness. Ruttman was only 19, two years below the minimum age requirement, when he raced at Indianapolis for the first time in 1949, having 'borrowed' his cousin's birth certificate. Three years later he became the youngest ever winner of the Indy 500, guiding J.C. Agajanian's Offy-engined 'upright' Kuzma dirt car to victory.

Pete Weismann, a true character as well as a pioneer in the development of auto racing transmissions (especially of the transverse genre) through his Traction Products company, died after a short illness on November 22, 1996. Weismann was 63.

Charlie Wright, 39, widely admired and hugely popular driver of Honda's hospitality coach on the CART circuit, died suddenly of a heart attack while racing karts with his friends on February 20, 1997. 'Good-time Charlie' had just set the fastest lap of the day!

Engineering's Mercedes IC108D perhaps offered the most compliant characteristics so far as the drivers were concerned. And while most pundits reckoned the latest Honda HRR might have lacked a little in terms of horsepower, it made up for any minor deficiency with awesome reliability. In the final reckoning, Honda drivers claimed the top three positions in the PPG Cup points table and Mercedes took the coveted CART Manufacturers Championship for the first time. Each of the three automobile giants now has one title to its credit.

Toyota, unquestionably, still lagged behind the acknowledged 'Big Three'

at season's end, yet its quest to make up ground had been hindered by a serious fire at its Aisen Seiki plant in Japan. Nevertheless, progress was apparent. The latest RV8B motor displayed improved characteristics toward the end of the season, while Toyota affirmed the seriousness of its intentions by hiring some high-quality personnel and expanding the scope of its Japanese involvement. The fruits of its labor are likely to be realized in 1998.

So far as the chassis were concerned, Reynard displayed a clear superiority in '97, leading an impressive 76 percent of the total laps. Nevertheless, the Penske PC26 was at least a match on the short

Photos: Michael C. Brown

Emerson Fittipaldi announces his retirement

Emerson Fittipaldi enjoyed his most successful season in the CART series in 1989 *(right)* when he won the PPG Cup at the wheel of a Patrick Racing-entered Penske PC18-Chevrolet.

ovals, while the newest addition to the fold, Swift Engineering, produced a worthy adversary which won, sensationally, on its debut at Homestead. After a successful 1996 season, Lola Cars suffered a disastrous time in 1997. Its latest T97/00 failed to live up to expectations, and it wasn't until the final race of the year that exhaustive efforts to improve the handling characteristics demonstrated any appreciable breakthrough.

The safety aspects of the various cars were enormously impressive – in line with the constant refinement of CART's rules package, which in 1997 provided for additional padding around the cockpit opening (to protect the driver's head); enhanced resistance of the chassis with regard to puncture damage; and mandatory use of an energy-absorbing seat. Structural integrity was tested by the usual quota of high-impact accidents, and the only serious injury was sustained by Christian Fittipaldi, who suffered a broken leg at Surfers Paradise. Bearing in mind the enormity of Fittipaldi's wreck, the Swift did an outstanding job of minimizing his injuries.

The final, crucial element of the teams' basic equipment package, tires, saw Firestone and Goodyear continue to engage in a battle which had been renewed in 1995 following a cessation of 'hostilities' for some 20 years. Statistically, there didn't seem to be too much between their respective products – at least in the early stages of the

EMERSON Fittipaldi's driving career is officially over. He made the announcement less than a month after sustaining his second serious back injury within the space of just 14 months. The 50-year-old Brazilian, who has two Formula 1 World Championships, one PPG CART World Series title and two Indianapolis 500 victories to his credit, has not raced since suffering spinal injuries in an accident on the opening lap of the 1996 Marlboro 500 at Michigan Speedway. On September 7, he was once again hospitalized with vertebral damage after crashing his ultralight plane in Brazil.

'Last year I received a message from God; this time it was an order,' said Fittipaldi, referring to the suggestion he should perhaps refrain from such precarious activities.

Fittipaldi will be remembered fondly as one of the sport's all-time greats. Few drivers have come close to matching his list of accomplishments, and certainly none with as much flair and class and *joie de vivre*. He remains one of the sport's true gentlemen. He can be infuriating at times – and is almost invariably late for appointments – yet he overcomes any shortcomings with his disarming charm and that characteristic broad, teasing grin.

Fittipaldi accumulated a total of 14 Formula 1 victories as well as 22 PPG Cup race wins, the most recent of which came at Nazareth in 1995. He has enjoyed equal success out of the cockpit and proved to be a magnificent ambassador both for his country and his sport. It was he, after all, who introduced CART to an enthusiastic new audience in South America, and later was responsible for making the Rio de Janeiro event a reality.

Fittipaldi, in time, is expected to make a complete recovery from his injuries. And in between his myriad and varied business interests he has agreed to manage the career of promising 21-year-old countryman Helio Castro-Neves, who finished a close second in the 1997 PPG-Firestone Indy Lights Championship. So much for a peaceful retirement!

season. Only once in 17 races, at Toronto, did one company (Firestone) lead every single lap. Later, though, Firestone established a clear superiority by winning the final 11 races in a row. The Goodyear engineers have pledged to make a comeback in 1998, but they will do so without the assistance of Team Rahal, which committed itself to a switch immediately following the season finale.

'This is not a decision we took light-ly or made hastily,' declared team owner Bobby Rahal. 'It was with a great deal of analysis and consideration, not to mention a fair amount of lost sleep, that we determined to make the move. The overwhelming current competitiveness of this series magnifies the minute advantages that arise from circumstances like the tire war.'

The series played host to a pair of exciting new venues in 1997: Gateway International Raceway, just across the

mighty Mississippi river from St. Louis; and California Speedway, situated in the shadow of the San Gabriel Mountains some 70 miles east of Los Angeles. Both facilities are top-notch, serving important marketplaces and enhancing still further the demographic qualities of the PPG Cup series. Next year the progression will be continued as CART exerts its influence on the Far East for the first time, hosting an event at the magnificent new Twin Ring Motegi oval just north of Tokyo, Japan; and spreads its wings into Texas with an exciting new street course venue in downtown Houston. Additional races, of course, will dictate a heavier burden for the teams, yet the benefits for fans and sponsors alike will be substantial.

Individual race attendances once again reached record levels in 1997, although, curiously, the blossoming interest did not tend to be reflected in the network television ratings. CART President Andrew Craig promised to address that crucial issue, and with the introduction of a new 'lifestyle' show, 'Inside CART,' which airs on Fox Sports, as well as a concerted advertising blitz, positive strides already have been made toward broadening the series' appeal still further. Certainly, in terms of competitiveness, the PPG CART World Series has never been better. And logic suggests that the sport will maintain its upward spiral in 1998.

Jeremy Shaw
Dublin, Ohio
October 1997

1998 PPG CART WORLD SERIES SCHEDULE

March 15	Marlboro Grand Prix of Miami, Metro-Dade Homestead Motorsports Complex, Fla.
March 28	Budweiser 500, Twin Ring Motegi, Japan
April 5	Toyota Grand Prix of Long Beach, Calif.
April 26	Bosch Spark Plug Grand Prix Presented by Toyota, Nazareth Speedway, Pa.
May 10	Rio 400, Emerson Fittipaldi Speedway, Nelson Piquet International Raceway, Rio de Janeiro, Brazil
May 23	Motorola 300, Gateway International Raceway, Madison, Ill.
May 31	Miller 200, The Milwaukee Mile, Wis.
June 7	ITT Automotive Detroit Grand Prix, Mich.
June 21	Budweiser/G.I. Joe's 200 Presented by Texaco Havoline, Portland International Raceway, Ore.
July 12	Medic Drug Grand Prix of Cleveland, Ohio
July 19	Molson Indy Toronto, Ontario, Canada
July 26	U.S. 500 Presented by Toyota, Michigan Speedway, Brooklyn, Mich.
August 9	Miller Lite 200, Mid-Ohio Sports Car Course, Lexington, Ohio
August 16	Texaco/Havoline 200, Road America, Elkhart Lake, Wis.
September 6	Molson Indy Vancouver, B.C., Canada
September 13	Grand Prix of Monterey Presented by Texaco/Havoline, Laguna Seca Raceway, Calif.
October 4	Texaco Grand Prix of Houston, Texas
October 18	IndyCarnival Australia, Surfers Paradise, Queensland, Australia
November 1	Marlboro 500 Presented by Toyota, California Speedway, Fontana, Calif.

Subject to alteration

Face your fears.

Live your dreams.

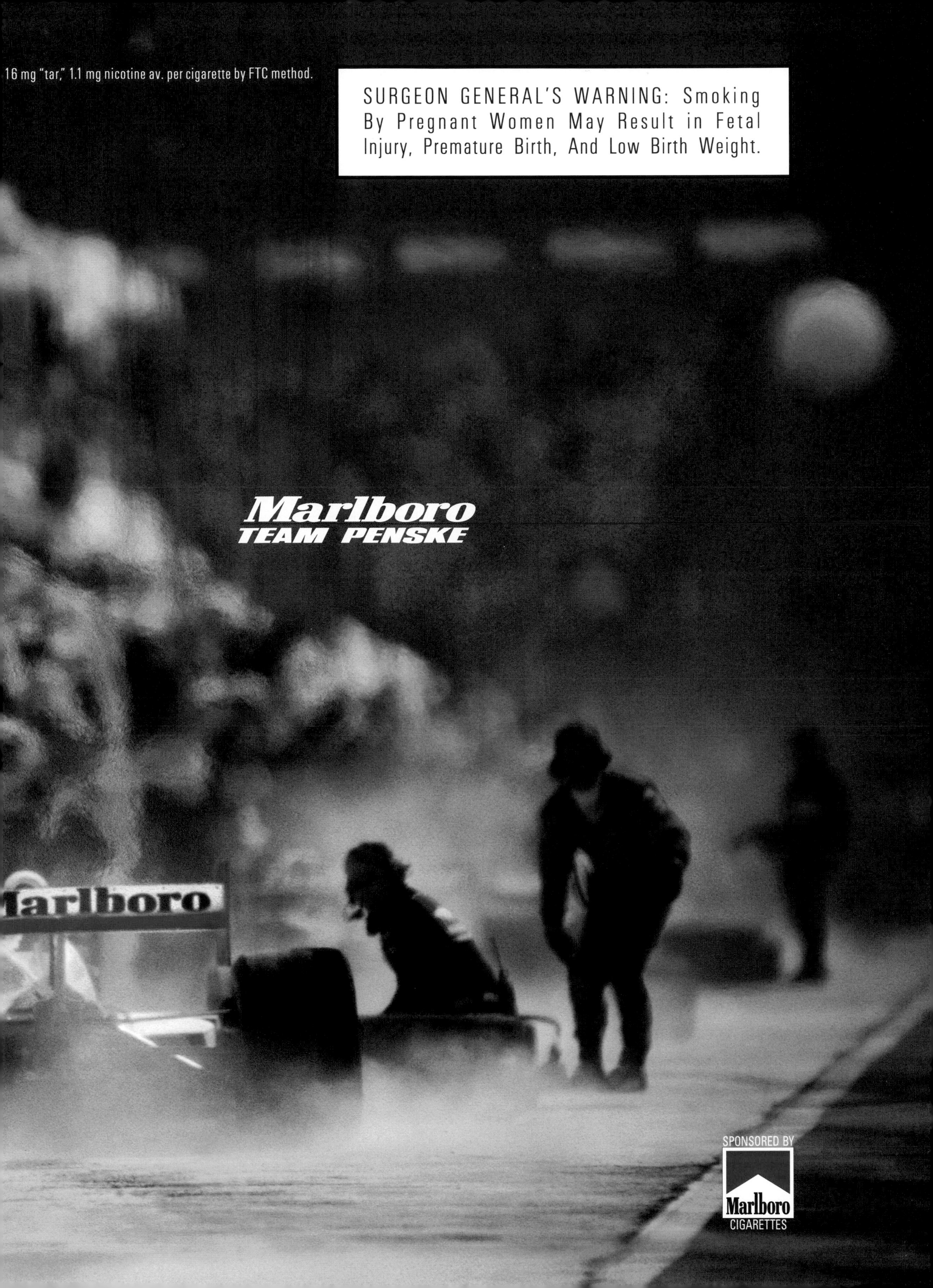

16 mg "tar," 1.1 mg nicotine av. per cigarette by FTC method.

Marlboro
TEAM PENSKE

Marlboro

SPONSORED BY

Marlboro
CIGARETTES

PPG ON

PARADE

Left: Come rain or shine, on road courses, temporary circuits, short ovals and superspeedways, the PPG Pace Cars have become an integral part of the CART raceday program.

Below: The 1997 PPG Cup champion, Alex Zanardi, receives the prestigious trophy from PPG Vice-President, Automotive Coatings, Rich Zahren.

PPG Industries, CART series title sponsor, celebrated another successful season of PPG Cup competition in 1997.

As the only sponsor of the PPG CART World Series with a direct identification with every car, driver, team member and race site, PPG is a key part of the continued growth and success of the series.

The centerpiece of the PPG program, and indeed the centerpiece of the CART season, is the PPG Cup, presented annually to the series champion.

'The PPG CART World Series is a complete test of driver, team and equipment,' said PPG's Director of Motorsports Marketing, Mike Sack. 'To win the PPG Cup, a team must succeed on four distinct types of tracks: short ovals, superspeedways, temporary circuits and permanent road courses. It is the quality of the teams and drivers and the distinct challenges encountered at each event which make the PPG Cup so special. Just look at the roster of PPG Cup champions. It is a virtual "Who's Who" of open-wheel racing.'

The level of PPG Cup competition increased yet again in 1997 with 16 different drivers taking podium finishes during the season. Alex Zanardi became the ninth different driver to claim the title in the past ten seasons.

Some of the firsts and highlights of the season included:

• Closest finish in PPG Cup history – Portland (Blundell–de Ferran–Boesel)

• Youngest race winner in history – Greg Moore at Milwaukee

• First ever PPG Cup victories for Mark Blundell, Mauricio Gugelmin and Greg Moore

• First team to successfully defend the PPG Cup since 1987 – Target/Chip Ganassi Racing

• Successful debuts at two important new venues, Gateway (St. Louis) and Fontana (Los Angeles)

Through its innovative and unsurpassed PPG Pace Car team and drivers, PPG provides the finest and best prepared pace cars in motorsports. And in the process, PPG has helped to provide thousands of team and event sponsors, elected officials, media and guests with the thrill of lapping CART race tracks in their colorful, specially prepared vehicles at speeds in excess of 100 miles per hour.

Photos: Michael C. Brown

A long-time supporter of women in motorsports, PPG enlisted several of its talented PPG Pace Car team members to serve as drivers of the official pace vehicle at most 1997 CART events. Drivers Trisha Hessinger, Margie Eatwell, Gail Truess and Kelly LaFollette performed admirably while receiving additional attention for their efforts.

The popular PPG Colorful Character program recognized promoters Ralph Sanchez, Jim Haynes, Bud Stanner and Phil Heard, team owner Derrick Walker, Tasman Racing's Christine Horne, Toyota's Les Unger, journalist Mike Harris, photographer Ron Hussey and the man who brought the donuts, PPG Cup winner Alex Zanardi.

At season's end PPG acknowledged that, in renewing its CART commitment through 1999, it had generously offered CART a rare win–win opportunity, in keeping with its selfless tradition. Under the new agreement, the world's leading provider of paint, plastics and resins to the automotive industry offered CART the opportunity to seek a more broadly based marketer as CART title sponsor. At the same time, PPG vowed to continue to support CART and to uphold the rich history and tradition of the PPG Pace Cars and PPG Cup.

A list of recent PPG Cup champions

Year	Driver	Team
1997	Alex Zanardi	Target/Chip Ganassi Racing
1996	Jimmy Vasser	Target/Chip Ganassi Racing
1995	Jacques Villeneuve	Team Green
1994	Al Unser Jr.	Marlboro Team Penske
1993	Nigel Mansell	Newman/Haas Racing
1992	Bobby Rahal	Rahal-Hogan Racing
1991	Michael Andretti	Newman/Haas Racing
1990	Al Unser Jr.	Galles-Kraco Racing
1989	Emerson Fittipaldi	Patrick Racing
1988	Danny Sullivan	Penske Racing
1987	Bobby Rahal	TrueSports
1986	Bobby Rahal	TrueSports
1985	Al Unser	Penske Racing
1984	Mario Andretti	Newman/Haas Racing
1983	Al Unser	Penske Racing
1982	Rick Mears	Penske Racing
1981	Rick Mears	Penske Racing
1980	Johnny Rutherford	Hall Chaparral

tom anderson
ON TARGET

TARGET/CHIP GANASSI RACING

by John Hopkins

FOR a team to repeat as champion in any racing series is a significant achievement. To do it in the highly competitive PPG CART World Series is especially noteworthy.

But in 1997 Target/Chip Ganassi Racing became the first team to win back-to-back CART titles since TrueSports accomplished the feat exactly a decade ago as Italian Alex Zanardi followed up teammate Jimmy Vasser's 1996 title success.

In the eyes of Target/Chip Ganassi Managing Director Tom Anderson, continuity and consistency played critical roles in the team's repeat performance. While many of its rivals made switches in the chassis, engine or tire department, Target/Chip Ganassi Racing stayed committed to the Reynard/Honda/Firestone combination that had proven so overwhelmingly successful in 1996.

'Even though other engine builders closed the gap to Honda in terms of power,' says Anderson, 'they didn't in reliability. And the way the competition is now, you have got to finish all the time if you're going to be champion. That was key to Jimmy's title in 1996 and it helped Alex a great deal this year.

'We had more of a competitive advantage in 1996 than we did this year, but we had continuity in the team personnel, especially on the higher levels.'

Zanardi was heavily favored to take the PPG Cup in 1997 after claiming the previous season's Rookie of the Year title and winning two of the last four races. But his season didn't start out with great promise. Although he won the third round in Long Beach, Zanardi was only fifth in the point standings after the first eight races of the year, five of which had been held on the daunting short ovals.

'We were in some races where Alex had conflicts and he struggled to get back up in the points,' Anderson says. 'It might have appeared like we were in trouble from the outside but a lot of things were going right for [Paul] Tracy.

'I don't think we expected to score big with Alex on the short ovals. We just wanted to stay close in the points. The short ovals take more experience than Alex has. We knew the middle portion of the season would be more to Alex's liking. That's where he made his breakthrough last year.'

Indeed, Zanardi hit his stride as the season entered its second half. He scored his second win of the year in Cleveland, finished second to Mark Blundell at Toronto's Molson Indy and then reeled off a string of three straight victories at the U.S. 500, the Miller 200 at Mid-Ohio and Elkhart Lake's Texaco/Havoline 200 to put himself in command of the points lead.

'I don't know if it was any one thing that turned it around,' says Anderson. 'I think we took a step back, realized it was going to be a long summer and just settled in and relaxed. We didn't do a lot of development, there was no budget for it. It was just a matter of doing the basics really well and getting the most out of what we had.'

While Zanardi's season picked up momentum by the middle of the summer, teammate Vasser's year took much longer to come around. After finishing on the podium in the season opener at Homestead, the defending champion was bedeviled by bad luck in the early races and fell into a slump in the middle of the season. Rumors flew that he would not be returning to the team in 1998.

'I think late in the season, when he was mathematically out of the points race and he had decided he was going to stay with us next year, Jimmy turned things around,' Anderson says. 'Julian Robertson came up with a good setup for Vancouver and Jimmy took it from there.'

After a strong run in Vancouver, Vasser picked up his first win in over a year at Laguna Seca.

Nunn's tale

WHEN Target/Chip Ganassi Racing was casting about for a replacement for Bryan Herta late in the 1995 season, Alessandro Zanardi did not rate highly on team engineer Morris Nunn's list. In fact, Nunn was not at all interested in having the Formula 1 outcast on the team.

Nunn didn't know a lot about Zanardi, except that he was Italian. And Nunn's experiences with Italian drivers, dating back to his days as a Formula 1 team owner, hadn't been very positive.

'I found them to be pretty fiery in the car,' he recalls.

'Don't get me wrong, they're fun people. But coming from England, where we're very calm and steady, working with an Italian was not what I had in mind.'

It didn't take Nunn long to change his opinion. The veteran engineer reluctantly agreed to give Zanardi a test on the road course at the Homestead Motorsports Complex in Florida and was quickly impressed by what he saw.

'I expected him to come out of the last turn and onto the front straight with the car sideways and the wheels spinning,' Nunn says. 'Instead, it was the exact opposite. From the word go he only used the power that the chassis would put to the ground. He didn't overdrive the chassis. He was very, very good at being super-smooth.'

Nunn also found Zanardi to be particularly adept at the delicate task of setting up his car.

'His feedback was excellent,' he says. 'We would always go forward based on his information.'

The collaboration between Nunn and Zanardi bore fruit in 1997 with the PPG Cup title. Additionally, Zanardi scored a victory in the U.S. 500 at Michigan Speedway, giving Nunn a win in every major 500-mile CART event. Zanardi's increasing success brought with it new challenges, however.

'As we had more success, I didn't have Alex as much as I would have liked,' Nunn explains. 'After qualifying on Saturday, he'd be gone as soon as the session ended for a press conference or sponsorship function. Before, we would spend more time together talking about the car. And we'd often go out to dinner and talk about it some more. That's the kind of relationship I like to have with a driver.'

Nunn has become a very big fan of Zanardi and, interestingly, it is that fire which he initially feared which has impressed him the most.

'He's kind of the complete driver,' Nunn explains. 'Bryan Herta I would put in the Chris Amon mold. He's very fast, he can sort the car and he has good racecraft. Alex has all of those but in addition he never gives up. He hasn't been coasting for a championship and that's something I admire about him.

'His only fault, if I can find one, is that he might be a little impatient when he comes to going by people. But I think the cars have outpaced the circuits. We need more tracks like Cleveland [Burke Lakefront Airport]. At least spectators can see the circuit all the way around and it invites people to overtake. The Vancouver track was for Formula Fords, really.'

It appears doubtful that Nunn will attempt to repeat his PPG Cup triumph with Zanardi in 1998. He has told team owner Ganassi that he doesn't want to engineer a car next year and although he might remain with the team in another capacity he admits that the busy series schedule is starting to take its toll.

'I'm burnt out,' he admits. 'I've been doing this for 35 years. The travel gets to you, and it's not getting any better.

'Maybe I'll just take a year off, you never know. When you're working so hard during the season you feel tired and frustrated. But once you get away from it you become bored.'

Left: Managing director Tom Anderson has his eyes fixed on a third successive PPG Cup championship for Target/Chip Ganassi Racing in 1998.

Below: Veteran race engineer Morris Nunn notes detailed changes to the setup of Alex Zanardi's spare car during practice as the never-ending quest for perfect handling continues.

'I think if Jimmy had the opportunity, he would redo his winter,' Anderson continues. 'As the series champion, he committed himself to a lot and by the middle of May I was scratching my head and wondering if he had done the right thing. We want to be careful this winter with Alex, and we'll talk about that heavily.

'But the problems you incur by winning are good problems to have.'

While Zanardi and Vasser experienced differing fortunes during the year, Robertson says the two made an excellent combination in the team.

'It's incredible how well those two guys get along,' he says. 'When you're racing with a two-car team, you're always going to bring home one loser. Sometimes it's easier coming back with two losers. They were both very competitive, but they shared everything.

'Alex brings with him a special talent of being very personable with the guys around him.'

Anderson doesn't discount the possibility of a 'three-peat' by the Target/Chip Ganassi team. Although it appears likely that Zanardi's race engineer, Morris Nunn, will not be back, the rest of the championship package will remain in place.

'I just think about it in terms of winning the championship in 1998,' says Anderson. 'I'm not looking at it as winning three in a row.

'What we did this year won't win it for us next year,' he cautions. 'The other teams made a lot of improvements this year but we stayed pretty much the same as in 1996. We'll need plenty of help out of Honda, plenty of help out of Reynard and plenty of help out of Firestone. In our engineering department, instead of relying on just one person, we'll have to spread that load. You don't just go out and get another Morris Nunn.'

One thing Anderson doesn't think will be a problem will be motivating the team to put in the effort required to pick up yet another PPG Cup title.

'The big thing around here is that none of the veterans have forgotten the agony of defeat,' he stresses. 'In the middle management we have five guys with about 120 years of combined racing experience and we bond the young guys together. We understand what it's like to lose, and be beaten really bad. We know we're very, very fortunate to have what we have right now.'

Photos: Michael C. Brown

We've Got It Covered!

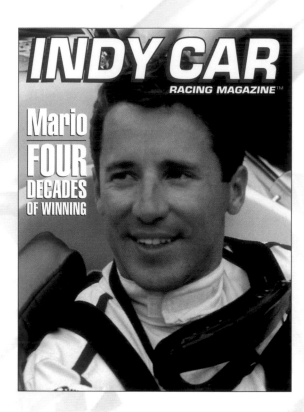

DREAM SEASON II

In the last two years, Firestone has produced a remarkable record of accomplishments in CART racing:

- In 1997 competition, drivers on Firestone tires won 13 of 17 races, earned 11 poles, swept the podium three times and won the season championship.
- In 1996 competition, drivers on Firestone tires won 10 of 16 races, earned 12 poles, swept the podium three times and won the season championship.
- Firestone-equipped drivers won every road and street course event in 1997.
- Firestone drivers led the majority of laps both years: 1,321 of 2,259 laps in 1997; 1,077 of 2,005 laps in 1996.
- Firestone drivers won every CART race in June, July, August and September of 1997.
- Firestone's rain tire proved itself in 1997, giving Firestone-equipped drivers a clear advantage in the wet at Portland.

Considering the familiar Firestone logo was absent from Indy car competition for 21 years, the achievements are even more incredible.

"The last two years have surpassed all our expectations," said Bridgestone/Firestone Motorsports Director Al Speyer. "When we announced in 1993 that we would test in 1994 and begin racing again in 1995, we knew we could develop a competitive program. We just didn't realize that we would do it as quickly as we have."

Shortly after the Firestone Tire & Rubber Company was founded in 1900, Firestone tires began appearing at race tracks. Ray Harroun, in his Marmon Wasp, drove on Firestone tires to win the inaugural Indianapolis 500 in 1911. Since then, Firestone has been on the Indy 500 winner's car 50 times – a cherished record unmatched by any other tire manufacturer. The last two wins came in 1996 and 1997, provided by Buddy Lazier and Arie Luyendyk.

Firestone-shod cars won 43 consecutive Indy 500s between 1920 and 1966, and remained competitive until 1974, when it retired from the series. The company was purchased by

Bridgestone Corporation in 1988, and in 1990 Bridgestone and Firestone operations in the U.S. were consolidated as Bridgestone/Firestone, Inc. Headquartered in Nashville, Tenn., the company has invested more than $1.5 billion in new equipment, facilities and technologies.

Technical centers around the globe share information to design, develop and produce some of the world's finest tires for a wide variety of applications. More than 8,000 different types and sizes of tires feature the Bridgestone, Firestone, Dayton and associate brand labels, including fitments for go-karts, giant earth-moving equipment, airplanes, off-road vehicles, trucks, passenger vehicles and other applications. The company also produces a variety of rubber products, including building materials, dams, marine fenders and shock absorbing devices.

"Our research, development and manufacturing teams keep us the world leader in the rubber industry," Speyer said. "Racing provides great visibility for our products and an important research tool for our engineers. Innovations allowing us to win on the track are moved to consumer tire applications more frequently than you might imagine, permitting us to maintain and attract customers. The L.L. Carbon component of our unique UNI-T technology is a direct example of race tire to street tire evolution."

In addition to its presence in CART and the IRL, the company participates in a growing number of racing series. Bridgestone Potenza tires are showcased in Formula One while Dayton Daytona tires are used in the Indy Lights series. Bridgestone Battlax tires have earned respect in motorcycle competition, while the company's other logos appear in FIA GT racing and other series.

"Our growing presence in motorsports is good for everyone," Speyer said. "It creates a higher level of competition and forces all participants to work harder for wins. That's healthy for the sport and exciting for the fans."

Speyer said the competition to produce better tires was most obvious when Mauricio Gugelmin exceeded 242 mph on Firestone Firehawks during a 1997 practice session in California.

"We'll keep looking for innovations to keep Firestone drivers in front," Speyer said. "Isn't that what racing is all about?"

Firestone®
America's Tire Since 1900

FIRESTONE WI

Record 50th Indy 500 V

1911
Ray Harroun

1913
Jules Goux

1920
Gaston Chevrolet

1921
Tommy Milton

1922
Jimmy Murphy

1928
Louis Meyer

1929
Ray Keech

1930
Billy Arnold

1931
Louis Schneider

1932
Fred Frame

1938
Floyd Roberts

1939
Wilbur Shaw

1940
Wilbur Shaw

1941
M. Rose, F. Davis

1946
George Robson

1952
Troy Ruttman

1953
Bill Vukovich

1954
Bill Vukovich

1955
Bob Sweikert

1956
Pat Flaherty

1962
Rodger Ward

1963
Parnelli Jones

1964
A.J. Foyt

1965
Jim Clark

1966
Graham Hill

50 WINS — A RACING LEGEND AT THE INDY 500 — Firestone

**1997 Winner
Arie Luyendyk**

IS INDY AGAIN
tory For Firestone Tires

1923
Tommy Milton

1924
L. Corum, Joe Boyer

1925
Pete De Paolo

1926
Frank Lockhart

1927
George Souders

1933
Louis Meyer

1934
Wild Bill Cummings

1935
Kelly Petillo

1936
Louis Meyer

1937
Wilbur Shaw

1947
Mauri Rose

1948
Mauri Rose

1949
Bill Holland

1950
Johnnie Parsons

1951
Lee Wallard

1957
Sam Hanks

1958
Jimmy Bryan

1959
Rodger Ward

1960
Jim Rathmann

1961
A.J. Foyt

1969
Mario Andretti

1970
Al Unser

1971
Al Unser

1996
Buddy Lazier

On May 27, 1997, Firestone challenged—and shattered—the ultimate Indy 500® record. Our own. Firestone Firehawk™ racing tires chalked up an astonishing 50th Indianapolis 500® win for the brand that has become an American Legend...from Indy, to the interstates, to the street where you live.

Firestone returned to the Indy 500® because we knew the challenges of competition bring out the best, in our people and our tires. The same challenging spirit that leads us into the fiercely competitive world of Indy racing also drives our search for new consumer tire technologies. What we've learned along the way allows us to create an exciting new line-up of outstanding tires for your car.

We'd like to congratulate Arie Luyendyk on winning the 1997 Indy 500 on Firestone Firehawk racing tires, and salute all the teams and drivers that chose to compete on Firestone tires. And to everyone across America who chooses to drive on Firestone tires every day, thanks for being part of our winning tradition. Firestone. The Legend.

Race-Winning Firestone Firehawk™
Indy Racing Slick & Firestone
Firehawk SS10™ Street Tire

Firestone
America's Tire Since 1900

Firestone Firehawk™ Indy Racing
Rain Tire & Firestone Firehawk
SZ50™ Ultra-High Performance Tire

FIREHAWK™

**BORN AT INDY.
DRIVEN EVERYWHERE.**

FIRESTONE ACCEPTS THE CHALLENGE...
AND YOU WIN!

THE LESSONS WE LEARN ON RACE DAY ARE IN THE TIRES YOU COUNT ON EVERY DAY.

With a record 50 wins at the Indy 500,® Firestone knows Indy racing like no other tire company. And if we can develop the kind of quick acceleration, grip and stability required for Indy racing tires, just imagine how well our line of Firehawk street performance radials will perform for you. Firehawk performance tires, including the new, ultra-high performance Firehawk SZ50 with **UNI-T,**™ the **U**ltimate **N**etwork of **I**ntelligent **T**ire **T**echnology, are speed rated from S to Z and specifically engineered for crisp handling and legendary performance. Stop by your local Firestone retailer and check out the complete Firehawk line today. And congratulations to all Indy teams racing on Firestone Firehawk tires. We wish you much success.

**Firehawk
Racing Slick**

**Firehawk
SS10 Street Tire**

Firestone®
America's Tire Since 1900

**Original Firehawk
Indy Racing Rain Tire**

**Firehawk SZ50 Ultra-
High Performance Tire**

Indy 500® and Indy® are registered trademarks of the Indianapolis Motor Speedway.

TOP TEN DRIVERS

The ever-escalating intensity of the PPG CART World Series makes ranking the Top 10 Drivers an increasingly formidable task. The easy way out would be simply to adopt the final PPG Cup rankings. But that's not the *Autocourse* way. In the following pages, Editor Jeremy Shaw offers his personal ranking of the best of the best, taking into account their individual performances, their level of experience and the equipment at their disposal

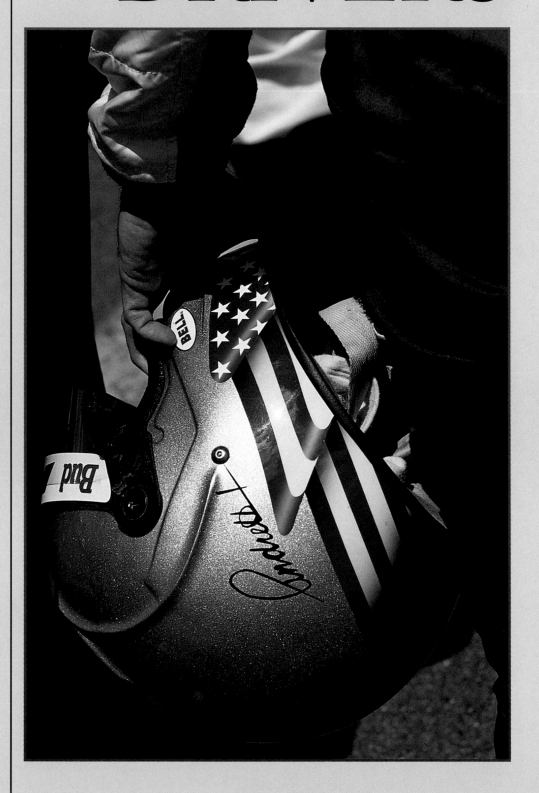

Photographs by Michael C. Brown

1

alex zanardi

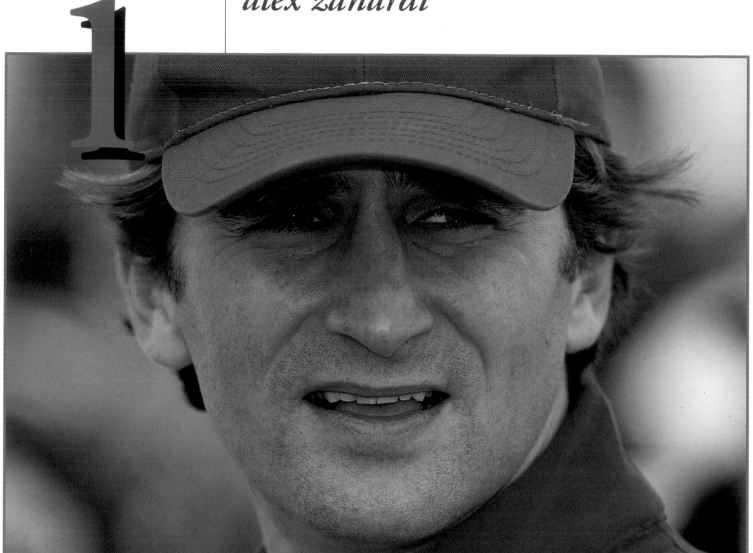

Alex Zanardi

Date of birth: October 23, 1966

Residence: Monte Carlo, Monaco

CART starts in 1997: 16

PPG Cup ranking: 1st

Wins: 5; Poles: 4; Points: 195

ALESSANDRO Zanardi began the year as a red-hot favorite to win the PPG Cup title. Rightly so. He had shown prodigious pace during a rookie campaign which yielded three wins and six poles. A concerted winter testing program was equally productive, ensuring that Zanardi was both well prepared and brimful of confidence prior to the opening race.

He promptly secured the pole at Homestead and repeated the feat at Surfers Paradise to establish a new CART record of six consecutive poles (dating back to Mid-Ohio in 1996). In the following race at Long Beach he qualified second but once more etched his name in the history books: It was his 11th straight front row start. Quite remarkable. Yet Zanardi was brought back to earth at the quirky Nazareth oval, managing only 21st on the grid. The short ovals, indeed, remained his Achilles Heel. He was out-paced by teammate Jimmy Vasser both at Nazareth and at Milwaukee, and in the latter event was involved in a war of words with Paul Tracy following an incident during practice. The pair also had clashed while dicing for the win in Australia. Suddenly, the burden of being the championship favorite seemed to be weighing heavily upon his shoulders.

Zanardi slipped to fifth in the standings after nine races, 31 points adrift of Tracy; but then came a spectacular revival. He posted a brilliant drive at Cleveland, recovering from two penalties to snatch victory, and after a second-place finish in Toronto, he took command of the series with another hat-trick of wins. The 30-year-old Italian was involved in a couple of controversial clashes, just as he was during his rookie season, but overall he was an impressive and deserving champion.

2

gil de ferran

Gil de Ferran

Date of birth: November 11, 1967

Residence: Fort Lauderdale, Fla.

CART starts in 1997: 17

PPG Cup ranking: 2nd

Wins: 0; Poles: 2; Points: 162

FIVE crashes within the first three race weekends represented an inauspicious start to Gil de Ferran's new relationship with no-nonsense team owner Derrick Walker. Ditto his championship aspirations. The only good news was that de Ferran at least was running quickly on each occasion. And to be fair, the accidents were not always his fault.

'I was getting a lot of criticism, particularly from the Brazilian press,' recalls de Ferran, 'so I said, well, let me do my own analysis and see if this criticism is valid. I tend to listen to a lot of people, but at the end of the day I sit down and look at the facts and draw my own conclusions; and when I looked at all the separate incidents, I could not see anything that was common – except there were these huge accidents and I was in the middle of them!'

Rather than allow himself to become overwhelmed by the consequences, de Ferran put his head down, maintained his focus, and slowly worked his way into contention. The relationships with both Walker and race engineer Bill Pappas, who had transferred with de Ferran from Hall Racing, were crucial to his reemergence as a championship challenger. Honda reliability also played a vital role. In the 10 races between Gateway and Vancouver, the Brazilian recorded seven top-three finishes.

De Ferran, along with Michael Andretti and Bryan Herta, was among a very few drivers who regularly made the best of their Goodyear tires, which, especially in the latter part of the season, proved to be no match for the Firestones. In 1998 de Ferran and Walker Racing will be a serious threat for the PPG Cup title.

3

mauricio gugelmin

Mauricio Gugelmin

Date of birth: April 20, 1963

Residence: Fort Lauderdale, Fla.

CART starts in 1997: 17

PPG Cup ranking: 4th

Wins: 1; Poles: 3; Points: 132

MAURICIO Gugelmin displayed much more than just speed in 1997. He was in every sense a team leader, whose positive attitude and tireless work ethic played a prominent role in transforming Bruce McCaw's PacWest Racing Group operation from one which had merely shown great promise into a regular contender.

Gugelmin accumulated an impressive record in qualifying. He was the only driver to start among the top 10 in each of the 17 races. His average grid position, 4.235, was significantly better than the next best, Zanardi, at 6.938. Gugelmin was versatile too, recording poles on such diverse tracks as the Rio 'roval', the Elkhart Lake road course and the Fontana superspeedway.

Luck, however, seemed to be all too rarely on his side. At Homestead, after qualifying on the front row, he lost ground to a dramatic oversteer in the early stages; in Rio, after being down-on-power from the start, he abruptly – and inexplicably – lost control under braking; and then, famously, in Detroit, his team's bold attempt to complete the distance on a single fuel stop came up about a mile short. Later, in the U.S. 500, he was the class of the field until losing time due to a faulty spark box.

Gugelmin also failed to score at Surfers Paradise, where he spun while attempting to relieve Jimmy Vasser of second place. But rather than attempt to pin the blame elsewhere, the classy Brazilian simply came clean: 'I just made a mistake.'

When Gugelmin finally claimed his first victory, in Vancouver, his happiness was shared by virtually the entire CART contingent. There could be no more fitting tribute to one of the most popular men on pit road.

greg moore

4

Greg Moore

Date of birth: April 22, 1975

Residence: Maple Ridge, B.C., Canada

CART starts in 1997: 17

PPG Cup ranking: 7th

Wins: 2; Poles: 0; Points: 111

G REG Moore burst onto the PPG Cup scene impressively in 1996 and built upon that solid foundation in 1997. Among his many attributes are a refreshing honesty, a maturity beyond his 22 years and Job-like patience. Moore came tantalizingly close to a maiden CART victory during his rookie season and continued to flirt with success during the early part of 1997 – despite a late switch from Lola to Reynard. He finished a close second in two of the first five races. On the down side, he was pushed off the road by Paul Tracy at Long Beach and sustained a puncture while leading in the late stages at Gateway. But Moore kept his wits about him. Prior to the season he had determined that a top-five finish in each race would keep him in contention for the ultimate prize, the PPG Cup title. He never lost sight of that goal. Sure, he had suffered a few disappointments, but he never doubted the ability of either himself or his crew. The wins, he felt certain, would come in due course.

Sure enough, in round seven, on the famed Milwaukee Mile, Moore took advantage of excellent strategy and held off a determined challenge from no less an adversary than Michael Andretti. His patience had paid off. A week later in Detroit he won again after both PacWest cars ran out of fuel on the final lap.

Sadly, the second half of the season turned into a nightmare. Moore finished only one of the final eight races, when he was second at Mid-Ohio. He was pushed off the road in Toronto and made mistakes both at Road America and at Vancouver. Engine failures accounted for his retirements in the other three races. But his time will surely come.

5

michael andretti

Michael Andretti

Date of birth: October 5, 1962

Residence: Nazareth, Pa.

CART starts in 1997: 17

PPG Cup ranking: 8th

Wins: 1; Poles: 0; Points: 108

INCREDIBLE though it seems, Michael Andretti now is regarded as one of the CART elders. In terms of both race wins and poles, he remains, by a substantial margin, the most successful active participant. His tally of 211 starts is exceeded only by longtime friend and rival Al Unser Jr. (237) and Bobby Rahal (245). How time flies!

By rights, Andretti should have won more than the solitary PPG Cup title he claimed in 1991. And judging by the manner in which he began the 1997 season, with a victory, many pundits expected him to remain in contention for that long-awaited second championship. The latest Ford/Cosworth XD engine clearly offered substantially more power – and, crucially, improved reliability – compared with '96, while the new Swift 007.i chassis seemed to match up well against its primary rival, the Reynard. Tires, however, often seemed to be a limiting factor. And Lady Luck.

At Long Beach, the usually flawless Newman/Haas crew let him down by employing incorrectly calibrated tire pressure gauges which caused a succession of tire failures. In Brazil he was sidelined by an engine problem; at Michigan he fell victim to a broken transmission. On both occasions he displayed race-winning potential. Ultimately, however, in attempting to keep pace with the Firestone-shod cars ahead of him at Road America and Vancouver, Andretti committed rare errors of judgment.

Andretti posted typically tigerish performances at Homestead, Milwaukee and Michigan, and while the legendary blinding pace in qualifying has mysteriously escaped his grasp in recent years – his last pole, incredibly, came at Long Beach in '95 – he remains one of the series' most widely feared and respected competitors.

6

mark blundell

Mark Blundell

Date of birth: April 8, 1966

Residence: Scottsdale, Ariz.

CART starts in 1997: 17

PPG Cup ranking: 6th

Wins: 3; Poles: 0; Points: 115

AFTER seven races, Mark Blundell had garnered a meager 11 PPG Cup points and had been regularly outpaced by teammate Mauricio Gugelmin. He lay a distant 16th in the standings despite a promising start to the season which had seen him qualify fifth both at Homestead and at Surfers Paradise. Blundell, though, had not matched those performances in the races. But why? No one seemed quite sure. Least of all Blundell. All he knew for certain was that the car was not handling to his liking. And while he languished in the lower reaches of the top 20, teammate Gugelmin, using the exact-same equipment, was a regular pace-setter. The effect on Blundell's confidence was devastating.

The root of his problems boiled down to the fact that the studious, methodical approach favored by his newly assigned race engineer, Jim Hamilton, did not sit well with the intensely ambitious, impatient and increasingly frustrated Englishman. A change was evidently needed. Nevertheless, perhaps no one could have predicted the astonishing turnaround in Blundell's fortunes after the capable Hamilton moved on to concentrate on development projects and technical director Allen McDonald stepped in to take charge of the Motorola Reynard. Whether by coincidence or not, Blundell qualified a respectable 11th at Milwaukee and, for the first time, began to develop a 'feel' for the short ovals. Then, in Detroit, he shadowed Gugelmin and came within 200 yards of scoring a momentous victory.

Next came the breakthrough win at Portland, where Blundell took advantage of a perfect strategic call and drove magnificently despite the treacherous track conditions. He never looked back. His drive in Toronto, where he led virtually throughout, was flawless. At last, Blundell's true talents, largely untapped these past 10 years, had emerged.

7 | *jimmy vasser*

Jimmy Vasser

Date of birth: November 20, 1965

Residence: Las Vegas, Nev.

CART starts in 1997: 17

PPG Cup ranking: 3rd

Wins: 1; Poles: 0; Points: 144

I WRESTLED long and hard over where to place Jimmy Vasser in the Top 10 ranking. On the one hand he didn't come close to matching the achievements of Target/Chip Ganassi teammate Alex Zanardi. One win, two seconds and a pair of thirds doesn't sound especially impressive when matched against Zanardi's tally of five wins, six additional top-five finishes and four poles. Nevertheless, while the California-born Vasser did not enjoy the kind of title defense he had anticipated, he did display a great deal of heart and resilience. And in the end, a victory and two strong runner-up finishes from the last three races allowed him to rebound from a disappointing eighth position in points to take a firm grasp on third place in the final PPG Cup table.

In reality, Vasser drove consistently well. He began with a third-place finish at Homestead and was running second in Australia before being taken out by Gugelmin. At Long Beach he fought back to ninth after losing a lap in the early going, due to a puncture. In Rio he soldiered on despite the fact a broken engine fitting was leaking oil onto his right-rear tire.

After struggling on the short ovals during his championship season, Vasser worked hard to overcome that deficiency – and was largely successful, finishing fifth at Nazareth and third in Milwaukee. However, a preponderance of oval track tire-testing perhaps restricted his ability to extract the maximum potential from his car on the other types of circuit, and it wasn't until late in the season that he and engineer Julian Robertson finally agreed that simply adopting Zanardi's setup was not the optimal solution. Their driving styles were too disparate. Once the penny dropped, Vasser recovered his true form.

paul tracy

Paul Tracy

Date of birth: December 17, 1968

Residence: Parker, Ariz.

CART starts in 1997: 16

PPG Cup ranking: 5th

Wins: 3; Poles: 2; Points: 121

WHAT to make of Paul Tracy's season? The mercurial Canadian began the year full of optimism following a promising winter test program, and while he couldn't match Andretti's Swift in the first race at Homestead, he proclaimed himself delighted after finishing second: 'We know we've got a good short-oval car and we know we've got a good road course car,' declared Tracy. 'We knew this kind of track was going to be a thorn in our side. Obviously, it still isn't a win but we ran strong and we were in the hunt the whole time. It's nice to get some points in the bag. Now we can get going.'

Sure enough, Tracy was embroiled in a tight battle for the lead in Australia with Zanardi – until they tangled. Tracy came off worst. He was involved in several incidents, too, at Long Beach, earning himself a $25,000 fine, but recovered to finish seventh. Precisely mirroring the achievement of Michael Andretti in '96, Tracy rebounded to win impressively at Nazareth. He proceeded to add two more victories, plus a pole at Milwaukee, and opened up a commanding lead in the PPG Cup standings. Marlboro Team Penske was back. With a vengeance. Or so it seemed.

But it was virtually all downhill from there. Perhaps the writing was on the wall at Milwaukee, where Tracy's Goodyear-tired Penske was overhauled by the more consistent Firestone-shod Reynard of Moore. In the latter part of the season, even the enormously brave Canadian managed only one top-10 qualifying effort. For love or money, neither he nor Unser was able to make the car work on the succession of road and street circuits. But can a car that wins three races be that bad?

bryan herta

9

Bryan Herta

Date of birth: May 23, 1970

Residence: New Albany, Ohio

CART starts in 1997: 17

PPG Cup ranking: 11th

Wins: 0; Poles: 2; Points: 72

ODD, one might suggest, for a driver with only two top-five finishes and one podium result (a third place at Cleveland) to be represented among the Top 10. But the facts bear closer examination. For the second successive year, Bryan Herta produced some stunning performances during the second half of the season, including two poles which left the remainder of the Goodyear contingent scratching their heads. The second of these, indeed, at Laguna Seca Raceway, one of the more technically demanding circuits on the entire schedule, saw Herta's Shell Reynard-Ford a staggering 1.160 seconds clear of the next fastest Goodyear representative.

'How did he do that?' questioned an astonished Gil de Ferran.

'I wish I knew,' smiled Herta. 'If I did, I'd bottle it and take it everywhere else.'

Herta had little to cheer about during the opening half of his second campaign with Team Rahal. The reasons were complex and, admits Herta, not readily understood, but the fact is that the team once again failed to secure a good setup for the short ovals. Herta and teammate Bobby Rahal (who was desperately unlucky not to win the Rio 400) took some time to dial in their Reynards for the road courses, and later their frustrations were heightened by constant revisions to the specification of their tires as the Goodyear engineers strove to maintain pace with the Firestone opposition. Nevertheless, Herta amassed a qualifying record throughout the second half of the season which was bettered only by Zanardi and Gugelmin.

10 | *scott pruett*

Scott Pruett

Date of birth: March 24, 1960

Residence: Crystal Bay, Nev.

CART starts in 1997: 17

PPG Cup ranking: 9th

Wins: 1; Poles: 2; Points: 102

FOR the second straight year, Scott Pruett began his season with a bang and finished it with a whimper. Three top-five results in a row catapulted the deserving Californian to the top of the PPG Cup standings, which in itself represented a remarkable achievement given the fact that the vast majority of an intensive winter testing program was rendered useless by the Patrick team's shocking (at the time) decision to switch from Lola to Reynard little more than a month before the first race. Subsequent results, of course, revealed the move to have been especially astute, since the Lola soon came to be regarded as a dog.

But Pruett was unable to sustain the fast start. He continued to qualify well, gathering a record bettered only by Gugelmin and Zanardi, but struggled on several of the oval tracks which dominated the first half of the season. His confidence also took a knock at Gateway when fading brakes caused him to crash heavily while holding down sixth place. Several other incidents also took their toll. At Portland, for example, after qualifying superbly on the pole, he never looked comfortable in the wet on raceday and spun twice, falling to 17th. He endured a heavy hit, too, at Michigan and crashed out of the race in Vancouver.

In stark contrast to 1996, the vastly improved Ford/Cosworth engine proved both quick and reliable. The only failure came in Detroit, after he had started from the front row. The Reynard 97I was clearly the chassis of choice, as were the Firestone Firehawk tires. Somewhere along the line, though, something was missing. And it's hard to pinpoint exactly what that was.

COSWORTH

CASTINGS

ENGINEERING

MANUFACTURING

RACING

WORLD CLASS WORLD WIDE

COMMITTED TO BE FIRST . . .

IN celebrating its 100th anniversary, Goodyear can reflect that its entire history encompasses the development and evolution of the automobile for the everyday motorist. The company's leading position in the automotive industry is supported by a commitment to engineering, research and development, and a long-term involvement in international motor racing.

The company is firmly established as number one in racing worldwide with a successful program that encompasses Formula 1, Indy cars, stock cars, sports cars, sprints, drag racing and off-road racing.

Goodyear was founded in 1898 by 38-year-old Frank A. Seiberling in Akron, Ohio. He named the company 'Goodyear' in honor of Charles Goodyear who, almost 60 years earlier, had discovered vulcanization, a process of 'cooking' gum rubber and sulphur to make a stable rubber end product.

From its beginnings in a small strawboard factory with 13 employees and a product line of horseshoe pads, bicycle and carriage tires and poker chips, Goodyear has grown into a global force operating plants in 28 countries and topping $13 billion in sales. Products include tires, chemicals and industrial rubber products.

Almost from the outset of motorized competition, Goodyear was quick to appreciate that lessons learned on the race track could feed back into the general tire manufacturing process. Charlie Metz used Goodyear tires on

GOODYEAR 100 1898-1998

Top: Howdy Wilcox, winner at Indianapolis in 1919, qualified his Peugeot at an average speed of 101.01 mph.
Right: Goodyear advertising from the early period.
Below: More than seven decades on, Goodyear still leading the way, as Jacques Villeneuve takes the victory in the 1997 Argentine Grand Prix.

his Stutz to finish third in the Indianapolis 500 as early as 1913, although it was not until six years later that the world's largest tire and rubber company became really serious about the world's largest motor race.

A major development effort by Goodyear engineers resulted in the production of tires which helped competitors break the magic 100 mph barrier at Indianapolis in 1919. Howdy Wilcox, who qualified his Peugeot at 101.01 mph, won the race on Goodyear rubber at an average speed of 88.05 mph. Just to confirm the company's superiority, nine of the top 10 finishers

were on Goodyear rubber – and two went the distance without a tire change, regarded as an almost unbelievable feat at the time!

Thereafter, the company gradually scaled down its motor racing involvement and it dropped out of the sport in 1922. It was not until the early 1950s that Goodyear began to

reconsider its attitude toward motor racing. Surveys conducted around that time indicated that Goodyear had a strong appeal to middle-aged and older customers, with its products having an image of dependability and reliability.

Yet the management decided it was time to develop a more dynamic corporate image. Thus was born the 'Go, Go Goodyear' advertising and promotional campaigns and at the same time the company made a return to motor racing after an interval of over three decades.

Goodyear has been the leading supplier to auto racing for nearly 30 years. In 1957, the company appeared in the stock car racing arena and quickly established itself as a competitive force. By 1960, it had furnished the winning tire in the Daytona 500 in what is now the prestigious NASCAR Winston Cup Series championship trail. By 1962, Goodyear was the dominant NASCAR tire supplier, and the company celebrated its 1000th NASCAR Winston Cup victory in 1995 with driver Jeff Gordon.

Goodyear tires appeared in Grand Prix racing for the first time in 1960, when Lance Reventlow, the millionaire son of Woolworth heiress Barbara Hutton, used the company's rubber for his lavishly over-ambi-

GOOD YEAR 100
1 8 9 8 - 1 9 9 8

Top: Richard and Lee Petty, legends both in NASCAR, run together on the banking at Darlington in 1960.
Below left: One of America's finest, the great A.J. Foyt, was instrumental in bringing Goodyear to the Indianapolis Motor Speedway, winning the race in 1967 on Goodyears – the start of three decades of almost total tire dominance in this legendary arena.
Below right: Richie Ginther, the pint-sized Californian who brought Goodyear its maiden Grand Prix victory in Mexico City in 1965.

tious F1 foray to Europe. Disappointingly, his front-engined Scarabs were a year or so behind the times. The rear-engined F1 revolution was in full swing and the cars proved to be a failure.

Although by now Goodyear was a proven competitor on the NASCAR trail, its first post-war foray onto the international racing scene came at Indianapolis in 1963. The 1961 Indy 500 winner A.J. Foyt was frustrated that Firestone had produced some special tires for the trend-setting new Lotus-Fords driven by Jim Clark and Dan Gurney, but at the same time declined to supply them for his own front-engined machine. Foyt urged Goodyear to begin an Indy tire development program and he won the first race of the 1964 season on Goodyears in Phoenix. Just three years later, Foyt would speed to victory in his Goodyear-shod Coyote to register the company's first Indy 500 win in over four decades. From 1972 onwards, Goodyear's total domination of the Indy 500 would remain unchallenged for almost a quarter of a century, with Goodyear celebrating its 100th consecutive CART win in October 1981 with Rick Mears at Watkins Glen; the 200th win in July 1988 with Al Unser Jr., at the Mead-

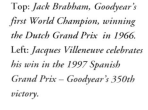

owlands, followed by the 300th in September 1994, again with Al Unser Jr., at Vancouver, B.C.

At the close of the 1997 CART racing season, Goodyear has registered a total of 328 wins. With the company racing against tire competitor Bridge-stone/Firestone in the CART PPG World Series since the start of the 1995 season, the two tiremakers have split the wins.

Having a tire competitor in any racing series changes the basic way Goodyear handles its support of that series. Instead of a conservative, consistent tire that works well and doesn't become a factor in the outcome of a race, competition demands a product that will add speed and grip and be a major element in a winning pack-age. 'It's a different philosophy and a definite challenge,' says Stu Grant, general manager of racing worldwide.

In CART, evolutionary tire changes were made in con-struction and compounds for nearly every CART track in 1997, with the Goodyear entries proving to be durable and consistent on a variety of chassis and at a number of new race tracks.

But, as Goodyear faces continued competition in CART, the IRL and F1, the 1998 tire develop-ment program will continue to evolve in order to meet the competitive requirements.

Looking back again at Goodyear's early years in Formula 1, it was in 1964 that the company established its international racing division in Wolverhampton, Great Britain. An intensive program of F1 competition would be sustained for the next 15 years from that location, before being consolidated in the Akron Technical Center. In 1965, Goodyear struck up a partnership with both the Brabham and Honda F1 teams, Richie Ginther posting the company's maiden Grand Prix victory at Mexico City in what was the final race of the 1.5-litre Formula 1.

In 1966, Goodyear marked its first F1 World Championship, with Jack Brabham dominating the season. The success was repeated the following year by Brabham's teammate Denny Hulme.

F1 success continued, with Goodyear introducing the first slick-treaded tire into the series in 1971 in the French Grand Prix, a race won by Jackie Stewart on his way to his first World Championship title on Goodyear rub-ber, a feat repeated in 1973.

Niki Lauda logged Goodyear's 100th F1 victory at Hock-enheim in 1977. The 200th came in 1987 at the Australian GP with Gerhard Berger. Number 300 was scored in 1994 by Damon Hill at the Spanish GP. In 1997, Goodyear has faced a determined challenge from a new rival, Bridge-stone. It has responded to this competition by stepping up its technical development and has dominated the battle for the World Champi-onship. In May, Jacques Villeneuve scored the company's 350th Grand Prix victory in the Spanish GP at Barcelona.

Goodyear's commitment to the ever-changing technical challenges of Grand Prix tire engineering will be sustained into

Top: *Jack Brabham, Goodyear's first World Champion, winning the Dutch Grand Prix in 1966.* Left: *Jacques Villeneuve celebrates his win in the 1997 Spanish Grand Prix – Goodyear's 350th victory.*

1998 when new regulations demand grooved dry weather tires as part of a package intended to reduce Grand Prix car lap speeds. Yet the company is confident that it will consolidate its proven track record of transferring advanced technology from its racing activities to its road car products.

'We are extremely proud of Goodyear's dominant F1 victory record against competition in 1997,' says Stu Grant. 'We intend to be victorious and are backing up that goal with an aggressive Eagle tire development program supported by major capital investments to support our race teams in 1998 and beyond.

'We will deal with tire rule changes and challenges in all series, knowing we have the best people on the job and that our technical centers in the US, Japan and Luxembourg are linked to share critical data.'

The conviction that the technical knowledge derived from participating in racing is relevant to the ordinary motorist is exemplified by Goodyear's latest-generation high-performance road tire, the Goodyear Eagle F1. Unlike racing tires, which are specifically developed for either dry or wet track conditions, tires used by the everyday motorist require supreme versatility and dependability in all driving conditions. Consequently Goodyear's high-performance road tires must provide high levels of dry weather grip and directional stability, combined with a tread design which efficiently evacuates the water to pro-

Top: **Goodyear Technical Center at Akron, Ohio, where the Eagle race tires are produced. The intense development and testing of these tires in the heat of competition brings swifter benefits to the ordinary motorist as technology is transferred from the track to the road.**
Below: **Steve Myers (left), director of racing tire sales and marketing, with Stu Grant, general manager of racing worldwide.**

vide maximum performance in heavy rain.

'Much of what we learn with race tires in terms of handling, cornering and overall response, we can transfer to the design of tires that operate at lower speeds and in a less demanding environment,' explains Pierre Kummer, the company's director of tire technology for Europe, based at Goodyear's Technical Center in Luxembourg.

'For Goodyear, motor sport represents the ultimate testing environment. Only many years of experience, the most modern technology and the never-flagging enthusiasm of our engineers and researchers guarantee success.'

Walt Curtiss, director of the Akron Technical Center, says, 'It is no secret why design, development and manufacturing of Goodyear's race tires are located at the Akron Tech Center. Proximity to core research, developing new technologies, the feedback from race tire development and racing experience offer a synergy that benefits the consumer's street tire and world-class race drivers on the track.

'This ability to get fast technology transfer in every area from manufacturing capability to high-tech computer-aided performance simulation keeps Goodyear on the leading edge in all arenas of competition.'

Stu Grant confirms the link between passenger and racing

tires. 'The customer is the ultimate beneficiary of our racing involvement,' he says. 'The leading edge technology developed in racing benefits all of the company's tire development programs in one form or another.'

Of course, extensive experience in CART and other series has confirmed Goodyear's view that the rewards of racing are evenly divided between commercial and technical benefits. It is a well established fact that brand awareness for Goodyear's products is enhanced if there is opposition from a rival manufacturer, as there has been in CART for the past three seasons.

Looking ahead, Goodyear's racing department is confident that it will continue to produce a top-quality tire which works well across the wide range of cars being supplied, and is not simply tailored for the individual performance of one high-profile machine. The company's engineers continually fine-tune the del-

Top: Goodyear Eagle racing rain tires for CART are tested under controlled track conditions.
Left and above right: Tire engineers at work in just two of the motor sport arenas contested by Goodyear: CART and NASCAR.
Below: The enormously successful Goodyear Eagle F1 tires, winners of more than 350 Grand Prix races and fitted to 1997's World Championship-winning car.

icate balance between tire construction and rubber compounds to provide the best tire for constantly changing CART racing vehicles. The cars may evolve from year to year, but tire designers focus one step ahead when it comes to optimizing car/tire performance.

In general terms, Goodyear's race tire division balances the need to look months ahead with the immediate requirement to have subtly improved tire performance at the next race on the calendar. There is always one carefully planned compound available for each individual race in F1, CART and the IRL, which is supplemented by an optional compound, to ensure that every possible variation in track and weather conditions is confidently anticipated prior to each event.

'While the results of next weekend's race are certainly important, we are focused ahead,' says Stu Grant. 'I am optimistic and excited about the future. Racing helps inspire a winning spirit among members of our global Goodyear family. We are committed to be first, not second, in everything we do as a company.'

Goodyear is the leading competitor in many fields of motor sport worldwide. Its famous tires have brought countless victories in such diverse motor sport disciplines as (clockwise from top left) Formula 1, CART, NHRA drag racing, the Indy Racing League, NASCAR Winston Cup and NASCAR Craftsman Truck racing.

PACWEST RACING GROUP

OVERNIGHT SUCCESS

by David Phillips

IT took the best part of five years, but the PacWest Racing Group finally became an overnight success in 1997, scoring its first four victories in CART competition and placing fourth and sixth in the PPG Cup points standings. PacWest's stretch run saw one or both of its cars finish on the podium in seven of nine races after Mark Blundell's dramatic win at Portland in mid-June.

Patience proved to be a key to success after PacWest's formative seasons had been marked by promise and frustration. Having previously founded a successful aviation insurance company (Forbes Westar), a regional airline (Horizon Air) and, with his brothers, McCaw Cellular Communications, team owner Bruce McCaw brought an enviable entrepreneurial track record to CART when he and partners Tom Armstrong, Wes Lematta and Dominic Dobson founded PacWest in late 1993. McCaw knew Rome wasn't built in a day; he was also wise enough to allow the people he put in charge of the team to do their jobs.

'I've been a very strong believer in the group of people we've had since the middle of 1995,' he says. 'Back then we had some people wearing several hats; sooner or later you gotta get everybody wearing one hat, not three or four, and build the support in the organization to get the job done.

'So I think we've tried to spend some time on how we're organized. This is an easy business to get involved in every single decision. Sometimes you have to force yourself not to do that all the time.'

McCaw and his associates made a savvy choice in naming John Anderson to run the team's racing operations. A veteran team manager whose resume includes time spent with the likes of Forsythe, Galles/Kraco and A.J. Foyt

Enterprises, Anderson brought valuable experience to the PacWest organization. He'd seen dilettante team owners come and go, and he was convinced the PacWest Group meant business.

'What struck me immediately was that these were successful businessmen who wanted to run a racing team from a sound business footing,' says Anderson. 'They weren't drivers trying to make it as team owners, or rich guys who wanted to see their names in the paper a few times and then disappear. These guys were serious.'

That business background translates into more than a tough-minded approach to the bottom line; it also involves growing the company from within – by taking advantage of its human resources and giving its talented people every opportunity to advance.

'Part of Bruce's background is that he likes to see people move from here to there in the company,' says Anderson. 'He puts you in a position and says, "This is what I want done, you figure out how." He may not agree with your approach to something, but if you can make a convincing case he'll go with it.'

Steve Fusek and Paul 'Ziggy' Harcus are prime examples of the PacWest system. Formerly team coordinator at Walker Racing, Fusek joined PacWest in 1996 and has since risen to vice-president of business operations. Harcus, meanwhile, was chaffing in his role as crew chief at PacWest until he was named team manager of the team's fledgling Indy Lights program in 1996.

'I told Bruce that Ziggy was going to go somewhere else if we weren't careful,' recalls Anderson. 'We agreed he was a guy we didn't want to lose, so we looked to see if there was a way to create a situation to keep him.'

Of course, all the good people in the

Mark Blundell's season took off after technical director Allen McDonald *(right)* assumed the role of race engineer on the #18 Motorola Reynard-Mercedes.

Experienced team manager John Anderson *(far right)* has played a key role in PacWest's success.

Mauricio Gugelmin was out of luck at Surfers Paradise *(bottom)* but by season's end his run of misfortune had finally been broken.

Opposite: Bruce McCaw and Mark Blundell celebrate their victory in the season finale at the California Speedway.

world working together at peak efficiency still need the right tools to do the job. After a 1996 season which saw PacWest work wonders with the reliable but under-powered Ford/Cosworth XB engine, the team switched to Mercedes-Benz power.

'Part of this whole process is to get further up in the pecking order with your vendors,' says McCaw. 'This was a real opportunity to become perhaps a more important element in the Mercedes program than we would have been with Cosworth.'

PacWest also switched tire brands, and its Firestone-shod Reynard-Mercedes were among the pace setters in pre-season tests. Yet the team's legacy of unfulfilled promise continued. Mauricio Gugelmin routinely qualified in the front rows but couldn't buy, beg, borrow or steal a victory. Blundell, meanwhile, was curiously off the pace in the early races. The team had the equipment to win – as Greg Moore showed in his Reynard-Mercedes – but needed a final tweak on the personnel front.

That came with a mid-season decision to shuffle assignments for Jim Hamilton and Allen McDonald. Hamil-

ton had moved from All American Racers to PacWest, while McDonald had joined PacWest as technical director, having formerly worked with the Footwork/Arrows Formula 1 team. Half a dozen races into the '97 season the working relationship between Hamilton and Blundell was not producing results, thus Hamilton assumed a greater role in the team's R&D programs while McDonald took over as race engineer on the Motorola car.

'When you've got good people, just because one particular thing isn't working the way you want it to doesn't mean there's anything wrong with the people,' says McCaw. 'There's multiple personalities involved in these things, and we found that making some changes made a lot of things work a lot better.

'Since we began this team we have moved a number of people to a level and scope of responsibility that they've never had in their life. It's one thing to have good people, the next thing is to get 'em working together and making good decisions.'

Ironically, a bold decision that backfired put PacWest over the hump.

That was the team's quest to run the Detroit race on one pit stop. Thanks to the gamble, Gugelmin and Blundell leapfrogged from fourth and sixth to first and second at mid-race. They remained in front going into the final lap. But Gugelmin sputtered to a halt a mile from the finish, handing the lead to Blundell, who ran out of fuel within sight of the checkered flag.

'Detroit helped instill some of the confidence that we were a team that was ready to win races,' says McCaw. 'Sort of that mental shift from saying, "Gee, I *hope* we can win" to, "Gee, I *know* we can win."

'I'd love to have the points we threw away at Detroit, but on the same hand it was going for a win, not with one car but *really* going for it. It was right for the team. Everybody was ready for it, and I think what to me was most important was that the strategy was developed throughout the team.

'Under those circumstances, had it worked and had we only pulled it off with one car, I think it would have maybe imbalanced the team. It was better to go for the whole enchilada and it was either going to work or it wasn't.'

It didn't, but a week later Gugelmin dominated the early, rainy portion of the Portland race and Blundell stormed through from an exquisitely timed pit stop for slick tires to pip Gil de Ferran by 0.027s on a drying track for PacWest's maiden win.

'To do it right after Detroit was great,' says McCaw.

'Portland was a great race. A friend of mine was talking to me about the race and I said, "If the conditions start changing, I think we'll surprise a lot of people, because we've got two guys who can adapt to those conditions very, very well."

'The skill of going through changing conditions really shows the depth of drivers. Obviously, right to the bitter end I still thought Mo was the guy who was going to pull it off. But he got a little bottled up and couldn't get temperature in his tires as fast as he wanted. He had a squirrely car but he still brought it home. Another lap and it would have been a whole different race again.'

A month later Blundell led virtually from flag to flag at Toronto to earn his second win. Any skeptics unconvinced

Photos: Michael C. Brown

Right: Mark Blundell's commanding victory in Toronto confirmed that his brilliantly opportunist win in Portland a month earlier had been no fluke.

Below right: Mauricio Gugelmin has been with the team since 1995 and his maiden CART win gave Bruce McCaw particular pleasure.

Bottom: Victories on a road course, a temporary circuit and a superspeedway have confirmed that Mark Blundell is ready to mount a concerted challenge for the PPG Cup in 1998.

by PacWest's Detroit gamble and Blundell's Portland *tour de force* had to admit the team had come of age.

'It just solidified and took the perception of the fluke out of the Portland win,' notes McCaw. '[Tasman Motorsports owner] Steve Horne told me at Portland, "You got one, the next one will be right around the corner."'

Two items remained on the PacWest agenda for 1997. One of them was to bring Gugelmin that elusive first victory. He looked like a winner at Michigan before suffering an electrical problem, then settled for the fourth second-place finish of his CART career at Road America. Finally, everything fell into place at Vancouver. Gugelmin tigered his way past Michael Andretti at the start, then had a front row seat when early leader Alex Zanardi took to the escape road. After the PacWest crew got the better of Jimmy Vasser and Target/Chip Ganassi Racing on the final round of pit stops, 'Big Mo' cruised to an emotional victory.

'The wins were all special in their own right,' says McCaw. 'But in some ways that was the one we were all waiting for the most. Not to take anything away from Mark, but we'd been so close so many times with Mo and to finally win one . . . I was just so happy for him.'

A month later, Blundell took care of the other item on PacWest's list of things to do, scoring the team's first oval win and its first victory in a 500-mile race at the Marlboro 500.

And so the 1998 season beckons. Unlike last year, there are no sweeping changes planned for the PacWest line-up, least of all in the cockpit as both Gugelmin and Blundell have commit-ted to contracts which will see them driving for McCaw & Co. through the end of 1999.

For now, however, PacWest's sights are focused on 1998. With four wins under its belt, the team has higher aspirations for the coming year.

'Clearly our focus and our priorities have shifted from just being a race-winning team to being a championship team,' says McCaw. 'We have as good a shot at the championship next year as any team out there. And that's where we're headed. I just wish the season had started in Portland: I think our results in the last half of the season have been as strong as anybody's.

'But you have to take things one step at a time. If I'd have told people a year ago we were going to run for the championship, they'd have thought I was nuts – including the people on the team. It was a jump we probably weren't ready to make. But today we have an organization from top to bottom that absolutely believes and knows that we will be contenders for the championship, so that's where our head is.'

Photos: Michael C. Brown

BUILDING FOR THE FUTURE

A STRONG business is built from the bottom up. Without a strong foundation, the pinnacle is weak and vulnerable.

When Brown & Williamson Tobacco became involved in motorsports, it realized a strong base was necessary to achieve its marketing goals and support the continued growth of the sport in the United States.

Right: Barry Green, President of Team KOOL Green.

Below: The KOOL Indy Lights pair of Chris Simmons and Mark Hotchkis.

Bottom: KOOL partners Toyota in support of the Formula Atlantic series.

That's why it took a proactive role in developing opportunities for individuals and series to prosper through its support of the grassroots level of development of American drivers and open-wheel development series.

What began as a two-car Team KOOL Green effort in the 1996 PPG Firestone Indy Lights Championship, blossomed in 1997 into a comprehensive program that impacts all phases of open-wheel racing in this country.

At the peak is the high profile CART program, featuring races in the global markets of Australia, Brazil, the United States and Canada (and Japan in 1998). Almost 2.5 million spectators attended the 17 races in 1997 and more than 1 billion fans in 100 countries were exposed to the sport.

A level below CART was the three-car Team KOOL Green Indy Lights effort in the CART official development series – the PPG Firestone Indy Lights Series. In 1997, the Indy Lights effort was complemented by co-sponsorship – with Toyota Motor Sales of America – of the Formula Atlantic series, one of the longest-running open-wheel racing series anywhere and a series recognized world-wide as the proving ground for many of the sport's top drivers. Another building block to stabilize the foundation!

Jacques Villeneuve and his late father, Gilles, made their initial mark in Atlantic cars. So too, did CART Indy car stars such as Bobby Rahal, Greg Moore and a host of others.

Complementing the driver development efforts in Indy Lights and Atlantics was the Team Green Academy, operated in conjunction with the Derek Daly SpeedCentre at the Las Vegas Motor Speedway. Barry and Kim Green created the Academy to provide opportunities for aspiring American drivers who might not otherwise have the financial resources to learn their trade and move up through the open-wheel ranks. Over time, this program coupled with KOOL's driver development efforts will undoubtedly yield a stable of American drivers vying for seats in the premier open-wheel class of racing – the CART World Series.

Right: Part of the KOOL hospitality program includes in depth pit and paddock tours for the VIP guest.

Far right: The KOOL Balloon, a distinctive sight at race meetings and competitor in the KOOL Balloon Racing Series (inset below).

OTHER foundation elements of KOOL's program included the Reporter's Club and the KOOL Balloon Racing Series. The Reporter's Club focused on providing the media with the necessary support to perform their critical role of keeping fans apprised of the latest news about open-wheel racing in the United States. The KOOL Balloon Racing Series, a ten event series of hot-air balloon races at major CART race events, provided a new and unique method of entertaining fans and building interest in the sport.

Rounding out KOOL's program was its world-class hospitality program at each CART event, which exposes KOOL's business partners, a new set of influential corporate executives, to the sport.

ON THE RIGHT TRACK

THE 17 race PPG CART World Series featured stops in Brazil, Australia and Canada as well as 13 events in the United States.

1997 saw Team KOOL Green field a Reynard-Honda for three-time IMSA champion Parker Johnstone in all 17 rounds of the PPG CART World Series. The combination was a promising one, bringing together the team that won the 1995 PPG Cup with Johnstone, one of IMSA's winningest drivers and a man who won the pole position for the 1995 Michigan 500 in the first oval race of his career.

The season got off to a promising start, with Johnstone running competitively throughout the opening round at the Homestead Motor Sports Complex only to finish eighth after losing a couple of laps to the leaders as a result of a cut tire.

However, Homestead proved to be a precursor to a season in which the Team KOOL Green Reynard-Honda earned just 5 top ten finishes as Johnstone and Team KOOL Green were unable to match the pace of championship leaders Alex Zanardi, Gil de Ferran, Jimmy Vasser, Michael Andretti and Paul Tracy with any regularity. As was the case at Homestead, on those occasions when the KOOL Reynard-Honda was in a position for a top finish, misfortune usually intervened. Despite the intervention of misfortune, the KOOL Reynard-Honda prevailed to finish 10 of the 17 races in the points, and 16th overall in the championship.

But while victory on the track is the ultimate goal of every race team and an integral element of most racing sponsorships, it is not the ultimate litmus test of KOOL's multi-faceted program. The scope of KOOL's racing efforts extends well beyond the boundaries of the PPG CART World Series program to Indy Lights, Atlantics, and the ancillary efforts designed to support and enhance the overall initiative.

Triple IMSA champion Parker Johnstone headed the CART challenge in Team KOOL Green's Reynard–Honda.

KOOL's multi-faceted involvement in the PPG Firestone Indy Lights Championship is emblematic of this two-fold approach to racing, as represented by Team KOOL Green's entries for drivers Mark Hotchkis (below), Naoki Hattori and Chris Simmons as well as the KOOL Rookie Challenge, Race Challenge, and KOOL Move of the Race contingency awards.

1997 was the second year of Team KOOL Green's Indy Lights effort, with Simmons returning for his sophomore season with the team, joined by Indy Lights veteran Hotchkis and exciting newcomer Hattori with support from Brown & Williamson Tobacco of Japan. The trio enjoyed a successful campaign with at least one driver finishing in the top 10 in 12 out of the 13 races in addition to 5 podium finishes. Mark Hotchkis earned 1 pole on the way to 7th in the Indy Lights points standings, while Chris Simmons earned his first career pole and a total of 2 poles en route to 6th in the points race, and Naoki Hattori enjoyed a solid rookie campaign that netted 16th in the points standings.

Team KOOL Green ran a three-car Indy Lights team in 1997. Drivers were (from left to right) Chris Simmons, Mark Hotchkis and Naoki Hattori.

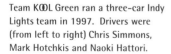

IN addition to the impact of Hotchkis, Simmons and Hattori's on-track efforts, KOOL's impact on the Indy Lights series was manifested in its contingency awards. Over the course of the season, KOOL distributed some $65,000 in its Rookie Challenge, Move of the Race and Race Challenge awards. Following the final round of the championship at California Speedway, impressive rookie Cristiano da Matta took home the KOOL Racing and KOOL Rookie Challenge seasonal awards totaling $25,000.

That pattern was repeated in the KOOL/Toyota Atlantic Championship where KOOL served as the co-title series sponsor and also awarded some $24,000 over the course of the 12 race season to winners of the KOOL Rookie Challenge and KOOL Move of the Race competitions. That sum was augmented by the $25,000 presented to Alex Barron as winner of both the KOOL "Series Cup Award" and "Rookie Challenge Winner" as well as the $15,000 KOOL "Racing Challenge Award" presented to Alex Tagliani as the non-rookie with the highest points total.

Never viewing their Team KOOL Green Indy Lights program and ancillary support programs for Indy Lights and the KOOL/Toyota Atlantic Championship as substantially different, KOOL considers all involvement as part of an integrated American driver development program. The Team KOOL Green sponsorship is a direct sponsorship of American driving talent providing a stepping stone for that talent to rise into Indy car racing, whereas sponsorship of Atlantics and involvement in Indy Lights contingency programs is a broad-brush approach of supporting two series that have as their objective developing drivers for the future of Indy car racing. Different elements – but all part of the driver development vision and methodology.

KOOL's multi-faceted sponsorship program extended into numerous innovative awards and incentives for both the Indy Lights and the KOOL/Toyota Atlantic series.

TEAM GREEN ACADEMY

PERHAPS the most innovative element of the driver development initiative is Team Green's own Team Green Academy. Team Green owner Barry Green has long been known for his ability to develop some of racing's finest young talents including Michael Andretti and Jacques Villeneuve. Working in concert with Derek Daly SpeedCentre (DDS) driving school, the Team Green Academy identifies 25 of America's most promising racing drivers from a variety of disciplines and invites them to participate in a comprehensive training and development program at the Las Vegas Motor Speedway. Five finalists are then selected from the initial group for a final competition with the outstanding talent selected for ongoing support from the Academy in the subsequent racing season, including financial backing from KOOL and coaching and tutoring support from DDS.

The Class of '97 saw drivers Matt Sielsky and Jeff Shafer selected to drive KOOL-sponsored cars in the U.S. National Formula Ford 2000 Championship. Sielsky earned 4 poles and finished second in the championship, while Shafer won the Phoenix round of the series as well as one pole position and finished 12th in the points race.

The Team Green Academy is a fresh and unique approach to grassroots development of open-wheel drivers in the United States. The program includes advanced on-track driving training and evaluation, technical training, physical and mental evaluation by Human Performance International (HPI) in Daytona Beach, Florida, and media training conducted by Aviva Diamond.

"There's a huge reservoir of driving talent in this country," Barry Green says. "But due to the tremendous diversity in the sport, developing drivers have a tough time making a name for themselves, because team owners face a difficult task of identifying new talent. The goal of the Team Green Academy is to support the development of American driving talent for the benefit not only of the drivers and Team Green, but also for the benefit of motor racing in general."

Four-time Indy car champion and former F1 titleist Mario Andretti lauds Green's efforts, "I have never seen as comprehensive a driver development program. Team Green and Derek Daly will give a huge boost to the future of American motorsports. I applaud and support them."

Above: Jeff Shafer (foreground) and Matt Sielsky, Team Green Academy graduates, were selected to drive in the U.S. National Formula Ford 2000 Championship with KOOL sponsorship support.

Sielsky (left) finished second in the championship.

Below: The final five. New racing talent chosen by the Team Green Academy pose with Parker Johnstone and the Team KOOL Green Reynard–Honda.

BEHIND THE SCENES

K OOL entered into motorsports realizing there were a lot of other people participating in the sport, many for quite some time. Responding to the challenge of "How do we get noticed?" KOOL focused on doing new and innovative things.

One of KOOL's most visible trackside presences during the past two seasons has been the Reporter's Club, a full service motorcoach facility for use by the writers and photographers who cover the CART, Indy Lights and Atlantic series. The coach has work stations, meeting rooms, telephones, fax and copy machines as well as computers with access to Speednet Pro available to working journalists. Breakfast and lunch are served during the three day weekends at the track, and Sunday mornings feature the unique "Stars of Tomorrow" breakfasts in which drivers from the Indy Lights and Atlantics series, together with other rising stars, are invited to meet with the media.

"Sure, at the end of the day we're hoping to get exposure out of that," says Bert Kremer, Manager, Sponsorships for Brown & Williamson Tobacco. "But we don't expect every journalist who comes into the motorcoach to walk away and write an article about KOOL. What we would like to happen – and I think there's enough indication that it is happening – if we facilitate the job the media has to do, if we help them to do their job more effectively, then it helps grow the sport and we benefit too."

Above: Oasis of calm. Luxurious state-of-the-art meeting rooms allow for business meetings to be conducted away from the whirlwind of activity that is naturally a part of race weekends.

Top: The Elkhart Lake KOOL barbecue served host to many members of the racing community.

Left: Full media service available to journalists from within the KOOL motorcoach.

Another less apparent dimension to the KOOL Racing Program is symbolized by Brown & Williamson's state-of-the-art hospitality unit featuring meeting rooms, marble floors, hardwoods, 2 full bathrooms, a shower, a full commercial kitchen, a 12' x 12' deck, three 70" and one 50" built-in big screen televisions.

The hospitality unit is the centerpiece to KOOL's ability to utilize its racing program to enhance its business-to-business relationships with suppliers, retailers and other business partners. Less visible to the racing fan, but still an important aspect of a sponsorship program, KOOL again sought to break out of the pack. Looking around the paddock, they saw what was being done and decided to set a new benchmark.

Says Kremer, "Our trade program focuses objectively, on being better than anyone else in that paddock. Brown & Williamson and KOOL are first class and very quality-driven. So when we bring our VIP customers to an event, we want to ensure everyone walks away with an experience that clearly communicates a world-class image.

Above: KOOL hospitality area caters to VIP guests both in the open and under cover.

Left: Sunday morning means "Stars of Tomorrow" at the Reporter's Club.

RISING ABOVE THE CROWD

THE newest and most unique element to the KOOL Racing Program has been the 1997 KOOL Balloon. At 10 races throughout the United States, balloons entered by approximately 20 corporate sponsors, from a range of industries, competed for a total of $120,000 in seasonal prize funds.

Working to devise promotion programs that would help KOOL "surround" the series, the awesome 15 story tall KOOL Indy car balloon and the KOOL Balloon Racing Series was yet another interesting way to do something fun and innovative and something that had not existed in CART in any way, shape or form.

Indeed, one could say much the same thing about the whole KOOL Racing Program. From the PPG CART World Series to the PPG Firestone Indy Lights Championship, KOOL/Toyota Atlantic Championship, Team Green Academy to the contingency awards, KOOL Reporter's Club, KOOL Balloon Racing Series and its many supporting programs, KOOL's racing effort is arguably the most ambitious sponsorship and marketing program ever seen in American open-wheel racing.

TEAM-BY-TEAM ●

review

by Jeremy Shaw

A total of 18 different teams, employing 34 drivers,

Target/Chip Ganassi Racing

Base: Indianapolis, Ind.

Drivers: Jimmy Vasser, Alex Zanardi, Arie Luyendyk

Sponsor: Target Stores

Chassis: Reynard 97I

Engines: Honda Indy V8

Tires: Firestone

Wins: 6 (Zanardi 5, Vasser 1);

Poles: 4 (Zanardi 4)

PPG Cup points: 339

Zanardi 195 (1st), Vasser 144 (3rd)

alex zanardi

jimmy vasser

CHIP GANASSI

TARGET/Chip Ganassi Racing employed a simple credo in 1997: If it ain't broke, don't fix it. Jimmy Vasser and Alex Zanardi had enjoyed a mutually enjoyable and successful relationship during their first season together in '96, resulting in a maiden PPG Cup title for Vasser and an impressive third-place finish, plus Rookie of the Year honors, for Zanardi. The alliance continued to blossom in 1997, despite a further intensification of the series' competitiveness, and was similarly successful, albeit with the relative positions transposed.

In terms of equipment, the new Reynard 97I chassis was clearly dominant, as were the latest breed of Firestone Firehawk tires. Honda, meanwhile, did not enjoy the same kind of superiority as in 1996. Consequently, the team and drivers had to work rather harder for their laurels.

Two other key elements of success – consistency and reliability – were retained, along with valuable stability in terms of personnel. Ganassi and his high-profile race weekend partner, former NFL superstar Joe Montana, once again left the day-to-day chores in the capable hands of managing director Tom Anderson and team manager Mike Hull, while race engineers Morris Nunn (Zanardi) and Julian Robertson (Vasser) took charge of setups and worked closely with their respective crew chiefs, Rob Hill and Grant Weaver.

There was some turnover in terms of mechanics, especially on the #1 car, which didn't help Vasser's peace of mind, but the only failure on either car all year came at the U.S. 500 when Vasser fell victim to a broken transmission. Remarkable.

Ganassi did not have a huge budget and his financial resources were spent wisely, with the emphasis upon maximizing the benefits of the available equipment rather than seeking any 'unfair advantage.' One of the team's primary aims going into the season was to improve its performance on the short ovals. It was partially successful as Vasser posted personal bests of fifth at Nazareth and third in Milwaukee. Zanardi, though, continued to struggle, and it was only after the midseason sequence of oval races had been completed that the Italian truly came on song.

JULIAN ROBERTSON & TOM ANDERSON

ALEX ZANARDI

JIMMY VASSER & ALEX ZANARDI take on tires and fuel at Homestead

Photos: Michael C. Brown

NICE GUYS
ONLY FINISH LAST
IF THEY'RE SLOW.

Alex Zanardi not only won this year's PPG CART World Series Championship, he won the hearts of fans with his warmth, humor and commitment to causes like St. Jude Children's Research Hospital.

TARGET

PacWest Racing Group

Base: Indianapolis, Ind.
Drivers: Mauricio Gugelmin, Mark Blundell
Sponsors: Hollywood, Motorola
Chassis: Reynard 97I
Engines: Mercedes-Benz IC108D
Tires: Firestone
Wins: 4 (Blundell 3, Gugelmin 1);
Poles: 3 (Gugelmin)
PPG Cup points: 247
Gugelmin 132 (4th), Blundell 115 (6th)

mauricio gugelmin

mark blundell

BRUCE McCAW

THE mantle of 'Most Improved Team' in the PPG Cup series in 1997 was claimed comfortably by the organization headed by accomplished businessman Bruce McCaw. As with Target/Chip Ganassi Racing, a well-structured management provided the cornerstone of PacWest's success. Under McCaw's expert guidance, veteran team manager John Anderson remained in charge of the expanded Indianapolis base, while Russell Cameron, formerly chief mechanic for Mauricio Gugelmin, was promoted to the role of overall crew chief. The new posting provided a valuable link between the universally respected 'Ando' and the individual crews headed by former Atlantic racer Mark Moore (Gugelmin) and ex-TWR/Galles wrench Butch Winkle (Mark Blundell).

The engineering department was strengthened substantially over the winter. Englishman Allen McDonald, formerly with TWR-Arrows in Formula 1, assumed the post of technical director, while chassis dynamics expert Jim Hamilton moved to Indianapolis from Southern California after concluding a lengthy liaison with All American Racers. Hamilton originally was assigned to work as Blundell's race engineer, while PacWest stalwart Andy Brown continued his partnership with Gugelmin which had begun fully a decade earlier in F3000. Soon, though, after Hamilton was reassigned to developmental duties and McDonald took charge of Blundell's Motorola car, the proper chemistry was in place and the results followed.

The most significant changes, of course, were in terms of equipment, with McCaw forging new partnerships during the offseason with Mercedes-Benz and Firestone. Gugelmin, in particular, developed an immediate affinity with the new combination. He posted some impressive lap times in winter testing and qualified solidly on the front row for the opening event at Homestead.

Blundell, too, was delighted to renew his association with Mercedes, having established an excellent rapport during the 1995 Formula 1 season when he stood in for Nigel Mansell at McLaren. The Englishman took rather longer to reap the full benefits, although, paradoxically, it was he who scored the team's first-ever victory – at Portland in June.

MARK BLUNDELL

MAURICIO GUGELMIN

Brahma Sports Team/Patrick Racing

Base: Indianapolis, Ind.
Drivers: Scott Pruett, Raul Boesel
Sponsor: Brahma
Chassis: Reynard 97I
Engines: Ford/Cosworth XD
Tires: Firestone
Wins: 1 (Pruett); Poles: 3 (Pruett 2, Boesel 1)
PPG Cup points: 193
Pruett 102 (9th), Boesel 91 (10th)

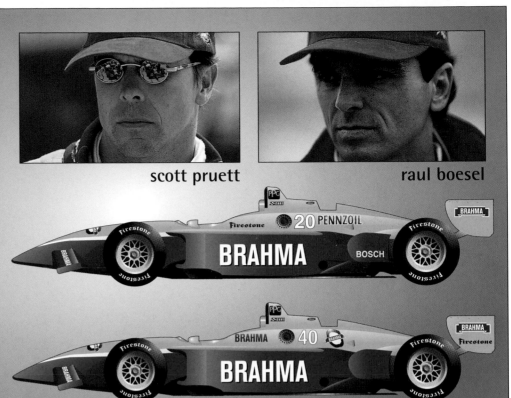

scott pruett

raul boesel

PAT PATRICK

PRUETT tasted victory in Australia

RAUL BOESEL

Photos: Michael C. Brown

SUBSTANTIAL sponsorship from Brahma, South America's largest brewery, ensured an expansion to two cars (as well as a fresh identity) for the team formerly known as Patrick Racing. Consequently, vastly experienced Brazilian Raul Boesel joined the operation following a couple of disappointing seasons with Team Rahal and Team Green. Scott Pruett remained as lead driver for the fourth straight year.

The organization was overseen, as usual, by veteran chief mechanic-turned-general manager Jim McGee. Other key players such as Steve Newey (team manager/technical director) and Tony Van Dongen (crew chief) ensured stability during the necessary expansion. Tom German (race engineer) and Donny Lambert (chief mechanic) took responsibility for the #20 car while veteran John Ward, formerly technical director for Dan Gurney's All American Racers, and the equally experienced Mikes Sales looked after the respective chores on Boesel's sister #40 machine.

The team's biggest challenge came in the six weeks leading up to the start of the season. Lola's new T97/00 chassis had failed to live up to expectations during an extensive winter testing program, and in an unprecedented – and extraordinarily bold – switch, Patrick decided to ditch the cars and start afresh with a new fleet of Reynards. The first 97I was delivered just in time for Spring Training at Homestead. The drivers immediately felt more comfortable in the Reynard, whereupon Pruett finished a fine fifth at Homestead, then followed up with an excellent victory in Surfers Paradise.

Pruett moved atop the PPG Cup standings after finishing third at Long Beach, while Boesel's confidence received a much-needed boost when he led the race convincingly during the middle stages. Boesel led also at Nazareth, then finished fifth in Rio and secured the pole at Gateway. The prospects looked extremely bright. But for the second straight season, the team failed to build upon its early successes. Boesel was unable to match his teammate's consistency in qualifying and both drivers were blighted by a series of accidents and/or engine problems.

SCOTT PRUETT confers with his engineers during practice

an engine that produces more than 800 hp while enduring

500 miles at nearly constant full throttle. Or were we?

Mercedes-Benz is the "Official Car of CART."

Mercedes-Benz

Motorsport

Marlboro Team Penske

Base: Reading, Pa.
Drivers: Al Unser Jr., Paul Tracy
Sponsor: Marlboro
Chassis: Penske PC26
Engines: Mercedes–Benz IC108D
Tires: Goodyear
Wins: 3 (Tracy 3); Poles: 2 (Tracy 2)
PPG Cup points: 188
Tracy 121 (5th), Unser 67 (13th)

al unser jr.

paul tracy

ROGER PENSKE

O H my, what a disappointment! As with Pat Patrick's team, the season began promisingly for Roger Penske as Paul Tracy finished strongly in second place at Homestead and diced for the lead at Surfers Paradise. Unser, meanwhile, rebounded from an engine failure and a lost wheel (oops) in the opening two events to finish fourth at Long Beach. Next time out at Nazareth, Tracy sped to an accomplished victory – the first of three straight which elevated him into the lead of the PPG Cup standings – while Unser backed him up in third. After a dismal 1996 season, Marlboro Team Penske appeared to be firmly back in contention for the championship.

But the remainder of the campaign was little short of disastrous. Neither driver could find a handle on his PC26 for the road or street course events and Unser continued to be plagued by reliability problems. Even the two superspeedway events in Michigan and California provided scant satisfaction, save for a steady rather than spectacular run to fourth by Tracy in the U.S. 500.

Unser, of course, has never been noted as a particularly good qualifier. But in the final eight races he managed a best of 14th on the grid at Road America. In Vancouver, where he traditionally shines, Unser languished in 22nd – his worst ever starting position on a road course in 16 years of CART competition. The two-time PPG Cup champion wasn't much quicker in the race, posting the 17th fastest lap, although he did provide another perfect example of his own sublime talent, as well as the tenacity and strategic excellence of Penske Racing, by climbing through the field to finish fifth.

There has been an unusually high staff turnover in Reading during recent years. Nevertheless, led by newly promoted general manager Chuck Sprague and technical director Nigel Beresford, the team was unstinting in its efforts to claim that elusive 100th race victory. It's a shame the milestone remained beyond reach. It would have been a fitting tribute to the incomparable Karl Kainhofer, who finally retired after more than 30 years as Penske's right-hand man.

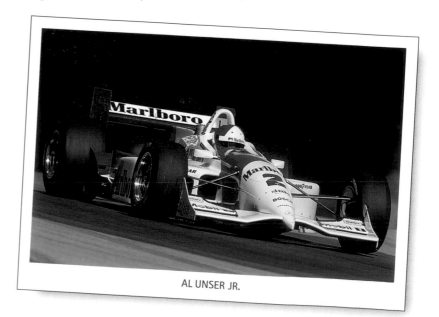

Both TRACY and UNSER made the podium at Nazareth

PAUL TRACY

AL UNSER JR.

Photos: Michael C. Brown

Inside INDYCARS

FOR TECHNICAL ANALYSIS OF THE INDYCAR SCENE...

RACECAR ENGINEERING

1 9 9 7 | Vol 7 No 3 | UK £3.50 | USA $7.95

Swift Startles CART Kingpins

FIRST US-MADE CAR TO WIN FOR 14 YEARS

Suspensions in F1
ONE, TWO AND THREE SPRING SYSTEMS

Ford's Wild Horse
TOM GLOY RACING TRANS-AM MUSTANG

FOR WINNERS ONLY!

- IRL NISSAN INFINITI V8 ENGINE MANAGEMENT SYS
- A ONE-MAN RACECAR MANUFACTURER ● COMPOS

RACECAR ENGINEERING

1 9 9 7 | Vol 7 No 4 | UK £3.50 | USA $7.95

Bad Vibrations for Formula 1!
PROBLEMS WITH NEW REAR IMPACT STRUCTURES

Seat's Title Defence
THE 2-LITRE IBIZA 'EVO 2' RALLY KIT CAR

Pilbeam Moving Up
STATE-OF-THE-ART FACILITY AT BOURNE

FOR WINNERS ONLY!

CLASS OF '97 CART Indycars

CART Indycars

RACECAR ENGINEERING

1 9 9 7 | Vol 7 No 8 | UK £3.50 | USA $7.95

WORLD RALLY CAR SPECIAL

CLASS OF 97

97 World Rally Cars

FOR WINNERS ONLY!

- OPTIMISING RACECAR SUSPENSION SYSTEMS
- RILEY & SCOTT ENTERS INDY RACING LEAGUE
- WIND TUNNEL RESEARCH FOR THE AMATEUR

YOU CANNOT AFFORD TO MISS IT!

Archive issues and full subscription details on **WWW.LINK HOUSE.CO.UK**

RACECAR ENGINEERING is published by Link House Magazines, Link House, Dingwall Avenue, Croydon, CR9 2TA, England Tel (44)(0) 181 597 0181 Fax (44)(0) 181 597 4040

Newman/Haas Racing

Base: Lincolnshire, Ill.
Drivers: Michael Andretti, Christian Fittipaldi, Roberto Moreno
Sponsors: Kmart, Texaco/Havoline, Budweiser
Chassis: Swift 007.i
Engines: Ford/Cosworth XD
Tires: Goodyear
Wins: 1 (Andretti); Poles: 0
PPG Cup points: 163
Andretti 108 (8th), Fittipaldi 42 (15th),
Moreno 13 (of 16, 19th)

michael andretti

christian fittipaldi

CARL HAAS

N common with the Patrick and Penske teams, Newman/Haas Racing began the season with high hopes of claiming the PPG Cup title. Preseason testing with the new Swift 007.i was limited due to its relatively late completion, but the car's vital signs were extremely healthy. Sure enough, the potential was fulfilled in its very first race as Michael Andretti sped to a sensational debut victory at Homestead.

Surprisingly, that success remained the high water mark. Andretti added a third in Australia and runner-up finishes at Nazareth, Milwaukee and Detroit, but his championship aspirations were dented by several mechanical failures and a couple of self-inflicted accidents. There was also a bizarre error at Long Beach where the team's tire pressure gauges had been incorrectly calibrated, leading to a series of blown tires.

Fittipaldi's accident at Surfers Paradise, where he suffered a badly broken right leg, also served to interrupt the team's progress . . .

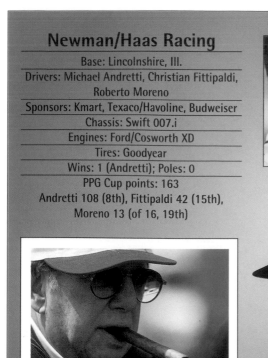

MICHAEL ANDRETTI

ROBERTO MORENO

Paul gives Christian the film star treatment!

although, having said that, Roberto Moreno did perform admirably as substitute. The experienced Brazilian drove especially well at Long Beach, his home race in Rio, where he qualified a career-best second, and Detroit, where he started on row two and finished fifth.

When Fittipaldi returned to the fray at Portland, it was as if he had never been away. He was perhaps fortunate to be greeted on his comeback by rain, which most assuredly reduced the g-loadings – and once again highlighted his prodigious wet-weather skills – yet the 26-year-old still displayed true grit by withstanding considerable pain from his still-healing injury. Other sterling performances came at Cleveland, where he would surely have finished on the podium but for an airjack failure, and at Road America, where he was hindered by electronic woes.

CHRISTIAN FITTIPALDI

Fast Crowd.

Want to run with the elite? Better know something about performance. The kind of performance that keeps Texaco out in front on the track and off. With products like Havoline Formula^3 motor oil. And CleanSystem^3 high performance gasolines. It's all about pushing limits. Because for performers, success doesn't stop at the finish line. Add more life to your car.

Walker Racing

Base: Indianapolis, Ind.
Driver: Gil de Ferran
Sponsors: Valvoline, Cummins
Chassis: Reynard 97I
Engines: Honda Indy V8
Tires: Goodyear
Wins: 0; Poles: 2
PPG Cup points: 162 (2nd)

gil de ferran

DERRICK WALKER

Race engineer BILL PAPPAS with GIL DE FERRAN

DERRICK Walker's organization truly came of age in 1997. The lack of even a solitary race victory represented a travesty, since Gil de Ferran drove consistently well (after a somewhat rocky start) and the crew never failed to present him with a reliable, efficient car. As with several other teams, the Goodyear tires appeared to be the only weak link, although, to his credit, de Ferran largely resisted the temptation to use that as excuse for not visiting Victory Lane.

Walker Racing was much changed from the team which endured such a disappointing time in 1996. De Ferran, of course, was new, joining the Indianapolis operation following Jim Hall's decision to retire from active participation, as was race engineer Bill Pappas, who had developed a close bond with de Ferran during the previous two years. Pappas' no-nonsense approach melded perfectly with Walker's own philosophy, and he struck an instant rapport with engineering coordinator Rob Edwards, who along with team manager Ron Meadows and crew chief Dan Miller provided the organization with vital stability.

De Ferran was instrumental in ensuring Walker's new relationship with Honda, which paid off in spades. The only engine problem all year came toward the end of the final race at Fontana, and by that stage second place in the PPG Cup championship already had been clinched.

'This has been a fantastic season for us all the way around,' declared de Ferran after finishing sixth in the Marlboro 500. 'We've been right up front, just like today, and that I enjoy very much. These things happen in racing. Sure, we had a chance to win the race, but more importantly we had a fantastic car and unbelievable [pit] stops.'

For sure, the best is yet to come.

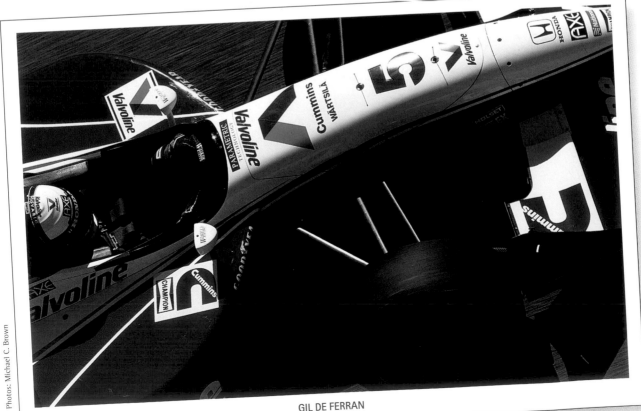

Photos: Michael C. Brown

GIL DE FERRAN

WHEN YOU RACE, IT'S WHAT'S INSIDE THAT COUNTS: GUTS, DETERMINATION AND OIL.

For all its spectacle, racing is truly about things that are hard to see. Like the .003 inch of oil that protects your engine. At Valvoline, we've been sweating the details for 130 years so Gil de Ferran can trust his instincts without worrying about his engine. That's an edge we can give to every driver, regardless of how fast you go. The guts and determination? Well, that's a different story.

The #1 Choice Of Top Mechanics.

People Who Know Use Valvoline.

Team Rahal

Base: Hilliard, Ohio
Drivers: Bobby Rahal, Bryan Herta
Sponsors: Miller Lite, Shell Oil Products
Chassis: Reynard 97I
Engines: Ford/Cosworth XD
Tires: Goodyear
Wins: 0; Poles: 2 (Herta)
PPG Cup points: 142
Herta 72 (11th), Rahal 70 (12th)

bobby rahal

bryan herta

BOBBY RAHAL: Team boss and driver

GOING into the new season, Bobby Rahal continued his penchant for change by switching from Mercedes-Benz engines to Ford/Cosworth. It was the sixth time he had begun a new campaign with a different equipment package since establishing his own race team, initially in partnership with Carl Hogan, in late-1991.

When Rahal made the announcement, at the conclusion of the 1996 season, it was greeted with some surprise, since the Mercedes appeared to come on strongly in the latter part of the year while the Ford continued to suffer reliability problems. The latest XD, however, surpassed all expectations. Team Rahal lacked neither horsepower nor reliability in '97.

The team took a couple of races to properly come to grips with the new Reynard-Ford combination, and during the season the engineers appeared to be flummoxed on several occasions when, after establishing a good baseline setup during testing, they were presented with all-new Goodyear tires for the race weekends.

By and large, Rahal and his young protege, Bryan Herta, proved to be closely matched. And equally unlucky. Rahal came close to ending his long victory drought in Rio, when he dominated the race before running out of fuel just over one lap from the finish. Cruel. Herta, meanwhile, qualified twice on the pole, at Mid-Ohio and Laguna Seca (where, incredibly, he was a full second clear of the next fastest Goodyear contender), only to run into tire difficulties on both occasions.

BRYAN HERTA

BOBBY RAHAL

Consequently, at the conclusion of the season Rahal confirmed his latest equipment change by switching allegiance from Goodyear to Firestone.

'This is certainly not a decision we took lightly or made hastily,' said Rahal. 'It was with a great deal of analysis and consideration, not to mention a fair amount of lost sleep, that we determined to make the move.'

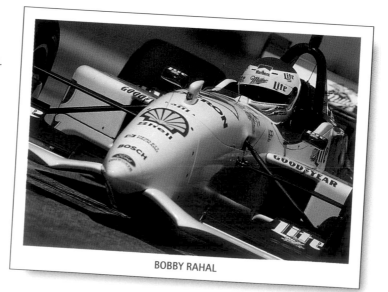

BOBBY RAHAL

Photos: Michael C. Brown

When asked his biggest aggravation in life Bryan Herta replied, "traffic." We said, "perfect."

Player's/Forsythe Racing

Base: Indianapolis, Ind.
Driver: Greg Moore
Sponsors: Player's Ltd./Indeck
Chassis: Reynard 96I/97I
Engines: Mercedes-Benz IC108D
Tires: Firestone
Wins: 2; Poles: 0
PPG Cup points: 111 (7th)

greg moore

JERRY FORSYTHE

Team manager TONY BRUNETTI

A COUPLE of weeks after Pat Patrick announced he would forsake his new Lolas in favor of Reynards, Jerry Forsythe's team followed suit. The decision came in early February, after Greg Moore had languished in 23rd position during the traditional 'Spring Training' open test session at the Metro-Dade Homestead Motorsports Complex.

'We didn't have a great time at the test,' admitted Player's/Forsythe Racing General Manager Neil Micklewright with admirable restraint, 'so we took a close look at the whole situation to see if there was anything missing. We figured the Lola just lacked overall downforce in comparison to the Reynard. We got to a point in Spring Training where Greg wasn't scaring himself any more, but we weren't getting any quicker. We were just struggling and we couldn't see any way out of the mess.'

With less than a month to go before the first race, also at Homestead, the Phil Lepan-led crew lost no time in rescuing one of its '96 Reynards from show-car duties and refettling it for competition. Moore responded by qualifying fourth, despite minimal testing, and finishing in the same position.

Moore's remarkable partnership with Steve Challis, his friend, confidant – and race engineer – since his Formula Ford days, once again paid off as the pair got to grips with their new 97I, which was delivered just in time for the race in Australia. Moore this time finished second and remained a staunch challenger for victory throughout the season. His title hopes ultimately were halted by a series of incidents and engine problems, but not before he had won two races and marked both himself and the team as potential champions.

Full service for GREG MOORE by the Player's/Forsythe crew

Photos: Michael C. Brown

More Power, More Service, More Support, More Choices, More of Everything!

INDECK POWER EQUIPMENT COMPANY

Does it all, from small boilers to large turnkey power plants. Indeck is the WORLD'S LARGEST supplier of rental boilers and pre-packaged boilers up to 250,000 lbs/hr (lease, rent, purchase). In addition to designing/building complete water treatment and combustion control systems for new and retrofit plants, Indeck provides rental generators, chillers and compressors.

Contact: Marsha Fournier, 800-446-3325

INDECK OPERATIONS, INCORPORATED

Service With an Owner's Perspective. There is no better choice for Operation and Maintenance Services than Indeck Operations. Consistently leading the industry in safety, availability, reliability and cost control, the skilled teams from Indeck offer unequaled service to power producing and manufacturing facilities.

Contact: Paul Corwin or Frank Shapiro, 800-275-5658

INDECK ENERGY SERVICES, INCORPORATED

Independently owned power plants have now become the source of electric generation in half of all new plant installations. Indeck Energy Services, Inc. is a leading developer, owner and operator of cogeneration (steam plus electricity) and independent power plants. Learn more about the enormous benefits of independent power and cogeneration.

Contact: Tom Campone, 800-275-5658

INDECK CAPITAL, INCORPORATED

Indeck Capital combines experience and knowledge in providing financial services to the power industry. Indeck Capital, the General Partner of the Indeck North American Power Fund, enhances the value of power generating assets by improving operations, optimizing fuel arrangements, maximum monetization of equity, and aggressive power marketing.

Contact: John Salyer, 847-459-4250

Greg Moore drives the *INDECK* sponsored  car #99

Tasman Motorsports Group

Base: Hilliard, Ohio

Drivers: Andre Ribeiro, Adrian Fernandez

Sponsors: LCI International, Marlboro, Tecate, Quaker State

Chassis: Lola T97/00 & Reynard 97I

Engines: Honda Indy V8

Tires: Firestone

Wins: 0; Poles: 0

PPG Cup points: 72

Ribeiro 45 (14th), Fernandez 27 (18th)

andre ribeiro

adrian fernandez

STEVE HORNE

ANDRE delighted with third at Toronto

Race engineer DON HALLIDAY

Photos: Michael C. Brown

ANDRE Ribeiro's season was split into two very distinct halves. For the first eight races he achieved next to nothing with the recalcitrant Lola chassis. The final nine events, by contrast, were altogether more fruitful after team owner Steve Horne bit the bullet and acquired a Reynard 97I (which had previously seen service primarily as a test hack with Walker Racing).

Oh, boy, what a difference the new car made! Whereas his best qualifying effort of the season thus far had netted 13th on the grid, Ribeiro started eighth on his first appearance with the Reynard at Cleveland. He admitted to several mistakes while still getting used to the car and so wound up out of the points in 13th, but he had made his point.

'I think people can now see our problem was not with the drivers, the team, the engineers or the tires,' declared the Brazilian pointedly. 'It was the car.'

Ribeiro finished third in his next race at Toronto, and led convincingly in the U.S. 500 until becoming one among several Reynard customers to be sidelined by a transmission problem. He drove well, too, at Elkhart Lake before being inadvertently punted off the road by Raul Boesel; finished a strong fourth at Laguna Seca, despite tangling with Scott Pruett in the late stages; and dominated much of the season finale at Fontana before running out of fuel inside the final 100 miles.

RIBEIRO in his LCI/Marlboro Lola-Honda

THE LCI INDY CAR CAN TRAVEL 344 FEET IN ONE SECOND.

LCI INTERNATIONAL KNOWS THE IMPORTANCE OF EVERY SECOND IN A LONG DISTANCE RACE.

So, it's no surprise that they are the first major telecommunications company to bill your long distance calls in one second increments after an initial sixty seconds. Stop paying for time you don't use on your long distance calls when you switch to LCI. Plus, sign up today and receive a FREE LCI racing jacket. Call now and join the winning team.

SIGN UP TODAY AND RECEIVE A FREE RACING JACKET

1-800-LCI-LONG

LCI International®
A very different telecommunications company.

ADRIAN FERNANDEZ leads the similar Tasman Lola of teammate ANDRE RIBEIRO

T HE second Tasman Motorsports Group driver, Adrian Fernandez, meanwhile, was left to his own devices with the Lola, since there were apparently no other new Reynard chassis available at that late stage in the season. To their credit, Fernandez, race engineer Diane Holl (still the only female engineer in the CART pit lane) and the entire Tecate/Quaker State team, led by Andy Jones, soldiered on as best they could. Lola continued to produce new parts in a bid to improve performance, but none of them had the desired effect until the final race of the year, when a new underwing brought about a remarkable transformation. Suddenly, the car responded. By then, of course, Fernandez's self-confidence was at a low ebb, but in the race he produced one of the single most impressive performances of the season as he gradually got to grips with the car's effectiveness and rewarded his team and sponsors with a magnificent podium finish.

ADRIAN FERNANDEZ

Engineer DIANE HOLL and tire specialist KENNY SZYMANSKI share a joke

Labatt USA wants to stop
and say "thanks" to
Adrian Fernandez.

Just one
problem.

Adrian
doesn't like
to stop.

Labatt USA, proud sponsor of the Tecate car, salutes Adrian Fernandez.

The Tecate/Quaker State Team and The Tasman Motor Sports Group.

Hey, when you race, it's nice to have people behind you.

TECATE
QUAKER STATE

©1996 Labatt U.S.A. Darien, CT

Tasman

Labatt

Darien, CT 203-656-1876

CERVEZA
TECATE
IMPORTED BEER
PRODUCT OF MEXICO
12 FL. OZ. (355 ml)

Team KOOL Green

Base: Indianapolis, Ind.
Driver: Parker Johnstone
Sponsors: KOOL, Klein Tools
Chassis: Reynard 97I
Engines: Honda Indy V8
Tires: Firestone
Wins: 0; Poles: 0
PPG Cup points: 36 (16th)

parker johnstone

BARRY GREEN

TONY CICALE

BARRY Green's organization moved into a brand-new state-of-the-art shop over the winter, secured major sponsorship from the KOOL brand of Brown & Williamson, regained the services of vastly experienced race engineer Tony Cicale, switched its tire allegiance to Firestone, joined forces with Honda, the defending Manufacturers Champion, and entrusted Parker Johnstone with the driving duties. After suffering through a dismal campaign with Raul Boesel in '96, Green seemed set to turn his fortunes around.

But the relationship between the loquacious Johnstone and the understated Cicale never really got into top gear.

The season started out promisingly enough, with Johnstone qualifying seventh and finishing eighth in the opening race. Yet perhaps the tone was set during the first full-course caution of the year. Johnstone had made a pit stop immediately before the yellow lights flashed on. By the time he had rejoined, the #27 car had fallen a lap behind the leaders, who duly pitted during the caution. According to newly introduced regulations, however, after the race leaders had taken on service and rejoined in line *behind* Johnstone, any cars *in between* the pace car and the race leader *should* have been waved past the pace car and allowed to circle around the race track in order to take up position at the back of the pack. But the officials neglected to follow the correct procedure; and Green, still cursing his luck for pitting a couple of laps before the caution, failed to notice the error. So Johnstone remained a lap down and was unable to make up the deficit.

The likable Oregonian scored points in 11 of the 17 races including all of those he finished, which represented a respectable achievement – but he was involved in more than his fair share of incidents. The conflict with Cicale also sapped his confidence, so Johnstone rarely displayed the flair he had exhibited with the under-funded Brix/Comptech team on occasion in '96.

PARKER JOHNSTONE

Photos: Michael C. Brown

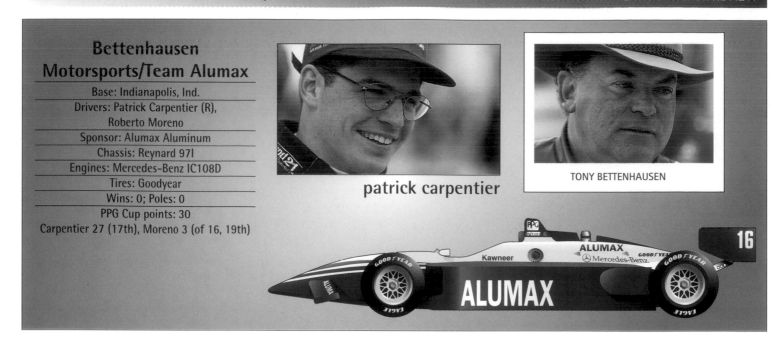

Bettenhausen Motorsports/Team Alumax

Base: Indianapolis, Ind.
Drivers: Patrick Carpentier (R), Roberto Moreno
Sponsor: Alumax Aluminum
Chassis: Reynard 97I
Engines: Mercedes-Benz IC108D
Tires: Goodyear
Wins: 0; Poles: 0
PPG Cup points: 30
Carpentier 27 (17th), Moreno 3 (of 16, 19th)

patrick carpentier

TONY BETTENHAUSEN

TOM BROWN

P ATRICK Carpentier achieved one of his goals by securing the Jim Trueman Rookie of the Year Award – the second time team owner Tony Bettenhausen has achieved the accolade in six years (joining Stefan Johansson in 1992). The reigning Player's/Toyota Atlantic champion also displayed simply awesome pace on the ovals. On the road courses, however, to his intense frustration, the 26-year-old French-Canadian never even remotely extracted the maximum potential from his Alumax Reynard-Mercedes.

Strange. Carpentier had shown equal prowess on both road courses and ovals with Lynx Racing in 1996, winning nine of 12 Atlantic races, and he had proven impressive during his initial test with Bettenhausen at Sebring, where he gained the nod in the face of stiff opposition from European Formula 3000 contenders Jorg Muller, Allan McNish and Tom Kristensen.

Preseason testing had gone well. Carpentier struck up a good rapport with technical director Tom Brown, who joined Bettenhausen's newly expanded team after more than 10 years with Penske Cars, and posted some extremely promising test times. He ran well, too, at Homestead, where he qualified and finished ninth, comfortably best of the three rookies in attendance. But at Surfers Paradise he languished a dismal 20th on the grid. At Long Beach he was 21st. Then he qualified a superb third at Nazareth. And so the trend continued. He finished a brilliant second at Gateway, beaten only by an inspired Tracy, who swept past with just two laps remaining, but never qualified better than 19th on any road or street course.

The team brought in experienced Brazilian Roberto Moreno to try to pinpoint the difficulty, whereupon Carpentier promptly broke his collarbone in a bicycle accident and was obliged to sit out two races. Moreno duly filled in and ran among the top 10 on both occasions.

PATRICK CARPENTIER brought Tony Bettenhausen's Alumax Reynard tantalizingly close to victory at Gateway

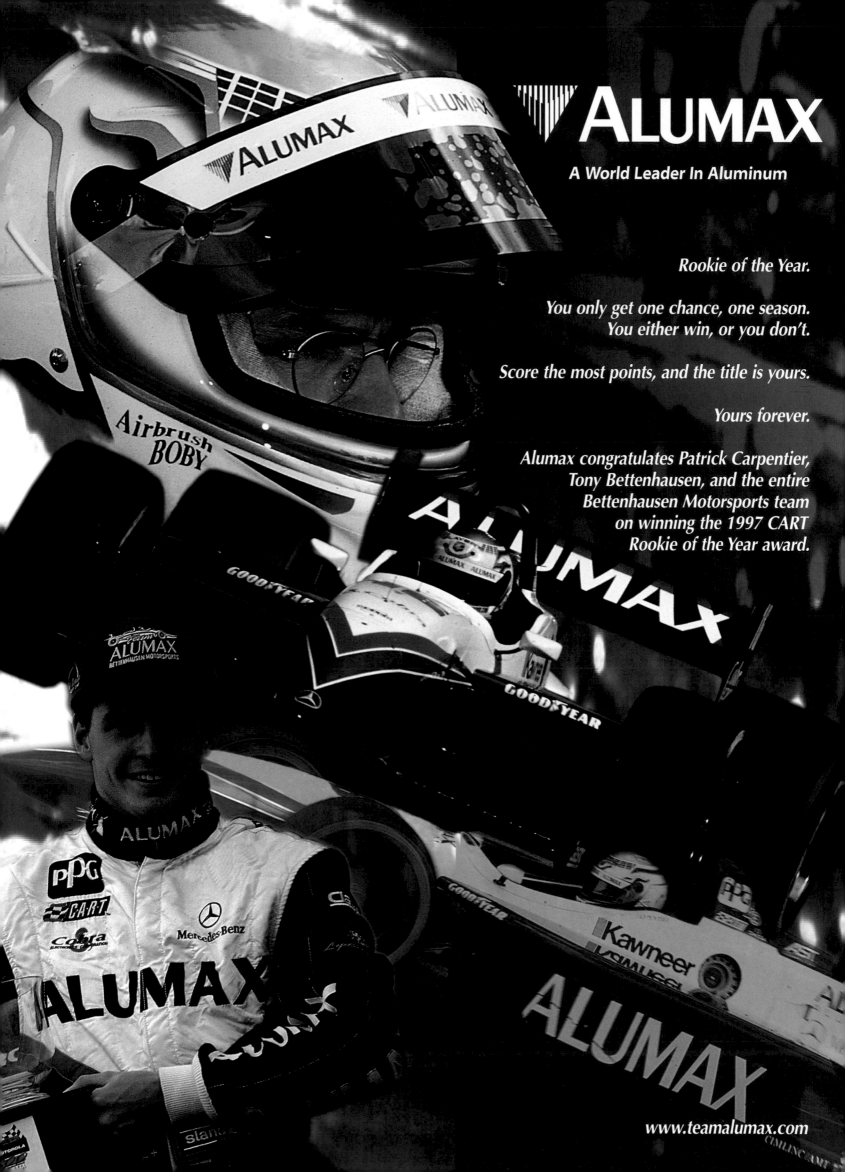

Hogan Racing

Base: Indianapolis, Ind./St. Louis, Mo.
Drivers: Dario Franchitti (R), Robby Gordon
Sponsor: Hogan Motor Leasing LLC
Chassis: Reynard 97I
Engines: Mercedes-Benz IC108D
Tires: Firestone
Wins: 0; Poles: 1 (Franchitti)
PPG Cup points: 15
Franchitti 10 (22nd), Gordon 5 (26th)

dario franchitti

CARL HOGAN

Photos: Michael C. Brown

EVEN though Carl Hogan was left high and dry when Roger Penske elected not to continue their partnership beyond the end of the 1996 season, during which Hogan Penske Racing had entered a car for Emerson Fittipaldi (and Jan Magnussen), he wasn't ready to quit the sport. Instead, he decided to go it alone. Hogan, who won a pair of Formula 5000 championships in the early 1970s, contacted his friends at Mercedes-Benz and was recommended the services of Dario Franchitti. The 23-year-old Scotsman had been an integral part of the Mercedes Junior Team, competing for two years in the recently concluded International Touring Car series; but he was anxious to return to open-wheel racing. Here, it seemed, was a perfect match.

Doug Peterson, formerly co-owner of Brix/Comptech Racing, was placed in charge of the new team which was capably managed by the experienced Peter Scott. Other key members included crew chief Shad Huntley, engineer Steve Conover (both ex-Comptech) and rookie race engineer Alan Langridge.

The final pieces were put into place mere days before Spring Training, whereupon Franchitti quickly impressed the team with his determination and willingness to listen and learn. Progress was rapid. Excellent strategy by Hogan allowed Franchitti to be on the road toward victory at Gateway, in only his sixth race, until hobbled by a broken transmission. He later qualified on the pole at Toronto and ran strongly in several other races, only to be involved in a series of accidents.

The entire team worked well together, although shortly before the end of the season it became apparent that Franchitti had decided his future lay elsewhere – apparently with Team KOOL Green. An aggrieved Hogan promptly fired the Scot and replaced him with Robby Gordon, who had endured a less than successful rookie season in NASCAR Winston Cup and was desperately seeking a way back into CART competition. Gordon drove impressively to an eighth-place finish at Fontana, notching the team's best result of the year.

DARIO FRANCHITTI

Broken car – and, at season's end, broken dreams

ROBBY GORDON

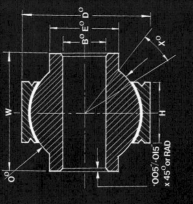

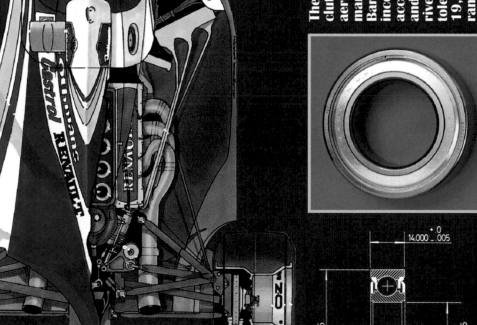
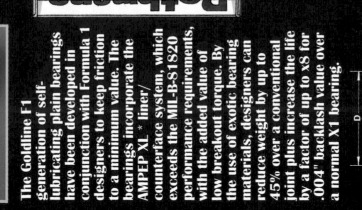

All American Racers

Base: Santa Ana, Calif.
Drivers: Juan Fangio II, P.J. Jones
Sponsors: Castrol, Jockey
Chassis: Reynard 96I/97I
Engines: Toyota RV8A/RV8B
Tires: Goodyear
Wins: 0; Poles: 0
PPG Cup points: 12
Fangio 9 (23rd), Jones 3 (28th)

juan fangio II

p.j. jones

DAN GURNEY

The #98 car of P.J. JONES is refueled by the AAR crew

D AN Gurney's team underwent substantial change following a disappointing return to the PPG Cup series in 1996. Several prominent and long-standing team members departed the organization, including chief engineer John Ward and vehicle dynamics expert Jim Hamilton. Gone, too, was the Eagle chassis, which had failed to live up to expectations. Gurney instead ordered Reynard chassis and gathered a new technical regime headed by Matt Cranor. Bernie Marcus (working with Juan Fangio II) and Gerald Tyler (P.J. Jones) stepped in as race engineers. AAR stalwart Gary Donahoe remained as team manager, with Gary Martin taking overall responsibility for the crew and John Scherry and Derek Ige overseeing the #36 and #98 cars respectively.

The team was obliged to use '96 motors for the first four races, and although the latest Toyota engines remained markedly inferior to the competition, they did exhibit improved power and reliability as the season progressed. The drivers, meanwhile, maintained a good attitude and continued to work hard.

'The one benefit about being down on power,' said Jones, 'is that you work extra-hard on the car.'

Indeed, the AAR Reynards displayed excellent handling characteristics which enabled Fangio and Jones to lap with admirable consistency – for as long as their engines lasted. Fangio scored points in four different races, including 10th-place finishes at Detroit and Road America, and once again confirmed he belongs at this level. Jones had to wait until the final 500-mile race at California Speedway before adding another three points to the team's tally. He, too, displayed a good turn of speed and established an excellent rapport with Tyler. With some more horsepower, AAR will feature strongly.

Photos: Michael C. Brown

JUAN FANGIO II

Castrol is a world leader in the specialist field of lubricants. Our partnership with Toyota in motorsport enables us to test products to extreme limits. The information gathered during races provides vital data for ongoing development programmes, resulting in new lubricant technology.

Our mission is to provide car owners worldwide with high performance, premium quality, technology led products which aim to both enhance performance and provide high levels of engine protection.

TOYOTA

Castrol

PARTNERS IN MOTORSPORT

MCI/Arciero-Wells Racing

Base: Rancho Santa Margarita, Calif.
Drivers: Max Papis, Hiro Matsushita
Sponsors: MCI, Panasonic, Duskin
Chassis: Reynard 96I/97I
Engines: Toyota RV8A/RV8B
Tires: Firestone
Wins: 0; Poles: 0
PPG Cup points: 12
Papis 8 (24th), Matsushita 4 (27th)

max papis

hiro matsushita

CAL WELLS III

FRANK ARCIERO

N EEDLESS to say, there was an intense rivalry between the Cal Wells III/Frank Arciero-owned team and fellow Toyota stalwart AAR, both relying on the underpowered engines and being based within a few miles of each other in Southern California. Honors, it has to be said, were quite evenly shared. Each scored a dozen PPG Cup points during the season. 'Mad Max' Papis, for Arciero-Wells, recorded the best overall result, eighth in the U.S. 500, while AAR scored points on five occasions to Arciero-Wells' four. Papis enhanced his growing reputation by qualifying fastest of the Toyota contingent on 10 occasions (to the four of Fangio and three of Jones), although it should be said that the AAR duo made good progress in the second half of the season when all three Toyota cars proved very closely matched. Businessman/racer Hiro Matsushita, who rejoined the operation after a one-year sojourn with Payton/Coyne, was not in the same league as the other three true professionals. Nevertheless, he recorded a remarkable sequence of eight consecutive finishes after taking delivery of his '97 Reynard and the latest RV8B motor at Gateway. Matsushita's best result was a ninth in the attrition-filled U.S. 500.

The extremely professional-looking Arciero-Wells organization expanded dramatically to cope with its additional entry. The vastly experienced Gordon Coppuck remained in charge of technical duties, ably assisted by ex-Lola engineer Iain Watt. Crew chiefs Bharat Naran (Papis) and Brad Filbey (Matsushita) performed sterling duty under the direction of Richard Buck, who added yet more credibility after working for many years with Al Unser Jr. at Penske Racing.

Make no mistake, the MCI-sponsored team will become a serious contender – as soon as Toyota finds the horsepower to compete on level terms with the established might of Ford/Cosworth, Honda and Mercedes-Benz/Ilmor.

GORDON COPPUCK

HIRO MATSUSHITA

MAX PAPIS

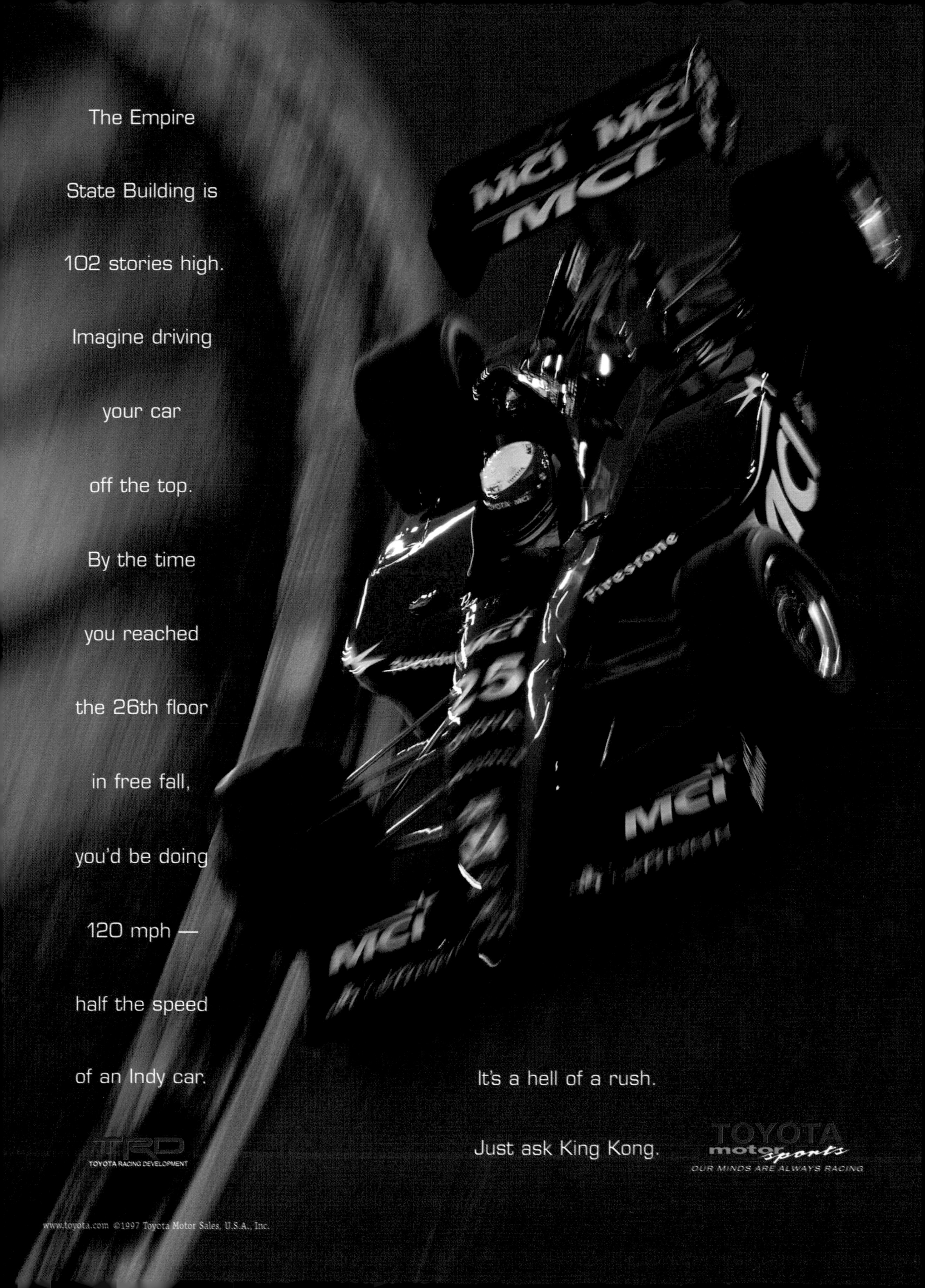
The Empire
State Building is
102 stories high.
Imagine driving
your car
off the top.
By the time
you reached
the 26th floor
in free fall,
you'd be doing
120 mph —
half the speed
of an Indy car.
It's a hell of a rush.
Just ask King Kong.
TRD
TOYOTA RACING DEVELOPMENT
TOYOTA
motor sports
OUR MINDS ARE ALWAYS RACING
www.toyota.com ©1997 Toyota Motor Sales, U.S.A., Inc.
MCI
Firestone
25

Davis Racing

Base: Midland, Texas
Driver: Gualter Salles (R)
Sponsors: Indusval, Marlboro
Chassis: Reynard 96I/97I
Engines: Ford/Cosworth XD
Tires: Goodyear
Wins: 0; Poles: 0
PPG Cup points: 10 (20th)

gualter salles

GERALD DAVIS

SALLES' promise was masked by retirements

Photos: Michael C. Brown

GERALD Davis, formerly team manager for Hall Racing, knew what he was letting himself in for when he decided to strike out on his own. At least to some degree. But perhaps he didn't foresee all the pitfalls. After a time-consuming cul-de-sac when one prospective partner failed to deliver the promised financial package, Davis joined forces with Jorge Cintra, promoter of the Hollywood 400 event in Rio de Janeiro, a few weeks prior to the start of the season. The alliance enabled him to proceed with his original intention of hiring talented Indy Lights graduate Gualter Salles.

Based in the same premises which previously housed Jim Hall's CART team, and employing several of the same people, including crew chief Alex Hering and race engineer Chuck Matthews, Davis Racing made steady progress. Financial resources, however, remained precious, and resulted in Davis selling his backup Reynard which had been damaged in a crash at Milwaukee. The team's continued existence also owed much to the generosity of Hall, who supplied a vital lifeline toward the end of the season. Nevertheless, both team and driver showed well, with a best finish of seventh at Laguna Seca representing real promise for the future.

Della Penna Motorsports

Base: Indianapolis, Ind.
Driver: Richie Hearn
Sponsors: Ralphs, Food 4 Less
Chassis: Lola T97/00, Swift 007.i
Engines: Ford/Cosworth XD
Tires: Goodyear
Wins: 0; Poles: 0
PPG Cup points: 10 (21st)

richie hearn

JOHN DELLA PENNA

RICHIE HEARN – impressive in the Lola

IF there was to be a prize for the most resilient CART team in 1997, John Della Penna's tight-knit team would have to be a prime contender. The enterprising Argentinian assembled a top-notch group headed by experienced team manager/engineer David Cripps and crew chief Phil Howard. The only problem was that despite some impressive preseason testing performances, their new Lola turned out to be a dud. Even so, former Toyota Atlantic champion Richie Hearn reaffirmed his promise as a rising star by posting some fine drives during his first full CART season, most notably at Nazareth where he ran as high as fifth before becoming entangled in a crash involving Johnstone and Boesel.

Della Penna confirmed he will rely on Swift chassis for '98, and as part of the deal he was able to equip Hearn with the original prototype 007.i for the final race at Fontana. Sadly, the car got away from Hearn in practice, so he was once again consigned to the Lola. Team and driver deserved better.

Payton/Coyne Racing

Base: Plainfield, Ill.
Drivers: Michel Jourdain Jr., Roberto Moreno, Paul Jasper, Christian Danner, Charles Nearburg, Dennis Vitolo
Sponsors: Herdez, Mexlub, Viva Mexico!, Data Control, HYPE, SmithKline Beecham
Chassis: Lola T97/00 & Reynard 97I
Engines: Ford/Cosworth XD
Tires: Firestone
Wins: 0; Poles: 0
PPG Cup points: 8
Vitolo 6 (25th), Danner 1 (27th), Jourdain 1 (28th)

charles nearburg   christian danner   paul jasper

michel jourdain jr.

DALE COYNE & WALTER PAYTON

WALTER Payton and Dale Coyne were unable to match the third-place finish achieved by Roberto Moreno in the '96 U.S. 500, but their team continued to make forward strides, especially with Michel Jourdain Jr., who, despite his meager experience, emerged as a potential star toward the end of the season.

The small team confirmed it meant business by purchasing a pair of Reynards in midseason, once it had become apparent the Lola was a lost cause. The transformation, as with Tasman, was remarkable. Jourdain established an excellent rapport with vastly experienced driver-turned-race engineer David Morgan, and while the youngster's only PPG Cup point came at Michigan, he shone at Mid-Ohio, Laguna Seca and, especially, in the season finale at Fontana, where he qualified fifth and ran as high as third. Keep an eye on this team and driver for '98. Ironically, Payton/Coyne's best result came with the Lola, which Dennis Vitolo drove steadily to a hard-earned seventh at Michigan. Christian Danner was impressive despite a long lay-off from open-wheel competition, while rookies Paul Jasper and Charles Nearburg were, frankly, over-matched.

Project Indy

Base: Brownsburg, Ind.
Drivers: Dennis Vitolo, Arnd Meier (R)
Sponsors: SmithKline Beecham, Hasseroder Pils, JAG, Marcelo
Chassis: Lola T97/00
Engines: Ford/Cosworth XD
Tires: Goodyear
Wins: 0; Poles: 0
PPG Cup points: 1 Meier (29th)

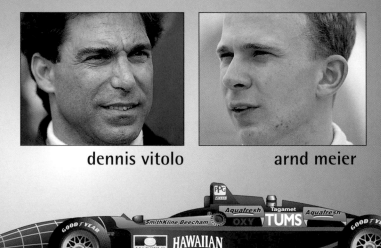

dennis vitolo   arnd meier

ANDREAS LEBERLE

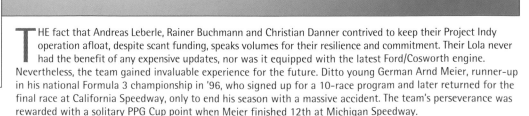

THE fact that Andreas Leberle, Rainer Buchmann and Christian Danner contrived to keep their Project Indy operation afloat, despite scant funding, speaks volumes for their resilience and commitment. Their Lola never had the benefit of any expensive updates, nor was it equipped with the latest Ford/Cosworth engine. Nevertheless, the team gained invaluable experience for the future. Ditto young German Arnd Meier, runner-up in his national Formula 3 championship in '96, who signed up for a 10-race program and later returned for the final race at California Speedway, only to end his season with a massive accident. The team's perseverance was rewarded with a solitary PPG Cup point when Meier finished 12th at Michigan Speedway.

Dennis Vitolo also contested a handful of races with support from pharmaceutical giant SmithKline Beecham.

Reynard

Production base: Bicester, England; U.S. base: Indianapolis, Ind.
Number of cars built in 1997: 38
Wins: 13
(Zanardi 5, Blundell 3, Moore 2, Pruett, 1, Gugelmin 1, Vasser 1);
Poles: 15
(Zanardi 4, Gugelmin 3, de Ferran 2, Pruett 2, Herta 2, Boesel 1, Franchitti 1)

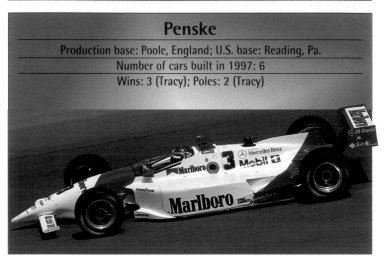

MALCOLM Oastler's Reynard 97I, the fourth generation of CART chassis designed by the English-resident Australian, represented a logical evolution of the successful 96I which had captured eight wins and 11 poles. Outwardly, the car appeared quite similar to its predecessor, although several detail modifications ensured compliance with the latest regulations pertaining to aerodynamics and driver safety – specifically in the cockpit area. The most dramatic change was the introduction of an all-new transverse six-speed gearbox, which reduced the polar moment of inertia and lowered the center of gravity (both longitudinally and vertically).

The car was extraordinarily successful, winning 13 of the 17 races – in the hands of six different drivers representing four teams – and all but two poles. Reynards led 1,717 laps during the season (76.01 percent of the total of 2,259), and most significantly, they did so with six different combinations of engines and tires. Reynard easily claimed its third successive CART Constructors Cup title.

Originally, 10 teams had intended to purchase Reynards, but two (Patrick and Forsythe) defected from Lola prior to the first race and two more (Payton/Coyne and Tasman) joined the throng by season's end.

Penske

Production base: Poole, England; U.S. base: Reading, Pa.
Number of cars built in 1997: 6
Wins: 3 (Tracy); Poles: 2 (Tracy)

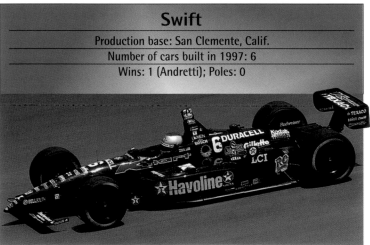

FOLLOWING its first winless campaign in 20 years, Marlboro Team Penske began the season in an optimistic frame of mind. The PC26 chassis, designed by Nigel Bennett (with input from John Travis, who switched across from Lola Cars toward the end of 1996 and will take charge of the Penske design team in 1998), had shown well during an intensive winter test program. The car appeared to be more consistent and user-friendly than the unloved PC25. It also compared favorably in back-to-back testing with a '96 Reynard which had been acquired with precisely that purpose in mind.

A great deal of emphasis had been placed on the aerodynamic balance of the new car, and in the early-season races, the PC26 seemed to be a match for the latest Reynard. Tracy finished second at Homestead and was competitive in the early street circuit races. He then added three straight wins to take an 18-point lead in the PPG Cup standings after six events. But that was as good as it got. The team reputedly clocked close to 100 days of testing without ever managing to regain its early-season form.

Swift

Production base: San Clemente, Calif.
Number of cars built in 1997: 6
Wins: 1 (Andretti); Poles: 0

THE prototype Swift chassis was completed only a couple of weeks before Spring Training at Homestead, and several early test outings, especially on the road courses, were plagued by gearbox problems. Nevertheless, Michael Andretti was confident of a good showing for the attractive David Bruns-designed 007.i, which also incorporated valuable input from aerodynamicist Mark Hanford and experienced Newman/Haas engineers Peter Gibbons and Brian Lisles.

'I think we can win the first race,' declared Andretti. 'I think we're probably going to qualify fifth or so, but if all things remain equal, I think we can win the race.'

Andretti was a little off in his qualifying prediction – he started only 14th – but quickly moved forward in the race before claiming a sensational debut victory for Swift Engineering. It was the first win for an American-built chassis in 14 years. Curiously, that was to remain the car's only triumph, although Andretti led strongly in Rio, Michigan and Fontana before being sidelined by mechanical woes on each occasion. The Swift also frequently appeared to utilize its Goodyear tires rather better than the phalanx of Reynards.

Lola

Production base: Huntingdon, England; U.S. base: Indianapolis, Ind.
Number of cars built in 1997: 16
Wins: 0; Poles: 0

HOW are the mighty fallen. One year ago, the Lola T96/00 was reckoned to be at least the equal of the Reynard 96I. Customer teams liked what they saw during the build process of the 1997 challenger, despite the arrival of a new and relatively unproven design team headed by Ben Bowlby and Lola Cars founder Eric Broadley. Jerry Forsythe's team was so impressed it decided to switch allegiance from Reynard.

Initial testing seemed to go well. But then word began to filter through to the effect that some teams were unhappy. The car was not responding as expected. Pat Patrick was the first to jump ship. Then Forsythe.

Tasman's Steve Horne persevered, but soon it became apparent that the T97/00 was no match for the Reynard. But why? Opinions varied. The Lola engineers produced all manner of update kits, but none had the desired effect – until the final race at Fontana. Meanwhile, the company ran into dire financial difficulties and eventually was taken over by Irish businessman Martin Birrane, who will attempt to recreate the British constructor's former glory.

Mercedes-Benz

Production base: Brixworth,
England; U.S. base: Detroit,
Mich.
Wins: 9
(Tracy 3, Blundell 3,
Moore 2, Gugelmin 1);
Poles: 6
(Gugelmin 3, Tracy 2,
Franchitti 1)

WHAT a difference a year can make! After failing to win a race in 1996, Ilmor Engineering bounced back in spectacular style in '97 as its Mercedes-Benz IC108D motor proved to be the class of the field in terms of both horsepower and reliability. Chief designer Mario Illien knew he had been on the right track with his IC108C, and while the latest

engine boasted many new components, primarily due to the reduction to 40 inches of manifold boost pressure at all races (rather than just on the superspeedways, as in '95 and '96), the product was largely evolutionary. And extremely effective.

Mercedes had to wait until the fourth race before tasting victory – its first since the final race of the '95 season – then went on a tear, winning each of the next five and adding three more before the end of the season to comfortably secure the coveted Manufacturers Championship. Only once, indeed, at Cleveland, did Mercedes finish outside the top two. The IC108D led in all but two of the 17 races for a total of 914 laps (40.46 percent). Six different drivers, from five teams, shared the honors.

Honda

Production base: Santa Clarita,
Calif.
Wins: 6
(Zanardi 5, Vasser 1);
Poles: 6
(Zanardi 4, de Ferran 2)

THE Honda HRR motor represented a 'clean sheet of paper' design according to Robert Clarke, general manager of Honda Performance Development, and while it was surely not as dominant as the previous year's HRH, it was still a mighty effective piece. Reliability, once again, proved to be the engine's strong suit. Only two engine-induced retirements were

recorded on racedays in 1997 (Johnstone at Detroit and Fernandez at Mid-Ohio), and in fact, when Andre Ribeiro experienced a problem during practice at Laguna Seca, it meant that Steve Ragan's crew had to contemplate an unscheduled race weekend engine change for the first time since Tasman entered the PPG Cup series at the beginning of the 1995 season. Imagine that!

Popular opinion suggested that the Honda perhaps gave away a little in terms of ultimate horsepower to the Mercedes and Ford opposition. But it was strong enough to lead in 13 races for a total of 791 laps (35.02 percent). Furthermore, Honda-powered cars swept the top three positions in the PPG Cup championship through the efforts of Alex Zanardi, Gil de Ferran and Jimmy Vasser.

Ford/Cosworth

Production base: Northampton,
England; Torrance, Calif.
Wins: 2
(Pruett 1, Andretti 1);
Poles: 5
(Pruett 2, Herta 2, Boesel 1)

THE latest Ford/Cosworth XD boasted significantly more horsepower, vastly improved reliability and greater 'drivability' in comparison with 1996. The gains were achieved by virtue of both a revised induction system and a new electronics package developed jointly by Ford and Cosworth. Two straight wins provided a perfect start to the season, but the

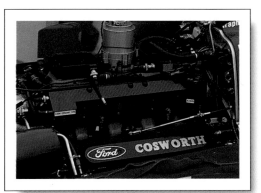

momentum could not be maintained and there were to be no more visits to Victory Lane. Consequently, Ford finished a distant third in the Manufacturers Championship. Nevertheless, the XD led in all except one race for a total of 554 laps (24.52 percent), and frequently appeared to have the legs of both the Mercedes and Honda opposition.

'I'm pleased with the engine performance,' summarized Ian Bisco, president of Cosworth USA. 'We took the pole at Michigan Speedway, which is generally recognized as an engine dyno. I think we had one of the best engines out there, but the results didn't show it.'

Crucial engine failures at Rio and Cleveland cost Michael Andretti dearly, but then, so too did a couple of uncharacteristic errors at Road America and Vancouver.

Toyota

Production base: Costa Mesa,
Calif. and Aisen Seiki, Japan
Wins: 0;
Poles: 0

FOR the first half of the season, frankly, Toyota seemed to have taken a step backward following its already disastrous initial campaign in 1996. All American Racers and Arciero-Wells began with a mixed bag of the older RV8A motors and the new RV8Bs, but both were plagued by diabolical reliability. During the entire season, the two teams conducted well

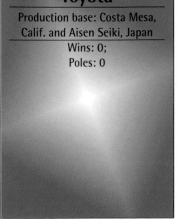
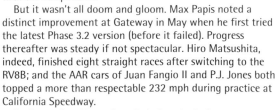

over 200 unscheduled engine changes between them. They were also substantially down on horsepower by comparison with the competition.

But it wasn't all doom and gloom. Max Papis noted a distinct improvement at Gateway in May when he first tried the latest Phase 3.2 version (before it failed). Progress thereafter was steady if not spectacular. Hiro Matsushita, indeed, finished eight straight races after switching to the RV8B; and the AAR cars of Juan Fangio II and P.J. Jones both topped a more than respectable 232 mph during practice at California Speedway.

Engineers from Toyota's technical center in Japan were more in evidence during the latter stages of the year, while the hiring of highly respected electronics guru John Faivre from Penske Racing provided further proof of Toyota's intentions.

Firestone

Production base: Akron, Ohio and
Tokyo, Japan
Wins: 13
(Zanardi 5, Blundell 3, Moore 2, Pruett 1,
Gugelmin 1, Vasser 1);
Poles: 13
(Zanardi 4, Gugelmin 3, de Ferran 2,
Pruett 2, Boesel 1, Franchitti 1)

FIRESTONE has made steady progress since reentering the Indy car marketplace in 1995 following a 20-year absence from the sport. After winning twice during its initial season, the multinational giant added 10 more wins in 1996 and increased the tally to 13 in '97, including an unbeaten sequence of 11 beginning at Milwaukee on June 1.

Impressively, a total of nine different drivers, representing six teams, garnered either a pole or a race victory on Firestone tires. The Firehawk radials also led in every one of the 17 races for a total of 1,321 laps, or 58.48 percent. Only once, however, in Toronto, did they lead every lap.

The Firestone engineers appeared to have made especially strong gains (by comparison with 1996) on the short ovals, which during the previous two years had been very much the domain of Goodyear. And in the second half of the season the Firehawks were substantially faster and more durable than the opposition on virtually every kind of race track. The only real problem occurred in the final race at California Speedway, where most of the Firestone teams suffered from blistered right-rear tires. But even then, the tires were apparently never in danger of falling apart. Neither did they lose any speed: 'The carcass integrity is really the key,' explained Al Speyer, Bridgestone/Firestone Director

of Motorsports. 'It's difficult to hit the mark exactly right every time and we missed the mark a little today. But it wasn't an integrity issue. We weren't telling people they had to come in [to the pits to change tires]. The tires [just] got too hot. This was our problem. We know it and we've got to work on it.'

Goodyear

Production base: Akron, Ohio
Wins: 4
(Tracy 3, Andretti 1);
Poles: 4
(Tracy 2, Herta 2)

AFTER more than two decades as the sole tire supplier in Indy car racing, Goodyear received a rude awakening in 1996 and '97. That is not to suggest, of course, that the Goodyear engineers expected Bridgestone/Firestone to be anything less than a formidable opponent. Far from it. The level of mutual respect between the two companies is substantial and Goodyear fully realized the seriousness of the challenge.

In 1996, the writing was on the wall as Firestone appeared to take a solid lead, especially in the latter part of the season. But Goodyear fought back. Strongly. In the first half of the 1997 season, there was little to choose between the two tire giants. Each claimed four wins from the opening eight races. At that stage Goodyear had led 716 laps to the 464 of Firestone. All of Goodyear's victories, however, came on oval tracks. The three street circuit races (plus one oval) fell to Firestone.

As the season progressed, the margin between the companies expanded – and not in Goodyear's favor. By the close, Firestone had far eclipsed Goodyear's laps-led tally; and on the road courses, only Bryan Herta seemed able to stem the Firestone tide.

Rumors began to circulate

to the effect that several Goodyear teams were seriously contemplating a defection to the Firestone camp. Indeed, immediately following the final race, Team Rahal and Della Penna Motorsports did exactly that. But Goodyear had every intention of fighting back, as evidenced by a major restructuring and personnel realignment within the tire development and marketing groups. The moves, said Stu Grant, general manager of racing worldwide, 'will allow this organization to provide quicker response time in a competitive environment.'

celebrating the M-FACTOR

During its first quarter-century, BMW Motorsport GmbH has powered winners from Grands Prix to touring cars, via Le Mans. *Jeremy Walton* **highlights an innovative BMW enterprise which returns to Grands Prix as the power behind Williams Grand Prix Engineering in the millennium.**

REWIND 25 years back to 1972, and discover a 25-year-old Emerson Fittipaldi winning his first World Championship for Lotus. Then, as now, Britain exported its music to the world, but back then the headline act was the Rolling Stones rather than Oasis.

As spring 1972 slipped into summer, German motorsport was rocked by the news that the architects of Ford Cologne's competition success – Herren Jochen Neerpasch and Martin Braungart – were to migrate south to Bavaria.

The Munich-based management of BMW AG – energised by former fighter pilot Bob Lutz – decided to formalise their extended support of motorsport, forming a new 'company-within-a-company'. Not for BMW the usual big banker's draft for an outside specialist. BMW Motorsport continued to rely on in-house talent, particularly in engine design, to reap results.

There was also a BMW pedigree dating back 44 years for utilising production components wherever possible. This philosophy took BMW into Grands Prix, where in 1983 their Motorsport division took the first World Championship for the driver of a turbocharged car, utilising an iron production cylinder block.

From May 1972 BMW Motorsport GmbH was charged with the job of bringing honour to the whirling white and blue roundel badge. The infant company responded by hauling in two European Championships in its first season of racing, in 1973.

A European Formula 2 title came courtesy of Jean-Pierre Jarier, along with the first of many BMW Motorsport seasons wedded to March at Bicester. During the years 1973-84 the company erased previous painful memories of Formula 2, dominating the 2-litre category between 1973 and 1982.

BMW M12/7 Motorsport-engineered units generated an astounding 70 victories. As with all official BMW Motorsport entries, including the forthcoming Grand Prix unit, those 10,000 rpm fours were developed by a team under the leadership of born and bred Munich resident, Paul Rosche.

These were not easy F2 wins, for both Renault and Honda fielded effective pedigree racing V6s against the BMW four-cylinder. Yet the BMW motor's low weight and wide torque curve saw it win five Formula 2 Championships and inspire a sixth title. BMW cylinder blocks actually won 76 races, because a Schnitzer unit behind Jacques Laffite additionally won six races and the 1975 title.

Apart from Laffite and his agile Martini, those BMW M-Power Champions were all March-mounted. They were: Frenchmen Jean-Pierre Jarier (1973) and Patrick Depailler (1974), followed by Italy's Bruno Giacomelli in 1978. Switzerland's Marc Surer secured the title in 1979 and Corrado Fabi took the final honours, in 1982.

The Good News was that 1973's European Championship success could be translated into orders for racing hardware, establishing the 2-litre Formula 2 engine as the one to buy. Production of these hand-built Munich masterpieces finally exceeded 500, most producing over 300 bhp apiece.

Jean-Pierre Jarier *(below)* took the BMW-powered March to the 1973 European Formula 2 Championship. It was to be just the start of a long run of successes in this category, and paved the way for M-GmbH ultimately to take the step into Grand Prix racing.

Top: Classic car. Classic pose. Classic circuit. The Hans Stuck/Jacky Ickx BMW CSL in flight at the 1974 Nürburgring 1000 Km.

Above: CSL turbo, Seventies style. This car was dubbed the world's fastest painting, courtesy of artist Frank Stella's eye-catching livery.

Above right: The 1973 European Touring Car Champion Toine Hezemans in the CSL at the TT race at Silverstone.

Right: The shape of things to come. A flame-snorting BMW 320 at Brands Hatch in 1978. This shape and its successors were to become a mainstay of touring car racing for the next two decades.

Left: Nelson Piquet in the M1 ProCar. These exotic machines, driven by the stars of the day, proved an entertaining support to many Grands Prix during 1979 and 1980.

Motorsport at Munich took its second 1973 debut season European Championship with the magnificent CSL coupé. This former paragon of understated elegance was developed to sprout Braungart's rapidly developed wings, splitters and hoops. Rosche and company dialled in 375 M-power horses and an extra half-litre from the classic straight six. The boldly striped ensemble equally rapidly earned both the European title (the first of six) and the affectionate sobriquet 'Batmobile'.

Drivers of Niki Lauda's calibre drove CSLs for the factory-favoured Alpina team. Factory aces Hans Stuck, Chris Amon, champion Toine Hezemans and the inevitable Dieter Quester did most of the winning, once the factory got into its crushing stride.

Soon nicknamed M-GmbH , the main company offshoot expanded commercially at virtually competition speed: in the beginning there were eight employees and earnings equated to $130,000 a year. In 1991 employees were counted by the hundred at two Munich sites trading on a turnover of $445 million! Today some 450 employees yield a turnover of $528 million, so M-business is big business in a niche market that is unique to BMW.

There was sustained BMW AG investment in the M-badge as a commercial proposition: during the 1978/79 winter the parent company injected £1.3 million in the original Preussenstrasse site to allow separate production facilities for M-Power and M cars. By 1986 business justified a second site, Garching, on a suburban trading estate in north-western Munich.

Initially the M5 was a hand-built Motorsport machine, along with the M3 convertible, but demand in the 1990s has required that the new M5 be a production item for the main company, just as the M3 saloon has always been in all but its early convertible guise.

What did M-GmbH sell in the Seventies? Anything from a key fob to serious racing hardware was the short answer, but some services were supplied to outsiders...

Surviving staff smile when they recall the prototype installation of BMW diesel engines into large American Fords. Huge sedans would wobble around BMW's test track, accompanied by tell-tale clouds of smoke, as BMW employees tried to detect some signs of performance in the American knee-jerk reaction to petrol economy worries.

BMW Motorsport survived on this strange Ford contract and more obvious applications of its expertise without redundancies. The M-division also shows long-term loyalty to its driving force: recently retired Roberto Ravaglia, the world's most successful touring car driver, was with them for 14 years and BMW also retain links with their Grand Prix and ProCar title winner, Nelson Piquet. Dieter Quester has raced BMWs for more than 30 years and regularly appeared in 1997 USA M3s.

Another Seventies adjunct to the main competition programme created two separate branches to the central M-GmbH organisation, which have secured increasing prominence for the M-branding. Highest profile have been the M-prefixed cars: the original M1, two generations of M3 in five bodies, the M5 in four body shapes, two generations of M535i and the much-loved M635CSi, dubbed the M6 in the USA.

A further offshoot of pioneering Motorsport labour was BMW Individual, a phenomenally successful commercial division which tailors non-production specifications to one in twenty customer orders.

Beginning as a VIP service to contracted star drivers, BMW Motorsport constructed increasingly sophisticated road cars. They featured unobtainable combinations of the mainstream product: the 5-series was the usual victim, growing 3- to 3.3-litre versions of BMW's sibilant straight six at a time when production was restricted to the smaller 528i.

Between the drivers and motor-sport mechanics, further advances in suspension and braking specification brewed, alongside racier steering wheels and clinging front seats to remind the contractees of their day jobs. These special product developments were particularly interesting to the main BMW AG set-up for their production potential, as Motorsport employed numerous production parts on a mix-and-match basis from elsewhere in the main company range.

The first M-car was the 1978-81 M1, but a larger engined 5-series (M535i) was in serial production by April 1980 and would found a line of ever-faster M5s. The latter peaked with the Frankfurt announcement in 1997 of a 400 bhp V8 version to replace ever-larger (3.8-litre) descendants of the 3.5-litre BMW racing six cylinders.

The marvellous M1, literally a Supercar, made the best of a bad job. A BMW contract had been assigned to Lamborghini and Italian subcontractors, with the idea of competing against Porsche in the ill-fated FIA Group 5 'Silhouette' Championship. Delays scotched that Group 5 race plan.

Thus the mid-engined M1 needed an exotic one-make race series to demonstrate its competition merits. ProCar was conceived by Neerpasch, in association with Bernie Ecclestone and Max Mosley, to support most major 1979-80 European Grands Prix.

Instead of the M1 attributes of 277 bhp and 162 street mph, ProCars proffered 470 bhp and 192 mph – and they made champions of then Brabham team-mates, Niki Lauda and Nelson Piquet.

As an individual competition car, the M1 came too late to offer Porsche consistent opposition. However, in the USA the charismatic Red Lobster team, with drivers Kenper Miller/David Cowart, demolished all their IMSA GTO class opposition for 1981. They also set new records for the number of category wins recorded in a season.

BMW also resorted to even wilder versions of the CSL: as the old warrior went out of production in 1975, it was fielded as the official factory car in America. Hans Stuck proved it could win at IMSA level and BMW netted the 1976 Daytona 24 Hours (a shortened race that foggy year) with ex-pat Briton Brian Redman on the team.

The most powerful BMW racing saloon to date, and the ultimate car/driver alliance for spectators, was the pairing of Ronnie Peterson and a monstrous CSL, one carrying the clout of a 3.2-litre twin-turbo six. The result was enough power – boost was *lowered* for 'only' 750 bhp! – to challenge even 'SuperSwede's' fabled reflexes, munching Silverstone's main straight at 178 mph in 1976...

At Dijon and Le Mans (it led...briefly!) the Peterson turbo CSL appeared in the graph paper design of American inventor/artist Frank Stella, part of a series of four American 'Art Cars' that BMW had backed since 1975. Contributing artists included Andy Warhol, and the sixth-placed M1 he decorated for 1979 recorded BMW's best overall result at Le Mans prior to the 1995 McLaren-BMW victory. Later, BMW extended the Art concept internationally and included road cars, as well as a 1993 M3 racing prototype.

A radically reworked 3-series was a predictable 1977-78 class (but not overall) winner in Group 5 trim, when it carried a 305 bhp Formula 2 motor. It sold strongly to privateers at £30,000 a copy. However, the 1977-79 need for 3-series speed in the domestic German Championship, and American national racing, led to a brace of very different turbocharged four-cylinders...and on to Formula 1 power.

Paul Rosche recalled, 'The M12/7 four-cylinder engine was developed in turbocharged form first for saloon car racing, and then – as the M12/13 series – for Grands Prix. So our Formula 2 experience in the single-seaters was important to us, as were the developments we made with McLaren (North America) and Schnitzer in saloon car racing.'

Left: The dart-shaped Brabham
BT52-BMW which propelled Nelson
Piquet to the 1983 World Championship.

Below: The four-cylinder turbocharged
Formula 1 engine.

Centre: Rosche in conference with Piquet.

Below far left: Piquet was still competitive
in 1984, taking two Grand Prix wins.

Bottom left: The BMW powerplant in situ.

Bottom right: Gerhard Berger scored
BMW's last Grand Prix win in the turbo
era with his Benetton in 1986.

The rock on which so much power would be built was the production iron block four, carefully aged to simulate 100,000 km (62,000 miles) and externally lightened. Schnitzer and other German specialists used 1.4 turbocharged litres to achieve German class success – former German journalist Harald Ertl won the 1978 title in a 410 bhp Schnitzer 3-series – while the American programme used 2-litre turbos that achieved over 600 bhp.

The German 1.4-litre programme and its short-stroke motors had most relevance to BMW's increasing Formula 1 aspirations, for Grand Prix operated a 1.5-litre turbo equivalency formula. Rosche remembered, 'The Schnitzer car of 1978 was interesting for us, so we got behind the 1979 GS Tuning 320 for Markus Hottinger.' This Jagermeister orange fireball won on its sixth outing and deployed a massive 610 bhp from its BMW Motorsport-supplied 1.4 turbo four.

Technically, it looked as though BMW had cracked open a path to Grand Prix success at low cost, for the motors used a tremendous amount of the uprated hardware found in their proven Formula 2 design.

Grand Prix life could never be that simple, though. A rugged course in character-building politics awaited Rosche and new BMW Motorsport manager Dieter Stappert for, in March 1980, Munich had signed to supply Brabham with the F1 power units.

By October 1980 Brabham-BMW had completed the first test runs at Silverstone with a unit rated at 557 bhp at 9500 rpm in the back of a converted BT49. The same British venue saw Nelson Piquet officially record the fourth-fastest time and more than 190 mph at the Grand Prix in July 1981.

As on so many subsequent occasions the engine was not raced, which tested the durability of the Paul Rosche-Gordon Murray working relationship immediately. It took some world class diplomacy from Dieter Stappert, public pressure from BMW management and a winter full of often explosive testing before the M12/13 unit was deemed ready for trial by Grand Prix.

That was at the January 1982 South African GP. Piquet's second-fastest practice time was encouraging, but not a reliable guide to race form. Piquet slid off after four laps and Brabham number 2, Riccardo Patrese, also retired. Not an auspicious start, but better than the three races which intervened before its next event!

Prevailing Grand Prix politics had played a part and the BMW unit was not raced again until the Belgian GP of May 1982. Belgium's bumpy Zolder circuit gave Brabham-BMW its first World Championship point for Piquet's sixth, but it was obvious that the motor's peaky power required soothing if it was to succeed on North America's tight street circuits.

America strained the BMW-Brabham alliance as Piquet failed to qualify on the Detroit doorstep of Motown. 'No Pain, No Gain' – but this was more like a prolonged torture session. There were enormous risks for BMW in the prestige market should the motor continue to misbehave.

BMW's board kept their nerve and, just a week later, were rewarded with their first victory! Deploying leading edge Bosch technology to monitor and manage their motor, BMW went into the record books with a win in the restarted Canadian GP of June 1982.

There were no more GP wins that season for BMW, but some compensation in the achievement of three pole positions and a brand new Gordon Murray design for 1983: the bold and beautiful Brabham BT52.

Bold because it was born with a pioneering pit-stop role, and because the crash-tested Brabham-BMW (another first) compensated for the loss of ground effect with almost 60 per cent of the weight shifted aft. It was beautiful in its arrow-inspired clean lines and looked a winner from the Brazilian opening round to the close of play in Murray's native South Africa.

Looking back in the summer of 1997 Gordon Murray commented, 'That was a very special moment...winning the championship with one driver and the race with the other. And that BMW beat Renault to the title, the first for a turbo car, for just a fraction of what the French were spending. That just made our Kyalami satisfaction complete, especially as I was on home turf.'

There should have been a lot more winning in 1984, and another world title. Brabham-BMW's undoubted pace saw Piquet pick up eight pole positions, but he only took two victories, in Canada and Detroit.

The root cause of BMW's previously unpublicised problems lay with a German supplier, but the consequent component change came too late to add another title. Subsequent seasons of ever-tightening legislation to lower turbo boost ensured that the four-cylinder would be uncompetitive against its V6 opposition, though it was still a quick proposition.

In 1987 a Benetton B186 rated at 900 race bhp and driven by Teo Fabi recorded 0-100 mph in 4.8 seconds in trials for *Road & Track* magazine. However, the figures enthusiasts remember for the BMW Motorsport 1.5-litre turbo are those for qualifying specials.

Paul Rosche recalled, 'The truth was that we were only brave enough to see the maximum of 1200 horsepower on our test bed at Preussenstrasse...' A pause for a quiet chuckle before Rosche grinned: 'As 1200 was the maximum on the scale, there was no point in going on. Besides, we were all scared what would happen if it exploded!'

From 1983 onwards BMW supplied Grand Prix engines for cars apart from Brabham, including Arrows (1984-86, then as Megatron BMW for 1987/88); ATS (1983-84) and Ligier (1987). Benetton's single 1986 season deploying Munich works motors was most significant: they scored the only GP win outside Brabham, but also the last M-Power GP victory, when Gerhard Berger won in Mexico.

Right: The Ravaglia/Pirro BMW 635CSi on the grid at Silverstone before the 1986 RAC Tourist Trophy race.

Far right: An unexpected highlight for BMW Motorsport came in 1987 when Bernard Bequin took the Prodrive BMW M3 to a superbly controlled victory on the Tour de Corse, a rare win for a non-factory organisation.

Below: Paul Rosche, for so long the engine mastermind behind M-GmbH's many sporting successes.

Overall the BMW M12/13 Formula 1 motor took nine Grand Prix wins, all but two recorded by Nelson Piquet. An excellent 14 pole positions were seized, with 11 coming from the Brazilian.

The faithful BMW CSL went on winning long after its production death. The Batmobile dropped only one European Touring Car title between 1973 and 1979. The CSL and Alpina/BMW were responsible both for Jaguar's non-winning run in its first assault on the European series (1976-77), and for sustaining the driving and business career ambitions of one Tom Walkinshaw. 'Mr TWR' returned to make sure Jaguar did become winners in the Eighties. You can take sportsmanship too far...!

BMW were so successful in the 1980s European Touring Car Championship that almost any of their cars – with varying support from Motorsport – appeared capable of netting the title for a variety of drivers, whatever the prevalent formula.

In 1980 the Group 2 smallest BMW, a 320, did the job to record the first of three successive Drivers' titles for Helmut Kelleners. Subsequent Euro Championships were racked up in the Group 2 BMW 635 coupé (1981), while the change to Group A in 1982 failed to stop either BMW or Kelleners winning, this time in an Eggenberger 528i four-door.

The Group A era saw the stiffest opposition to BMW in the European Championship. TWR fielded Mazda rotaries, Rover V8s and Jaguar V12s during the Eighties, with the two British marques regular outright winners. Volvo developed their super-quick 240 turbos, and GM-Holden allowed their mighty V8s to roam beyond Australia.

BMW Motorsport did not have the best products in the BMW showroom armoury to face this onslaught of touring car power, for their national sporting organisation, ADAC, would permit no rule-bending on homologation numbers. That meant the 635 coupé relied on its 12-valve engine at 285 reliable race horsepower, rather than redeveloping the 24-valve M635i, which gave 286 bhp on the street...and could yield 400 bhp in competition trim.

Nevertheless, BMW acquired the 1983 title with a Schnitzer-run BMW Motorsport 635CSi and – after an FIA recount – the same combination also conquered in 1986. For 1987 Ford became the threat, via turbocharged Cosworth power for the Sierra.

BMW Motorsport retaliated, designing both road and racing versions of the M3, a 3-series with production-based modifications that allowed BMW to meet turbo power with a normally aspirated 2.3-litre engine. The 200 bhp road version of the M3, under a team led by Thomas Ammerschlager (now engineering future products for BMW AG), was an enormous commercial success for the M-brand. They sold over 17,100 saloons – including 600 of the final 2.5-litre Sport Evo M3 – and almost 1000 M3 convertibles, these latter hand made at Motorsport.

Although the track version of the M3 was enormously successful, it utilised a lot of production technology. It was raced to victory in the German Championship twice, in 1987 and 1989, with full catalytic converter cleansing. The M3 also built on BMW's advanced Seventies work, featuring ABS braking in Nineties competition.

The M3 captured the only World Touring Car title for Drivers, too, when Roberto Ravaglia won in 1987, as well as the two final European Championships and national titles literally all around the world. The M3 was so versatile that Prodrive even resurrected an obsolete BMW tradition and made simple rear drive into a rally winner. Prodrive M3s won a World Championship round (Corsica) in the Eighties 4x4 turbo era – and national titles in France, Spain and Belgium.

The arrival of the 2-litre Super Touring car racing formula in Britain and the rest of the world also saw BMW switching 3-series models for competition and commerce. The M-people constructed over 85 racing E36 four-door saloons between 1992 and 1996 – and a few coupés for the 1992 British season, won by Tim Harvey.

BMW Motorsport-backed 'Threes' have won 2-litre titles in most countries that cater for the category, literally from Japan (Steve Soper, 1995) to Australia, via Britain. Here Joachim Winkelhock's 1993 *Autotrader* title was the third successive UK Championship win for BMW Motorsport-backed hardware.

The M3 became a six-cylinder (initially a 3 litre, now 3.2), but neither its sales rate nor its appetite for motorsport success have diminished. After winning the 1993 German national ADAC Championship with Johnny Cecotto in a 325 bhp version, the M3 transferred its competition affections to its biggest sales market: the USA.

Veteran preparation and race management specialist Thomas H. Milner, ironically working out of the old Jaguar Group 44 premises in Virginia, took the six-cylinder M3 on as an IMSA GT class racer in 1995 for Preparation Technology Group (PTG). Strongly backed by BMW North America, Milner persisted in adversity, as had Rosche and Murray in Grand Prix racing in the Eighties.

A consistently winning race reward materialised for the 380-400 bhp PTG M3s in 1996, taking the company's first national IMSA title since the early Eighties. PTG and BMW established such a strong winning streak that they enjoyed the marketing-led luxury of constructing four-door M3 winners, as well as the original coupés.

The McLaren BMW V12 F1 supercar was drawn by Gordon Murray as the ultimate road driving machine – not a racer. The F1 three-seater re-established a Murray working relationship with Rosche and BMW Motorsport at Preussenstrasse, after Gordon had scanned the world for possible power plants. Murray set strict size, power and weight parameters that only BMW Motorsport could meet. They rapidly developed a 627 bhp V12 of 6.1 litres which exceeded Murray's requirement for 100 bhp a litre.

Some one hundred McLaren-BMW F1s were built, including the racing prototype that made history in a winning Le Mans debut in 1995. Persuasion from privateers Thomas Bscher

Right: Joachim Winkelhock, a hugely popular driver in the Super Touring class, won championships for BMW in both Great Britain and Germany.

Below: Two BMWs head the pack as they thunder down to Eau Rouge at the start of the 1997 Spa 24 Hours race. The winning car *(front right)* was handled by Marc Duez, Eric Helary and Didier de Radigues.

Top right: The classic BMW M3 road car which met the aspirations of many driving enthusiasts in the late Eighties and early Nineties.

Centre right: 'Smokin' Jo' Winkelhock, a superstar in touring cars and one of the most popular drivers in motorsport.

Above: BMWs compete successfully all over the globe. A Valvoline-backed M3 heads into the night at the 1997 Daytona 24 Hours.

Above: Over the past three seasons, the McLaren-BMW F1 GTR has been a massive success. Since its competition debut in 1995 the F1, designed initially as the ultimate road car by Gordon Murray *(above right)*, has helped to breathe new life into GT racing and prompted other major manufacturers to enter this class of the sport and battle for honours.

Right: Back to the future! Nelson Piquet, his 1983 World Championship-winning Brabham-BMW, and Karl-Heinz Kalbfell at the official announcement of BMW's return to Grand Prix racing with Williams in the year 2000.

and Ray Bellm converted the McLaren into a racing winner of the BPR Global Cup in both 1995 and 1996, and it also commandeered the Japanese GT Championship of 1996.

That contract to supply the S70 M-Power 12 also led BMW to forge closer links with Britain. Rosche and Murray headed the Bracknell- and McLaren-based UK offshoot of M-GmbH: BMW Motorsport Ltd.

The British end tackled all touring car development work outside the engine bay for the 1996-97 seasons. Motorsport Ltd also further developed the 'long tail' McLaren for the 1997 FIA GT Championship, a series BMW and McLaren led for much of 1997 with a lower-weight-break (6-litre) version of the V12.

Although the GT programme has proved an unexpectedly successful triumph for the converted McLaren supercar, all attention is now centred on BMW Motorsport's new alliance with Williams. The aim is a Le Mans specification open sports car and 'other projects at the highest level of motor racing'. For this reason BMW Motorsport Ltd will move 'near the Williams facility in order to enable the two companies to work closely together', according to the September 1997 formal announcement about the BMW Williams Grand Prix engine.

Paul Rosche confirmed that the Preussenstrasse building, creative home to all these victorious engines, is already resounding to the birth cries of the first V10 BMW motors. As the best compromise between torque and power, the V10 has proven ability.

Led by Rosche, BMW Motorsport engineers will explore the V10's potential in private until late 1998, when the first BMW V10s will be installed in a Williams chassis. The 1999 season will see a full year of track and bench testing, with BMW Williams pursuing M-Power's second world title in the year 2000 season, and beyond.

It's been a rewarding first 25 years, but BMW Motorsport anticipate that the twenty-first century will hold even greater competitive and commercial prizes than did the twentieth century.

Position	Driver	Car	Tires	Homestead	Surfers Paradise	Long Beach	Nazareth	Rio de Janeiro	Gateway	Milwaukee	Detroit	Portland	Cleveland	Toronto	Michigan	Mid-Ohio	Road America	Vancouver	Laguna Seca	Fontana	Points total
1	Alex Zanardi (I)	Target/Chip Ganassi Racing Reynard 97I-Honda	FS	P7	P4	†1	11	4	4	13	26	11	P1	2	†1	†1	1	P4	3	NS	195
2	Gil de Ferran (BR)	Walker Valvoline/Cummins Reynard 97I-Honda	GY	22	5	P21	4	11	3	7	P†3	2	†2	25	3	6	3	3	5	6	162
3	Jimmy Vasser (USA)	Target/Chip Ganassi Racing Reynard 97I-Honda	FS	3	12	9	5	9	5	3	4	19	13	7	24	5	8	†2	†1	2	144
4	Mauricio Gugelmin (BR)	PacWest Racing Group Hollywood Reynard 97I-Mercedes	FS	6	17	2	9	P22	6	5	16	†6	15	6	6	7	P2	1	9	P4	132
5	Paul Tracy (CDN)	Marlboro Team Penske Penske PC26-Mercedes	GY	2	†19	7	P†1	1	1	P6	NS	7	7	10	4	27	28	28	26	26	121
6	Mark Blundell (GB)	PacWest Racing Group Motorola Reynard 97I-Mercedes	FS	14	8	13	19	8	24	12	17	1	9	†1	2	26	†16	7	2	1	115
7	Greg Moore (CDN)	Forsythe Player's Ltd./Indeck Reynard 96I-Mercedes	FS	4	–	–	–	–	–	–	–	–	–	–	–	–	–	–	–	–	111
		Forsythe Player's Ltd./Indeck Reynard 97I-Mercedes	FS	–	2	23	16	2	13	†1	1	5	24	23	27	2	18	17	24	13	
8	Michael Andretti (USA)	Newman/Haas Kmart/Texaco Havoline Swift 007.i-Ford XD	GY	†1	3	22	2	21	P11	2	2	8	23	4	21	8	26	16	27	19	108
9	Scott Pruett (USA)	Patrick Brahma Sports Team Reynard 97I-Ford XD	FS	5	1	3	10	3	19	9	24	P17	8	5	†14	9	5	18	16	7	102
10	Raul Boesel (BR)	Patrick Brahma Sports Team Reynard 97I-Ford XD	FS	17	7	8	8	5	†14	4	6	3	16	8	18	4	21	6	8	20	91
11	Bryan Herta (USA)	Team Rahal Shell Reynard 97I-Ford XD	GY	10	22	6	7	6	22	15	7	21	3	17	5	P†24	11	8	P6	21	72
12	Bobby Rahal (USA)	Team Rahal Miller Lite Reynard 97I-Ford XD	GY	16	10	10	6	†10	20	11	9	24	5	9	17	3	6	24	19	5	70
13	Al Unser Jr. (USA)	Marlboro Team Penske Penske PC26-Mercedes	GY	27	27	4	3	7	18	20	8	25	4	20	20	22	7	5	11	22	67
14	Andre Ribeiro (BR)	Tasman Motorsports LCI/Marlboro Lola T97/00-Honda	FS	12	6	14	26	15	10	26	25	13	–	–	–	–	–	–	–	–	45
		Tasman Motorsports LCI/Marlboro Reynard 97I-Honda	FS	–	–	–	–	–	–	–	–	–	14	3	23	10	22	10	4	†17	
15	Christian Fittipaldi (BR)	Newman/Haas Kmart/Budweiser Swift 007.i-Ford XD	GY	26	NS	–	–	–	–	–	–	4	6	11	16	21	4	9	21	9	42
16	Parker Johnstone (USA)	Team KOOL Green Reynard 97I-Honda	FS	8	21	5	17	12	7	25	20	9	10	12	25	12	23	11	12	11	36
17	*Patrick Carpentier (CDN)	Bettenhausen Alumax Aluminum Reynard 97I-Mercedes	GY	9	15	15	12	NS	2	8	15	16	12	16	15	15	27	–	–	NS	27
17	Adrian Fernandez (MEX)	Tasman Tecate Beer/Quaker State Oil Lola T97/00-Honda	FS	13	11	11	23	26	8	24	27	10	17	14	26	23	12	19	23	3	27
19	Roberto Moreno (BR)	Payton/Coyne Data Control Lola T97/00-Ford XD	FS	24	–	–	–	–	–	–	–	–	–	–	–	–	–	–	–	–	16
		Newman/Haas Kmart/Budweiser Swift 007.i-Ford XD	GY	–	–	24	14	18	25	10	5	–	–	–	–	–	–	–	–	–	
		Bettenhausen Alumax Aluminum Reynard 97I-Mercedes	GY	–	–	–	–	–	–	–	–	–	–	–	–	–	–	15	10	–	
20	*Gualter Salles (BR)	Davis Racing Marlboro/Valvoline Reynard 96I-Ford XD	GY	15	–	–	–	–	–	–	–	–	–	–	–	–	–	–	–	–	10
		Davis Racing Marlboro/Valvoline Reynard 97I-Ford XD	GY	–	24	18	24	19	12	22	21	23	19	18	10	20	13	26	7	14	
20	*Dario Franchitti (GB)	Hogan Racing LLC Reynard 97I-Mercedes	FS	25	9	12	13	27	17	16	13	26	11	P26	19	11	25	13	13	–	10
20	Richie Hearn (USA)	Della Penna Ralphs/Food 4 Less Lola T97/00-Ford XD	GY	11	13	27	18	14	9	23	23	14	28	27	22	13	9	22	25	15	10
23	Juan Fangio II (RA)	All American Racers Castrol/Jockey Reynard 96I-Toyota RV8A	GY	20	20	26	15	–	–	–	–	–	–	–	–	–	–	–	–	–	9
		All American Racers Castrol/Jockey Reynard 97I-Toyota RV8B	GY	–	–	–	–	20	23	21	10	22	21	19	11	25	10	12	15	NS	
24	Max Papis (I)	Arciero-Wells Racing MCI Reynard 97I-Toyota RV8B	FS	19	14	25	22	13	26	19	11	28	27	15	8	14	15	20	14	12	8
25	Dennis Vitolo (USA)	Project Indy SmithKline Beecham Lola T97/00-Ford XD	GY	23	–	NS	NQ	–	–	–	–	–	–	–	–	–	–	27	20	–	6
		Payton/Coyne Racing Lola T97/00-Ford XD	FS	–	–	–	–	–	–	–	–	28	7	–	–	–	–	–	–	–	
		Payton/Coyne SmithKline Beecham Lola T97/00-Ford XD	FS	–	–	–	–	–	–	–	–	–	–	–	–	–	–	–	–	16	
26	Robby Gordon (USA)	Hogan Racing LLC Reynard 97I-Mercedes	FS	–	–	–	–	–	–	–	–	–	–	–	–	–	–	–	–	8	5
27	Hiro Matsushita (J)	Arciero-Wells Panasonic/Duskin Reynard 96I-Toyota RV8A	FS	21	25	20	25	23	–	–	–	–	–	–	–	–	–	–	–	–	4
		Arciero-Wells Panasonic/Duskin Reynard 97I-Toyota RV8B	FS	–	–	–	–	–	15	17	19	15	20	22	9	19	24	14	28	23	
28	P.J. Jones (USA)	All American Racers Castrol/Jockey Reynard 96I-Toyota RV8A	GY	28	26	16	21	–	–	–	–	–	–	–	–	–	–	–	–	–	3
		All American Racers Castrol/Jockey Reynard 97I-Toyota RV8B	GY	–	–	–	–	16	21	14	14	20	25	21	28	17	14	25	17	10	
29	Christian Danner (D)	Payton/Coyne Lola T97/00-Ford XD	FS	–	–	–	–	–	–	12	27	–	–	–	–	–	–	–	–	–	1
		Payton/Coyne Reynard 97I-Ford XD	FS	–	–	–	–	–	–	–	–	–	–	–	–	–	–	–	23	–	
29	Michel Jourdain Jr. (MEX)	Payton/Coyne Herdez/Mexlub/Viva Mexico! Lola T97/00-Ford XD	FS	18	18	17	20	17	16	27	–	–	–	–	–	–	–	–	–	–	1
		Payton/Coyne Herdez/Viva Mexico! Lola T96/00-Ford XD	FS	–	–	–	–	–	–	–	22	–	–	–	–	–	–	–	–	–	
		Payton/Coyne Herdez/Viva Mexico! Reynard 97I-Ford XD	FS	–	–	–	–	–	–	–	–	12	18	13	13	18	20	21	22	18	
29	*Arnd Meier (D)	Project Indy Hasseroder Pils/Marcelo Lola T97/00-Ford XD	GY	–	16	–	–	25	NS	–	18	18	22	24	12	16	19	–	–	25	1
	*Charles Nearburg (USA)	Payton/Coyne Nearburg Exploration Lola T97/00-Ford XD	FS	–	–	–	–	–	–	–	–	–	26	–	–	–	–	–	–	–	0
		Payton/Coyne Nearburg Exploration Reynard 97I-Ford XD	FS	–	–	–	–	–	–	–	–	–	–	–	–	–	NS	17	–	18	–
	*Paul Jasper (USA)	Payton/Coyne Hype/US Long Distance Lola T97/00-Ford XD	FS	–	23	19	NQ	24	NQ	18	–	–	–	–	–	–	–	–	–	–	0
	Arie Luyendyk (NL)	Target/Chip Ganassi Racing Reynard 97I-Honda	FS	–	–	–	–	–	–	–	–	–	–	–	–	–	–	–	24	–	0

Bold type indicates car still running at finish

* rookie   † led most laps   P pole position   NQ did not qualify   NS did not start

Lap Leaders (Number of races led)

1	Alex Zanardi	338	(10)
2	Paul Tracy	336	(6)
3	Mauricio Gugelmin	212	(8)
4	Michael Andretti	197	(6)
5	Gil de Ferran	165	(8)
6	Jimmy Vasser	153	(5)
7	Greg Moore	142	(5)
8	Mark Blundell	138	(5)
9	Bobby Rahal	137	(3)
10	Andre Ribeiro	135	(2)
11	Raul Boesel	90	(4)
12	Scott Pruett	66	(5)
13	Bryan Herta	54	(5)
14	Dario Franchitti	47	(3)
15	Patrick Carpentier	39	(2)
16	Richie Hearn	4	(1)
17	Arnd Meier	2	(1)
18	Christian Fittipaldi	2	(1)
19	Gualter Salles	1	(1)
20	Roberto Moreno	1	(1)

Nations Cup

1	United States	252
2	Brazil	238
3	Italy	197
4	Canada	190
5	England	115
6	Mexico	27
7	Scotland	10
8	Argentina	9
9	Japan	4
10	Germany	2
11	Holland	0

Manufacturers Championship

1	Mercedes	316
2	Honda	290
3	Ford	230
4	Toyota	15

Constructors Championship

1	Reynard	346
2	Penske	156
3	Swift	143
4	Lola	45

Jim Trueman Rookie of the Year

1	Patrick Carpentier	27
2	Gualter Salles	10
3	Dario Franchitti	10
4	Arnd Meier	1
5	Paul Jasper	0
6	Charles Nearburg	0

FACTS & FIGURES

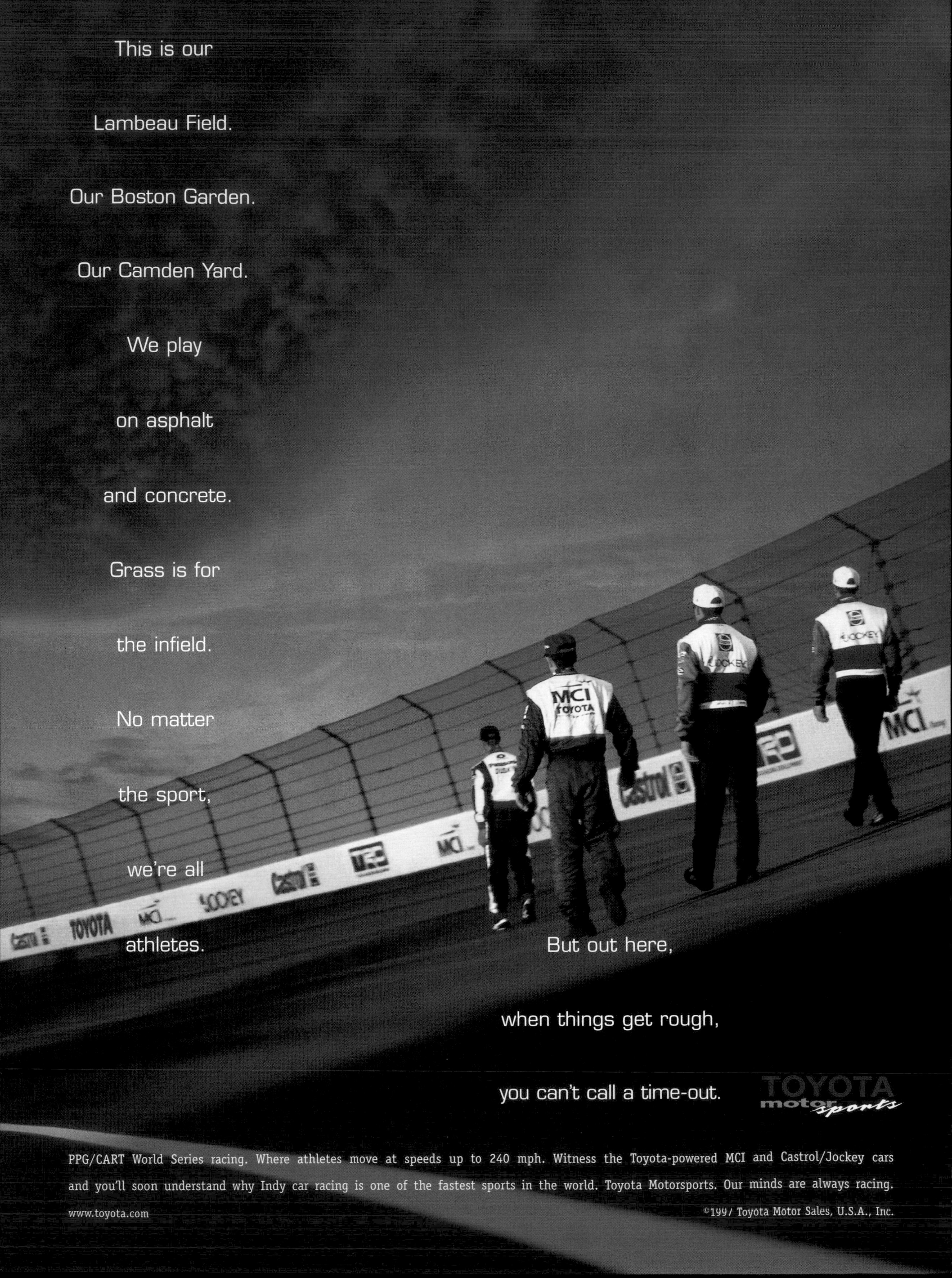
This is our
Lambeau Field.
Our Boston Garden.
Our Camden Yard.
We play
on asphalt
and concrete.
Grass is for
the infield.
No matter
the sport,
we're all
athletes.
But out here,
when things get rough,
you can't call a time-out.
TOYOTA motor sports
PPG/CART World Series racing. Where athletes move at speeds up to 240 mph. Witness the Toyota-powered MCI and Castrol/Jockey cars and you'll soon understand why Indy car racing is one of the fastest sports in the world. Toyota Motorsports. Our minds are always racing.
www.toyota.com
©1997 Toyota Motor Sales, U.S.A., Inc.

Michael C. Brown

HOMESTEAD

Helped by slick work from Tim Bumps and
the rest of the Kmart/Texaco Havoline pit
crew, Michael Andretti gave the new
Swift a sensational debut victory.
Photo: Michael C. Brown

HISTORY has a curious habit of repeating itself. Three years after earning a place in the record books with a sensational debut victory for the brand-new Reynard chassis, Michael Andretti achieved an identical feat in the opening round of the 1997 PPG CART World Series, this time with Newman/Haas Racing's Kmart/Texaco Havoline Swift 007.i.

Andretti didn't dominate the proceedings, as he had done with the Reynard 94I at Surfers Paradise; instead, he qualified a mediocre 14th among the 28-car field for the Marlboro Grand Prix of Miami. But a few subtle changes to the Swift's setup after qualifying – and prior to the final warmup practice session on Sunday morning – provided a remarkable transformation.

'I really felt good after the first run this morning,' declared Andretti. 'The car felt totally different to the way it had been the whole rest of the weekend. I just had a smile on my face. I

knew we had a car to get the job done.'

Andretti was on the move from the moment the green flag waved. He passed a half-dozen cars on the very first lap, then snuck past Greg Moore's Player's Reynard-Mercedes for seventh place on lap two. Al Unser Jr. (Marlboro Penske-Mercedes), Parker Johnstone (KOOL Reynard-Honda) and Mauricio Gugelmin (Hollywood Reynard-Mercedes) fell victim in quick succession between laps nine and 13, and after hounding defending race and series champion Jimmy Vasser's Target Reynard-Honda relentlessly for almost 20 laps, Andretti grasped his opportunity on lap 32 to slip into third place. Now only Vasser's pole-winning teammate, Alex Zanardi, and Gil de Ferran, at the wheel of Derrick Walker's backup Valvoline/Cummins Reynard-Honda due to a heavy crash in qualifying, lay ahead.

Zanardi had taken off into a clear

Series champion Jimmy Vasser opened the defense of his title with a strong third place for Target/Chip Ganassi Racing.

Below left: Proud parent. Designer David Bruns could feel quietly satisfied with the Swift's first PPG Cup outing.

lead during the early stages, his initial jump assisted by a first-lap squabble for second place between de Ferran and Gugelmin. The Italian seemed to be in a class by himself as he extended his advantage to more than four seconds inside nine laps.

Gugelmin and Vasser were glued to de Ferran's tail for the first dozen or so laps – until Gugelmin's car began to oversteer. His team had perceived the need for some additional ducting to the rear uprights following practice, but a compensatory aerodynamic change to the nose of the car had proved insufficient under race conditions. The Brazilian's predicament was eased by an adjustment during the first pit stop, by which time he had slipped to eighth, but it wasn't until the final stint, following another change, that he really began to feel comfortable. And by then it was too late to offer a serious challenge for the lead.

Zanardi's advantage remained intact

until he encountered a group of slower cars which allowed de Ferran to edge steadily closer. On lap 32, de Ferran swept through into the lead. Andretti relieved Vasser of third place at virtually the same instant, then quickly reduced the four-second gap to Zanardi. The Swift soon moved past the Reynard with ease.

Andretti next set his sights on de Ferran, only for his charge to be halted by the first full-course caution of the day after rookie Dario Franchitti smote the wall heavily in Turn Two with Carl Hogan's brand-new Reynard-Mercedes.

The young Scotsman, who, thankfully, emerged unscathed, had hitherto given a solid account of himself, despite a total lack of prior oval track experience. Franchitti, indeed, was running happily in 11th, just behind fellow rookie Patrick Carpentier's similar Alumax Reynard-Mercedes, when he made the classic mistake of attempting to move off line to give some room for

the race leader, de Ferran, who was looming large in his mirrors and about to put him a lap down.

The interlude enabled all the front-runners to make scheduled pit stops. All, that is, except for Johnstone, who had pitted under green a couple of laps earlier. Johnstone lost a lap in the process. Nevertheless, according to the CART rules, after everyone else had taken on service and rejoined in line behind Johnstone, the #27 Reynard should have been waved past the pace car in order to take up its rightful position at the tail end of the lead lap.

Unfortunately, Barry Green & Co. were still cursing their luck at the timing of the caution and, in the heat of the moment, failed to realize that the CART officials had neglected to follow the correct procedure. So Johnstone remained one lap in arrears.

The top three positions were unchanged after the pit stops, with de Ferran leading Andretti and Zanardi, whose car had gone loose toward the end of the first stint. Paul Tracy emerged in fourth, due to typically expert work by Jon Bouslog and the Marlboro Team Penske crew. He was followed by Vasser, Gugelmin and Moore, who had lost a couple of positions in the shuffle. Pat Patrick's pair of Brahma Sports Team Reynard-Fords, driven by Scott Pruett and Raul Boesel, plus the impressive Carpentier, also were on the lead lap.

The leaders stayed in close formation until lap 69, when de Ferran sped onto the back straightaway in pursuit of the lapped cars of Max Papis (MCI Reynard-Toyota) and Dennis Vitolo (SmithKline Beecham Lola-Ford). Papis swept past Vitolo shortly before the entry to Turn Three, but as de Ferran attempted to do likewise, he was side-swiped by Vitolo, who had been forced into taking evasive action as Papis slowed more suddenly than he anticipated on the entry to the corner. An instant later, the erstwhile leader's Reynard was into the retaining wall.

'The car was perfect today,' lamented de Ferran. 'I was out there running my own pace. Everything was going well. It would have been so nice to begin my association with Walker with a win. We were capable of winning, and I can't tell you how disappointed I am.'

The incident allowed Andretti to take over the lead, which he maintained with a comfortable advantage of between four and five seconds through the middle stages. Zanardi ran alone in second, with Tracy holding off Pruett and Gugelmin in a tight battle for third.

On lap 106, Andretti peeled into the

QUALIFYING

An intensive program of winter testing and development had taken the PPG CART World Series to a new level of competitiveness prior to the new season, as exemplified by the practice times at Homestead. Mauricio Gugelmin (28.144 seconds/194.045 mph) and Bobby Rahal topped the time sheets – ironically after their respective teams had effectively exchanged powerplants during the off-season, with PacWest switching to Mercedes-Benz and Team Rahal aligning itself with Ford/Cosworth. Alex Zanardi's Honda-powered 97I made it three Reynards at the front, all with different engines. Next were Marlboro Penske-Mercedes teammates Al Unser Jr. and Paul Tracy. Incredibly, Rahal was separated from Richie Hearn's 20th-placed Ralphs/Food 4 Less Lola-Ford by less than a half-second!

Qualifying was no less exciting.

Zanardi set the standard by posting a magnificent 28.000s, but when Gugelmin, next in the lineup, recorded a 28.112s on his first flying lap, it seemed as though Zanardi's string of four consecutive poles, dating to the end of the 1996 season, was about to come to an end. Gugelmin, however, could manage 'only' 28.025s on his second lap. It was not enough.

'That's qualifying on an oval,' said the philosophical Brazilian. 'Two one-hundredths. It could go either way. It's not frustrating because nothing was wrong with my car. That's as fast as it would go. It just shows how competitive everything is.'

Gil de Ferran also came tantalizingly close with Derrick Walker's Valvoline/Cummins Reynard-Honda, stopping the clocks at a sizzling 28.050s on his first flying lap. There was palpable tension as de Ferran sped into Turn One on his next lap . . . which quickly turned to horror as the Brazilian understeered wide and slammed into the retaining wall. De Ferran was fortunate to emerge unscathed.

Zanardi's pole was secure, as was a new CART record of nine consecutive front row starts, eclipsing the previous mark set by Bobby Unser in 1979-80 and Bobby Rahal in 1985.

Greg Moore turned a startling lap to be fourth fastest in his year-old Reynard-Mercedes, while Mark Blundell produced a truly heroic effort for PacWest after struggling throughout practice with his '97 Motorola Reynard-Mercedes.

'To be honest, I've never been so scared in all my life,' said the steely Briton, 'and that's the honest truth.'

Safety fears prove unfounded

WHEN the PPG Cup series made its first visit to the Metro-Dade Homestead Motorsports Complex in 1996, the cars ran in conventional short-oval aerodynamic configuration, which meant large, street course-type wings producing high levels of downforce. This time, in a bid to promote safety and reduce cornering speeds, CART mandated the use of low-downforce superspeedway-type wings.

Interestingly, average lap speeds were remarkably similar – at least in qualifying. Straight-line speeds were higher, up to around 210 mph, due to the reduced drag, while cornering speeds were trimmed to around 170 mph.

Prior to the race weekend, however, Bobby Rahal *(right)* was among very few drivers who declared the move a positive step. So far as he was concerned, the smaller wings would make the cars harder to drive and perhaps a little less forgiving, which, he reasoned, would place a premium on driver ability.

It was, therefore, ironic that Rahal should struggle harder than most on raceday. He had been among the quickest contenders during practice and qualifying, but come the race his car quickly developed a dangerous loose condition. The #7 Miller Lite Reynard-Ford eventually finished a distant 16th.

Many of Rahal's peers had expressed concern about competing at such high speeds with minimal downforce – especially as the effectiveness of the tiny speedway wings would be compromised still further by high ambient temperatures and a gusty wind which prevailed throughout the weekend.

But when some drivers suggested that the benefits of the change might be offset by fewer overtaking opportunities, Jimmy Vasser begged to differ: 'I don't think it will be a problem,' declared the defending series champion. 'When it comes down to the race, I think we'll find ways to overtake. We always do.'

And so it proved. The Marlboro Grand Prix of Miami passed without undue incident. It was not the crash-fest some had feared. Furthermore, the race order changed frequently and dramatically during the early stages. Sure, the closing laps were somewhat processional, but that was primarily due to the fact a true pecking order had emerged – and Michael Andretti took full advantage as he sped to an accomplished victory for Newman/Haas Racing, Swift, Ford/Cosworth and Goodyear.

Red faces after restart confusion

THE outcome of the first race of the season was unfortunately clouded in controversy following a botched restart procedure during the third and final full-course caution of the afternoon.

The problems occurred as a result of the fact that most of the front-runners already had made pit stops under green. In doing so, all bar erstwhile point-man Michael Andretti had fallen a lap behind the new leader Paul Tracy, who, along with only Jimmy Vasser and Greg Moore, had not yet taken on service.

The opportunity to stop under yellow allowed all three to do so without losing a lap. They duly emerged from the pits and took up formation behind Andretti, who had already stopped and therefore had been able to regain the advantage.

Up ahead, meanwhile, and trapped behind the pace car, were Scott Pruett, Mauricio Gugelmin, Alex Zanardi and Raul Boesel. By rights, they should have been waved past the pace car and allowed to position themselves behind the other contenders on the lead lap. But before this could take place, chief starter Jim Swintal was instructed to display the crossed flags, which is the signal for the drivers to adopt a two-by-two formation prior to the restart with only the unlapped cars on the inside line.

Thus, when Andretti, on cue, moved to the front of the pack, Pruett, Gugelmin, Zanardi and Boesel were all put one lap down, and despite protestations from their respective crews, that was the lineup when the green flag finally was shown on lap 123.

In reality, the overall positions were not compromised.

Nevertheless, the foursome should have been able to take the restart immediately behind the race leaders – and that was the focus of their respective teams when the arguments continued into the stewards' room long after the race had been completed.

Several hours later, in a bid to redress the balance, the CART officials decided to declare the finish as of 147 laps, despite the fact that Andretti, Tracy, Vasser and Moore actually completed 148. The next three (excluding Boesel who had retired with engine trouble) were therefore shown as finishing on the same lap, which explains the inordinately large time differential in the final box-score.

pit lane for a routine change of tires and a fresh load of methanol. Crucially, rapid work by Tim Bumps and the boys enabled Andretti to rejoin just in front of the new race leaders, Zanardi and Tracy.

When Zanardi made for the pits on lap 108, a recalcitrant wheel nut caused him to lose a lap to Tracy, who was deliberately stretching his fuel load as far as it would go. The strategy paid off moments later as the yellow lights flashed on. Papis had ground to a halt, out of fuel, on the pit entrance road.

At that point only Tracy, Moore and Vasser, who was out of sequence on pit stops after picking up a puncture during the previous yellow, had not yet made pit stops. The full-course caution enabled them to take on service without losing a lap. While they did so, however, Andretti, the only other driver still on the same lap, duly regained the lead.

Following a period of confusion while the field was sorted out prior to the restart, Andretti accelerated clear of Tracy and immediately posted a series of laps at better than 180 mph. The Pennsylvanian remained in command to record his 36th CART victory, easily the most among active drivers.

'I pretty much knew we had it under control after the last restart, so I just wanted to keep a nice, consistent pace,' he said. 'To be honest, I felt confident, even with de Ferran there. I felt like our car was a little bit better than his.'

Tracy remained behind the lapped car of Pruett in the closing stages, so was in no position to mount a serious bid for the lead. Still, the Canadian was more than content with second after a mature performance.

'It's the first time I've ever finished the first race of the season,' noted Tracy, 'so that's encouraging. It's nice to get some points in the bank.'

Vasser, too, was happy to settle for third ahead of Moore, who drove a fine race in Jerry Forsythe's year-old Reynard 96I following the team's late decision to ditch its new Lolas, which had not lived up to expectations during testing.

'It sounds kind of funny,' said Moore, 'we're disappointed with fourth. We thought we had a run at winning the thing. Realistically, with a '96 car and just two days of running here, that's a pretty good result. [Race engineer] Steve [Challis] and I sat down and figured out if we finished in the top five in every race, we'll win the championship. That's what we did today.'

Pruett finished strongly in fifth to ensure a fine result for Brahma in its new association with Patrick Racing. Teammate Boesel also looked set for a top-10 finish until his engine failed just a couple of laps from the checkers. Zanardi finished sixth on the road but, correctly, was penalized 25 seconds for passing Gugelmin during the chaotic final yellow, which effectively redressed the situation.

All of those finishing one lap down argued vehemently that they had been robbed of a chance to challenge for the win by the snafu during the final caution. But the leaders were turning laps of similar speed as the race wound toward its conclusion, and with such equality – and almost no slower traffic to cause any delays – overtaking was nigh impossible. Andretti, it seemed, was firmly in control.

HOMESTEAD SNIPPETS

Photos: Michael C. Brown

• NEW RULES for the 1997 season, mandating additional padding around the drivers' helmets and energy-absorbing seats, received a vote of approval from Gil de Ferran *(left)*, who endured heavy accidents both in qualifying and the race. 'CART did a fantastic job with the rule changes,' he declared. 'Unfortunately I got to test that twice this weekend. I feel totally fine. Last year I would have had a big headache and my ears would be ringing for ages.'

• In marked contrast to the early stages of the 1996 season, the latest FORD/COSWORTH XD engine displayed a dramatic improvement in terms of both horsepower and reliability. 'It's definitely been quite a culture shock from last year when we were hiding in our bunkers,' joked Ford/Cosworth chief engineer Steve Miller.

• 'It's funny,' said ALEX ZANARDI after clinching his fifth consecutive CART pole, 'I always thought I was a much, much stronger racer [than qualifier], but it looks like I'm not a bad qualifier either.'

• Honors among the two TIRE MANUFACTURERS, Firestone and Goodyear, were shared as Firestone secured the pole and Goodyear the top two positions in the race. Firestone, meanwhile, filled the next six places.

• MAX PAPIS, first onto the track in single-car qualifying, was justifiably delighted with his time of 28.784s – almost three-quarters of a second faster than his previous best aboard Arciero-Wells Racing's under-powered MCI Reynard-Toyota *(right)*. 'When I saw the exit speed in Turn One [on the dash display], I thought, oh, very fast,' said the Italian with a huge smile after securing 17th on the grid in his very first appearance on an oval. 'My foot was coming up by itself so I said, "No, no, down, down!" The car was stuck very well, but I think if I lift, I will get push, so I kept my foot down. So it was good, I'm very 'appy.'

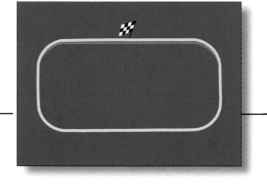

PPG CART WORLD SERIES • ROUND 1
MARLBORO GRAND PRIX OF MIAMI PRESENTED BY TOYOTA

METRO-DADE HOMESTEAD MOTORSPORTS COMPLEX, HOMESTEAD, FLORIDA

MARCH 2, 147 laps – 222.999 miles

Place	Driver (Nat.)	No.	Team Sponsors Car-Engine	Tires	Q Speed	Q Time	Q Pos.	Laps	Time/Status	Ave. (mph)	Pts.
1	Michael Andretti (USA)	6	Newman/Haas Kmart/Texaco Havoline Swift 007.i-Ford XD	GY	190.978	28.596s	14	147 †	1h 38m 45.666s	135.478	21
2	Paul Tracy (CDN)	3	Marlboro Team Penske Penske PC26-Mercedes	GY	189.862	28.764s	16	147 †	1h 38m 49.067s	135.400	16
3	Jimmy Vasser (USA)	1	Target/Chip Ganassi Racing Reynard 97I-Honda	FS	192.968	28.301s	6	147 †	1h 38m 55.250s	135.259	14
4	Greg Moore (CDN)	99	Forsythe Player's Ltd./Indeck Reynard 96I-Mercedes	FS	194.004	28.150s	4	147 †	1h 38m 57.246s	135.214	12
5	Scott Pruett (USA)	20	Patrick Brahma Sports Team Reynard 97I-Ford XD	FS	191.776	28.477s	11	147	1h 39m 17.613s	134.751	10
6	Mauricio Gugelmin (BR)	17	PacWest Racing Group Hollywood Reynard 97I-Mercedes	FS	194.869	28.025s	2	147	1h 39m 29.485s	134.483	8
7	Alex Zanardi (I)	4	Target/Chip Ganassi Racing Reynard 97I-Honda	FS	195.043	28.000s	1	147 §	1h 39m 54.002s	133.933	7
8	Parker Johnstone (USA)	27	Team KOOL Green Reynard 97I-Honda	FS	192.887	28.313s	7	146	Running		5
9	*Patrick Carpentier (CDN)	16	Bettenhausen Alumax Aluminum Reynard 97I-Mercedes	GY	192.404	28.384s	9	146	Running		4
10	Bryan Herta (USA)	8	Team Rahal Shell Reynard 97I-Ford XD	GY	189.678	28.792s	18	146	Running		3
11	Richie Hearn (USA)	21	Della Penna Ralphs/Food 4 Less Lola T97/00-Ford XD	GY	186.237	29.324s	21	146	Running		2
12	Andre Ribeiro (BR)	31	Tasman Motorsports LCI/Marlboro Lola T97/00-Honda	FS	186.695	29.252s	20	146	Running		1
13	Adrian Fernandez (MEX)	32	Tasman Tecate Beer/Quaker State Oil Lola T97/00-Honda	FS	185.673	29.413s	22	146	Running		
14	Mark Blundell (GB)	18	PacWest Racing Group Motorola Reynard 97I-Mercedes	FS	193.132	28.277s	5	145	Running		
15	*Gualter Salles (BR)	77	Davis Racing Marlboro/Valvoline Reynard 96I-Ford XD	GY	189.658	28.795s	19	145	Running		
16	Bobby Rahal (USA)	7	Team Rahal Miller Lite Reynard 97I-Ford XD	GY	191.514	28.516s	12	144	Running		
17	Raul Boesel (BR)	40	Patrick Brahma Sports Team Reynard 97I-Ford XD	FS	192.744	28.334s	8	143	Engine		
18	Michel Jourdain Jr. (MEX)	19	Payton/Coyne Herdez/Mexlub/Viva Mexico! Lola T97/00-Ford XD	FS	183.459	29.768s	23	143	Running		
19	Max Papis (I)	25	Arciero-Wells Racing MCI Reynard 97I-Toyota RV8B	FS	189.730	28.784s	17	133	Running		
20	Juan Fangio II (RA)	36	All American Racers Castrol/Jockey Reynard 96I-Toyota RV8A	GY	182.362	29.947s	25	122	Running		
21	Hiro Matsushita (J)	24	Arciero-Wells Panasonic/Duskin Reynard 96I-Toyota RV8A	FS	179.704	30.390s	26	88	Engine		
22	Gil de Ferran (BR)	5	Walker Valvoline/Cummins Reynard 97I-Honda	GY	194.695	28.050s	3	68	Accident		
23	Dennis Vitolo (USA)	64	Project Indy SmithKline Beecham Lola T97/00-Ford XD	GY	176.407	30.958s	27	62	Engine		
24	Roberto Moreno (BR)	34	Payton/Coyne Data Control Lola T97/00-Ford XD	FS	no speed	no time	28	62	Handling		
25	*Dario Franchitti (GB)	9	Hogan Racing LLC Reynard 97I-Mercedes	FS	191.306	28.547s	13	44	Accident		
26	Christian Fittipaldi (BR)	11	Newman/Haas Kmart/Budweiser Swift 007.i-Ford XD	GY	189.981	28.746s	15	40	Oil leak		
27	Al Unser Jr. (USA)	2	Marlboro Team Penske Penske PC26-Mercedes	GY	192.167	28.419s	10	27	Electrical		
28	P.J. Jones (USA)	98	All American Racers Castrol/Jockey Reynard 96I-Toyota RV8A	GY	183.366	29.783s	24	26	Engine		

* denotes Rookie driver   † lap count readjusted due to improper alignment of field prior to restart on lap 123   § includes 25-second penalty for passing under yellow

Caution flags: Laps 45–58, accident/Franchitti; laps 68–76, accident/de Ferran and Vitolo; laps 110–122, tow/Papis. **Total:** three for 36 laps.

Lap leaders: Alex Zanardi, 1–31 (31 laps); Gil de Ferran, 32–68 (37 laps); Michael Andretti, 69–105 (37 laps); Zanardi, 106–107 (2 laps); Paul Tracy, 108–112 (5 laps); Andretti, 113–147 (35 laps). **Totals:** Andretti, 72 laps; de Ferran, 37 laps; Zanardi, 33 laps; Tracy, 5 laps.

Fastest race lap: Michael Andretti, 29.697s, 183.897 mph on lap 131.

Championship positions: 1 Andretti, 21; **2** Tracy, 16; **3** Vasser, 14; **4** Moore, 12; **5** Pruett, 10; **6** Gugelmin, 8; **7** Zanardi, 7; **8** Johnstone, 5; **9** Carpentier, 4; **10** Herta, 3; **11** Hearn, 2; **12** Ribeiro, 1.

Ω
OMEGA
OFFICIAL TIMEKEEPER OF CART

SURFERS PARADISE

PPG CART WORLD SERIES • ROUND 2

Scott Pruett profited from a clash between front row starters Alex Zanardi and Paul Tracy to claim the second win of his CART career at the wheel of Pat Patrick's Brahma Reynard.

Michael C. Brown

plete restart led to heated discussions up and down pit lane. Indeed they continued long into the evening as several teams filed a protest.

The restart was a blessing for several drivers, including front row qualifier Paul Tracy, who, a couple of corners on from the scene of Fittipaldi's crash, had slid into the wall while in pursuit of race leader Alex Zanardi's Target Reynard-Honda. Parker Johnstone, whose KOOL Reynard-Honda had sustained a puncture following contact with Pruett in a separate incident on the opening lap, also was granted a reprieve and was able to take up his original grid position.

Zanardi and Tracy again took off into the lead when the race was finally restarted. Third qualifier Jimmy Vasser was obliged to lift off the throttle when Target Reynard-Honda teammate Zanardi appeared to check up momentarily before the green flag, giving Greg Moore the opportunity to slip past in his Player's Reynard-Mercedes as the field accelerated toward the Sunbelt Chicane. Mauricio Gugelmin, who again qualified strongly in his Hollywood/PacWest Reynard-Mercedes, held down fifth place at the completion of lap one, followed by Pruett, Johnstone and the second PacWest car of Mark Blundell.

Zanardi, like the majority of the Firestone contingent, had chosen to qualify on the softer prime tires and took full advantage as he edged clear of Tracy in the opening laps. Soon, though, Tracy, on the soft Goodyear optionals, began to close. By lap six, Tracy was hard on Zanardi's tail, looking for a way past. Two early full-

course cautions worked in Zanardi's favor, but eventually, on lap 19, he locked up his brakes on the entry to Dime Turn, slid wide on the exit and allowed Tracy clear passage as the pair accelerated along the short straight toward Bartercard Turn and the ocean front. Tracy romped clear to the tune of almost three seconds as he crossed the start/finish line at the completion of lap 19, whereupon Zanardi was saved from further ignominy by another full-course yellow.

This time everybody took the opportunity to make their first scheduled pit stops. Tracy, who survived a scare when he clipped Johnstone's car exiting his pit box, resumed ahead of Zanardi, who wisely switched to the more durable Firestone compound. Bryan Herta's Shell Reynard-Ford jumped up to third for the restart by virtue of the fact he had already visited the pit lane (after being forced off the road by Gualter Salles' spinning Indusval Reynard-Ford) and did not require an additional stop.

Herta couldn't match the pace of the two leaders at the restart and soon began to slip down the order. Then his day came to a premature end when Johnstone attempted an impossible move under braking for Dime Turn. Blundell's Motorola Reynard also was an innocent victim. Out came the yellow flags one more time.

The restart on lap 34 saw Tracy still leading from Zanardi, Moore, Vasser, Pruett and Michael Andretti, who had started a lowly 11th in the Homestead-winning Kmart/Texaco Caltex Swift-Ford. Gugelmin ran next, seventh, having lost a couple of places during

FIRST Alex Zanardi and then Paul Tracy held the upper hand during a dramatic Sunbelt IndyCarnival, but at the end of the day it was Scott Pruett who emerged with the victory after a typically workmanlike performance aboard Pat Patrick's Brahma Sports Team Reynard-Ford/Cosworth. Pruett, who had battled through all manner of difficulties during the two days of practice and qualifying, took over at the front after Tracy and Zanardi clashed while disputing the lead. He also took advantage of two excellent pit stops by Donny Lambert's crew, then kept his calm in the closing stages to ensure a fine win, the second of his CART career.

'This was a real team effort,' praised Pruett. 'We had a lot of problems this weekend but we worked very hard and had a good car for the race. That's one aspect of this sport that we tend to forget is how much of it comes down to

teamwork. We're always practicing pit stops, trying to make them better because, as we saw today, races are won or lost in the pits.'

A total of seven full-course cautions served to break up the action. The proceedings also were delayed by almost an hour following an accident at the beginning of lap two which left Christian Fittipaldi with a badly broken right leg.

Fittipaldi's eighth-placed Kmart/Budweiser Swift had come into contact with the pursuing Gil de Ferran's Valvoline/Cummins Reynard-Honda on the curving main straightaway in front of the pits, sending Fittipaldi's car headlong into the barriers at the end of pit lane. The Swift withstood the huge impact remarkably well, but a mass of debris littering the track left the officials with little alternative but to display the red flag.

CART Chief Steward Dennis Swan's subsequent decision to order a com-

Pruett overcomes the odds

SCOTT Pruett endured all manner of difficulties in Pat Patrick's Brahma Sports Team Reynard-Ford/Cosworth throughout practice and qualifying. His problems began in the opening session on Friday when a broken drive-flange on his primary car triggered a catastrophic gearbox failure which forced him to rely upon his backup 97I for the remainder of the weekend. Pruett was therefore content after setting the third best time in Friday qualifying. 'We lost some of our momentum having to switch from one car to the other,' said Pruett. 'It took a little bit away, but we're real happy with the performance of the engine and the overall reaction of the car. Now we have to use what we learned today to go quicker on day two.'

Sure enough, Pruett set the fastest time on Saturday morning, although his hopes of challenging for the pole were dashed when his car ground to a halt after the very first lap of qualifying on Saturday afternoon. A spark box failure was eventually diagnosed as the cause.

The Patrick team faced a dilemma, since it had already withdrawn Pruett's time from Friday due to a decision to switch to the more durable 'optional' Firestone tires. The only solution was to haul out teammate Raul Boesel's spare car, and without time to make any adjustments – nor even install his own seat – Pruett returned to the fray. Seventh on the grid represented a remarkable effort.

'All I did was pitch and catch,' said Pruett. 'There was no fluidity in what I was doing. I just did the best I could. It's really disappointing because we had a good shot at the pole. I'm not saying we'd have got it but we'd have been fighting for it.'

Photos: John Morris/Mpix Photography

Christian Fittipaldi suffered a badly broken leg when his Kmart/Budweiser Swift smashed into the barriers after making contact with Gil de Ferran's Valvoline Reynard at the start of the second lap.

the stops when his egress was inadvertently hindered by one of Vasser's crew members in the adjacent pit box.

The scrappy race was interrupted once again just a handful of laps later when Juan Fangio's Castrol/Jockey Reynard caught fire following yet another Toyota engine failure. The latest caution triggered the second round of pit stops. This time CART debutant Arnd Meier emerged, somewhat surprisingly, in the lead with Andreas Leberle's Project Indy Lola-Ford after eschewing the opportunity to make a pit stop.

The young German rookie responded by leaving his braking too late for the Sunbelt Chicane immediately following the restart on lap 42. While Meier took to the escape road, the close-pursuing Tracy also missed his braking point and ended up bouncing across the curbs. Tracy retained the lead, but only as far as Dime Turn, where Zanardi dived for the inside, brakes locked. When he slithered wide on the exit, Tracy took the opportunity to pull alongside in a virtual carbon copy of their earlier tussle for the lead. This time, as they approached Bartercard Turn, the two cars made contact and went spinning.

Zanardi, despite making solid contact with the tire wall, was able to rejoin at the back of the pack. Tracy, though, was out with damaged suspension. Not surprisingly, their individual views on the incident varied substantially.

'As soon as he saw me, he came across my right front and spun himself out,' claimed Tracy.

'I want to give Paul the benefit of the doubt,' countered Zanardi, 'because I could not feel a hard hit and the track is very bumpy there. It is possible to spin just from the bumps.'

What was indisputable was the fact that Pruett had inherited the lead. Vasser and Gugelmin had taken advantage of a miscue during Moore's final pit stop to move into second and third places, although that didn't last long as Gugelmin's bid to demote the defending series champion at Dime Turn succeeded only in forcing both cars into the escape road.

'I just made a mistake,' admitted the honorable Brazilian. 'We were running pretty good and I was really going for the win. I was trying to pass Jimmy, locked up, and the car came around.'

Both rejoined at the back of the pack, whereupon Vasser posted an incredible charge, despite bent suspension, to claim one PPG Cup point for a 12th-place finish.

QUALIFYING

Alex Zanardi set a blistering pace during qualifying on Friday as he completed the session an astonishing 1.082 seconds faster than his nearest challenger, Christian Fittipaldi's Kmart/Budweiser Swift-Ford. Zanardi's Target Reynard-Honda remained at the top of the charts throughout most of the final half-hour on Saturday until, with little more than four minutes remaining, Paul Tracy vaulted ahead with a lap at 1m 36.140s.

'I like to go for my final run with about 10 minutes to go,' said Tracy, who had languished a distant 11th on Friday, 'because everybody's usually in the pits putting on fresh tires at that time, so the track's a lot clearer.'

The ploy, however, allowed Zanardi one last chance to secure the pole and keep his streak alive. The Italian rose to the challenge brilliantly, using every inch of the race track – and the curbs – as he posted a 1m 35.940s on his final lap.

'I'm so 'appy for the 'ole team,' said Zanardi after earning a new CART record sixth straight pole, eclipsing the record held jointly by Mario Andretti and Danny Sullivan. 'They've worked very 'ard from the first moment I joined this team and now we're getting to see the results.

'It's amazing [to beat the record]. It's unfortunate we have to race tomorrow. Otherwise we could celebrate now!'

Tracy was content with a place on the front row of the grid, having made a dramatic improvement to his Marlboro Penske-Mercedes. Jimmy Vasser, the defending race and PPG Cup series champion, improved by almost two seconds to jump from sixth to third. He was joined on row two by the impressive Greg Moore aboard Jerry Forsythe's new Player's Reynard-Mercedes, which had been given only a brief shakedown run in Arizona before making the long haul to Australia.

'We're learning every time we go out,' said Moore. 'It is different to the '96 car but we're getting there.'

Mark Blundell improved from a distant 14th on Friday to annex fifth on the grid – exactly equal to Moore's best – aboard Bruce McCaw's identical Motorola Reynard-Mercedes/Firestone package.

A disappointed Andre Ribeiro had to settle for sixth place at the flag after Alex Zanardi and Gil de Ferran slipped past on the last lap.

Bottom: Young Canadian Greg Moore maintained his bright start to the season by taking the runner-up spot in Jerry Forsythe's new Reynard.

Photos: Michael C. Brown

'I thought I would have to pull in the pits,' related Vasser, 'because it's no fun being out there at 180 mph and just being along for the ride, but I decided it wasn't worth the boos and hisses from my mechanics if I parked the race car.' Brave man.

By now it had become apparent that the scheduled 65-lap distance would not be completed before the mandatory two-hour time limit. Thus, at the completion of lap 55, the white flag was

shown, signifying one lap to go. But the CART officials had miscalculated. As Pruett accelerated out of the final corner for the 56th time, almost a minute remained on the clock. So the hapless chief starter, Jim Swintal, was ordered to display the white flag one more time. The race leader was not amused.

'The last lap I was really careful, just giving myself plenty of room at every turn,' explained Pruett, 'and then, just as I was firing it up coming out of the last turn, [general manager] Jim [McGee] said there was going to be another white. That caught us out a bit. We had to pick up the pace again.'

A close-following Moore, having halved a two-second deficit to Pruett during the previous three laps, could sense the chance for his long-overdue first CART victory. But Pruett was up to the challenge. The Brahma Reynard was inch-perfect on its 57th and final, final lap. Pruett's victory was assured.

Moore had to be content with second place after another excellent performance which brought his fourth podium finish since joining the PPG Cup circuit at the beginning of the 1996 season. The youngster finished well clear of Andretti, who was content to take it easy in the closing laps.

'I just backed off because I knew I couldn't pass them,' said Andretti.

Not so Zanardi, who somehow muscled his way from 17th on lap 44 to fourth at the finish line,

displacing both de Ferran and Andre Ribeiro on the final lap. Ribeiro, who had driven a fine race in the LCI/Marlboro Lola-Honda, was particularly upset, having held fourth position with one lap to go, only to be boldly usurped by Zanardi less than a half-mile from the finish line. The loss of momentum also allowed de Ferran to squeak through.

CART official under fire

CART Chief Steward Dennis Swan, who had assumed the post following the retirement of Wally Dallenbach at the end of the 1996 season, was under siege for the second straight race – this time as a result of his decision to order a complete restart following Christian Fittipaldi's crash.

After the race, Swan was greeted by an official protest from Newman/Haas Racing, Hogan Racing, Team Rahal, Brahma Sports Team and Bettenhausen Motorsports, who collectively argued the race should have been resumed on lap three, in single-file order and without allowing drivers to take up their original grid positions.

The teams' argument was based upon CART Rule 6.20.5B, which states: '. . . unless all race cars . . . have completed at least one officially scored lap . . . the race will be restarted in its entirety.' And in this case, every car had completed one lap before the red flag was displayed.

Swan's stance was based upon additional wording within the rule-book which refers to the right to order a complete restart if the race leader had not completed two laps prior to the red flag. In this instance, Zanardi was on his second lap. 'The stewards interpreted that as an "and/or," ' explained Swan, 'which is not what it says. It says "or." '

Swan, furthermore, had a sound reason for his ruling: 'We weren't trying to doctor anything. We came here to race. To take two front-running competitors [Paul Tracy and Gil de Ferran] out of the race was not what we came here to do.

'But,' he added with admirable honesty, 'upon further reading of the rules, I had to agree with [the teams]. We [the stewards] were incorrect.'

Fortunately, the matter was resolved reasonably amicably as the teams agreed among themselves to rescind the protest.

'[The stewards] admitted they made a mistake and we decided not to pursue it,' said Newman/Haas Team Manager Lee White. 'There didn't seem to be much point. You can't re-run the race. [To continue with the protest] wasn't going to achieve anything. We'll just make sure that any ambiguity in the rules is fixed.'

A little later in the evening, shortly after returning to his hotel, the unfortunate Swan began to experience chest pains and was rushed to the nearby Gold Coast Hospital. Swan remained under close observation for a week, then flew home to Detroit where he underwent an angioplasty. Dallenbach meanwhile agreed to resume the duties of chief steward during Swan's enforced absence.

SURFERS SNIPPETS

Photos: Michael C. Brown

• **DARIO FRANCHITTI** was the top rookie finisher despite stalling the engine at one pit stop, attracting a 'drive-through' penalty for exceeding the pit lane speed limit and a quick spin. Franchitti *(left)* then stormed from 17th to ninth inside the final eight laps. 'The kid is something else,' praised Hogan Racing General Manager Doug Peterson.

• **CHRISTIAN FITTIPALDI**'s car virtually exploded into a mass of composite bits and pieces after slamming head-on into a wall at the end of the pit lane. It then rebounded onto the track and careered on down the road, sustaining another very hard hit with the wall before coming to rest in the middle of the Sunbelt Chicane, perhaps a quarter-mile from the original point of impact. The Swift 007.i chassis, however, absorbed the twin impacts remarkably well. The driver cell remained intact, and even though the left-side suspension was torn from the car, no debris penetrated the carbon/Kevlar tub. Fittipaldi's injuries, incidentally, were caused when his lower right leg became trapped within the pedal assembly.

• **PAUL JASPER**, a 27-year-old graduate of Toyota Atlantic competition, acquitted himself well during his CART debut in one of Payton/Coyne Racing's Lolas, despite being plagued by a variety of niggling mechanical problems.

• Picture perfect weather on the Queensland Gold Coast *(right)* resulted in an **IMPRESSIVE TURN-OUT** of 91,664 fans on raceday as well as a record four-day weekend total of 226,130.

• Hogan Racing engineer **STEVE CONOVER** spent the weekend in a Surfers Paradise hospital having suffered a broken bone in his neck when he was bowled over by a wave just a few hours after his arrival in Australia the previous Tuesday. Conover was lucky, and in fact he returned to work with the team one week later in Long Beach wearing a halo restraint collar.

• A highlight of the spectacular **NO FEAR AIR SHOW** was an awesome 'dump and burn' routine performed by an F-111 fighter on Sunday afternoon. The trick consisted of the pilot jettisoning fuel at extremely low altitude, then igniting it with the application of the after-burners, which resulted in a lengthy fireball behind the rapidly climbing – and accelerating – fighter.

PPG CART WORLD SERIES • ROUND 2
GOLD COAST SUNBELT INDYCARNIVAL

SURFERS PARADISE STREET CIRCUIT, QUEENSLAND, AUSTRALIA

APRIL 6, 57 laps – 159.315 miles

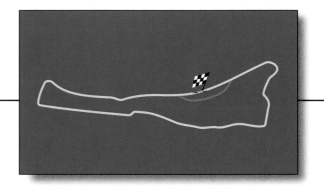

Place	Driver (Nat.)	No.	Team Sponsors Car-Engine	Tires	Q Speed	Q Time	Q Pos.	Laps	Time/Status	Ave. (mph)	Pts.
1	Scott Pruett (USA)	20	Patrick Brahma Sports Team Reynard 97I-Ford XD	FS	103.913	1m 36.831s	7	57	2h 01m 04.678s	78.948	20
2	Greg Moore (CDN)	99	Forsythe Player's Ltd./Indeck Reynard 97I-Mercedes	FS	103.996	1m 36.754s	4	57	2h 01m 05.362s	78.941	16
3	Michael Andretti (USA)	6	Newman/Haas Kmart/Texaco Havoline Swift 007.i-Ford XD	GY	103.337	1m 37.371s	12	57	2h 01m 15.939s	78.826	14
4	Alex Zanardi (I)	4	Target/Chip Ganassi Racing Reynard 97I-Honda	FS	104.878	1m 35.940s	1	57	2h 01m 19.505s	78.787	13
5	Gil de Ferran (BR)	5	Walker Valvoline/Cummins Reynard 97I-Honda	GY	103.387	1m 37.324s	11	57	2h 01m 20.268s	78.779	10
6	Andre Ribeiro (BR)	31	Tasman Motorsports LCI/Marlboro Lola T97/00-Honda	FS	103.046	1m 37.646s	14	57	2h 01m 21.488s	78.766	8
7	Raul Boesel (BR)	40	Patrick Brahma Sports Team Reynard 97I-Ford XD	FS	102.131	1m 38.521s	19	57	2h 01m 22.312s	78.757	6
8	Mark Blundell (GB)	18	PacWest Racing Group Motorola Reynard 97I-Mercedes	FS	103.996	1m 36.754s	5	57	2h 01m 22.840s	78.751	5
9	*Dario Franchitti (GB)	9	Hogan Racing LLC Reynard 97I-Mercedes	FS	103.103	1m 37.592s	13	57	2h 01m 28.237s	78.693	4
10	Bobby Rahal (USA)	7	Team Rahal Miller Lite Reynard 97I-Ford XD	GY	103.649	1m 37.078s	10	57	2h 01m 30.602s	78.668	3
11	Adrian Fernandez (MEX)	32	Tasman Tecate Beer/Quaker State Oil Lola T97/00-Honda	FS	102.863	1m 37.819s	15	57	2h 01m 34.400s	78.627	2
12	Jimmy Vasser (USA)	1	Target/Chip Ganassi Racing Reynard 97I-Honda	FS	104.333	1m 36.441s	3	57	2h 01m 34.869s	78.622	1
13	Richie Hearn (USA)	21	Della Penna Ralphs/Food 4 Less Lola T97/00-Ford XD	GY	101.647	1m 38.990s	20	57	2h 01m 42.888s	78.535	
14	Max Papis (I)	25	Arciero-Wells Racing MCI Reynard 97I-Toyota RV8B	FS	100.694	1m 39.927s	22	57	2h 01m 44.203s	78.521	
15	*Patrick Carpentier (CDN)	16	Bettenhausen Alumax Aluminum Reynard 97I-Mercedes	GY	101.029	1m 39.595s	21	57	2h 01m 46.445s	78.497	
16	*Arnd Meier (D)	64	Project Indy Hasseroder Pils/Marcelo Lola T97/00-Ford XD	GY	98.342	1m 42.316s	27	57	2h 02m 02.753s	78.322	
17	Mauricio Gugelmin (BR)	17	PacWest Racing Group Hollywood Reynard 97I-Mercedes	FS	103.843	1m 36.896s	8	57	2h 02m 18.780s	78.151	
18	Michel Jourdain Jr. (MEX)	19	Payton/Coyne Herdez/Mexlub/Viva Mexico! Lola T97/00-Ford XD	FS	98.772	1m 41.871s	26	43	Transmission		
19	Paul Tracy (CDN)	3	Marlboro Team Penske Penske PC26-Mercedes	GY	104.660	1m 36.140s	2	41	Accident		
20	Juan Fangio II (RA)	36	All American Racers Castrol/Jockey Reynard 96I-Toyota RV8A	GY	100.639	1m 39.981s	23	37	Engine fire		
21	Parker Johnstone (USA)	27	Team KOOL Green Reynard 97I-Honda	FS	103.976	1m 36.772s	6	35	Suspension		
22	Bryan Herta (USA)	8	Team Rahal Shell Reynard 97I-Ford XD	GY	102.784	1m 37.895s	16	29	Accident		
23	*Paul Jasper (USA)	34	Payton/Coyne Hype/US Long Distance Lola T97/00-Ford XD	FS	100.481	1m 40.138s	24	24	Transmission		
24	*Gualter Salles (BR)	77	Davis Racing Indusval/Marlboro Reynard 97I-Ford XD	GY	102.334	1m 38.325s	18	17	Accident		
25	Hiro Matsushita (J)	24	Arciero-Wells Panasonic/Duskin Reynard 96I-Toyota RV8A	FS	97.884	1m 42.795s	28	16	Electrical		
26	P.J. Jones (USA)	98	All American Racers Castrol/Jockey Reynard 96I-Toyota RV8A	GY	100.114	1m 40.505s	25	15	Engine fire		
27	Al Unser Jr. (USA)	2	Marlboro Team Penske Penske PC26-Mercedes	GY	102.446	1m 38.218s	17	10	Lost wheel		
NS	Christian Fittipaldi (BR)	11	Newman/Haas Kmart/Budweiser Swift 007.i-Ford XD	GY	103.791	1m 36.945s	9	–	Did not start/accident		

*denotes Rookie driver

Caution flags: Laps 7–8, accident/Salles and Herta; laps 10–12, accident/Jourdain and Hearn; laps 19–22, realign tire barrier; laps 30–32, accident/Johnstone, Herta and Blundell; laps 38–40, fire/Fangio; laps 42–43, accident/Zanardi and Tracy; lap 50, spin/Gugelmin. **Total:** seven for 18 laps.

Lap leaders: Alex Zanardi, 1–18 (18 laps); Paul Tracy, 19–39 (21 laps); Arnd Meier, 40–41 (2 laps); Scott Pruett, 42–57 (16 laps). **Totals:** Tracy, 21 laps; Zanardi, 18 laps; Pruett, 16 laps; Meier, 2 laps.

Fastest race lap: Alex Zanardi, 1m 38.026s, 102.646 mph on lap 37.

Championship positions: 1 Andretti, 35; **2** Pruett, 30; **3** Moore, 28; **4** Zanardi, 20; **5** Tracy, 17; **6** Vasser, 15; **7** de Ferran, 10; **8** Gugelmin, 9; **9** Ribeiro, 8; **10** Boesel, 6; **11** Johnstone and Blundell, 5; **13** Carpentier and Franchitti, 4; **15** Herta and Rahal, 3; **17** Hearn and Fernandez, 2.

Ω
OMEGA
OFFICIAL TIMEKEEPER OF CART

Only in America

ALEX Zanardi began the year as one of the firm favorites for PPG Cup honors following a spectacular second half of his rookie campaign in 1996 during which he qualified on the front row for eight consecutive races and claimed six top-three finishes. Zanardi duly kicked off his sophomore season with two more poles, only to be frustrated each time in his quest for victory. So his triumph in Long Beach was even more satisfying.

'This [win] is very, very important for us,' he said. 'I believe we had a very fast car in Homestead; I believe we had the best car in Surfers and we didn't win. Today, we had a fantastic car but other people were very, very competitive with us and I believe we won the race in the pits. The performance of the 'ole team was fantastic.

'I believe this is very, very important for morale because when you keep getting close but you never win, then you start to think that something is wrong; you start to think you are unlucky; you start to think that everything is going to go wrong at the last minute, so it is good that we finally break the ice.'

As a measure of his delight, Zanardi celebrated by performing a spectacular tire-burning 'donut' in front of the packed grandstands in Turn One.

'It's fantastic when you win a race,' explained Zanardi, smiling broadly, in his charismatic, lisping, Italian accent. 'I'm delighted because it's the first time for me to win a race without dominating the race; we won just because everything worked perfect. It's the first time that we donate the $5,000 to St. Jude's Hospital [children's charity under a special sponsorship arranged by Target Stores] and I'm very, very proud to be the first to win this money.

'The crowd here this weekend was amazing. It's a fantastic event and I had to please the fans a little bit.

'I want to dedicate this win also to a race fan. The other night I went to a restaurant with some friends and when I asked for the check, the waiter said, "Don't worry, a racing fan took care of it." I said what do you mean, where is he? "He left half an hour ago." I was absolutely amazed. Only in America!'

1 - ZANARDI   2 - GUGELMIN   3 - PRUETT

LONG BEACH

QUALIFYING

Gil de Ferran experienced another action-packed weekend before finally emerging with his first pole since joining Derrick Walker's team at the beginning of the season. On Friday, the track record holder clipped almost a full second from his 1996 standard to end the session well clear of Mauricio Gugelmin.

'I'm a little surprised how well Gil went,' admitted Gugelmin, 'but I think I have a good idea where he found the time and I think we can improve when more rubber goes down.'

Not so. 'I don't know what happened,' said Gugelmin on Saturday after slipping to third on the grid behind Alex Zanardi. 'Normally the track gets better on the second day. It got worse. I lost traction in my car and it was loose this afternoon.'

De Ferran, meanwhile, did not take to the track on Saturday afternoon after being involved in a heavy crash during morning practice. The incident occurred on Shoreline Drive, immediately after the flat-out right-hand curve, when de Ferran pulled out to pass the slower car of Hiro Matsushita and was suddenly confronted by countryman Gualter Salles' stricken Indusval Reynard-Ford, which had lost power and was coasting to a halt.

'It was the scariest moment of my life,' said de Ferran. 'I pulled out from behind Hiro and all I saw was this parked car . . .'

Fortunately, both drivers emerged unscathed, although de Ferran's primary car sustained heavy damage.

The crew wheeled out its backup Valvoline/Cummins Reynard-Honda, but if de Ferran had ventured out of the pits, he would have been obliged to withdraw his time from Friday and start afresh. Wisely, therefore, de Ferran sat anxiously in the pits, hoping no one would beat his time.

Zanardi certainly tried, even spinning at one stage and bending a toe-link, which his crew changed in double-quick time, but his best came up almost four tenths shy of the coveted pole.

Scott Pruett jumped from 10th on the provisional grid to fourth with Pat Patrick's Brahma Reynard-Ford, followed by the two Newman/Haas Swift-Fords of Michael Andretti and Roberto Moreno. Team Rahal's Bryan Herta and Bobby Rahal were a mere 0.004s apart in seventh and eighth, fractionally ahead of four other cars also within the 52.0s bracket.

ALEX Zanardi narrowly failed in his bid for a seventh consecutive CART pole during qualifying for the 23rd Annual Toyota Grand Prix of Long Beach, but he more than made amends with a flawless performance on raceday. The Italian's cause was assisted by two excellent pit stops by Rob Hill's crew, after which he guided Chip Ganassi's Target Reynard-Honda to the checkered flag some 3.82 seconds clear of Mauricio Gugelmin's Hollywood/PacWest Reynard-Mercedes.

'I don't believe we had overall the best car today but we definitely beat the opposition in the pit lane,' said a joyful Zanardi. 'I have to give thanks to my guys for doing a fantastic job – actually a perfect job.'

In the early stages of the race, as in qualifying, Zanardi had to give best to Gil de Ferran, who made a good jump from the pole and led handily into Turn One with Derrick Walker's Valvoline/Cummins Reynard-Honda. Zanar-

di duly tucked in behind, chased by Gugelmin and Michael Andretti (Swift-Ford/Cosworth), who nipped past Scott Pruett (Brahma Reynard-Ford) on the drag race toward the first turn. Roberto Moreno, meanwhile, after qualifying a fine sixth in the second Newman/Haas

Swift, found himself shuffled down to 11th within the first couple of corners.

The early laps saw de Ferran maintaining a comfortable margin of around 1.5 seconds over Zanardi, with Gugelmin content to follow a similar distance in arrears. Andretti held sta-

Bottom: Mauricio Gugelmin took second place after a highly competitive showing with the ambitious PacWest team's Hollywood Reynard-Mercedes.

tion close behind the third-placed Brazilian until, on lap 12, his left-rear tire suddenly exploded at close to maximum speed on Shoreline Drive. Andretti did a masterful job of maintaining control before limping slowly back to the pits for a fresh set of Goodyears. The incident cost Andretti a lap to the leaders but he continued to run strongly until experiencing an identical failure on lap 36 – and another on lap 70. This time he called it a day.

'We exploded three tires and we reckoned three was enough,' said Andretti. 'We were lucky not to put it in the wall.'

No immediate cause was apparent, although a subsequent investigation by Newman/Haas Racing revealed its tire pressure gauges to have been incorrectly calibrated. The actual tire pressures were therefore significantly lower than prescribed.

'It's embarrassing,' admitted chief engineer Peter Gibbons.

Strips of rubber fly from the disintegrating left-rear tire of Michael Andretti's black Swift as the 1991 PPG Cup champion limps back to the pits. A spate of punctures ended his chances of adding to his points total.

'We threw away some valuable [PPG Cup] points.'

Adding to the team's misery, Moreno suffered yet another blown tire before ending his day on lap 49 with his Kmart/Budweiser car parked solidly against the wall in Turn Four.

Defending race champion Jimmy Vasser also was forced to pit early due to a left-rear Firestone failure, although his problem apparently was caused by contact with Paul Tracy during the early jostling for position. Vasser, too, lost a lap before rejoining.

De Ferran was unconcerned by the travails of others. Instead he eked out an advantage of almost four seconds over Zanardi before making his first pit stop on lap 26, during a full-course caution necessitated by a clash between 'fellow' Canadians Greg Moore and Paul Tracy in Turn Six. The pair had been disputing seventh place before Tracy dived for the inside under braking.

'There was nowhere for me to go,' claimed a disgruntled Moore. 'He went straight and hit me, pushing me into the tire wall.' Moore resumed several laps in arrears before being forced out for good by a faulty fuel pump.

Pat Patrick's team opted to hedge its bets during the caution. Pruett, in common with all the other front-runners, pulled onto pit lane for service, whereas teammate Raul Boesel did not. The Brazilian duly inherited the lead for the restart.

Behind, Zanardi emerged in second place by virtue of an ultra-quick stop which enabled him to rejoin ahead of de Ferran. Gugelmin and Pruett were fourth and fifth, followed by a resurgent Bobby Rahal (Miller Lite Reynard-Ford), who moved ahead of teammate Bryan Herta when the youngster stalled the engine as he attempted to rejoin. Curiously, Rahal's fine run was handi-

Moreno's big break

ROBERTO Moreno, a veteran of Formula 1 and CART competition, returned unexpectedly to the fray at Long Beach after being tabbed by Carl Haas and Paul Newman to act as a substitute for Christian Fittipaldi, who had been injured in the first-lap crash at Surfers Paradise the previous weekend.

'Moreno has lots of testing and racing experience,' explained Haas. 'Myself, Paul and the entire team feel terrible about Christian being injured. We hope he recovers quickly and is back driving for us soon.

'We're glad Roberto was available on such short notice. We know we're putting him into a pressure situation but we feel confident that he will do a good job for us this weekend.'

Moreno, who contested the first race of the season at Homestead with Payton/Coyne Racing but missed the Gold Coast IndyCarnival after his sponsorship plans fell flat, rose to the task admirably.

'The car feels really good,' declared the 38-year-old Brazilian after setting eighth fastest time during the first session on Friday morning. 'I need some time to get used to it. At the beginning of the session they had me bed some brakes and pads to get acquainted with the car.

'The car is so different. I can brake much later than usual, which will take time to get used to. The power is unbelievable. I drove with a Ford/Cosworth XB Series II [last year]. The XD is quite an improvement. I ran the Firestone tires last season so that's another change [Newman/Haas runs on Goodyears]. This whole package is a new ball-game altogether. It's great.'

Moreno qualified a magnificent sixth, less than one-tenth of a second and one position behind Andretti, and also set the fourth fastest lap of the race before crashing on lap 49.

'The overall experience was fantastic,' he concluded. 'In a very short time I was able to get used to the car and the team helped me fit in quickly. That was half the challenge. It's amazing how much easier it is to race when you have a good, quick car.'

capped by an identical problem during his second pit stop.

'We've had some clutch problems all weekend,' explained Herta. 'It's like an on/off switch and it just caught me out.' Herta's Shell Reynard-Ford regained the fray in ninth behind Mark Blundell (Motorola Reynard-Mercedes) and Parker Johnstone (Team KOOL Green Reynard-Honda).

Boesel gave his confidence a much-needed boost by leading strongly until making his own stop for fuel and fresh tires on lap 40. Unfortunately, a problem connecting the refueling nozzle cost him 17 valuable seconds. He had fallen to 17th position by the time he rejoined.

Zanardi, who had taken the opportunity to switch to the more durable Firestone 'option' tires, took over out in front and effectively controlled the remainder of the 105-lap race.

'We knew that Gil was going to be very, very strong,' related Zanardi. 'My tires started to give up just a little bit, but I have to say that Gil was running at a faster pace than me. Then when I came in, we did not simply change the tires, we also adjust[ed] the balance of

the car. I improved my pace by an average of half a second a lap, and that's why I was able then to keep Gil behind me and sometime actually pull away from him.'

Zanardi did relinquish the lead – once again to Boesel – after pitting for service on lap 68, but it was only a matter of time before the out-of-sequence Brahma car made its second stop. Vasser, who was also on a different pit stop strategy following his early unscheduled visit, took over the lead for 10 laps before making his final stop on lap 94.

Moments earlier, de Ferran's afternoon came to a premature halt when he clouted the tire wall in Turn One. He was running fourth at the time after being passed by Gugelmin during the second round of pit stops.

'It was my mistake,' admitted a crestfallen de Ferran. 'I got too close to the guys in front under braking, lost the front downforce, locked up and I went straight. I couldn't stop.

'The car was good,' he continued. 'We lost a position in the pits but that didn't really worry me. I was just try-ing to stay close to Mauricio to keep the pressure on.

'I apologize profusely to the guys. I promise it won't happen again.'

Prior to de Ferran's demise, Gugelmin had been inching gradually closer to Zanardi, reducing the deficit from more than five seconds to less than two over a 10-lap period. But then he encountered some slower traffic. The gap immediately rose again to over three seconds, at which point Gugelmin wisely opted to settle for second, equalling his career-best CART finish.

'We're pushing very hard to get a win, but this time I kept it under con-trol,' said Gugelmin, referring to his error one week earlier in Australia. 'Alex was just a bit quicker today and I couldn't do anything.'

Pruett was equally delighted to fin-ish third, especially since his fourth consecutive top-five finish, dating back to the end of the 1996 season, was enough to move him into the lead of the PPG Cup point standings.

'Even though we didn't win, we've been on a pretty good roll of late,' summarized Pruett. 'A lot of things happened with our team over the win-ter and all of it has been very, very positive. Obviously we have a new sponsor, Brahma, and we have new cars, Reynards, after switching from Lola. Most importantly, Ford and Cos-worth have been working extremely hard on the engine. We now have an engine and car package which has been running very, very well, very consistently. I couldn't be happier.'

Fourth place was claimed by Al Unser Jr., who was relieved to score his first PPG Cup points of the season following an otherwise disappointing weekend for Marlboro Team Penske. Unser, six times a winner on the streets of Long Beach, qualified a dis-tant 15th but made up ground steadily during the race. His progress was assisted by typically astute strategy from Roger Penske, who realized Unser was being held up by a train of cars headed by Blundell at two-thirds dis-tance and called him into the pits for his final pit stop at the earliest possible opportunity.

When Unser resumed, with a clear track in front of him, he was able to circulate fast enough to move ahead of Blundell, Johnstone and Herta by the time they, too, had stopped for fuel and fresh tires.

'Finally we have some points under our belt,' noted Unser. 'We're ready to go nowhere but up from here.'

Tracy benefited from an identical strategy but was forced to conserve fuel in his final stint and, in doing so, overworked his tires. He indulged in a quick spin on lap 94, falling behind Unser and Johnstone, then was passed for sixth by Herta just three laps from the finish.

'It was a long, hard race,' concluded Tracy. 'The last 10 laps I was just doing my best to hold on.'

Zanardi, too, had some concerns as he paced himself toward the checkered flag and his fourth career CART victory.

'On the last pit stop I asked for an extra turn of front wing and that was probably a mistake,' he explained. 'Right at the end the car was over-steering. I had to push my car to the limit to try to keep that advantage on Mauricio, who was running fantastic towards the end.'

LONG BEACH SNIPPETS

• Following his accident on Saturday morning, **GIL DE FERRAN** was obliged to use his backup car for the race. The same chassis, Reynard 97I-011, already had been crashed during the race at Homestead and in the aborted start at Surfers Paradise . . .

• **PARKER JOHNSTONE** *(right)*, who starred at Long Beach in 1996, finishing a career-high second, was almost equally delighted this year *(left)* after his close battle with Al Unser Jr. 'I tell you, running with Al, that's the epitome of what racing should be,' said Johnstone. 'Two guys out there, going at it clean, but not giving an inch and not taking one. The thing that made me feel good is that as soon as we crossed the finish line, Al backed off, turned to me and gave me the thumbs-up. It's a big deal, because he's one of my heroes.'

• **BRYAN HERTA**, who retired from the race at Surfers Paradise following an incident with Johnstone, discovered after the long flight back to North America that he had sustained a broken right thumb. Herta was fitted with a brace for the weekend, and despite some pain he enjoyed his most competitive outing of the season to date, finishing a strong sixth in Team Rahal's Shell Reynard-Ford/Cosworth.

• Steve Horne's **TASMAN MOTORSPORTS GROUP** experienced a disappointing weekend with its recalcitrant Lola-Hondas. Nevertheless, the Tasman team still emerged with three victories as rising Brazilian star Helio Castro Neves took the PPG-Firestone Indy Lights honors and Australian Neil Crompton added a brace of wins on his debut with Tasman's Honda Accord in the Super Touring Championship.

• **PAUL TRACY** was slapped with a $25,000 fine by CART Chief Steward Wally Dallenbach following the Canadian's involvement in three separate incidents on raceday. 'We did exactly what all the drivers wanted us to do,' said Dallenbach. 'They wanted to clean up the rough driving, and that's my job. I hope the message was sent out not only to Paul but to everybody that we will not tolerate this type of driving.'

• Former racer and long-time Air Force officer **MIKE FISHER**, who joined the CART organization as executive vice-president of racing at the beginning of the season, relinquished his duties soon after the Long Beach weekend by mutual agreement with CART President Andrew Craig.

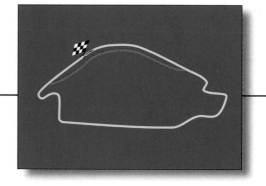

PPG CART WORLD SERIES • ROUND 3
23rd TOYOTA GRAND PRIX OF LONG BEACH
LONG BEACH STREET CIRCUIT, CALIFORNIA

APRIL 13, 105 laps – 166.530 miles

Place	Driver (Nat.)	No.	Team Sponsors Car-Engine	Tires	Q Speed	Q Time	Q Pos.	Laps	Time/Status	Ave. (mph)	Pts.
1	Alex Zanardi (I)	4	Target/Chip Ganassi Racing Reynard 97I-Honda	FS	110.512	51.665s	2	105	1h 46m 17.792s	93.999	21
2	Mauricio Gugelmin (BR)	17	PacWest Racing Group Hollywood Reynard 97I-Mercedes	FS	110.341	51.745s	3	105	1h 46m 21.612s	93.943	16
3	Scott Pruett (USA)	20	Patrick Brahma Sports Team Reynard 97I-Ford XD	FS	110.235	51.795s	4	105	1h 46m 33.251s	93.772	14
4	Al Unser Jr. (USA)	2	Marlboro Team Penske Penske PC26-Mercedes	GY	108.438	52.653s	15	105	1h 46m 38.320s	93.598	12
5	Parker Johnstone (USA)	27	Team KOOL Green Reynard 97I-Honda	FS	109.409	52.186s	13	105	1h 46m 38.693s	93.592	10
6	Bryan Herta (USA)	8	Team Rahal Shell Reynard 97I-Ford XD	GY	109.766	52.016s	7	105	1h 46m 41.881s	93.646	8
7	Paul Tracy (CDN)	3	Marlboro Team Penske Penske PC26-Mercedes	GY	109.659	52.067s	11	105	1h 46m 43.034s	93.629	6
8	Raul Boesel (BR)	40	Patrick Brahma Sports Team Reynard 97I-Ford XD	FS	109.652	52.070s	12	105	1h 46m 43.986s	93.615	5
9	Jimmy Vasser (USA)	1	Target/Chip Ganassi Racing Reynard 97I-Honda	FS	109.703	52.046s	10	105	1h 46m 47.173s	93.568	4
10	Bobby Rahal (USA)	7	Team Rahal Miller Lite Reynard 97I-Ford XD	GY	109.758	52.020s	8	105	1h 46m 48.418s	93.550	3
11	Adrian Fernandez (MEX)	32	Tasman Tecate Beer/Quaker State Oil Lola T97/00-Honda	FS	107.303	53.210s	20	105	1h 46m 55.376s	93.449	2
12	*Dario Franchitti (GB)	9	Hogan Racing LLC Reynard 97I-Mercedes	FS	108.085	52.825s	17	105	1h 47m 01.731s	93.356	1
13	Mark Blundell (GB)	18	PacWest Racing Group Motorola Reynard 97I-Mercedes	FS	108.529	52.609s	14	104	Running		
14	Andre Ribeiro (BR)	31	Tasman Motorsports LCI/Marlboro Lola T97/00-Honda	FS	107.769	52.980s	19	104	Running		
15	*Patrick Carpentier (CDN)	16	Bettenhausen Alumax Aluminum Reynard 97I-Mercedes	GY	107.297	53.213s	21	104	Running		
16	P.J. Jones (USA)	98	All American Racers Castrol/Jockey Reynard 96I-Toyota RV8A	GY	106.767	53.477s	24	103	Running		
17	Michel Jourdain Jr. (MEX)	19	Payton/Coyne Herdez/Mexlub/Viva Mexico! Lola T97/00-Ford XD	FS	107.160	53.281s	22	102	Engine		
18	*Gualter Salles (BR)	77	Davis Racing Indusval/Marlboro Reynard 97I-Ford XD	GY	108.059	52.838s	18	99	Tires		
19	*Paul Jasper (USA)	34	Payton/Coyne Hype/US Long Distance Lola T97/00-Ford XD	FS	106.765	53.478s	25	99	Running		
20	Hiro Matsushita (J)	24	Arciero-Wells Panasonic/Duskin Reynard 96I-Toyota RV8A	FS	101.654	56.167s	28	96	Running		
21	Gil de Ferran (BR)	5	Walker Valvoline/Cummins Reynard 97I-Honda	GY	111.313	51.293s	1	93	Accident		
22	Michael Andretti (USA)	6	Newman/Haas Kmart/Texaco Havoline Swift 007.i-Ford XD	GY	110.152	51.834s	5	70	Withdrawn		
23	Greg Moore (CDN)	99	Forsythe Player's Ltd./Indeck Reynard 97I-Mercedes	FS	109.726	52.035s	9	60	Fuel pump		
24	Roberto Moreno (BR)	11	Newman/Haas Kmart/Budweiser Swift 007.i-Ford XD	GY	109.988	51.911s	6	48	Accident		
25	Max Papis (I)	25	Arciero-Wells Racing MCI Reynard 97I-Toyota RV8B	FS	105.080	54.336s	26	39	Engine		
26	Juan Fangio II (RA)	36	All American Racers Castrol/Jockey Reynard 96I-Toyota RV8A	GY	106.805	53.458s	23	27	Electrical		
27	Richie Hearn (USA)	21	Della Penna Ralphs/Food 4 Less Lola T97/00-Ford XD	GY	108.436	52.654s	16	3	Engine		
NS	Dennis Vitolo (USA)	64	Project Indy SmithKline Beecham Lola T97/00-Ford XD	GY	103.294	55.275s	27	–	Accident		

* denotes Rookie driver

Caution flags: Laps 16–21, off course/Moreno; laps 25–28, accident/Moore; laps 41–44, fire/Papis; laps 51–55, accident/Moreno. **Total:** four for 19 laps.

Lap leaders: Gil de Ferran, 1–25 (25 laps); Raul Boesel, 26–39 (14 laps); Alex Zanardi, 40–68 (29 laps); de Ferran, 69 (1 lap); Boesel, 70–82 (13 laps); Jimmy Vasser, 83–93 (11 laps); Zanardi, 94–105 (12 laps). **Totals:** Zanardi, 41 laps; Boesel, 27 laps; de Ferran, 26 laps; Vasser, 11 laps.

Fastest race lap: Alex Zanardi, 52.895s, 107.942 mph on lap 64 (Record).

Championship positions: 1 Pruett, 44; **2** Zanardi, 41; **3** Andretti, 35; **4** Moore, 28; **5** Gugelmin, 24; **6** Tracy, 23; **7** Vasser, 19; **8** Johnstone, 15; **9** Unser Jr., 12; **10** de Ferran, Herta and Boesel, 11; **13** Ribeiro, 9; **14** Rahal, 6; **15** Blundell and Franchitti, 5; **17** Carpentier and Fernandez, 4; **19** Hearn, 2.

Michael C. Brown

NAZARETH

1 – TRACY

2 – ANDRETTI

3 – UNSER

A thrilled Paul Tracy celebrates his commanding victory – the first for Marlboro Team Penske since September 1995 – with his joyful pit crew.

ticular shortcomings within the organization. At Road America last season, Unser led to within a mile of the finish line before his engine expired amidst a cloud of oil smoke. The two-time PPG Cup champion also remained stoically in contention for the $1 million champion's check until the final race at Laguna Seca. Tracy, too, came close to victory on several occasions.

At Nazareth, finally, the cards fell in his favor. Tracy qualified comfortably on the pole and led an impressive 186 of the race's 225 laps. But that tells only half the story. For in the closing stages, 28-year-old Tracy came under intense pressure from Andretti, who was intent upon repeating his 1996 victory on the quirky, three-cornered

oval situated little more than a mile away from his home in the Pennsylvania countryside.

Andretti, after passing Tracy for the lead on lap 35, had been forced to make an unscheduled pit stop to change a punctured tire; but he fought back from a one-lap deficit in magnificent style. By lap 178, with less than 50 miles remaining, Andretti was shadowing the leading Penske's every move as they ducked and weaved their way past slower cars at speeds approaching 190 mph.

Tracy, who estimated he had completed as many as 10,000 miles of testing for Penske at Nazareth, faced one of the toughest challenges of his career.

'There's no traffic when you're out

QUALIFYING

Paul Tracy was in a class by himself throughout practice and qualifying.

'There's not really much to say,' declared Tracy after posting a best lap of 19.198s (187.520 mph) in the opening session on Friday, almost 0.3s faster than his closest challenger. 'We had a good tire test here earlier in the month. The car was pretty much *au point* right off the truck. We really haven't messed with it too much since.'

Tracy took advantage of the near-perfect weather conditions, cool and clear, as he continued to chip away at his times in each session. Finally he stunned the entire paddock by dipping as low as 18.769s (191.806 mph) during practice on Saturday morning, when only Patrick Carpentier's Team Alumax Reynard-Mercedes was within even a half-second of the #3 Marlboro Penske-Mercedes. Tracy almost matched that in qualifying (18.831s/191.174 mph) as he comfortably claimed the 11th pole of his career.

'He is special,' praised the Penske team's technical advisor (and three-time PPG Cup champion), Rick Mears. 'Al [Unser Jr.] leaves himself just a little bit of a cushion – until it matters – whereas Paul, he just has to see how far he can go.'

Michael Andretti made good progress with Newman/Haas Racing's Kmart/Texaco Havoline Swift-Ford/Cosworth, despite an engine blow-up on Saturday morning, to set the second fastest time in qualifying.

'I feel pretty good,' said Andretti after securing only his second front row starting position in his last 24 races. 'The car's been performing very well. We feel pretty confident for tomorrow.'

Rookie Carpentier maintained his excellent form by taking third on the grid and matching the best ever qualifying performance (achieved by Stefan Johansson at Portland in 1993) for team owner Tony Bettenhausen. Gil de Ferran would start alongside on row two, followed by Brazilians Mauricio Gugelmin and Raul Boesel. Al Unser Jr., in the second Marlboro Penske, had to be content with seventh on the grid.

'My car obviously isn't as good as Paul's,' he noted. 'He did an awesome job today. He did a little more fine-tuning and got more out of his car than I did.'

P AUL Tracy ended a sequence of 20 races without a victory for team owner Roger Penske by guiding his #3 Marlboro Penske PC26-Mercedes to a hard-earned success at Nazareth Speedway over hometown hero Michael Andretti's Kmart/Texaco Havoline Swift-Ford/Cosworth. The win laid to rest the second longest drought since Penske established his Indy car operation in 1971.

'It feels good to get the monkey off our back,' said Tracy. 'This team hasn't had the best car – or the best overall package – for the past couple of years, but everybody's worked real hard to get us back on top. The guys on the team and everybody at Mercedes and Goodyear have dug their heels so hard into the ground it kind of felt like quicksand. It's a relief to finally get the team, and Mercedes, back into Victory Lane.'

In truth, the perceived lack of success by Marlboro Team Penske was more a function of the ever-increasing competitiveness of the PPG CART World Series – and a paucity of what is termed 'racing luck' – than any par-

Michael C. Brown

there testing,' he said, 'and no Michael sitting right behind you. There's no way you can simulate that.'

The pressure was heaped onto the mercurial Canadian's shoulders. How would he cope?

One year ago, Tracy had been leading handsomely until briefly losing concentration as he sped toward his pit for routine service. The memory of his car, brakes locked, sliding into the pit wall and collecting three crew members has continued to haunt him, even though no one was seriously injured. At the back of his mind, too, was the reality of being slapped with a $25,000 fine

by CART Chief Steward Wally Dallenbach following his involvement in three separate incidents during the previous race in Long Beach.

This time there was no hint of a miscue. Tracy was flawless in traffic, although there was one close call on lap 215, with just 10 to go, as the two leaders came upon Andretti's teammate, Roberto Moreno. The Brazilian, who had been struggling all day long, was caught in no man's land on the exit of Turn Three, causing Tracy to jink left at the last moment in order to complete the pass.

'He was right in the middle of the

track,' said Tracy. 'I didn't know which way to go. There really wasn't a lot of room on the outside so I had to go inside, so I cut across to the low side and looked in my mirror and Michael was right there behind me.'

Andretti, indeed, at precisely that moment was attempting to find a way past Tracy on the inside line: 'It was very close,' said Andretti, who was forced to lift abruptly from the throttle. 'I almost ran into the back of him.'

That was as close as Andretti came to snatching the lead, although it wasn't for the lack of trying.

'I had everything for Paul except for

time,' said Andretti, whose hopes of a last-lap bid for glory were dashed by the yellow lights after Juan Fangio's Castrol/Jockey Reynard suffered yet another blown Toyota engine. 'I think we had the best car out there. At the beginning of a run, Paul was quicker in clean air. In traffic, I was quicker. I pulled everything out [in the closing stages]. I went to a lower gear, I changed the crossweight, I made the car loose and just went for it.'

Under the circumstances, Andretti was content with second, especially as the 16 points enabled him to regain the lead in the PPG Cup standings.

Raul Boesel gets a helping hand from his Brahma Sports Team mechanics as he accelerates back into the race after routine service.

Following a number of unfortunate incidents in the early-season races, Gil de Ferran *(bottom)* was pleased to take fourth-place points with Derrick Walker's Valvoline/Cummins Reynard-Honda.

'We'll take it after losing a lap and coming back the way we did,' concluded Andretti with a smile. 'Can't complain too much.'

Unser couldn't match the pace of the two leaders as the race reached toward its climax, but he, too, was reasonably pleased after garnering his first podium finish of the season.

'I figured those two guys were going to get into it pretty heavy,' said Unser. 'I just didn't want to be involved.'

Gil de Ferran was the only other unlapped finisher in fourth place following a solid afternoon's work aboard Derrick Walker's Valvoline/ Cummins Reynard-Honda.

'You have to bear in mind that this has been probably my most difficult circuit in my first two years,' related the Brazilian, 'so to finish on the lead lap and be quite competitive, I'm really happy. I couldn't match Paul and Michael but I was pretty much on Al's pace. I'm just ecstatic. The team did a fantastic job in the pits; they were right on the mark. Overall, it was a very good weekend for us.'

Several other drivers also had a good day. Among the most impressive was Richie Hearn, who climbed as high as fifth with John Della Penna's Ralphs/Food 4 Less Lola-Ford following a protracted battle with Bobby Rahal's Miller Lite Reynard-Ford. Unfortunately, Hearn, in common with Mauricio Gugelmin, lost a couple of laps while making a scheduled pit stop under green-flag conditions on lap 140 – just before the field was brought under the control of the pace car due to a spin by Parker Johnstone, whose Team KOOL Green Reynard-Honda had been inadvertently nudged by a close-following Unser. Hearn fell to 12th prior to the restart, and shortly afterward was unable to avoid an incident in Turn Three when Johnstone and Boesel collided as the significantly faster Brazilian was attempting to make a pass for position.

Boesel performed a miraculous save in Pat Patrick's Brahma Reynard-Ford, but Johnstone wasn't so lucky as he spun backward into the wall, taking the innocent Hearn with him.

Jimmy Vasser, after starting 12th in Chip Ganassi's Target Reynard-Honda, moved up the order in Hearn's shadow and was running fifth, having just been lapped by Tracy, at the time of the Johnstone/Hearn incident. He was able to make his pit stop under the ensuing caution and maintain his position to the finish.

'I guess fifth isn't too bad considering where we started,' said the defending PPG Cup champion with a shrug of the shoulders.

Team Rahal filled the next two positions, Rahal just ahead of Bryan Herta's Shell Reynard-Ford. Boesel enjoyed another good run to eighth ahead of Gugelmin, who, if not for the unfortunate timing of Johnstone's spin, would have finished significantly higher in PacWest's Hollywood Reynard-Mercedes.

Pruett took 10th, also one lap adrift. The #20 Brahma car ran respectably for most of the distance, and especially toward the end as Pruett matched the pace of the race leaders. Even so, it was not enough to prevent him from slipping to second place in the point standings behind Andretti. Tracy, meanwhile, moved into third following his impeccable drive to victory.

'This is exactly where we want to be at this point in the season,' said Tracy, basking in the glow of his best ever start to a PPG Cup campaign. 'We have a really good car this year and I'm looking forward to the next few races which are all on oval tracks.'

Marlboro Team Penske colleague Unser was similarly upbeat after his strong third-place finish: 'The snake-bite that we had [last year] is healed,' said Unser, a gleam in his eye, 'so now we can get back to the "normal" Penske way, which is, hopefully, dominating everything!'

Carpentier the ascending star

PATRICK Carpentier began his rookie season with a solid ninth-place finish for Bettenhausen Motorsports/Team Alumax at Homestead in March. But then he struggled to come even close to the front-running pace on the two street circuits in Surfers Paradise and Long Beach. Consequently, team owner Tony Bettenhausen and chief engineer/team manager Tom Brown hastily arranged a test session prior to the race weekend at Nazareth on the tight Putnam Park road course near Indianapolis.

'There's nothing you can do about Surfers Paradise and Long Beach except forget them,' declared Bettenhausen, 'but we still have street races at Detroit, Cleveland, Toronto and Vancouver to go on the schedule. So even though we've been trying to figure out what happened in the first two street races, we're also trying to prepare for the future.'

Brown and company made a few subtle adjustments to the car and found some dramatic improvements in terms of lap times. Carpentier, in turn, benefited enormously from the boost in confidence, as evidenced when the 25-year-old French-Canadian set a startling second fastest time in the opening practice session at Nazareth on Friday.

'I just lack technical feedback right now,' admitted Carpentier, who, incidentally, had won both of his two previous races at Nazareth Speedway, driving for Lynx Racing in the Player's Toyota Atlantic Championship. 'I think that Tom learned a lot about my style of driving [at Putnam] and I learned more about how to set up an Indy car. There is so much difference between Atlantic cars and Indy cars in terms of horsepower, and that translates into how you set up the car. The one thing I've changed this weekend, compared to Long Beach and Australia, is that I just drive the car; I leave the setup to Tom.'

Carpentier maintained his form by qualifying an excellent third behind only Paul Tracy and Michael Andretti. He moved up to second place when Andretti made an unscheduled pit stop on lap 53, but then cost himself all hope of a representative finish when he had difficulty in maneuvering around Tracy's stationary Penske in the adjacent pit box during his first routine stop.

Here endeth the streak(s)

PAUL Tracy's triumph *(below)* in the 11th Annual Bosch Spark Plug Grand Prix represented a record-extending 97th for Penske Racing, the most successful team in Indy car history; but the first since teammate Al Unser Jr. collected the checkered flag at Vancouver in September 1995. The losing streak was Roger Penske's longest since 1975, when Tom Sneva broke a 25-race winless spell which included the entire 1974 season.

'This was the greatest race of my life,' said an ecstatic – and relieved – Tracy. 'I did everything I could to hold off Michael [Andretti].'

One other streak also came to an end at Nazareth: Alex Zanardi's record-setting sequence of front row starts, which had reached 11 dating back to Portland in June, 1996. Moreover, as a measure of the PPG Cup series' overall competitiveness, the Italian could manage no better than 21st on the grid aboard Chip Ganassi's previously rampant Target Reynard-Honda.

Zanardi had struggled to obtain a comfortable balance on the car during practice, and his predicament in single-car qualifying was worsened by the fact that the previous runner, Juan Fangio II, had suffered a major engine failure as he took the checkered flag with Dan Gurney's Reynard-Toyota. There followed a lengthy clean-up before Zanardi was able to take to the track.

'It was difficult,' said a philosophical Zanardi. 'It was just bad luck. Somebody had to be next and it just happened to be me. It's a shame but that's the way it goes.

'To be perfectly honest, it probably didn't make that much difference. We knew that this race was going to be a tough test for us, and it's turning out that way.'

Zanardi ran respectably in the race but was unfortunate to be lapped by the race leader immediately before a full-course caution during the early stages. He was never able to make up the lost ground, although he did salvage a couple of useful PPG Cup points after finishing 11th.

'When you get lapped by the leader and then, in the next turn, it goes yellow, it is not your day,' declared Zanardi, who admitted: 'I still have a lot to learn about the short ovals.'

Photos: Michael C. Brown

NAZARETH SNIPPETS

• Roger Penske's **NAZARETH SPEEDWAY** took on a completely fresh ambience with the addition of a huge new grandstand opposite the pits. The impressive aluminum and steel structure rises almost double the height of the previous grandstand and affords a spectacular view from the vast majority of its 37,000 seats.

• For the second straight race, **MICHAEL ANDRETTI** was forced to make an unscheduled pit stop during the early stages. Unlike at Long Beach, however, this time the culprit was merely a cut tire. The potential for any more damaging consequences was negated by the Swift's on-board wheel sensors (developed originally by Penske Racing and Epic Technologies) which detected the loss of air pressure and relayed the information directly to the Newman/Haas team's computer in pit lane.

• **DARIO FRANCHITTI** qualified only 18th, but by virtue of a brave strategy devised by team owner Carl Hogan, he was elevated into second place following the first round of pit stops. The 23-year-old Scotsman rose to the task and lapped consistently quickly until being forced to make his second stop under green. Worse, he stalled the engine, which cost him a couple of laps.

• **PAYTON/COYNE RACING** endured a tough week with Michel Jourdain Jr.'s Herdez/Mexlub/Viva Mexico! Lola-Ford. The problems began on Tuesday, when a test session in Milwaukee was cut short by a blown engine, causing the Mexican to spin into the wall. The car was repaired in time for Nazareth, only for progress once again to be hindered by a succession of engine woes.

• The **TASMAN** team had some new wing pieces for its recalcitrant Lolas. Andre Ribeiro managed to break into the top 10 during practice, but on raceday he was sidelined even before the green flag by a broken tripod joint within the drive-train. An identical failure later caused teammate Adrian Fernandez to crash in Turn Two.

• **RAUL BOESEL** led his second race in a row as a result of the pit stop strategy chosen by his Brahma crew. The decision probably cost him a shot at a top-five finish, but it certainly provided a further boost to his growing confidence: 'It's great to lead again,' said Boesel after finishing eighth. 'Some time it will be on the last lap!'

PPG CART WORLD SERIES • ROUND 4
BOSCH SPARK PLUG GRAND PRIX PRESENTED BY TOYOTA

NAZARETH SPEEDWAY,
PENNSYLVANIA

APRIL 27, 225 laps – 225.000 miles

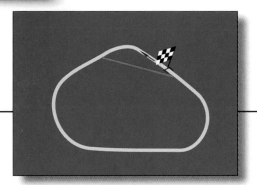

Place	Driver (Nat.)	No.	Team Sponsors Car-Engine	Tires	Q Speed	Q Time	Q Pos.	Laps	Time/Status	Ave. (mph)	Pts.
1	Paul Tracy (CDN)	3	Marlboro Team Penske Penske PC26-Mercedes	GY	191.174	18.831s	1	225	1h 53m 31.337s	118.919	22
2	Michael Andretti (USA)	6	Newman/Haas Kmart/Texaco Havoline Swift 007.i-Ford XD	GY	187.862	19.163s	2	225	1h 53m 31.864s	118.910	16
3	Al Unser Jr. (USA)	2	Marlboro Team Penske Penske PC26-Mercedes	GY	185.739	19.382s	7	225	1h 53m 32.587s	118.898	14
4	Gil de Ferran (BR)	5	Walker Valvoline/Cummins Reynard 97I-Honda	GY	186.964	19.255s	4	225	1h 53m 36.090s	118.836	12
5	Jimmy Vasser (USA)	1	Target/Chip Ganassi Racing Reynard 97I-Honda	FS	183.234	19.647s	12	225	1h 53m 37.429s	118.285	10
6	Bobby Rahal (USA)	7	Team Rahal Miller Lite Reynard 97I-Ford XD	GY	185.366	19.421s	8	224	Running		8
7	Bryan Herta (USA)	8	Team Rahal Shell Reynard 97I-Ford XD	GY	185.347	19.423s	9	224	Running		6
8	Raul Boesel (BR)	40	Patrick Brahma Sports Team Reynard 97I-Ford XD	FS	186.095	19.345s	6	224	Running		5
9	Mauricio Gugelmin (BR)	17	PacWest Racing Group Hollywood Reynard 97I-Mercedes	FS	186.326	19.321s	5	224	Running		4
10	Scott Pruett (USA)	20	Patrick Brahma Sports Team Reynard 97I-Ford XD	FS	184.087	19.556s	11	224	Running		3
11	Alex Zanardi (I)	4	Target/Chip Ganassi Racing Reynard 97I-Honda	FS	179.928	20.008s	21	223	Running		2
12	*Patrick Carpentier (CDN)	16	Bettenhausen Alumax Aluminum Reynard 97I-Mercedes	GY	187.461	19.204s	3	223	Running		1
13	*Dario Franchitti (GB)	9	Hogan Racing LLC Reynard 97I-Mercedes	FS	180.886	19.902s	18	222	Running		
14	Roberto Moreno (BR)	11	Newman/Haas Kmart/Budweiser Swift 007.i-Ford XD	GY	180.505	19.944s	20	218	Running		
15	Juan Fangio II (RA)	36	All American Racers Castrol/Jockey Reynard 96I-Toyota RV8A	GY	173.770	20.717s	25	214	Engine		
16	Greg Moore (CDN)	99	Forsythe Player's Ltd./Indeck Reynard 97I-Mercedes	FS	184.426	19.520s	10	194	Running		
17	Parker Johnstone (USA)	27	Team KOOL Green Reynard 97I-Honda	FS	180.950	19.895s	17	190	Accident		
18	Richie Hearn (USA)	21	Della Penna Ralphs/Food 4 Less Lola T97/00-Ford XD	GY	182.593	19.716s	14	190	Accident		
19	Mark Blundell (GB)	18	PacWest Racing Group Motorola Reynard 97I-Mercedes	FS	181.196	19.868s	16	178	Accident		
20	Michel Jourdain Jr. (MEX)	19	Payton/Coyne Herdez/Mexlub/Viva Mexico! Lola T97/00-Ford XD	FS	174.022	20.687s	24	111	Engine		
21	P.J. Jones (USA)	98	All American Racers Castrol/Jockey Reynard 96I-Toyota RV8A	GY	174.174	20.669s	23	96	Fuel system		
22	Max Papis (I)	25	Arciero-Wells Racing MCI Reynard 97I-Toyota RV8B	FS	176.939	20.346s	22	81	Engine		
23	Adrian Fernandez (MEX)	32	Tasman Tecate Beer/Quaker State Oil Lola T97/00-Honda	FS	180.569	19.937s	19	58	Accident		
24	*Gualter Salles (BR)	77	Davis Racing Indusval/Marlboro Reynard 97I-Ford XD	GY	182.769	19.697s	13	34	Accident		
25	Hiro Matsushita (J)	24	Arciero-Wells Panasonic/Duskin Reynard 96I-Toyota RV8A	FS	171.420	21.001s	26	23	Black flag		
26	Andre Ribeiro (BR)	31	Tasman Motorsports LCI/Marlboro Lola T97/00-Honda	FS	182.463	19.730s	15	4	Transmission		
NQ	Dennis Vitolo (USA)	64	Project Indy SmithKline Beecham Lola T97/00-Ford XD	GY	170.810	21.076s	27	–	Did not qualify		
NQ	*Paul Jasper (USA)	34	Payton/Coyne Hype/US Long Distance Lola T97/00-Ford XD	FS	168.492	21.366s	28	–	Did not qualify		

* denotes Rookie driver

Caution flags: Laps 1–2, debris; laps 6–11, debris; laps 13–17, spin/fluid spill/Moore; laps 35–44, accident/Salles; laps 59–69, accident/Fernandez; laps 82–88, oil/Papis; laps 144–152, spin/Johnstone; laps 180–188, accident/Blundell; laps 192–205, accident/Johnstone, Hearn; laps 223–225, engine fire/Fangio. **Total:** 10 for 76 laps.

Lap leaders: Paul Tracy, 1–34 (34 laps); Michael Andretti, 35–52 (18 laps); Tracy, 53–63 (11 laps); Raul Boesel, 64–84 (21 laps); Tracy, 85–225 (141 laps). **Totals:** Tracy, 186 laps; Boesel, 21 laps; Andretti, 18 laps.

Fastest race lap: Paul Tracy, 19.987s, 180.117 mph on lap 20 (Record).

Championship positions: 1 Andretti, 51; **2** Pruett, 47; **3** Tracy, 45; **4** Zanardi, 43; **5** Vasser, 29; **6** Gugelmin and Moore, 28; **8** Unser Jr., 26; **9** de Ferran, 23; **10** Herta, 17; **11** Boesel, 16; **12** Johnstone, 15; **13** Rahal, 14; **14** Ribeiro, 9; **15** Blundell, Carpentier and Franchitti, 5; **18** Fernandez, 4; **19** Hearn, 2.

RIO

1 – TRACY

2 – MOORE

3 – PRUETT

PPG CART WORLD SERIES • ROUND 5

QUALIFYING

The Brazilian crowd had much to celebrate on Saturday evening as two of their own, Mauricio Gugelmin and Rio-born Roberto Moreno, emerged fastest from an exciting session of qualifying which saw the top 17 cars separated by less than one second.

Intriguingly, the pair had twice before shared the front row – in 1987, when they both drove for Ron Tauranac's Ralt-Honda team in Formula 3000. Moreno had been the top dog on those occasions, at Silverstone and Brands Hatch in England, but this time it was Gugelmin who claimed the honors with a magnificent lap of 171.912 mph in Bruce McCaw's Hollywood Reynard-Mercedes.

'As a professional racing driver you just go out and do the best you can every weekend,' said Gugelmin after securing his first pole since his F3000 days, 'but for sure you tend to be a little more focused and you try a little harder when you're in your home country.'

Moreno, still substituting for the injured Christian Fittipaldi, was equally delighted after also securing his best ever starting position for a CART event: 'It's a fantastic feeling but it's all happening a bit too fast for me,' said Moreno with a broad smile. 'Unfortunately, Christian got hurt. It's a good opportunity for me to replace him but I'm surprised I have been able to adapt so quickly because we didn't have time to do any testing. I owe so much to the Kmart/Budweiser team, first of all for having me and secondly for teaching me so much in such a short time.'

For the third consecutive race, Team Rahal's Bobby Rahal and Bryan Herta qualified alongside each other, this time sharing row two with identical times and speeds. Team owner Rahal claimed the third starting position due to what he described as 'executive privilege.' In fact, he earned the place due to a faster second lap of qualifying.

'This is getting ridiculous,' quipped Rahal. 'We were a thousandth of a second apart [in practice] this morning and about the same at Long Beach and Nazareth.'

Photos: Michael C. Brown

Bobby Rahal maintains his slim advantage over Paul Tracy as the race enters its closing stages. Rahal's Miller Lite Reynard was to run short of fuel with just over a lap remaining.

PAUL Tracy took a leaf out of Danny Sullivan's book by overcoming an early spin and emerging with a finely judged victory – his second in as many races – in the Hollywood Rio 400. Tracy's cause aboard Roger Penske's Marlboro Penske-Mercedes was assisted by excellent fuel consumption as well as a little good fortune when series veteran Bobby Rahal, who had dominated the race in his Miller Lite Reynard-Ford/Cosworth, ran out of fuel with just over a lap remaining.

'He was driving a perfect line; he was flawless,' praised Tracy. 'I don't think we had enough straightaway speed to get by him so I had to keep the pressure on. If I hadn't put pressure on him, he might not have run out of fuel.'

The 133-lap race took a while to get going. First of all there was a melee even before the green flag when a group of midfield contenders collided as they accelerated off Turn Four in preparation for the start. Patrick Carpentier, Adrian Fernandez and Dario Franchitti were all done for the day. Brazilian favorite Andre Ribeiro lost a handful of laps while repairs were effected to his LCI International/Marlboro Lola-Honda. Parker Johnstone also was involved, although excellent work by Team KOOL Green permitted him to rejoin with a new nose section and without losing a lap.

Pole-sitter Mauricio Gugelmin's Hollywood Reynard-Mercedes led the way once the green flag was displayed on lap five. Rahal quickly usurped outside front row starter Roberto Moreno's Kmart/Budweiser Swift-Ford from sec-

ond place, while on the following lap an attempt by Tracy to dive inside Moreno under heavy braking for Turn One resulted in a quick gyration for the Brazilian. A close-following Bryan Herta (Shell Reynard-Ford) was obliged to spin in avoidance. Neither car was damaged. Moreno rejoined in 16th and Herta, following a pit stop, at the tail of the field in 24th.

The next attempt at a restart, on lap 10, was aborted when Tracy was caught unawares in Turn Four.

'We didn't get word it was going green,' claimed Tracy. 'I was cruising along in sixth [gear]. I bumped it down to second, jumped on [the throttle], spun the tires and looped it around.'

Once again there was no damage, despite a huge cloud of tire smoke as Tracy spun the wheels in frustration. He resumed in 10th.

Finally, with 13 laps in the books, the enthusiastic local fans were treated to some real racing action. Not that it was entirely to their satisfaction, as Rahal got a good run on Gugelmin and cruised past the local favorite into Turn One.

'Gugelmin tried to block me, so I just drove 'round the outside of him,' related Rahal proudly.

The race quickly settled into a pattern with Rahal lapping consistently in the low-41-second bracket and maintaining a comfortable margin of around one second over Gugelmin. Michael Andretti took advantage of the early incidents to move up to third in Newman/Haas Racing's Kmart/Texaco Havoline Swift-Ford, but already he knew there was something amiss.

'Right at the green flag I had no horsepower,' declared Andretti, who soon began to slip down the order. The erstwhile series leader soldiered on as best he could, but was forced out after 64 laps when the engine expired. 'It's disappointing because things looked so good all weekend,' he said, 'so what can you do?'

Scott Pruett moved into third place on lap 18 with his Brahma Reynard-Ford, soon to be followed by Greg Moore's Player's Reynard-Mercedes and the Honda-powered Valvoline Reynard of Gil de Ferran. Andretti and the two Penskes of Al Unser Jr. and Tracy ran next after 22 laps, pursued by Jimmy Vasser and Richie Hearn. The Californian had qualified a personal best 11th in John Della Penna's Ralphs/Food 4 Less Lola-Ford and was running well in 10th, despite a dangerous loose condition, until the car finally got away from him in Turn Four. Hearn, like Tracy before him, was able to resume without damage.

Several drivers took advantage of the ensuing full-course caution to make their first routine pit stops. Among them were Pruett and Brahma/Patrick Racing teammate Raul Boesel, who had been running 12th.

Rahal, meanwhile, continued to lead until making a pit stop, under green-flag conditions, on lap 42. Next time around, Gugelmin, Moore, de Ferran and Tracy all ducked into the pits together. There was almost a huge pile-up at pit exit as they attempted to rejoin at precisely the same time!

Once the cycle of stops had been completed, Pruett found himself out in the lead followed by fellow early pit-stoppers Moreno and Michel Jourdain Jr., who was running splendidly in Payton/Coyne Racing's Herdez/Mexlub/Viva Mexico! Lola-Ford. Next were Boesel, Johnstone, Gualter Salles and Hearn before a long gap to Rahal, first among those to have taken on service under the green.

The pattern of the race continued as Rahal regained the advantage when Pruett & Co. made their second pit stops, again under yellow, on lap 52, this time following a spin by Mark Blundell in Turn Four. A little later, Gugelmin, who had been troubled by a mysterious lack of boost, abruptly lost control when his car snapped sideways under braking for Turn One. Unfortunately, Moreno was making a pass at precisely the same moment. The two Brazilians collided, sending Gugelmin's car heavily into the tire barrier.

Following the sixth caution of the day, Rahal once more took off at the front of the field pursued by de Ferran, Tracy, Herta and Unser. Moore, who had lost several positions after his first pit stop, ran sixth ahead of the two Target Reynard-Hondas of Vasser and Alex Zanardi.

The status quo remained until the leaders were obliged to make their second round of pit stops – again under green-flag conditions. Pruett duly regained the point on lap 85, followed by Boesel, Jourdain and the Rio-born Salles, who, unfortunately, brought out the next caution one lap later when his Indusval Reynard's Ford engine exploded on the entry to Turn Four.

The oil spillage required a lengthy clean-up during which most of the field ducked onto pit lane for the final time. Once again there was a variety of divergent strategies. Pruett, Boesel, Jourdain and Hearn, for example, were on a different pit stop schedule to the main pack and needed to stop anyway. Rahal therefore reclaimed the lead ahead of Tracy, Herta, Moore and de Ferran, who had lost some time with a

Safety innovation proves highly effective

THE entire PPG Cup contingent was greeted by a host of improvements made since their first visit to Rio de Janeiro in 1996. For starters, the weather in May proved substantially more hospitable than during the inaugural visit in March, when temperatures – and especially the humidity – were much higher. Freshened garage areas, boasting additional awnings and new air-conditioned offices, also helped to make the experience altogether more enjoyable.

The most significant change – apart from the repaving of the notoriously bumpy Turns One and Four – was the introduction of an innovative barrier restraint system which comprised a relatively simple network of tire piles bound together by chicken-wire fencing. What was different, however, was that the entire mass was fronted by a thick layer of conveyor-belt rubber kept in place by a series of cables placed at 45 degrees to the angle of the wall in order to promote a cushioning effect.

'We had 10 drivers hit the walls during the weekend,' reported circuit director Tim Mayer, who assisted CART officials Kirk Russell and Wally Dallenbach in finalizing the design. 'I think we can say the system worked extremely well. Mauricio Gugelmin went in quite hard during the race in Turn One and he came over to me after getting out of the car and said, "That thing's unbelievable." He said he didn't really know what happened, he just knew he was spinning, so he braced himself, figuring it was going to be a really heavy hit, and he said it was just like braking heavily!'

Gugelmin's pole-winning Reynard sustained serious damage and required repairs to the monocoque, but no one was in any doubt the consequences would have been far more serious had he slammed into a concrete wall.

'It's an awesome step forward,' said veteran driver Mario Andretti. 'In my opinion, this is now the safest oval in the world. My hat's off to the CART folks.'

slightly slower pit stop. But as the caution dragged on, several teams opted to make a precautionary pit stop to top off the fuel and ensure they would have no difficulty in reaching the finish. Among them were Pruett, Vasser, Zanardi, Herta, Blundell and Unser. Everyone else kept their fingers crossed, in the full knowledge they would need some more laps of caution.

Their prayers appeared to be answered shortly after the restart on lap 98 when Jourdain, running strongly in fifth, was caught out by his Lola's fading brakes in Turn Four. The young Mexican valiantly pinched his car down low in order to avoid making contact with de Ferran, but lost control as he did so and spun into the tire-cushioned retaining wall.

But the pace car was out for only four laps before the track was cleared and the race was restarted. Several contenders knew they were still on the ragged edge in terms of fuel. Including Team Rahal. And Marlboro Team Penske.

All indications from the Team Rahal pit suggested its Miller Lite Reynard still required another lap or two of caution. Yet the team was committed to its strategy. Rahal continued to run out in front, with Tracy close behind.

The pace was consistent, in the mid-40s, and Rahal seemed to have the upper hand. But not quite enough fuel. Rahal's car finally ran dry at the end of the back straight on lap 132, allowing Tracy to sweep past as the Miller Lite Reynard coasted toward the pits. One lap remained. But having made his final stop just one lap after Rahal, would Tracy have enough fuel?

The answer was yes. Just.

'That was hard on the nervous system,' admitted Tracy's race engineer, Ian Reed. 'Our engine people made the call [not to make an additional pit stop], and basically we sat back and watched the fuel [consumption figures via the telemetry]. It kept going from plus to negative. Paul deserves a lot of credit because he figured out if he stayed in Rahal's draft it would help his mileage; and if he pushed Rahal hard he might run out of fuel. He used Rahal's car to break the air and forced him to use more fuel. If it came down to it, he'd have a go at the last corner. Fortunately it never came to that.'

Moore, like Tracy, made his final stop on lap 85, but held on to finish second.

'We were going for a three-stop strategy, but because of the yellows we ended up making two,' said Moore. 'We probably had enough fuel for one more lap.'

Pruett claimed the final podium position, nipping past Zanardi when the Italian was forced to take evasive action in Turn Four as de Ferran's Valvoline car ran dry with just two laps remaining. It was that kind of race.

Above: Paul Tracy lights up the rear tires of his Marlboro Penske as he accelerates away from his pit after routine service, sprinting ahead of Gil de Ferran's Valvoline/Cummins Reynard-Honda.

The Player's/Forsythe Racing team judged its fuel consumption perfectly, enabling Greg Moore *(left)* to inherit second place when Rahal was forced to pit a lap from the finish.

Profiting from others' misfortunes, Scott Pruett *(right)* maintained his PPG Cup championship challenge with third place in Pat Patrick's Brahma Reynard-Ford.

Frustration for Rahal

BOBBY Rahal was on the pace all weekend and came tantalizingly close to ending a streak of 70 races without a victory, dating back to Nazareth at the end of his third PPG Cup championship-winning season in 1992.

Rahal, 44, the oldest regular competitor on the circuit, took the lead from pole-sitter Mauricio Gugelmin at a restart on lap 14 and proceeded to run out in front of the field for 102 of the 133 laps. But it wasn't quite enough. His Miller Lite Reynard-Ford/Cosworth ran out of fuel with just over one lap remaining.

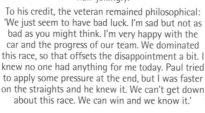

'I knew it would be close with our fuel,' admitted Rahal after finishing an unrepresentative 10th. 'My crew was working hard to calculate the number of laps of yellow that we needed. I just needed one more lap [of caution]. I pitted on lap 84 and Tracy pitted on lap 85. That was the difference.'

As the laps ticked away, Rahal was fully aware of his predicament. With just over a half-dozen laps remaining, there was a flicker of hope as the Toyota engine in P.J. Jones' Castrol/Jockey Reynard expired on the main straightaway. Jones, though, pulled off to the side of the road, safely out of harm's way. There was no caution.

'I'll have to get P.J. to park it in the middle of the straight next time,' quipped Rahal only half-jokingly.

To his credit, the veteran remained philosophical: 'We just seem to have bad luck. I'm sad but not as bad as you might think. I'm very happy with the car and the progress of our team. We dominated this race, so that offsets the disappointment a bit. I knew no one had anything for me today. Paul tried to apply some pressure at the end, but I was faster on the straights and he knew it. We can't get down about this race. We can win and we know it.'

Photos: Michael C. Brown

Greg Moore and Paul Tracy look back on the race's dramatic climax as they stand on the victory podium.

Below: The moment of truth. Parker Johnstone checks a printout of lap times during practice and discovers he is currently down in 16th place.

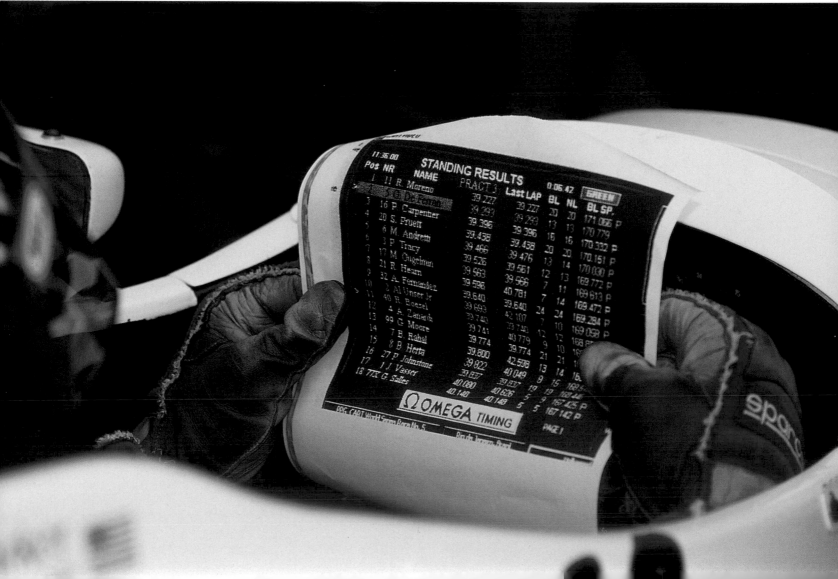

RIO SNIPPETS

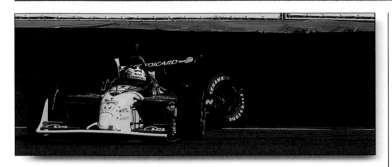

• One year after becoming the toast of Brazil following his sensational victory in the inaugural Rio 400, **ANDRE RIBEIRO** *(above)* was brought back to earth due to the inadequacies of the latest Lola chassis. Ribeiro's woes began early as he brought out the first caution of the weekend following a spin into the Turn One tire wall on Friday morning. Another 'off' on Sunday morning accounted for a second rear wing – as well as one more on-board camera – whereupon yet another wing, borrowed from the Della Penna team, was demolished in the accident prior to the green flag.

• **MICHEL JOURDAIN JR.** also experienced an eventful weekend which included three spins in Turn Four, a broken clutch cover and, on Friday afternoon, a holed radiator. Barry Brooke's crew worked wonders to fit a replacement in double-quick time, so the young Mexican could continue to gain valuable experience.

• In a bid to improve its cars' straight-line speed capability, **MARLBORO TEAM PENSKE** trimmed a half-inch off the PC26s' rear wings prior to the final warmup session on raceday morning. The results were immediately apparent as Paul Tracy and Al Unser Jr. picked up 3 mph.

• **EMERSON FITTIPALDI** *(right)*, out of action since suffering a broken bone in his neck when he crashed on the opening lap of the 1996 Marlboro 500, received one of the biggest cheers of the day when he drove the Acura NS-X PPG Pace Car prior to the start.

• **ALEX ZANARDI** was prevented from making a qualifying run when his Target Reynard-Honda encountered an electrical problem during the warmup laps. Zanardi aborted his run and pulled into the pits for repairs, but the maximum 90-minute allocation for the session had expired by the time everyone else had completed their qualifying attempts. Zanardi was obliged to start from the back of the grid along with Juan Fangio II, who experienced an engine failure, and Jourdain, who crashed in Turn Four on his first lap.

• **JIMMY VASSER** kept alive his streak of consecutive finishes dating back to Vancouver in 1995, but after running strongly for most of the race, the defending series champion was obliged to back off in the closing stages due to a broken engine fitting which leaked oil onto his Reynard's left-rear tire: 'I could smell the oil and it was smoking,' said Vasser. 'I was just hanging on.'

PPG CART WORLD SERIES • ROUND 5
HOLLYWOOD RIO 400

EMERSON FITTIPALDI SPEEDWAY/NELSON PIQUET INTERNATIONAL RACEWAY, JACAREPAGUA, BRAZIL

MAY 11, 133 laps – 247.912 miles

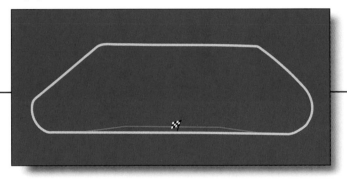

Place	Driver (Nat.)	No.	Team Sponsors Car-Engine	Tires	Q Speed	Q Time	Q Pos.	Laps	Time/Status	Ave. (mph)	Pts.
1	Paul Tracy (CDN)	3	Marlboro Team Penske Penske PC26-Mercedes	GY	170.531	39.350s	5	133	2h 10m 47.996s	113.721	20
2	Greg Moore (CDN)	99	Forsythe Player's Ltd./Indeck Reynard 97I-Mercedes	FS	170.367	39.388s	8	133	2h 10m 49.801s	113.695	16
3	Scott Pruett (USA)	20	Patrick Brahma Sports Team Reynard 97I-Ford XD	FS	170.371	39.387s	7	133	2h 10m 50.249s	113.689	14
4	Alex Zanardi (I)	4	Target/Chip Ganassi Racing Reynard 97I-Honda	FS	no speed	no time	26	133	2h 10m 51.088s	113.676	12
5	Raul Boesel (BR)	40	Patrick Brahma Sports Team Reynard 97I-Ford XD	FS	167.337	40.101s	18	133	2h 10m 54.351s	113.629	10
6	Bryan Herta (USA)	8	Team Rahal Shell Reynard 97I-Ford XD	GY	170.587	39.337s	4	133	2h 10m 54.513s	113.627	8
7	Al Unser Jr. (USA)	2	Marlboro Team Penske Penske PC26-Mercedes	GY	169.712	39.540s	9	133	2h 10m 58.128s	113.574	6
8	Mark Blundell (GB)	18	PacWest Racing Group Motorola Reynard 97I-Mercedes	FS	165.763	40.482s	20	133	2h 11m 02.305s	113.514	5
9	Jimmy Vasser (USA)	1	Target/Chip Ganassi Racing Reynard 97I-Honda	FS	168.756	39.764s	13	133	2h 11m 04.018s	113.489	4
10	Bobby Rahal (USA)	7	Team Rahal Miller Lite Reynard 97I-Ford XD	GY	170.587	39.337s	3	132	Running		4
11	Gil de Ferran (BR)	5	Walker Valvoline/Cummins Reynard 97I-Honda	GY	169.416	39.609s	10	132	Running		2
12	Parker Johnstone (USA)	27	Team KOOL Green Reynard 97I-Honda	FS	168.586	39.804s	14	132	Running		1
13	Max Papis (I)	25	Arciero-Wells Racing MCI Reynard 97I-Toyota RV8B	FS	164.101	40.892s	21	132	Running		
14	Richie Hearn (USA)	21	Della Penna Ralphs/Food 4 Less Lola T97/00-Ford XD	GY	169.326	39.630s	11	131	Out of fuel		
15	Andre Ribeiro (BR)	31	Tasman Motorsports LCI/Marlboro Lola T97/00-Honda	FS	168.375	39.854s	16	128	Running		
16	P.J. Jones (USA)	98	All American Racers Castrol/Jockey Reynard 97I-Toyota RV8B	GY	159.490	42.074s	25	126	Engine		
17	Michel Jourdain Jr. (MEX)	19	Payton/Coyne Herdez/Mexlub/Viva Mexico! Lola T97/00-Ford XD	FS	no speed	no time	27	98	Accident		
18	Roberto Moreno (BR)	11	Newman/Haas Kmart/Budweiser Swift 007.i-Ford XD	GY	171.031	39.235s	2	97	Engine		
19	*Gualter Salles (BR)	77	Davis Racing Indusval/Marlboro Reynard 97I-Ford XD	GY	169.168	39.667s	12	85	Engine		
20	Juan Fangio II (RA)	36	All American Racers Castrol/Jockey Reynard 97I-Toyota RV8B	GY	no speed	no time	28	80	Engine		
21	Michael Andretti (USA)	6	Newman/Haas Kmart/Texaco Havoline Swift 007.i-Ford XD	GY	170.509	39.355s	6	64	Engine		
22	Mauricio Gugelmin (BR)	17	PacWest Racing Group Hollywood Reynard 97I-Mercedes	FS	171.912	39.034s	1	56	Accident		1
23	Hiro Matsushita (J)	24	Arciero-Wells Panasonic/Duskin Reynard 96I-Toyota RV8A	FS	160.636	41.774s	22	46	Engine		
24	*Paul Jasper (USA)	34	Payton/Coyne Hype/US Long Distance Lola T97/00-Ford XD	FS	160.356	41.847s	23	36	Engine		
25	*Arnd Meier (D)	64	Project Indy Hasseroder Pils/J.A.G. Lola T97/00-Ford XD	GY	159.502	42.071s	24	23	Transmission		
26	Adrian Fernandez (MEX)	32	Tasman Tecate Beer/Quaker State Oil Lola T97/00-Honda	FS	168.008	39.941s	17	0	Accident		
27	*Dario Franchitti (GB)	9	Hogan Racing LLC Reynard 97I-Mercedes	FS	167.158	40.144s	19	0	Accident		
NS	*Patrick Carpentier (CDN)	16	Bettenhausen Alumax Aluminum Reynard 97I-Mercedes	GY	168.442	39.838s	15	0	Accident		

* denotes Rookie driver

Caution flags: Laps 1–3, multi-car accident before start; laps 6–9, spin/Herta and Moreno; laps 10–12, spin/Tracy; laps 23–27, spin/Hearn; laps 49–54, spin/Blundell; laps 57–61, accident/Gugelmin and Moreno; laps 86–97, spin/Salles; laps 99–103, accident/Jourdain. **Total:** eight for 43 laps.

Lap leaders: Mauricio Gugelmin, 1–13 (13 laps); Bobby Rahal, 14–41 (28 laps); Gugelmin, 42 (1 lap); Michael Andretti, 43–44 (2 laps); Bryan Herta, 45 (1 lap); Scott Pruett, 46–51 (6 laps); Gualter Salles, 52 (1 lap); Rahal, 53–83 (31 laps); Paul Tracy, 84 (1 lap); Pruett, 85–88 (4 laps); Rahal, 89–131 (43 laps); Tracy, 132–133 (2 laps). **Totals:** Rahal, 102 laps; Gugelmin, 14 laps; Pruett, 10 laps; Tracy, 3 laps; Andretti, 2 laps; Herta and Salles, 1 lap.

Fastest race lap: Gil de Ferran, 39.898s, 168.189 mph on lap 74 (Record).

Championship positions: 1 Tracy, 65; **2** Pruett, 61; **3** Zanardi, 55; **4** Andretti, 51; **5** Moore, 44; **6** Vasser, 33; **7** Unser Jr., 32; **8** Gugelmin, 29; **9** Boesel, 26; **10** de Ferran and Herta, 25; **12** Rahal, 18; **13** Johnstone, 16; **14** Blundell, 10; **15** Ribeiro, 9; **16** Carpentier and Franchitti, 5; **18** Fernandez, 4; **19** Hearn, 2.

Photos: Michael C. Brown

GATEWAY

1 – TRACY

2 – CARPENTIER

3 – DE FERRAN

Main photo: Greg Moore holds a tight line through one of the new track's challenging corners. A puncture ended the young Canadian's chances of victory.

Inset top: The 1997 PPG Cup field poses for a class photo before the Motorola 300.

Inset bottom left: Patrick Carpentier was more than happy with second place as the unstoppable Paul Tracy *(inset near left)* gave Roger Penske his 99th Indy car win.

ing included some strong words from well-respected CART Chief Steward Wally Dallenbach. A former race winner in his own right, Dallenbach made it perfectly clear he did not want to see a repeat of the melee which marred the start of the previous race in Brazil – or the previous year's embarrassing pace lap crash in the U.S. 500, which also took place on Memorial Day weekend. Sure enough, the front of the field was in perfect alignment as Boesel's Brahma Reynard-Ford led the 26-car grid toward starter Jim Swintal's green flag.

The 39-year-old Brazilian jumped immediately into the lead and quickly edged clear of Tracy, who in turn left Greg Moore's Player's Reynard-Mercedes to come under pressure from the second Marlboro Penske of Al Unser Jr.

Max Papis' MCI Reynard was first to fall by the wayside, due to yet another broken Toyota engine. The Italian was able to move his stricken car out of harm's way, but Roberto Moreno wasn't so fortunate a few laps later when his Kmart/Budweiser Swift-Ford succumbed to transmission failure and was stranded between Turns One and Two. Under the ensuing caution, Unser brought his car into the pits for attention to its rear wing. He rejoined but later was forced out by a broken transmission.

Boesel again set a fast pace at the restart, leading from Tracy, Moore and the two Target/Chip Ganassi Reynard-Hondas of Alex Zanardi and Jimmy Vasser which had moved up rapidly from 10th and ninth, respectively, on the grid.

After a couple of dozen laps, Moore began to make his move. First of all he passed Tracy into Turn Three, then swiftly closed on the race leader. Interestingly, Moore had chosen to qualify on the more durable of the two Firestone tires, whereas Boesel had selected the softer option. By lap 30, it had become apparent that Moore's choice was the better of the two, although just as he seemed poised to take the lead, on came the caution lights once more after Mark Blundell's Motorola Reynard slowed abruptly on the course due to an ignition problem.

Most of the field elected to make a pit stop during the yellow, whereupon Moore fell back behind the Ganassi pair due to a slight problem changing his right-front tire. Boesel, though, remained out in front until the next caution just a few laps later when Juan Fangio's Castrol/Jockey Reynard-Toyota expired expensively. Rookies Patrick Carpentier and Dario Franchitti also made pit stops on lap 42.

QUALIFYING

No clear favorite for the coveted pole position had emerged prior to Friday afternoon's one-at-a-time qualifying session. Paul Tracy had topped the speed charts at an average of 188.420 mph (24.265 seconds) during the final morning practice, but the top 11 drivers were blanketed by less than four tenths of a second.

Sure enough, qualifying began with a flourish as each of the first six competitors improved upon the previous best.

Tracy, fifth in the lineup, set the new standard with a second lap at 24.353s (187.739 mph), not quite as quick as his morning mark due to the higher ambient temperature. Raul Boesel was next to go. The Brazilian had been confident of being able to post a serious challenge. He was as good as his word, clipping a scant 0.029 seconds from Tracy's time to snatch the third pole of his CART career, his first since 1994 and his first with Pat Patrick's Brahma Sports Team Reynard-Ford.

'The car was comfortable from day one,' declared Boesel. 'Each session we just made little changes to stay with the track. My concern was not to lose speed in Turns One and Two because I knew my car was really fast in Three and Four. We made a small change to the aerodynamics, anticipating how hot it got, and it worked.'

Mauricio Gugelmin maintained his recent qualifying form by annexing third on the grid with the PacWest team's Hollywood Reynard-Mercedes. Greg Moore, after losing time on Friday morning due to a rare engine failure in his Player's Reynard-Mercedes, also served notice of his intentions by posting the fourth fastest time despite being one of very few contenders to choose the harder Firestone primary tires.

Patrick Carpentier, one of the stars at Nazareth, once again displayed his oval prowess by securing a place on row three of the grid with Tony Bettenhausen's Alumax Reynard-Mercedes. Al Unser Jr.'s Marlboro Penske ensured there would be five Mercedes-powered cars among the top six on the grid.

Parker Johnstone earned kudos by being the fastest of the Honda contingent, seventh for Team KOOL Green, followed by another rookie, Dario Franchitti, in the Reynard-Mercedes owned by locally based trucking magnate Carl Hogan. Next were the two Target/Chip Ganassi Reynard-Hondas of Jimmy Vasser and Alex Zanardi. As a measure of the level of competition, the top 13 qualifiers were blanketed by a mere 0.432 seconds.

PAUL Tracy ensured a fitting climax to a dramatic Motorola 300 at the brand-new Gateway International Raceway oval as he snatched the victory from fellow Canadian Patrick Carpentier with a sensational pass just two laps from the finish.

Tracy also had led during the early stages, taking over from pole-sitter Raul Boesel, who set a rapid pace prior to making his first pit stop. But the driver of Roger Penske's #3 Marlboro Penske-Mercedes later fell a lap behind the leaders when he was obliged to make his first scheduled pit stop under

green-flag conditions. Tracy was up to the challenge.

'The car was just really hooked up in the last part of the race,' said a jubilant Tracy after scoring his third consecutive victory. 'It was tough to lose a lap early with our pit strategy but we just kept our heads down and got to work.'

Perfect weather throughout the three days of practice and qualifying unfortunately gave way to cloudy skies on raceday, Saturday, but even the threat of rain by mid-afternoon failed to deter a capacity crowd of 45,000 from filling the imposing main grandstand.

The regular pre-race drivers' meet-

Sadly, Boesel's hopes of his long-overdue maiden CART victory were dashed a little later when his car's electrical system abruptly shut down. The crew eventually was able to resuscitate the Brahma car, but by then it was five laps in arrears of the leaders.

Already many of the top contenders were on differing pit stop strategies. Tracy, indeed, kept on going until he was obliged to stop under green on lap 65. Even though Jon Bouslog's crew performed its usual rapid service, Tracy was a lap down to new leader Zanardi by the time he rejoined.

Next it was Moore's turn to shine. The 22-year-old had blown past Vasser into Turn One on lap 59, and nine laps later he repeated the maneuver on Zanardi. Moore relinquished the lead by making his second pit stop on lap 77, but remained in contention for his first victory until picking up a puncture during the late stages. He deserved better than an eventual 13th-place finish.

'Today was very frustrating,' declared Moore. 'We had the guys covered today. It definitely would've been a good race between me and Paul at the end.'

Rookie Franchitti took advantage of shrewd strategy by team owner Carl Hogan and moved into the lead of a PPG Cup race for the first time on lap 77. The young Scotsman was far from overawed. Indeed, he extended a useful lead over Vasser before making his second pit stop, on schedule, after 96 laps.

Vasser, who had slipped ahead of teammate Zanardi during the earlier round of pit stops, duly took over the point from Franchitti. Ultimately, however, a decision not to take on fresh tires at his final scheduled fuel stop proved costly.

'We lost the balance of the car after that,' lamented Vasser. 'The car was quick all day long until the last stint.' Michael Andretti, who was making his 200th Indy car start, inherited the lead from Vasser and remained in front of the pack during an extended caution period due to light but persistent precipitation. Later, after the rain moved on and the race was resumed, his Kmart/Texaco Havoline Swift-Ford began to oversteer dramatically.

'What a day!' exclaimed Andretti after slipping to a disappointing 11th. 'I thought the engine was making funny noises and then we had a huge vibration. We were praying for a downpour [hoping the race would be stopped]. Everyone got by me after the restart because my car was so loose.'

The protracted full-course caution gave everyone an opportunity to plan their strategy for the closing stages. On lap 173, by which time the skies had brightened and it seemed likely the race would go the full distance, Carl Hogan pulled his master-stroke by signalling Franchitti into the pits.

'It was a tough call,' said Hogan. 'I knew what I wanted to do but I had to be careful I didn't call him in too soon, because we wanted to be sure we could make it to the finish without having to stop again.'

Franchitti fell to 15th place, last among those still on the lead lap, but by lap 199 he had regained the lead as, one by one, the other contenders were obliged to make pit stops of their own.

Franchitti gradually eked out a margin of more than three seconds over his nearest pursuer, Carpentier, who had pitted just a couple of laps after the Scotsman. But with just 26 laps remaining, Franchitti was forced out by a broken transmission.

'Obviously it's disappointing,' he said, 'but at least we showed what we are capable of. I couldn't believe how good the car was. It was just a dream to drive.'

Now it was Carpentier's turn to lead, and with Zanardi apparently unable to offer a serious challenge, the young French-Canadian was on course for a famous victory aboard Tony Bettenhausen's Alumax Reynard-Mercedes.

The gap from first to second stretched to as much as 2.5 seconds on lap 227; but Tracy was moving up menacingly. He had disposed of Gil de Ferran's Valvoline/Cummins Reynard-Honda and now was hard on the tail of Zanardi. Tracy's team had wisely elected to put on a fresh set of Goodyear tires during his final pit stop, on lap 198. The extra few seconds caused him to slip back to seventh position, but the newer rubber was to prove a significant benefit as the race drew toward its conclusion.

Tracy was able to carry phenomenal speed through Turns Three and Four, and after having one attempt to pass Zanardi rebuffed on lap 229, Tracy gathered himself once more before

Gil de Ferran was not quite able to match the pace of the leaders on this occasion but collected 14 valuable PPG Cup points with a third-place finish.

Below: A splash of methanol escapes from the nozzle of the fuel hose as Jimmy Vasser's Target Reynard-Honda receives service. The decision not to fit new tires at his last pit stop restricted the Californian to fifth place.

Overleaf: Rookies Patrick Carpentier and Dario Franchitti battle for the lead as they lap Parker Johnstone's KOOL Reynard.

Warm welcome for challenging new venue

CHRIS Pook's single-minded determination over the past 25 years has resulted in the Toyota Grand Prix of Long Beach becoming one of the world's premier racing spectacles. Furthermore, the Californian event's success has proved the catalyst in transforming what was once a seedy seaport into a bustling center for trade and tourism. More recently, the expatriate Englishman has set his sights on performing a similar miracle in a corner of St. Clair County, Ill.

An under-utilized, largely unprofitable road racing venue and drag strip has been in operation within the depressed city of Madison, right across the mighty Mississippi from St. Louis – and within sight of the famous Gateway Arch – since the 1960s. But not in its present guise. Pook took control of the facility in November 1994, and after attracting the support of both the local community and the Southwestern Illinois Development Authority, he began a complete reconstruction.

On Saturday, May 24, Pook's dream became a reality as the renamed and rejuvenated Gateway International Raceway hosted its first major event.

The brand-new oval is unlike any other on the CART tour. Quite apart from its length, at 1.27 miles, the track comprises two distinctly different corners, one banked at nine degrees and the other at 11 degrees.

So new was the facility that no testing had been permitted prior to the race meeting. CART therefore scheduled an additional day of practice on Wednesday, and while most of the session was spent cleaning away an abundant coating of lime, used to enhance the asphalt curing process, the track drew virtually unanimous praise from the drivers.

'It reminds me of the oval in Phoenix,' said pole-sitter Raul Boesel. 'It's very challenging. It's very fast, especially in Turns Three and Four where you can keep going faster and faster.'

The teams soon found that the new circuit permitted sustained cornering speeds exceeding five times the force of gravity – more than any other venue, including the high banks of Michigan Speedway. And once a racing 'groove' had emerged, drivers were able to run two-abreast into the corners.

The only real criticism concerned a paucity of such amenities as permanent restrooms and bridge access to the infield, although Pook made assurances that these aspects would soon be addressed as part of the facility's planned growth.

scorching past the Italian with imperious ease on lap 233.

Carpentier, meanwhile, was being urged from the pits to keep a close eye on his diminishing fuel load. Even so, Tracy was in irrepressible form. He used his clear advantage once again through Turns Three and Four, and ultimately squeezed past both Carpentier and the slower Panasonic/Duskin Reynard-Toyota of Hiro Matsushita in an audacious move with just a couple of laps remaining.

'We just had better grip,' said Tracy modestly. 'We decided to go with new tires at the final stop and that definitely paid off for us. We decided even if we gave up a couple of positions, we'd be able to get them back.'

Tracy did just that. Magnificently. And how the crowd loved it, providing both Tracy and Carpentier with a richly merited standing ovation on the victory podium.

'That was a great race,' beamed Carpentier after recording by far the best finish of his short CART career. 'I'm not disappointed at all. I'm extremely happy. Paul drove a great race. He deserved the win.'

GATEWAY SNIPPETS

• Neither ARND MEIER nor PAUL JASPER started the Motorola 300 after separate incidents during practice caused extensive damage to their respective Project Indy and Payton/Coyne Racing Lola-Fords.

• SCOTT PRUETT was running strongly in sixth place until fading brakes caused him to crash heavily between Turns One and Two on his 144th lap. Pruett, fortunately, was not injured. 'I went in there and the brake pedal went to the floor,' he reported. 'I thought I might be OK but it just came around on me. It was a big hit. I think [the lack of injury] says a lot about CART and their safety standards.'

• ADRIAN FERNANDEZ *(right)*, after being forced into his backup Tecate/Quaker State Lola-Honda following a fire in the Saturday warmup, drove solidly to finish eighth, his best result of the season thus far. Tasman teammate ANDRE RIBEIRO was two places farther back, sandwiching the Lola-Ford of Richie Hearn.

• Two days before the teams arrived for practice at Gateway, the directors of LOLA CARS announced they had placed the Huntingdon, England-based company into administration – the British equivalent of Chapter 11. Lola apparently had accumulated debts of almost $5 million as the result of a failed Formula 1 project.

• ALEX ZANARDI lost what appeared to be a certain third place on the final lap when his Target Reynard-Honda used up the last of its fuel.

• CART President Andrew Craig and Mark Reilly, vice-president of International Sales for ESPN, hosted a press conference to confirm that coverage of the PPG CART World Series in 1996 reached nearly 1 BILLION TELEVISION VIEWERS in 188 countries. The figures represented an average growth of seven percent over 1995.

• TOYOTA at last made what appeared to be a significant gain when Max Papis ran the latest Phase 3.2 version of the RV8B engine briefly during practice and qualifying. 'It's a definite improvement,' noted MCI/Arciero-Wells Racing Team Manager Richard Buck. 'It's got more horsepower – about 15 percent. It's the first big step we've made and it's the first time I've heard real enthusiasm in Max's voice.'

• Nextel Communications, Inc., the country's leading provider of fully integrated digital wireless communications, provided associate support during the Motorola 300 for the two PACWEST REYNARD-MERCEDES of Mauricio Gugelmin and Mark Blundell.

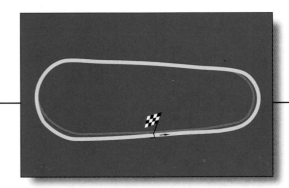

PPG CART WORLD SERIES • ROUND 6
MOTOROLA 300

GATEWAY INTERNATIONAL RACEWAY, MADISON, ILLINOIS

MAY 24, 236 laps – 299.720 miles

Place	Driver (Nat.)	No.	Team Sponsors Car-Engine	Tires	Q Speed	Q Time	Q Pos.	Laps	Time/Status	Ave. (mph)	Pts.
1	Paul Tracy (CDN)	3	Marlboro Team Penske Penske PC26-Mercedes	GY	187.739	24.353s	2	236	2h 37m 54.496s	113.884	20
2	*Patrick Carpentier (CDN)	16	Bettenhausen Alumax Aluminum Reynard 97I-Mercedes	GY	186.263	24.546s	5	236	2h 37m 56.887s	113.855	16
3	Gil de Ferran (BR)	5	Walker Valvoline/Cummins Reynard 97I-Honda	GY	183.533	24.911s	15	236	2h 37m 59.812s	113.820	14
4	Alex Zanardi (I)	4	Target/Chip Ganassi Racing Reynard 97I-Honda	FS	184.907	24.726s	10	236	2h 38m 00.628s	113.810	12
5	Jimmy Vasser (USA)	1	Target/Chip Ganassi Racing Reynard 97I-Honda	FS	185.086	24.702s	9	236	2h 38m 06.394s	113.741	10
6	Mauricio Gugelmin (BR)	17	PacWest Racing Group Hollywood Reynard 97I-Mercedes	FS	187.577	24.374s	3	236	2h 38m 06.906s	113.735	8
7	Parker Johnstone (USA)	27	Team KOOL Green Reynard 97I-Honda	FS	185.748	24.614s	7	236	2h 38m 08.088s	113.721	6
8	Adrian Fernandez (MEX)	32	Tasman Tecate Beer/Quaker State Oil Lola T97/00-Honda	FS	182.362	25.071s	18	236	2h 38m 15.226s	113.635	5
9	Richie Hearn (USA)	21	Della Penna Ralphs/Food 4 Less Lola T97/00-Ford XD	GY	184.863	24.756s	13	236	2h 38m 16.966s	113.614	4
10	Andre Ribeiro (BR)	31	Tasman Motorsports LCI/Marlboro Lola T97/00-Honda	FS	182.050	25.114s	19	236	2h 38m 17.623s	113.607	3
11	Michael Andretti (USA)	6	Newman/Haas Kmart/Texaco Havoline Swift 007.i-Ford XD	GY	184.899	24.727s	11	236	2h 38m 19.004s	113.590	3
12	*Gualter Salles (BR)	77	Davis Racing Indusval/Marlboro Reynard 97I-Ford XD	GY	180.206	25.371s	21	236	2h 38m 20.786s	113.569	1
13	Greg Moore (CDN)	99	Forsythe Player's Ltd./Indeck Reynard 97I-Mercedes	FS	186.643	24.496s	4	234	Running		
14	Raul Boesel (BR)	40	Patrick Brahma Sports Team Reynard 97I-Ford XD	FS	187.963	24.324s	1	231	Running		1
15	Hiro Matsushita (J)	24	Arciero-Wells Panasonic/Duskin Reynard 97I-Toyota RV8B	FS	no speed	no time	27	229	Running		
16	Michel Jourdain Jr. (MEX)	19	Payton/Coyne Herdez/Mexlub/Viva Mexico! Lola T97/00-Ford XD	FS	178.566	25.604s	24	216	Running		
17	*Dario Franchitti (GB)	9	Hogan Racing LLC Reynard 97I-Mercedes	FS	185.139	24.695s	8	210	Transmission		
18	Al Unser Jr. (USA)	2	Marlboro Team Penske Penske PC26-Mercedes	GY	186.035	24.576s	6	181	Transmission		
19	Scott Pruett (USA)	20	Patrick Brahma Sports Team Reynard 97I-Ford XD	FS	183.019	24.981s	17	143	Accident		
20	Bobby Rahal (USA)	7	Team Rahal Miller Lite Reynard 97I-Ford XD	GY	184.772	24.744s	12	103	Electrical		
21	P.J. Jones (USA)	98	All American Racers Castrol/Jockey Reynard 97I-Toyota RV8B	GY	174.032	26.271s	26	99	Out of fuel		
22	Bryan Herta (USA)	8	Team Rahal Shell Reynard 97I-Ford XD	GY	183.578	24.905s	14	73	Electrical		
23	Juan Fangio II (RA)	36	All American Racers Castrol/Jockey Reynard 97I-Toyota RV8B	GY	178.622	25.596s	23	37	Engine		
24	Mark Blundell (GB)	18	PacWest Racing Group Motorola Reynard 97I-Mercedes	FS	181.134	25.241s	20	28	Ignition		
25	Roberto Moreno (BR)	11	Newman/Haas Kmart/Budweiser Swift 007.i-Ford XD	GY	183.430	24.925s	16	8	Transmission		
26	Max Papis (I)	25	Arciero-Wells Racing MCI Reynard 97I-Toyota RV8B	FS	178.817	25.568s	22	4	Engine		
NS	*Arnd Meier (D)	64	Project Indy Hasseroder Pils/J.A.G. Lola T97/00-Ford XD	GY	178.079	25.674s	25	–	Accident in practice		
NQ	*Paul Jasper (USA)	34	Payton/Coyne Hype/US Long Distance Lola T97/00-Ford XD	FS	no speed	no time	–	–	Accident in practice		

* denotes Rookie driver

Caution flags: Laps 9–12, tow/Moreno; laps 29–34, tow/Blundell; laps 39–45, engine/Fangio; laps 74–80, tow/Herta and Boesel; laps 104–109, fire/Rahal; laps 119–134, moisture; laps 143–179, accident/Pruett and moisture; laps 196–200, tow/Franchitti. **Total:** eight for 88 laps.

Lap leaders: Raul Boesel, 1–41 (41 laps); Paul Tracy, 42–64 (23 laps); Alex Zanardi, 65–67 (3 laps); Greg Moore, 68–76 (9 laps); Dario Franchitti, 77–95 (19 laps); Jimmy Vasser, 96–122 (27 laps); Michael Andretti, 123–188 (66 laps); Vasser, 189–197 (9 laps); Franchitti, 198–209 (12 laps); Patrick Carpentier, 210–234 (25 laps); Tracy, 235–236 (2 laps). **Totals:** Andretti, 66 laps; Boesel, 41 laps; Vasser, 36 laps; Franchitti, 31 laps; Tracy and Carpentier, 25 laps; Moore, 9 laps; Zanardi, 3 laps.

Fastest race lap: Dario Franchitti, 25.312s, 180.626 mph on lap 86 (Establishes record).

Championship positions: 1 Tracy, 85; 2 Zanardi, 67; 3 Pruett, 61; 4 Andretti, 54; 5 Moore, 44; 6 Vasser, 43; 7 de Ferran, 39; 8 Gugelmin, 37; 9 Unser Jr., 32; 10 Boesel, 27; 11 Herta, 25; 12 Johnstone, 22; 13 Carpentier, 21; 14 Rahal, 18; 15 Ribeiro, 12; 16 Blundell, 10; 17 Fernandez, 9; 18 Hearn, 6; 19 Franchitti, 5; 20 Salles, 1.

Ω OMEGA
OFFICIAL TIMEKEEPER OF CART

MILWAUKEE

1 - MOORE   **2 - ANDRETTI**   **3 - VASSER**

Photos: Michael C. Brown

QUALIFYING

There was never any doubt that Raul Boesel's qualifying track record of 165.752 mph (21.719 seconds) would be pulverized. The only questions were when, by whom, and by how much?

One year after the Brazilian had set the standard in 1993, the cars were stripped of a significant amount of downforce as the CART officials attempted to keep the escalation of speeds in check; but subsequently the famous old fairgrounds track was repaved, making it substantially smoother. And faster. Paul Tracy *(above)* upped the ante to 176.058 mph (20.448s) during practice last year, although the official record remained intact due to persistent rain which caused qualifying to be canceled.

Speeds for '97 were up again, due to improvements made both by the engine manufacturers and the tire companies. Coolish temperatures and early afternoon cloud cover ensured near-perfect conditions for the Saturday qualifying session, and Tracy took full advantage as he ripped off a sensational first lap at 20.160 seconds, a new record average of 184.286 mph.

'We had a completely different setup on the car [today],' revealed Tracy, who had complained of persistent

understeer on Friday. 'We changed it this morning and we only got 40 minutes [of practice], so there's more [speed] there. We've been steadily improving the car and that's making it easier for me to drive. I'm not putting nearly as much effort into it as I was last year.'

Mauricio Gugelmin maintained his fine qualifying record – only once out of the top five in seven races – with his Hollywood Reynard-Mercedes, while former track record holder Boesel survived a lurid sideways slide in Turn Four to claim a position on row two with Pat Patrick's Brahma Reynard-Ford.

'The temperature changed from this morning and really made the car loose,' said Boesel. 'We thought we had a shot at the pole. If not for that hiccup, we may have had a chance, but I think we still have a good car for the race.'

Rookie Patrick Carpentier, fastest on Friday in the Alumax Reynard-Mercedes, opted to take only two warmup laps (to his rivals' three), but still lined up fourth, while fellow rookie Dario Franchitti displayed his growing affinity for the ovals by snaring seventh in Carl Hogan's similar car.

Moore makes history with maiden victory

GREG Moore was beginning to feel the pressure. The young man from Maple Ridge, B.C. had burst into the PPG CART World Series as a highly touted rookie in 1996; but after 22 races and numerous near misses, a victory had continued to elude him.

Never before had Moore experienced such a streak without taking the checkered flag. He had been a winner from virtually the first moment he began competing in Formula Ford in 1991. Four years later, in his last step before reaching the PPG Cup series, Moore absolutely dominated the PPG-Firestone Indy Lights Championship, claiming 10 of the 12 races.

Ever since then he had been widely tipped to become the youngest driver to win a race in CART history, eclipsing the mark set by Al Unser Jr. (at the age of 21 years, one month and 29 days) at Portland in 1984. But the clock was ticking. Finally, at the historic Milwaukee Mile, Moore achieved his aim with a superbly judged drive.

'It's exciting because Al Unser Jr. and Michael Andretti are the guys I beat to that honor of being the youngest,' said Moore, who bettered Unser's standard by a mere 19 days. 'It's neat to see that I've got my stuff together just as much as they did at such a young age. It's kind of exciting for the future. You look at that and you think there's a good possibility of me having a good future like Al Jr. and Michael.'

Moore also confessed to a feeling of relief after securing that elusive maiden triumph.

'In some ways it was a relief but it was also a dream come true,' he says. 'There was a lot of pressure on us – on the whole team – to win our first race. We all want to win; that's why we're in this business.

'Because we were so competitive a few times last year, and then to not get our win because of a mechanical failure or whatever, you just sort of get to the point where, argh! what do we have to do to win one of these things? But when we finally got it . . . it was welcome, let's put it that way.'

136

THE Miller 200 boiled down to a fascinating duel between Greg Moore and Michael Andretti. It was all about youth versus experience, patience versus aggression.

Jerry Forsythe's Player's Ltd.-backed team had taken a gamble on being able to complete the final 92 laps on a single tankful of methanol. Moore, therefore, had absolutely no margin for error as he chased after that elusive maiden CART victory. Newman/Haas Racing, meanwhile, had chosen a more conservative strategy, ensuring that Andretti had plenty of fuel after making a precautionary pit stop during a full-course caution on lap 134.

Andretti, the most successful driver in CART history with 35 wins to his credit, quickly stormed past Bobby Rahal, Raul Boesel and Jimmy Vasser, who also chose the fuel conservation route. It seemed only a matter of time before Moore, the 22-year-old sophomore, would succumb – either to Andretti's persistence or a lack of fuel. He did neither.

'I worked all my life to be here and win my first CART race,' said an ecstatic Moore. 'I'm so happy for the Player's team. The guys did a great job all weekend long. We gambled on pit stops and made the right decision.'

Fellow Canadian Paul Tracy, chasing a record-equalling fourth consecutive victory – as well as Roger Penske's 100th Indy car triumph – rocketed into the lead at the start; and following an early caution due to Michel Jourdain Jr.'s crash in Turn Four, the #3 Marlboro Penske-Mercedes soon eked out a margin of more than two seconds over Mauricio Gugelmin. The Brazilian once again was running strongly in PacWest's Hollywood Reynard-Mercedes, as was rookie Patrick Carpentier (Alumax Reynard-Mercedes), who followed closely in third ahead of Raul Boesel's Brahma Reynard-Ford and Moore, who was content to bide his time.

'I knew we had a good car in traffic,' related Moore. 'That's what we worked on all weekend. We weren't too worried about qualifying; we knew we didn't have the fastest car out there so I just wanted to settle into a rhythm and see what developed.' Smart young man.

On lap 25, Moore relieved Boesel of fourth place. Eight laps later he slipped past Carpentier. Gugelmin, too, fell victim to the flying Player's Ltd./Indeck Reynard-Mercedes. Now only Tracy remained in front – and the leader was experiencing difficulty as he attempted to work his way through slower traffic.

'The car was working good for the

137

Far right: Michael Andretti races wheel to wheel with his old rival, Al Unser Jr. The Penske driver's miserable season continued with another retirement, but second place kept Andretti in contention for the PPG Cup.

Bottom: The MCI Reynard-Toyota of Max Papis leaves a trail of flames as it slides to a halt after hitting the unforgiving wall.

first 25 laps or so,' declared Tracy, 'and then it started to push.'

On lap 40, after Tracy had spent five laps looking in vain for a way past Max Papis' MCI Reynard-Toyota, running 20th at the tail end of the lead lap, Moore saw an opportunity to make his move. The youngster sailed past both Tracy and Papis with contemptuous ease on the approach to Turn Three.

Moore soon began to edge clear of Tracy, and while Gugelmin, Carpentier and Boesel continued to fill the top five positions, Andretti was making his move toward the front after starting a lowly 14th in Newman/Haas Racing's Kmart/Texaco Havoline Swift-Ford/ Cosworth. Jimmy Vasser (Target/Chip Ganassi Reynard-Honda) and Roberto Moreno, in the second Newman/Haas Swift, also were in close attendance at one-quarter distance, as was Parker Johnstone until his Team KOOL Green Reynard-Honda suddenly began to oversteer violently. Johnstone slipped quickly to 12th, trying desperately to hold on until it was time for his first pit stop. But in vain. On lap 52, Johnstone lost control and crashed heavily in Turn Two.

'The car made a really swift transition from a huge push to neutral to loose to way loose,' reported Johnstone, who emerged unscathed.

The ensuing caution provided an opportunity for everyone else to take routine service – and shifted the focus onto the pit crews. The two leaders were situated at opposite ends of pit lane, with Tracy nearest to Turn One, and while Moore's stop was good, Tracy's was better. The Marlboro Penske thereby regained the lead from the Player's Reynard.

Tracy once again took off confidently at the restart. The gap grew quickly to almost four seconds before Moore began to reduce the deficit. By lap 74 the margin had dwindled to just a car length or so. Tracy fought tooth and nail to retain his advantage, but Moore finally got the better of him on lap 86.

The previous pit stops had seen some shuffling of positions a little lower down the order. Gugelmin still held third place, but excellent work by the crews of both Vasser and Al Unser Jr. enabled the two PPG Cup champions to move up into fourth and fifth. Unser, though, had reckoned without the tenacity of young Carpentier, who dived inside the Marlboro Penske at the end of the back straightaway. For not one, not two but three complete laps, Unser and Carpentier battled in absolutely side-by-side formation, neither giving an inch. Ultimately, it was Unser who had to concede the position.

Photos: Michael C. Brown

Moore, meanwhile, continued to set the pace until the next round of pit stops was triggered by another incident, this time involving Juan Fangio II, who lost control of his Castrol/Jockey Reynard-Toyota in Turn Four, spun, and took Gualter Salles' Indusval Reynard-Ford with him into the retaining wall. Salles remained in the car for several minutes but was later released from the infield hospital with nothing worse than a headache and some bruising to his leg.

Amazingly, the second pit stop sequence mirrored the first, with Tracy once again beating Moore out onto the track.

Moore first encountered trouble when he dropped the clutch and promptly broke first gear. Adroitly, he selected second, only to have to stand on the brakes as Bobby Rahal, running at the tail end of the lead lap in 12th position, pulled into his pit box directly in front of Moore. The cars did make contact, but fortunately without causing any significant damage.

Once again, Moore's fine work on the track had been undone. Tracy was back in the lead. But Moore, despite his relative lack of experience, remained unflustered.

'I knew that I was much faster than Paul once we got into traffic,' he said, 'so I was comfortable riding around behind him. He was struggling, no doubt about that, so I knew I was in pretty good shape.'

The race was restarted on lap 126, at which point it seemed fairly certain that everyone would require one more fuel stop in order to reach the finish. But when Papis became the latest casualty in Turn Four, bringing out the pace car one more time, the teams were faced with a dilemma: With the reduced pace under the caution, would they now have enough fuel to make it to the finish? Opinions varied. Tracy, Gugelmin, Andretti, Carpentier, Gil de Ferran, Scott Pruett and Moreno all elected to take on a splash of methanol. Moore, Vasser, Boesel, Mark Blundell and Rahal, by contrast, chose to take a gamble . . . although Blundell's team chickened out prior to the restart and elected to make a late stop which dropped him to the tail of the group.

Those who had chosen not to stop held the upper hand when the green flag waved on lap 145. Moore, despite driving in conservation mode, in sixth gear and with the fuel mixture on full lean, managed to stretch out his lead to more than five seconds over Vasser, who was employing an identical strategy. Andretti, though, was running flat out and rapidly moving up the order. He passed Gugelmin at the restart and made short work of Rahal and Boesel. Vasser proved to be a harder nut to crack, but Andretti moved up into second place on lap 182. By now just 18 laps remained. Moore was three seconds up the road.

Andretti, charging hard, soon began to eat up the gap between himself and the leader. But Moore refused to be flustered, despite being obliged to pay close attention both to his mirrors and his fuel gauge.

'It was a great race,' said Moore. 'I just kept my head down and raced as hard as I could.'

So did Andretti.

'I did the best I could do,' said the 1991 PPG Cup champion. 'I was driving as hard as I could and it just wasn't enough. All we wanted was a little bobble, but it never came.'

Moore, indeed, was flawless. He drove a perfect line and maintained his advantage like a seasoned veteran.

'I'm so happy,' said the youngster, justifiably ecstatic after claiming his long-awaited maiden CART victory. 'We had probably a cupful of fuel left. I knew Mikey was back there but I knew I was a little bit faster than him. My whole team just did a fantastic job. They figured out the fuel and then kept me informed. With about 12 laps to go they told me I was going to be OK, so I went for it.'

Vasser and Boesel also stretched their fuel to secure third and fourth, but poor Rahal didn't quite make it, running dry on the final lap and losing a hard-earned sixth.

'I can't believe it happened again,' said a frustrated Rahal, who lost a potential race victory in Rio in precisely the same fashion. 'We thought we were getting good mileage but it wasn't enough. Again, we needed another lap of yellow. But no luck. That's been the way all year for us.'

The Mears Gang is back!

TEAM Mears, a fledgling two-car Indy Lights operation formed at the start of the season by former Indy car drivers Rick Mears and his brother, Roger, for their respective sons, Clint and Casey, scored its first victory in Milwaukee as Clint led from flag to flag in round six of the extremely close-fought PPG-Firestone Indy Lights Championship. Coincidentally, Rick had scored his maiden Indy car success at the same track some 19 years earlier.

'I can honestly say I'm more excited now than I was in '78 when I scored my first Indy car win,' said the proud father. 'When you're in the car, you have a little bit of control about what's going on; when you're watching from the pits, you don't have any control. It's nerve-wracking.

'Watching Clint and Casey [who finished 10th] is just like when Roger and I were racing. It's a lot of fun. It's one of the reasons we formed this team.'

The two cousins showed tremendous promise when they began competing together in the California-based Jim Russell school series. Clint subsequently graduated into the Toyota Atlantic Championship with moderate results as a teammate to Richie Hearn at Della Penna Motorsports.

The 24-year-old didn't set the world alight during any of his first five starts in the PPG-Firestone Indy Lights Championship – indeed, on two occasions, on the street courses at Long Beach and Savannah, he started dead last – but in Milwaukee he more than made amends by qualifying his Penske Auto Centers/Mobil 1 Lola on pole position and then leading throughout the 90-lap race to record his first professional victory.

'It's real special for me to win on the same track that dad won his first Indy car race,' said Mears Jr., whose previous best result had been a seventh at Nazareth. 'This is just awesome.'

MILWAUKEE SNIPPETS

• AL UNSER JR.'s misfortunes continued as he was forced out of contention by a broken transmission – for the second straight race. Unser *(left)* had been running seventh prior to the failure.

• 'I keep pinching myself to make sure I'm awake,' quipped a delighted TONY BETTENHAUSEN after his young charge, Patrick Carpentier, posted the fastest practice time on Friday.

• There was an UGLY INCIDENT immediately following the Saturday morning practice session when Alex Zanardi, who struggled all weekend, stormed over toward Paul Tracy and let fly a stream of verbal abuse. The pair had not exactly been the best of friends since their clash in Australia and apparently had engaged in a couple of tit-for-tat incidents during the 45-minute session, each holding up the other while he was on a hot lap. The situation was later defused following an audience with CART Chief Steward Wally Dallenbach.

• Moore's victory was the fourth of the season for team owner JERRY FORSYTHE *(right)*, who, amazingly, had previously tasted success both in Indy Lights (David Empringham and Lee Bentham) and Toyota Atlantic (Alexandre Tagliani). Even more impressively, his second Atlantic driver, Bertrand Godin, completed the roster a couple of weeks later by winning in front of the F1 crowd in Montreal.

• TASMAN MOTORSPORTS GROUP owner Steve Horne *(left)* withdrew his pair of unloved Lolas, driven by Andre Ribeiro and Adrian Fernandez, from the race due to a diabolical handling imbalance. 'Both cars were very difficult to drive,' said an exasperated Horne. 'We were just an accident waiting to happen out there. Both of my drivers are capable of far better than this and they have my sympathy right now.'

• Some shuffling among the PacWest team saw Technical Director Allen McDonald take over specific race engineering duties for MARK BLUNDELL's Motorola Reynard-Mercedes, leaving Jim Hamilton to concentrate on development projects, his true forte. The change seemed to benefit Blundell, who remained among the top 10 for most of the weekend, although he eventually finished 12th due to a poorly timed final pit stop.

• Three of the top four finishers confounded their rivals by electing not to make PIT STOPS during the final caution period. Interestingly, those choosing to gamble represented each of the top three engine manufacturers: Mercedes-Benz (Moore), Honda (Vasser) and Ford/Cosworth (Boesel).

PPG CART WORLD SERIES • ROUND 7
MILLER 200

THE MILWAUKEE MILE,
WISCONSIN STATE FAIR PARK, W. ALLIS, WISCONSIN

JUNE 1, 200 laps – 200.000 miles

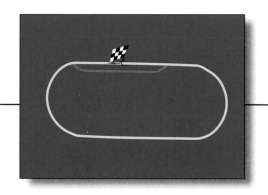

Place	Driver (Nat.)	No.	Team Sponsors Car-Engine	Tires	Q Speed	Q Time	Q Pos.	Laps	Time/Status	Ave. (mph)	Pts.
1	Greg Moore (CDN)	99	Forsythe Player's Ltd./Indeck Reynard 97I-Mercedes	FS	181.717	20.445s	5	200	1h 43m 32.873s	119.597	21
2	Michael Andretti (USA)	6	Newman/Haas Kmart/Texaco Havoline Swift 007.i-Ford XD	GY	178.392	20.826s	14	200	1h 43m 33.221s	119.590	16
3	Jimmy Vasser (USA)	1	Target/Chip Ganassi Racing Reynard 97I-Honda	FS	178.684	20.792s	12	200	1h 43m 43.739s	119.388	14
4	Raul Boesel (BR)	40	Patrick Brahma Sports Team Reynard 97I-Ford XD	FS	181.815	20.434s	3	200	1h 43m 45.394s	119.356	12
5	Mauricio Gugelmin (BR)	17	PacWest Racing Group Hollywood Reynard 97I-Mercedes	FS	182.252	20.385s	2	200	1h 43m 46.453s	119.336	10
6	Paul Tracy (CDN)	3	Marlboro Team Penske Penske PC26-Mercedes	GY	184.286	20.160s	1	200	1h 43m 48.459s	119.298	9
7	Gil de Ferran (BR)	5	Walker Valvoline/Cummins Reynard 97I-Honda	GY	178.324	20.834s	15	200	1h 43m 52.762s	119.215	6
8	*Patrick Carpentier (CDN)	16	Bettenhausen Alumax Aluminum Reynard 97I-Mercedes	GY	181.761	20.440s	4	200	1h 43m 53.158s	119.208	5
9	Scott Pruett (USA)	20	Patrick Brahma Sports Team Reynard 97I-Ford XD	FS	179.634	20.682s	8	200	1h 43m 53.616s	119.199	4
10	Roberto Moreno (BR)	11	Newman/Haas Kmart/Budweiser Swift 007.i-Ford XD	GY	179.123	20.741s	10	200	1h 43m 53.822s	119.195	3
11	Bobby Rahal (USA)	7	Team Rahal Miller Lite Reynard 97I-Ford XD	GY	178.444	20.820s	13	199	Running		2
12	Mark Blundell (GB)	18	PacWest Racing Group Motorola Reynard 97I-Mercedes	FS	179.089	20.745s	11	199	Running		1
13	Alex Zanardi (I)	4	Target/Chip Ganassi Racing Reynard 97I-Honda	FS	177.455	20.936s	17	199	Running		
14	P.J. Jones (USA)	98	All American Racers Castrol/Jockey Reynard 97I-Toyota RV8B	GY	173.973	21.355s	22	197	Running		
15	Bryan Herta (USA)	8	Team Rahal Shell Reynard 97I-Ford XD	GY	177.430	20.939s	18	196	Running		
16	*Dario Franchitti (GB)	9	Hogan Racing LLC Reynard 97I-Mercedes	FS	180.455	20.588s	7	196	Running		
17	Hiro Matsushita (J)	24	Arciero-Wells Panasonic/Duskin Reynard 97I-Toyota RV8B	FS	no speed	no time	27	194	Running		
18	*Paul Jasper (USA)	34	Payton/Coyne Hype/US Long Distance Lola T97/00-Ford XD	FS	163.875	22.671s	26	187	Running		
19	Max Papis (I)	25	Arciero-Wells Racing MCI Reynard 97I-Toyota RV8B	FS	176.461	21.054s	20	129	Accident		
20	Al Unser Jr. (USA)	2	Marlboro Team Penske Penske PC26-Mercedes	GY	179.409	20.708s	9	109	Transmission		
21	Juan Fangio II (RA)	36	All American Racers Castrol/Jockey Reynard 97I-Toyota RV8B	GY	174.595	21.279s	21	103	Accident		
22	*Gualter Salles (BR)	77	Davis Racing Indusval/Marlboro Reynard 97I-Ford XD	GY	177.574	20.922s	16	102	Accident		
23	Richie Hearn (USA)	21	Della Penna Ralphs/Food 4 Less Lola T97/00-Ford XD	GY	173.405	21.425s	23	77	Handling		
24	Adrian Fernandez (MEX)	32	Tasman Tecate Beer/Quaker State Oil Lola T97/00-Honda	FS	169.335	21.940s	24	73	Handling		
25	Parker Johnstone (USA)	27	Team KOOL Green Reynard 97I-Honda	FS	180.630	20.568s	6	51	Accident		
26	Andre Ribeiro (BR)	31	Tasman Motorsports LCI/Marlboro Lola T97/00-Honda	FS	176.544	21.044s	19	48	Handling		
27	Michel Jourdain Jr. (MEX)	19	Payton/Coyne Herdez/Mexlub/Viva Mexico! Lola T97/00-Ford XD	FS	167.457	22.186s	25	2	Accident		

* denotes Rookie driver

Caution flags: Laps 3–12, accident/Jourdain; laps 52–60, accident/Johnstone; laps 105–124, accident/Fangio and Salles; laps 132–144, accident/Papis. **Total:** four for 52 laps.

Lap leaders: Paul Tracy, 1–40 (40 laps); Greg Moore, 41–55 (15 laps); Tracy, 56–85 (30 laps); Moore, 86–108 (23 laps); Tracy, 109–134 (26 laps); Moore, 135–200 (66 laps). **Totals:** Moore, 104 laps; Tracy, 96 laps.

Fastest race lap: Paul Tracy, 21.728s, 170.987 mph on lap 127 (Record).

Championship positions: 1 Tracy, 94; **2** Andretti, 70; **3** Zanardi, 67; **4** Moore and Pruett, 65; **6** Vasser, 57; **7** Gugelmin, 47; **8** de Ferran, 45; **9** Boesel, 39; **10** Unser Jr., 32; **11** Carpentier, 26; **12** Herta, 25; **13** Johnstone, 22; **14** Rahal, 20; **15** Ribeiro, 12; **16** Blundell, 11; **17** Fernandez, 9; **18** Hearn, 6; **19** Franchitti, 5; **20** Moreno, 3; **21** Salles, 1.

Ω
OMEGA
OFFICIAL TIMEKEEPER OF CART

DETROIT

PPG CART WORLD SERIES • ROUND 8

Photos: Michael C. Brown

Main photo: PacWest teammates Mauricio Gugelmin and Mark Blundell both held the lead on the final lap but first one and then the other ran out of fuel, allowing Greg Moore *(inset left)* to grab the win.

his attention switched to Blundell's similar Motorola Reynard, which had taken over the lead with less than a half-lap remaining. By now the entire team was collectively holding its breath. Around the Fountain section of the track, Blundell continued to lead confidently. Only two corners remained. The engine picked up cleanly from the exit of Turn 11, and Blundell accelerated down the short straightaway alongside the Detroit River before jumping hard on the brakes for Turn 12. All he needed from there was a brief burst of power. Then he could surely coast home to the victory. But, incredibly, as the Englishman jumped on the throttle, the motor died. Instinctively, Blundell sawed at the steering wheel, hoping to pick up the final dregs of methanol. But to no avail. The scavenge system on a modern-day Indy car is so efficient that not even a thimble-full remained. The Reynard coasted onward, but not with enough momentum to hold back the snarling pack of cars that had been poised for just such an eventuality.

An incredulous Greg Moore, who had shadowed the PacWest pair throughout the final stint, swept past to secure his second PPG CART World Series victory in as many weekends with Jerry Forsythe's Player's Ltd./Indeck Reynard-Mercedes.

'This is unbelievable,' said Moore. 'I feel bad for PacWest, but hey, we've

had more than a few disappointments of our own. When I saw Mo slow down and then Mark, I was on the radio, screaming to my guys, "He's stopped! He's stopped!" Unbelievable.'

The dramatic 77-lap race had gotten off to a hesitant start due to three early full-course cautions. Two were caused by the Tasman pair, Andre Ribeiro and Adrian Fernandez, both of whom slid into the tire barriers in separate and unrelated incidents. Team boss Steve Horne was none too pleased. The third delay was due to debris in the vicinity of Turn Eight after a polystyrene brake marker board was blown from its mountings.

Pole-winner Gil de Ferran remained out in front through all the early mishaps. On a track which offers notoriously few opportunities for overtaking, the Brazilian was able to control the pace with Derrick Walker's Valvoline/Cummins Reynard-Honda. Scott Pruett followed closely in second with his Brahma Reynard-Ford, with Roberto Moreno also driving impressively in his final outing as substitute for the injured Christian Fittipaldi in Newman/Haas Racing's Kmart/Budweiser Swift-Ford.

Pruett, though, suffered yet more misfortune as he succumbed to an engine failure after just 25 laps. Fellow championship contender Alex Zanardi fared no better, falling victim to a first-corner nudge from rookie Dario

THE tension was almost unbearable. With just one lap remaining in the ITT Automotive Detroit Grand Prix, PacWest teammates Mauricio Gugelmin and Mark Blundell were at the head of a long train of cars, just as they had been for the previous half-hour after eschewing the opportunity to make a pit stop during what proved, crucially, to be the final full-course caution of the day on lap 51.

But did they have enough fuel?

'I was pretty apprehensive,' admitted PacWest team owner Bruce McCaw, who, in pursuit of that elusive first CART victory, was fully prepared to roll

the dice, gambling that his cars could make it to the finish. 'I think I stopped breathing when the white flag came out. We were right on the ragged edge.'

Gugelmin had been short-shifting, striving to stretch the supply of methanol as the laps wound down. But as he fed in the power at the exit of Turn Seven, leading onto the fastest part of the course, his Hollywood Reynard-Mercedes suddenly faltered and died. Its tank was dry.

McCaw, sitting atop his timing cart in the pits, anxiously watching his television monitor, winced as the Brazilian's car slowed abruptly. Then

QUALIFYING

A pair of suspenseful qualifying sessions, one each on Friday and Saturday, set the tone for the remainder of the weekend. Scott Pruett, who claimed his first-ever Marlboro Pole Award on Belle Isle in 1996, again set the pace in the first session, fastest aboard Pat Patrick's #20 Brahma Reynard-Ford at 1m 09.57s.

As usual, though, Saturday's final half-hour brought wholesale improvements. Alex Zanardi, who had slid off the road on Friday, was the first to eclipse Pruett's mark, only to be usurped a few minutes later by Roberto Moreno. The Brazilian was making the most of what would be his final appearance for Newman/Haas Racing prior to Christian Fittipaldi's return.

Tire wear was crucial on the 2.1-mile temporary circuit, especially as the promoters had spent a considerable amount of time and effort in grinding down the track surface to eliminate the worst of the bumps which have traditionally taken a high toll on both cars and drivers. Those actions, however, resulted in an abnormally abrasive surface, ensuring that the latest breed of soft tires would lose optimum traction after a maximum of two laps.

As time ticked away, Gil de Ferran made a substantial improvement in his Valvoline/Cummins Reynard-Honda, leaping to the top of the timing charts and securing his second pole of the season.

'There was a lot of pressure,' said the delighted Brazilian. 'We knew we would get only one good lap out of the tires. You either do it then or you don't do it at all. Obviously I'm very glad to start from the front because this is a difficult track to pass on. Having said that, I think the most important thing for tomorrow will be to manage the tires.'

Pruett's best on Saturday ended up just three hundredths slower than de Ferran, with Moreno a similar margin behind in third. Zanardi also was close behind, followed by Dario Franchitti, who improved upon his previous career-best for the third time in as many races. Michael Andretti wound up a frustrated sixth after spinning off in Turn 12 on his final lap while attempting to pass an unusually obstructive Bobby Rahal.

143

Gil de Ferran forces his Valvoline Reynard inside the Kmart/Budweiser Swift of Roberto Moreno, with Jimmy Vasser poised to pounce on the slightest slip.

Improved reliability allowed Max Papis *(bottom right)* to claim an 11th-place finish with the Toyota-powered MCI Reynard and earn his first points of the year.

Photos: Michael C. Brown

Championship leader forced to stand down

PAUL Tracy, who led the PPG Cup standings by a healthy 24-point margin prior to the ITT Automotive Detroit Grand Prix, was prevented from competing in the race by what were described by CART Director of Medical Affairs Dr. Steve Olvey as 'severe cervical muscle spasms associated with mild vertigo.'

Tracy set the fastest time during practice on Friday morning but already knew there was something amiss after complaining of dizziness and light-headedness while driving the car – especially under braking. The affliction worsened on Saturday, leading to a consultation with Dr. Olvey, who suggested the symptoms were consistent with some kind of viral infection. Tracy was prescribed rest as the primary means of alleviating the effects of the virus, and after sleeping for no less than 13 hours overnight, he felt sufficiently improved on Sunday morning to take part in the usual half-hour warmup session. But almost right away he knew there was no hope of completing the 77-lap race.

Tracy met once again with Dr. Olvey, after which team owner Roger Penske quickly made the decision to officially withdraw the #3 Marlboro Penske-Mercedes.

'Paul said he still had this dizziness and he was somewhat blacking out,' reported Penske. 'The first thing I thought about was his accident at Michigan [in 1996]. At the end of the day, we don't want to put him in jeopardy as an individual and we certainly have to think about the other 27 drivers that are out there today.'

Tracy, indeed, was on a plane home to Parker, Ariz. even before the race was under way.

'Obviously this is a huge disappointment for the entire Marlboro team, especially since we're in the battle for the PPG Cup championship and every point counts,' said Tracy before leaving for the airport. 'The good news is that Dr. Olvey said I should be better in a few days and be ready to race in Portland.'

In the meantime, two of Tracy's closest rivals in the title-chase, Greg Moore and Michael Andretti, finished in the top two positions to move within nine and eight points respectively.

Franchitti, while PPG Cup points leader Tracy was unable even to start the race due to an obscure virus which caused him severe neck spasms and dizzy spells throughout practice and qualifying.

As the race approached one-third distance it became apparent the Firestone tires were wearing rather better than the Goodyears. Teammates Bryan Herta and Bobby Rahal were the first pit visitors, on laps 23 and 24 respectively, soon to be followed by the race leader, de Ferran, and then the Newman/Haas pair. By lap 30, Franchitti had taken over the lead and was running strongly ahead of Moore, Gugelmin, Jimmy Vasser, Blundell, Parker Johnstone and Raul Boesel. All were equipped with Firestones. Next, a distant eighth following his pit stop, was de Ferran.

Franchitti ran confidently out in front until diving into the pits for routine service on lap 33. Unfortunately, a problem with the refueling nozzle dropped him to the tail of the field. The young Scot also was later delayed by another unscheduled pit stop due to a broken front wing. All hope of a strong finish was long gone, yet Franchitti refused to give up. He set the fastest lap of the race – by more than a second – as he scurried back up the order, rising as high as 11th on the final lap before his exuberance caused him to make a minor mistake which dropped him to an unrepresentative 13th behind Max Papis and Christian Danner. It had been an impressive show.

Moore stayed out one more lap than Franchitti before making his first pit stop – under caution after Richie Hearn lost control of his unforgiving Lola and crashed in Turn 11. The extra hot laps, allied to the consistency of his Firestone tires, enabled Moore to rejoin ahead of de Ferran, Moreno and Andretti. Next were Gugelmin and Blundell, who also pitted on lap 34.

After the restart, Moore soon began to edge away from de Ferran, who in turn was able to put a little distance between himself and the third-placed car of Moreno. Just as the race appeared in danger of degenerating into a boring procession, however, the yellow flags flew for a fifth time, on lap 51, after Hiro Matsushita's Panasonic Reynard-Toyota ground to a halt just before the pit entrance.

The race suddenly took on a completely fresh perspective as different teams chose to employ a variety of strategies. Moore, for example, led the charge onto pit lane but opted not to change tires.

'The tires were working great,' he said, 'so we decided it was worth trying to save a couple of seconds and hopefully move up a place or two, because on this circuit, with overtaking being so tough, track position is everything.'

Moore duly beat his rivals out of the pits, only to find himself in fourth position behind Gugelmin, Blundell

and Patrick Carpentier (Alumax Reynard-Mercedes). The top three had decided to try and make it to the finish with just a single fuel stop.

Much to the chagrin of the single-stoppers, the pace car remained out on the track for only a couple of laps. And shortly afterward, Carpentier's team realized their young charge wouldn't be able to complete the distance. On lap 67, the French-Canadian pulled onto pit lane for a splash of methanol. Unfortunately, any hope of a good finish was lost when Carpentier failed to stop on his marks, costing him at least 20 seconds while the crew repositioned the car to complete the refueling process.

Gugelmin and Blundell, meanwhile, stuck to their guns.

As the laps wound down and neither PacWest driver made a move to come into the pits, so rival teams began to wonder whether perhaps they could make it after all. Nevertheless, even as he acknowledged the white flag

It was an encouraging day all round for Toyota, Juan Fangio II – seen leading Arnd Meier in Project Indy's Lola-Ford – taking 10th place with Dan Gurney's Castrol/Jockey Reynard.

Photos: Michael C. Brown

signalling one lap to go, Moore was content to follow in their wheel-tracks.

'Basically, I was happy with third place,' admitted Moore. 'We were going to get good points. Detroit's never been a good race for me, so we decided to just pick up the points and go on to [the next race in] Portland where we feel pretty confident we can have a good race.'

But the final act was yet to be played out. It spelled heartbreak for Bruce McCaw and his two drivers. And joy for Moore and car owner Jerry Forsythe.

'We thought we should have won some races last year and we came close so many times,' said Forsythe. 'Our first one last week was almost more of a relief. It took the pressure off of Greg and the team. I knew the second win would come sooner and come easier, but to win one week later is just fantastic! We're so proud of Greg and the whole team.'

The final-lap drama enabled Andretti to take a hard-won second place, moving him within eight points of the absent Tracy. Andretti, though, was hanging on for dear life in the closing stages after electing not to change tires during his final pit stop. De Ferran, who did take on fresh rubber, finished third after passing Moreno just four laps from the finish in a bold maneuver which took him two corners to complete. The resultant loss of momentum also cost Moreno a place to Vasser.

'We almost had a shot at the podium but it was very difficult to hold onto the car,' said Moreno. 'I think fifth was a good result for the Kmart/Budweiser team.'

So near and yet so far

THE increasing intensity and competitiveness of the PPG CART World Series has led to the adoption of ever more ambitious pit stop strategies as the teams look for a decisive advantage in the quest for those elusive victories – witness each one of the four most recent events.

In Brazil, Bobby Rahal gambled on being able to reach the finish without a splash-and-go fuel stop. Unfortunately, his ploy came up a couple of miles short. Two weeks later, on the Gateway International Raceway oval, veteran entrant Carl Hogan made what appeared to be an inspired call for Dario Franchitti – only for the rookie to be stymied by a broken transmission. Fuel management also proved to be the key for Greg Moore in Milwaukee.

This time it was the turn of PacWest to roll the dice. 'It looked like a pretty good call,' said team owner Bruce McCaw *(right)*. 'It was close. We just needed something to come our way – a couple of laps of yellow – and it never happened.'

The team had done its homework. In McCaw's hands at the end of the race was a chart displaying the results of the previous years' races on Belle Isle. In almost every instance there had been at least one full-course caution in the later stages. This time there was none.

McCaw's brave effort had been thwarted by the lack of just a few ounces of fuel, but he remained unbowed: 'It was the right call. We knew we were gambling but the whole team made the decision. Last week [in Milwaukee] we went conservative and it went against us. We'd definitely do the same thing again.'

'We planned on one stop from the start,' concurred Mauricio Gugelmin, 'and it was the right decision. We just didn't get the yellow that normally comes at this place. But that's racing. I'm proud of my team, I'm proud of my guys.'

Teammate Mark Blundell, who ground to a halt less than 100 yards from the finish line, was equally stoic: 'I honestly thought I had it. I knew I was tight on fuel obviously, but when Mo ran out, I felt confident I could make it to the end. My hat's off to the team. We took the risk and it nearly came off.'

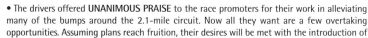

DETROIT SNIPPETS

• **CHRISTIAN DANNER** arrived in Detroit in his role as a co-owner of the Project Indy team, which returned to the fray after missing the race in Milwaukee due to Arnd Meier's crash at Gateway. But when rookie Paul Jasper vacated Payton/Coyne Racing's #34 Hype Lola, the charismatic German *(right)* was only too happy to step into the fray. Danner, who had not raced an Indy car for two years, showed remarkable form, actually proving fastest of the entire Lola contingent on Saturday morning! He drove well in the race, too, earning the team's first point of the season with a solid run to 12th.

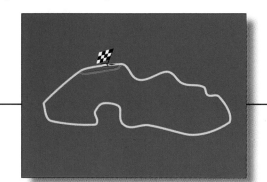

• **TOYOTA** also earned its best result of the season to date, with Juan Fangio II and Max Papis finishing 10th and 11th. Both, incidentally, were within a dozen seconds or so of the race winner. P.J. Jones and Hiro Matsushita also were still running at the finish.

• Moore's victory represented the fifth consecutive triumph for a Canadian driver. Consequently, the Maple Leafs held a handy 143–129 lead over the Americans in the CART **NATIONS CUP**.

• **MICHEL JOURDAIN JR.** drove one of Payton/Coyne Racing's '96 Lolas after his regular (unloved) '97 car was badly damaged at Milwaukee.

• The drivers offered **UNANIMOUS PRAISE** to the race promoters for their work in alleviating many of the bumps around the 2.1-mile circuit. Now all they want are a few overtaking opportunities. Assuming plans reach fruition, their desires will be met with the introduction of a new section of track which will extend beyond the current location of Turn Three, resulting in a much longer straightaway followed by a tight right-hand turn. The revised layout will rejoin the existing circuit at the present Turn Six.

• **BRYAN HERTA** lost a significant amount of time soon after his final pit stop, due to a stuck throttle sensor which caused his Ford/Cosworth engine to cut out. After refiring the motor, Herta guided Team Rahal's Shell Reynard from 15th place to seventh within the final 21 laps.

• Two days after the race in Detroit, **CHRISTIAN FITTIPALDI** climbed aboard the #11 Kmart/Budweiser Swift-Ford/Cosworth for the first time since his huge crash at Surfers Paradise. Fittipaldi, still wearing a cast to protect his broken right leg, acquitted himself extremely well during a two-day open CART test at Mid-Ohio and professed himself fit enough to return to action in Portland.

PPG CART WORLD SERIES • ROUND 8
ITT AUTOMOTIVE DETROIT GRAND PRIX

THE RACEWAY ON BELLE ISLE, DETROIT, MICHIGAN

JUNE 8, 77 laps – 161.700 miles

Place	Driver (Nat.)	No.	Team Sponsors Car-Engine	Tires	Q Speed	Q Time	Q Pos.	Laps	Time/Status	Ave. (mph)	Pts.
1	Greg Moore (CDN)	99	Forsythe Player's Ltd./Indeck Reynard 97I-Mercedes	FS	108.694	1m 09.553s	7	77	1h 52m 45.153s	86.047	20
2	Michael Andretti (USA)	6	Newman/Haas Kmart/Texaco Havoline Swift 007.i-Ford XD	GY	109.009	1m 09.352s	6	77	1h 52m 46.961s	86.024	16
3	Gil de Ferran (BR)	5	Walker Valvoline/Cummins Reynard 97I-Honda	GY	109.483	1m 09.052s	1	77	1h 52m 47.083s	86.022	16
4	Jimmy Vasser (USA)	1	Target/Chip Ganassi Racing Reynard 97I-Honda	FS	107.461	1m 10.351s	13	77	1h 52m 47.238s	86.020	12
5	Roberto Moreno (BR)	11	Newman/Haas Kmart/Budweiser Swift 007.i-Ford XD	GY	109.400	1m 09.104s	3	77	1h 52m 48.870s	86.000	10
6	Raul Boesel (BR)	40	Patrick Brahma Sports Team Reynard 97I-Ford XD	FS	107.129	1m 10.569s	14	77	1h 52m 49.507s	85.991	8
7	Bryan Herta (USA)	8	Team Rahal Shell Reynard 97I-Ford XD	GY	108.362	1m 09.766s	9	77	1h 52m 53.550s	85.940	6
8	Al Unser Jr. (USA)	2	Marlboro Team Penske Penske PC26-Mercedes	GY	106.952	1m 10.686s	16	77	1h 52m 54.522s	85.928	5
9	Bobby Rahal (USA)	7	Team Rahal Miller Lite Reynard 97I-Ford XD	GY	108.192	1m 09.876s	11	77	1h 52m 54.740s	85.925	4
10	Juan Fangio II (RA)	36	All American Racers Castrol/Jockey Reynard 97I-Toyota RV8B	GY	105.942	1m 11.360s	23	77	1h 52m 56.283s	85.906	3
11	Max Papis (I)	25	Arciero-Wells Racing MCI Reynard 97I-Toyota RV8B	FS	106.371	1m 11.072s	20	77	1h 52m 57.598s	85.889	2
12	Christian Danner (D)	34	Payton/Coyne Hype Lola T97/00-Ford XD	FS	106.228	1m 11.168s	21	77	1h 52m 57.915s	85.885	1
13	*Dario Franchitti (GB)	9	Hogan Racing LLC Reynard 97I-Mercedes	FS	109.111	1m 09.287s	5	77	1h 52m 58.568s	85.877	
14	P.J. Jones (USA)	98	All American Racers Castrol/Jockey Reynard 97I-Toyota RV8B	GY	105.398	1m 11.728s	24	77	1h 53m 46.171s	85.278	
15	*Patrick Carpentier (CDN)	16	Bettenhausen Alumax Aluminum Reynard 97I-Mercedes	GY	106.380	1m 11.066s	19	77	1h 54m 09.260s	84.990	
16	Mauricio Gugelmin (BR)	17	PacWest Racing Group Hollywood Reynard 97I-Mercedes	FS	108.540	1m 09.652s	8	76	Out of fuel		
17	Mark Blundell (GB)	18	PacWest Racing Group Motorola Reynard 97I-Mercedes	FS	108.323	1m 09.791s	10	76	Out of fuel		
18	*Arnd Meier (D)	64	Project Indy Hasseroder Pils/J.A.G. Lola T97/00-Ford XD	GY	103.118	1m 13.314s	27	75	Running		
19	Hiro Matsushita (J)	24	Arciero-Wells Panasonic/Duskin Reynard 97I-Toyota RV8B	FS	101.905	1m 14.187s	28	72	Running		
20	Parker Johnstone (USA)	27	Team KOOL Green Reynard 97I-Honda	FS	107.017	1m 10.643s	15	71	Engine		
21	*Gualter Salles (BR)	77	Davis Racing Indusval/Marlboro Reynard 97I-Ford XD	GY	106.073	1m 11.272s	22	61	Accident		
22	Michel Jourdain Jr. (MEX)	19	Payton/Coyne Herdez/Viva Mexico! Lola T96/00-Ford XD	FS	103.863	1m 12.788s	26	43	Accident		
23	Richie Hearn (USA)	21	Della Penna Ralphs/Food 4 Less Lola T97/00-Ford XD	GY	106.858	1m 10.748s	17	32	Accident		
24	Scott Pruett (USA)	20	Patrick Brahma Sports Team Reynard 97I-Ford XD	FS	109.435	1m 09.082s	2	25	Engine		
25	Andre Ribeiro (BR)	31	Tasman Motorsports LCI/Marlboro Lola T97/00-Honda	FS	106.857	1m 10.749s	18	10	Accident		
26	Alex Zanardi (I)	4	Target/Chip Ganassi Racing Reynard 97I-Honda	FS	109.268	1m 09.188s	4	1	Suspension		
27	Adrian Fernandez (MEX)	32	Tasman Tecate Beer/Quaker State Oil Lola T97/00-Honda	FS	105.210	1m 11.856s	25	0	Accident		
NS	Paul Tracy (CDN)	3	Marlboro Team Penske Penske PC26-Mercedes	GY	107.871	1m 10.084s	12	–	Driver illness		

* denotes Rookie driver

Caution flags: Laps 1–3, accident/Fernandez; laps 6–7, debris; laps 11–13, accident/Ribeiro; laps 33–40, accident/Hearn; laps 51–52, tow/Matsushita. **Total:** five for 18 laps.

Lap leaders: Gil de Ferran, 1–27 (27 laps); Roberto Moreno, 28 (1 lap); Dario Franchitti, 29–32 (4 laps); Greg Moore, 33–51 (19 laps); Mauricio Gugelmin, 52–76 (25 laps); Moore, 77 (1 lap). **Totals:** De Ferran, 27 laps; Gugelmin, 25 laps; Moore, 20 laps; Franchitti, 4 laps; Moreno, 1 lap.

Fastest race lap: Dario Franchitti, 1m 11.461s, 105.792 mph on lap 59 (Record).

Championship positions: 1 Tracy, 94; **2** Andretti, 86; **3** Moore, 85; **4** Vasser, 69; **5** Zanardi, 67; **6** Pruett, 65; **7** de Ferran, 61; **8** Gugelmin and Boesel, 47; **10** Unser Jr., 37; **11** Herta, 31; **12** Carpentier, 26; **13** Rahal, 24; **14** Johnstone, 22; **15** Moreno, 13; **16** Ribeiro, 12; **17** Blundell, 11; **18** Fernandez, 9; **19** Hearn, 6; **20** Franchitti, 5; **21** Fangio, 3; **22** Papis, 2; **23** Salles and Danner, 1.

PORTLAND

1 – BLUNDELL

2 – DE FERRAN

3 – BOESEL

Blundell claims first win

WHEN Mark Blundell overtook Gil de Ferran in the final, frantic dash to the checkered flag, the 31-year-old Englishman didn't realize the full implications of his maneuver.

'To be perfectly honest, with a couple of laps to go, [team manager] John Anderson had come over the radio and said the leader was six seconds in front,' related Blundell, 'and I didn't have a clue who the leader was, because he just said "the leader." So I was just going as quick as I could, and when I came up behind Gil, I didn't actually know he was leading the race. I just thought this was another guy I've got to pick off.

'When I saw the checkered flag, I wasn't sure. Normally the guys come on the radio and say "Good job" . . . or something else not quite so complimentary! Nothing came over the radio, so I thought, well, I'd better radio them and see where we finished, so, "Hey, guys, where did we come?" And nothing happened. About three corners later, all of a sudden somebody came on and said, "You won!" I went, na-ah! "You won!" And then I saw car #18 on the lap [leader] board and that was it. I mean, I gave the biggest ya-hoo on the radio! It was just great. Fantastic.

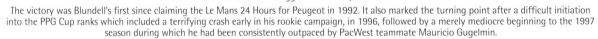

'It's been an unbelievable couple of weeks,' continued a jubilant Blundell. 'Detroit was a fantastic high for us – all but the last 300 feet – and then it was one of the biggest lows of my life. And now this!'

The victory was Blundell's first since claiming the Le Mans 24 Hours for Peugeot in 1992. It also marked the turning point after a difficult initiation into the PPG Cup ranks which included a terrifying crash early in his rookie campaign, in 1996, followed by a merely mediocre beginning to the 1997 season during which he had been consistently outpaced by PacWest teammate Mauricio Gugelmin.

'This win means a tremendous amount,' confirmed Blundell. 'I've been looking forward to winning a race for a while. When I came into CART racing with PacWest and Bruce [McCaw] last year, I felt we had the potential to win races. But last year was a tough season for us, we didn't really have as good a package as we would wish, but the team made some great changes over the winter and we've just been getting stronger and stronger – both me and Mauricio – and it's only been a matter of time before one of us would win a race.

'It means a fantastic amount to me to win in CART and to fly the flag for good old England. I feel really at home now and I'm looking forward to some more great results.'

Above: A moment to savor. England's Mark Blundell enjoys his maiden PPG Cup victory, having beaten Gil de Ferran by 0.027 seconds in the closest finish in CART history *(left)*.

Christian Fittipaldi *(opposite)* made a heroic comeback following the serious leg injuries he sustained in Australia, but had to settle for fourth place after opting to remain on wet-weather tires when the track dried out.

QUALIFYING

Two weeks earlier in Detroit, Scott Pruett had nabbed the provisional pole on Friday, only to be bested in the closing moments of the final session on Saturday by Gil de Ferran. The scenario in Portland seemed all too familiar. This time, however, after de Ferran usurped Pruett with less than three minutes remaining, the American had just enough time to respond with a spectacular new track record of 59.383s.

'It was pretty exciting from my standpoint,' said Pruett. 'When you're out there, you're giving it 110 percent. You're really taking some chances trying to yank off a quick lap.'

Earlier in the day, Pruett's previous best of 59.589s looked likely to be good enough. Practice on Saturday morning was held largely on a wet track, and when the first group of qualifiers took to the track at 12.30 p.m., the track remained quite damp. No one even came close to improving upon their Friday times.

'I was hoping it would rain all day,' smiled Pruett. 'And then about half an hour before qualifying was about to start I saw the blue sky and the sun peeking through the clouds and I said, "Guys, we've got to be ready to respond." We weren't going to go out unless people started running quickly – which they did almost right away.'

De Ferran was reasonably content with second on the grid with his Valvoline/Cummins Reynard-Honda, while the astonishing parity of equipment within the PPG Cup series was amply displayed by the fact four different chassis/engine/tire combinations filled the top four grid placings. Furthermore, the top 13 qualifiers were blanketed by less than one second.

Christian Fittipaldi was particularly impressive. The Brazilian was experiencing pain and discomfort from his right leg, still healing after being badly broken at Surfers Paradise in March. Nevertheless, Fittipaldi made spectacular progress before claiming a place on the inside of the second row of the grid with Newman/Haas Racing's Kmart/Budweiser Swift-Ford.

'Things have gone very well for me,' he said. 'Even though my leg is still broken and I am using a brace, I was pretty confident that we could go very quick.'

R EVENGE can be oh-so sweet. A mere two weeks after leading in Detroit and suffering the heartbreak of running out of fuel within sight of the finish line, Mark Blundell gained ample recompense by scoring a sensational last-gasp victory – the closest in CART history – at Portland International Raceway.

Changeable weather conditions provided an extra degree of excitement, although, ultimately, the Budweiser/G.I. Joe's 200 was decided by the timing of each team's final pit stop. It turned out to be a classic tortoise-and-hare contest.

With the entire field starting on grooved, wet-weather tires, pole-sitter Scott Pruett made full use of his clear vision to lead into the Festival Curves. Miraculously, there was no major incident at the notorious bottleneck, with Gil de Ferran slotting neatly into second place ahead of Mauricio Gugelmin. De Ferran, however, lasted only until lap two before spinning wildly into the infield before Turn One.

It was already apparent that the Goodyear Eagle wet-weather tires were no match for the Firestone Firehawks in heavy rain. Acknowledged rain-*meister* Christian Fittipaldi was driving brilliantly on his return to the series following the injury sustained at Surfers Paradise in March, but after only three laps even he was more than eight seconds adrift of the two leaders.

Gugelmin was content to allow Pruett to lead the way for the first four laps before powering past on the front straightaway. By lap 10, the inspired Brazilian had extended his lead to a whopping 11.5 seconds over Pruett. Dario Franchitti, though, was closing fast in third, and he, in turn, was coming under pressure from a charging Alex Zanardi, rapidly making up ground after being shuffled back to 11th place at the first corner.

Gugelmin's advantage was negated on lap 11 by the first of several full-course cautions, due to a marker cone having been dragged into the middle of the racing groove in Turn Two. The Hollywood Reynard-Mercedes quickly reestablished itself at the restart, however, leaving Pruett to hold off the attentions of Franchitti and Zanardi, who traded places on lap 15.

Blundell had moved into fifth immediately before the caution, ahead of Fittipaldi and Newman/Haas teammate Michael Andretti, who were leading the Goodyear 'class.' De Ferran also was in close attendance after his earlier gyration. The next best Goodyear runner was Paul Tracy in 12th.

'It was tough out there,' said the PPG Cup points leader. 'In the heavy rain, I was skating all over the place because I had no sidebite and no traction.'

When the rain intensified after 16 laps and standing water began to accumulate in a few locations, CART Chief Steward Wally Dallenbach wisely called once again for the pace car.

The running order remained unchanged when the race was restarted with 24 laps in the books. But not for long. On lap 28, Zanardi relegated Pruett with a bold move under braking in Turn One. Soon afterward, during another full-course caution made necessary when Christian Danner's Payton/Coyne Lola became stranded in the Festival Curves, the Italian's Target/Chip Ganassi pit crew stepped into the breach by completing its service faster than Gugelmin's PacWest team. Zanardi therefore moved to the head of the pack for the restart.

Zanardi and Gugelmin remained in close order for the next 33 laps,

although much of the time was spent under caution following a series of incidents. One of them saw Franchitti and Al Unser Jr. collide at the exit of the Festival Curves. Another yellow-flag period was caused by the stalled Brahma Reynard of Pruett, who had spun at the exit of Turn Nine. Shortly afterward, Bryan Herta was tipped into a spin at the Festival by Andre Ribeiro. Then P.J. Jones spun and stalled his ill-handling Reynard-Toyota.

During what turned out to be the final interruption of the afternoon, Zanardi's crew opted to call their man into the pits for routine service. By now it had become apparent the race would be halted at the two-hour mark, rather than run the full 98-lap distance, so the Italian had enough fuel to make it to the end. But what about tires? The rain clouds had departed toward the east and the track was beginning to dry, but not

yet enough to contemplate a change to slicks.

Furthermore, while the Goodyear contingent had been outclassed when the track was at its wettest, their tires, in turn, proved to be markedly superior in 'intermediate' conditions.

Zanardi's stop had enabled Gugelmin and Blundell to assume the top two positions after 60 laps. Coincidentally, as in Detroit, the PacWest Reynards were being shadowed by the similar Player's/Indeck car of Greg Moore, who had moved up stealthily into a challenging position. Tracy, too, was on the move as his Goodyear tires came into their own. By lap 62 he was up to third and closing on Blundell. At this stage all of the leaders required one more pit stop.

Tracy duly pulled onto pit lane next time around. Intriguingly, he chose to take on slick tires. But Tracy lasted only through the Festival Curves before los-

ing control and taking a long, lazy spin across the wet grass. He rejoined in a distant 15th, only to slide off the road again a couple of laps later.

'It was still awfully wet for cold, dry tires,' concluded Tracy after finishing seventh. 'It was really slippery. The conditions were pretty tough but we gave it our best shot.'

Raul Boesel, who had moved up to sixth in his Brahma Reynard-Ford, took the gamble for slicks a couple of laps after Tracy. He rejoined in 13th but soon began to turn some extremely fast lap times on the rapidly drying track.

Race leader Gugelmin followed Boesel into the pits for dry tires next time around, handing the lead briefly to Blundell before he, too, pulled in for slicks and a splash of methanol with 67 laps in the books – and less than 14 minutes remaining.

De Ferran, taking advantage of his durable Goodyear rain tires, inherited

the lead and was instructed by team owner Derrick Walker to try to make his rubber last. Fittipaldi employed an identical strategy. So, too, did Zanardi, although his Firestone wets already had begun to deteriorate.

Zanardi could not match the pace of the leading pair. By lap 74, he had fallen more than a dozen seconds behind and was seeking out the wettest sections of the track in a desperate attempt to cool his over-worked tires. Others, having changed to slicks, were as much as six seconds per lap faster.

Moore, Blundell and Boesel all closed in rapidly as Zanardi braked hard at the end of the front straight-away on lap 75; and in the inevitable incident, Zanardi slid straight across the gravel trap and out the other side. Blundell took advantage of the melee by also nipping past Moore into what was now third position. Five corners

later, Zanardi slithered wide onto the grass in Turn Five, costing him another handful of positions.

Blundell now had clear passage toward the two leaders, de Ferran and Fittipaldi, and even though they were almost seven seconds in front at the completion of lap 75, that margin was quickly eroded. The only problem for Blundell was the clock. A mere three minutes remained before the two-hour limit. Now it had become a race against time.

On lap 77, Blundell powered past Fittipaldi at the end of the curving back straightaway. The Motorola Reynard-Mercedes immediately closed onto the tail of de Ferran's Valvoline/Cummins Reynard-Honda, and as the two leaders flashed across the start/finish line they were greeted by Jim Swintal's white flag. Only one lap remained. And de Ferran had been kept fully apprised of the situation via radio. If he could just

stay in front of the Englishman for another 1.967 miles . . .

Blundell's task was made even more difficult by the fact that the prime overtaking point, under braking for the Festival Curves, was rendered a no-passing zone by a local yellow flag, warning of the stationary #1 Target Reynard of Jimmy Vasser, who had been punted into a spin a couple of laps from the finish.

De Ferran stuck grimly to his task, making sure he kept the door firmly closed in each of the remaining braking areas. So the outcome hinged on the final quarter-mile dash to the finish line.

'I pretty much knew what he was going to do because I would have done exactly the same thing,' related Blundell. 'He got off the gas a little earlier, to try to slow the pace down, but I jumped out of mine a little bit too, got the boost rolling and came off the turn just a snatch quicker. With the slicks

working, up to temperature, that just made all the difference. It was a drag race to the line. It's sheer traction at that point. But he was on wets – worn wets – and I was on slicks; and I came off the corner a whole bunch faster.'

Blundell gradually inched alongside de Ferran as they accelerated down the main straight before finally nosing ahead merely 100 yards or so before the finish line to ensure the closest victory in CART history – by a scant 0.027 seconds. Almost lost in the excitement, Boesel also was within a whisker of demoting de Ferran. As it was, Boesel finished third, just 0.055 seconds – less than a car length – behind Blundell. Fittipaldi and Moore also were just out of the frame in what was literally a photo-finish, while even Gugelmin and Tracy were barely more than three seconds behind in a breathless climax to what had been an enthralling auto race.

Raul Boesel flashed across the finish line in third place, a few feet behind the winner. It was a welcome return to the podium for the Brazilian, who was showing his true worth in Pat Patrick's Brahma Sports Team after a couple of lean years.

Overleaf: Having seen victory snatched from him at the death, Gil de Ferran was still waiting for his first win for the Walker team.

PORTLAND SNIPPETS

• A silent **AUCTION OF RACING MEMORABILIA** hosted a few days prior to the Portland race by PacWest principal Bruce McCaw and wife Jolene raised more than $31,000 for the Seattle Center Peace Academy.

Photos: Michael C. Brown

• Hogan Racing engineer **STEVE CONOVER**, who suffered a broken back in an accident on the beach at Surfers Paradise, was delighted after doctors removed his 'halo' head-brace. 'I'll miss the rearview mirrors,' quipped Conover, 'but I can learn to live with that!'

• Equipped with an ex-Team Rahal Reynard 97I chassis for the first time, Payton/Coyne Racing's **MICHEL JOURDAIN JR.** *(left)* posted a superb performance by climbing from 22nd on the grid to 10th inside the first 27 laps. The 20-year-old Mexican held on to claim his first-ever PPG Cup point despite fading with badly worn tires in the closing stages.

• After being routed by Goodyear in the last true test of **WET-WEATHER TIRES**, at Detroit in 1996, the Firestone engineers launched an intensive development program which included evaluation of no fewer than 40 different constructions and compounds. Much of the testing was carried out at Firebird Raceway, Ariz., where 400,000 gallons of water were pumped onto the track to simulate wet conditions.

• The hard-working **LOLA** engineers produced new rear uprights and other suspension components for their unloved T97/00 chassis, but the handling difficulties remained.

• **JIMMY VASSER**'s streak of 24 consecutive finishes came to an end when his Target Reynard-Honda was punted off the road a couple of laps before the finish. 'It's a shame the streak had to come to an end,' said Vasser *(below)*, who had been struggling in the drying conditions on well-worn Firestone wet-weather tires, 'but it's a real credit to my team and the equipment they gave me that we were able to go as long as we did.'

• **HIDEKI NODA** made a piece of history by winning the PPG-Firestone Indy Lights Championship event – the first victory both for himself and Indy Regency Racing team owner Sal Incandela. Noda thus became the first Japanese driver ever to win a CART-sanctioned event. 'His win is particularly appropriate as we look to conduct CART's first Japanese race – at Twin Ring Motegi – in 1998,' said CART President Andrew Craig.

PPG CART WORLD SERIES • ROUND 9

BUDWEISER/G.I. JOE'S 200
PRESENTED BY TEXACO/HAVOLINE

PORTLAND INTERNATIONAL RACEWAY,
OREGON

JUNE 22, 78 laps – 153.426 miles

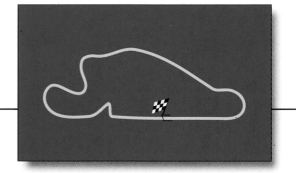

Place	Driver (Nat.)	No.	Team Sponsors Car-Engine	Tires	Q Speed	Q Time	Q Pos.	Laps	Time/Status	Ave. (mph)	Pts.
1	Mark Blundell (GB)	18	PacWest Racing Group Motorola Reynard 97I-Mercedes	FS	117.710	1m 00.158s	11	78	2h 00m 12.982s	76.575	20
2	Gil de Ferran (BR)	5	Walker Valvoline/Cummins Reynard 97I-Honda	GY	119.126	59.443s	2	78	2h 00m 13.009s	76.575	16
3	Raul Boesel (BR)	40	Patrick Brahma Sports Team Reynard 97I-Ford XD	FS	117.532	1m 00.249s	14	78	2h 00m 13.037s	76.574	14
4	Christian Fittipaldi (BR)	11	Newman/Haas Kmart/Budweiser Swift 007.i-Ford XD	GY	118.510	59.752s	3	78	2h 00m 14.051s	76.564	12
5	Greg Moore (CDN)	99	Forsythe Player's Ltd./Indeck Reynard 97I-Mercedes	FS	117.810	1m 00.107s	9	78	2h 00m 14.088s	76.563	10
6	Mauricio Gugelmin (BR)	17	PacWest Racing Group Hollywood Reynard 97I-Mercedes	FS	118.296	59.860s	4	78	2h 00m 16.021s	76.543	9
7	Paul Tracy (CDN)	3	Marlboro Team Penske Penske PC26-Mercedes	GY	117.540	1m 00.245s	13	78	2h 00m 16.125s	76.542	6
8	Michael Andretti (USA)	6	Newman/Haas Kmart/Texaco Havoline Swift 007.i-Ford XD	GY	118.116	59.951s	6	78	2h 00m 32.194s	76.372	5
9	Parker Johnstone (USA)	27	Team KOOL Green Reynard 97I-Honda	FS	115.329	1m 01.400s	19	78	2h 00m 45.099s	76.235	4
10	Adrian Fernandez (MEX)	32	Tasman Tecate Beer/Quaker State Oil Lola T97/00-Honda	FS	115.527	1m 01.295s	16	78	2h 01m 00.867s	76.070	3
11	Alex Zanardi (I)	4	Target/Chip Ganassi Racing Reynard 97I-Honda	FS	117.979	1m 00.021s	7	78	2h 01m 11.898s	75.955	2
12	Michel Jourdain Jr. (MEX)	19	Payton/Coyne Herdez/Viva Mexico! Reynard 97I-Ford XD	FS	114.322	1m 01.941s	22	78	2h 01m 26.104s	75.806	1
13	Andre Ribeiro (BR)	31	Tasman Motorsports LCI/Marlboro Lola T97/00-Honda	FS	115.194	1m 01.472s	20	77	Running		
14	Richie Hearn (USA)	21	Della Penna Ralphs/Food 4 Less Lola T97/00-Ford XD	GY	113.996	1m 02.118s	24	77	Running		
15	Hiro Matsushita (J)	24	Arciero-Wells Panasonic/Duskin Reynard 97I-Toyota RV8B	FS	112.925	1m 02.707s	27	77	Running		
16	*Patrick Carpentier (CDN)	16	Bettenhausen Alumax Aluminum Reynard 97I-Mercedes	GY	114.174	1m 02.021s	23	76	Running		
17	Scott Pruett (USA)	20	Patrick Brahma Sports Team Reynard 97I-Ford XD	FS	119.246	59.383s	1	76	Running		1
18	*Arnd Meier (D)	64	Project Indy Hasseroder Pils/J.A.G. Lola T97/00-Ford XD	GY	111.422	1m 03.553s	28	75	Running		
19	Jimmy Vasser (USA)	1	Target/Chip Ganassi Racing Reynard 97I-Honda	FS	117.973	1m 00.024s	8	74	Spun off		
20	P.J. Jones (USA)	98	All American Racers Castrol/Jockey Reynard 97I-Toyota RV8B	GY	115.333	1m 01.398s	18	74	Running		
21	Bryan Herta (USA)	8	Team Rahal Shell Reynard 97I-Ford XD	GY	117.571	1m 00.229s	12	74	Running		
22	Juan Fangio II (RA)	36	All American Racers Castrol/Jockey Reynard 97I-Toyota RV8B	GY	115.367	1m 01.380s	17	73	Running		
23	*Gualter Salles (BR)	77	Davis Racing Indusval/Marlboro Reynard 97I-Ford XD	GY	115.072	1m 01.537s	21	67	Engine fire		
24	Bobby Rahal (USA)	7	Team Rahal Miller Lite Reynard 97I-Ford XD	GY	117.722	1m 00.152s	10	39	Withdrawn		
25	Al Unser Jr. (USA)	2	Marlboro Team Penske Penske PC26-Mercedes	GY	116.803	1m 00.625s	15	34	Accident		
26	*Dario Franchitti (GB)	9	Hogan Motor Leasing Reynard 97I-Mercedes	FS	118.264	59.876s	5	34	Accident		
27	Christian Danner (D)	34	Payton/Coyne Racing Lola T97/00-Ford XD	FS	113.361	1m 02.466s	26	28	Transmission		
28	Max Papis (I)	25	Arciero-Wells Racing MCI Reynard 97I-Toyota RV8B	FS	113.665	1m 02.299s	25	26	Transmission		

* denotes Rookie driver

Caution flags: Laps 10–12, debris; laps 17–23, standing water; laps 29–33, tow/Danner; laps 35–37, accident/Unser and Franchitti; laps 45–46, tow/Pruett; laps 49–50, tow/Herta; laps 53–55, tow/Jones. **Total:** seven for 24 laps.

Lap leaders: Scott Pruett, 1–4 (4 laps); Mauricio Gugelmin, 5–30 (26 laps); Alex Zanardi, 31–53 (23 laps); Gugelmin, 54–65 (12 laps); Mark Blundell, 66 (1 lap); Gil de Ferran, 67–77 (11 laps); Blundell, 78 (1 lap). **Totals:** Gugelmin, 38 laps; Zanardi, 23 laps; de Ferran, 11 laps; Pruett, 4 laps; Blundell, 2 laps.

Fastest race lap: Raul Boesel, 1m 03.122s, 112.183 mph on lap 76.

Championship positions: 1 Tracy, 100; **2** Moore, 95; **3** Andretti, 91; **4** de Ferran, 77; **5** Zanardi and Vasser, 69; **7** Pruett, 66; **8** Boesel, 61; **9** Gugelmin, 56; **10** Unser Jr., 37; **11** Blundell and Herta, 31; **13** Carpentier and Johnstone, 26; **15** Rahal, 24; **16** Moreno, 13; **17** Fittipaldi, Ribeiro and Fernandez, 12; **20** Hearn, 6; **21** Franchitti, 5; **22** Fangio, 3; **23** Papis, 2; **24** Salles, Danner and Jourdain, 1.

Ω OMEGA
OFFICIAL TIMEKEEPER OF CART

Michael C. Brown

CLEVELAND

1 – ZANARDI

2 – DE FERRAN

3 – HERTA

Total commitment. Alex Zanardi's Target Reynard kicks up the dust as he closes on the slower car of Gualter Salles during the course of a superb recovery drive that yielded him a breathtaking victory.

'I was a man on a mission,' said Zanardi, who passed Gil de Ferran with six laps remaining to score an emphatic victory. 'I was just driving as hard as I could.'

Zanardi was on irrepressible form all weekend. And after securing the ninth $10,000 Marlboro Pole Award of his career, he was confident of being able to add the $90,000 roll-over bonus, unclaimed since Tracy won from the pole at Nazareth in April: 'I know we have the car, we have the speed. I just hope nobody tries to win the race at the first turn – or at least, if he does, he doesn't take me out with him.'

Zanardi's fears proved unfounded as the 28-car field funnelled cleanly into the notoriously tight, right-handed hairpin at the end of a massively wide start/finish straightaway. De Ferran's Valvoline/Cummins Reynard-Honda slotted into second, followed by Christian Fittipaldi, who made a fine start from fifth in his Kmart/Budweiser Swift-Ford. Portland winner Mark Blundell (Motorola/PacWest Reynard-Mercedes) ran next, although the Englishman lost three positions – to Bryan Herta (Shell Reynard-Ford), Paul Tracy (Marlboro Penske-Mercedes) and Michael Andretti (Kmart/Texaco Havoline Swift-Ford) – on lap two as he battled to adjust a balky fuel mixture knob in the cockpit.

Zanardi gradually extended his advantage over de Ferran, leaving de Ferran to come under pressure from Fittipaldi.

Tracy, meanwhile, after struggling throughout practice and qualifying with a persistent oversteer, found the car noticeably improved following some changes prior to the race morning warmup. The PPG Cup points leader battled his way from 10th to fifth inside the first two laps, and gained one more position on lap 11 when Herta was inadvertently pushed onto the grass at the exit of the final chicane by PPG Cup debutant Charles Nearburg, who was well off the pace in one of Payton/Coyne Racing's Lola-Fords.

The first and only full-course caution of the day came on lap 22 after Richie Hearn's Ralphs/Food 4 Less Lola blew its left-rear tire and spun into the barriers in Turn Nine.

Next time around, after consultation with his crew on the radio, Zanardi decided to duck into the pits for his first routine service. Unfortunately, he had failed to notice the red board with a large 'P' situated at the entrance to pit road which signified the pits were still officially closed for business due to some debris deposited during Hearn's spectacular exit.

A FTER winning the Friends of Jim Trueman Rookie of the Year Award in 1996, Alex Zanardi began the new season as one of the hot favorites for PPG Cup honors. But following a strong start to his sophomore campaign, the 30-year-old Italian's title aspirations were dented by a series of lackluster performances on the short ovals as well as some plain bad luck at both Detroit and Portland. Going into the Medic Drug Grand Prix of Cleveland, Zanardi was tied for fifth in the standings, 31 points behind series leader Paul Tracy, and was in desperate need of a turnaround in his fortunes.

Zanardi responded by qualifying his Target Reynard-Honda on the pole by a comfortable margin and establishing an appreciable cushion over his pursuers in the early stages. But then he was penal-ized – not once but twice – for separate pit lane violations. Zanardi fell to a distant 22nd. All hopes of a strong finish seemed to have been dashed.

'I wasn't, obviously, very happy,' he related, 'but I never thought that everything was lost. I didn't want my emotions to influence my driving. I let myself get mad after the race is over; until then I do whatever I can, I give 100 percent every single second.'

Sure enough, Zanardi provided one of the most astonishing solo performances of the season as he charged back into contention. He was clearly the fastest man on the track. By the end of the afternoon, Christian Fittipaldi was ranked second in the best lap report. Zanardi, however, had posted no fewer than 16 laps quicker than the Brazilian's best!

Tasman returns to prominence

STEVE Horne's Tasman Motorsports Group bounced back to prominence after Andre Ribeiro was equipped with a Reynard 97I chassis recently acquired from Walker Racing. The car, chassis 022, finished fifth at Surfers Paradise in the hands of Gil de Ferran and won the pole in Long Beach but did not race due to a ferocious crash during practice. Since then it had been relegated to test duties.

Ribeiro shook the car down only briefly at Mid-Ohio but immediately was more comfortable than in his regular Lola T97/00.

'The car feels light and easy to drive,' said Ribeiro, who ended the first day fifth on the provisional grid. 'And it's balanced. That's the big difference. If it's balanced, it's easier to have grip. We made some small changes and the car was very responsive. It was good to have this feeling again where small changes make a difference. We have a lot to learn about this car but there is definitely a lot of potential.'

Ribeiro rose as high as second during final qualifying before securing eighth on the grid. By comparison, his season-to-date best with the Lola had been 13th at Surfers Paradise. The Brazilian finished the race out of the points in 14th but remained optimistic for the remainder of the season.

'We definitely learned a lot,' he said. 'We were competitive in terms of lap times but because of a few mistakes I made, we lost some positions. I had problems with down-shifting and braking. The car was great and we should have finished higher, but this is my first race with this car and I am very pleased.'

Teammate Adrian Fernandez meanwhile persevered with the Lola, which boasted several dramatic developments for the race weekend in Cleveland, including a brand-new, stiffer gearbox casing made of aluminum rather than magnesium, and new rear uprights, bellhousing and other suspension components. Unfortunately, the new parts provided no real improvement.

'The car is still very difficult to drive,' said Fernandez. 'The back end just doesn't inspire any confidence. It's completely unpredictable.'

The Mexican retained a good attitude, despite his obvious disappointment, as he finished a lap down in 17th. Afterward, Ribeiro offered his sympathy: 'With our performance this weekend in the Reynard, I think people can now see our problem was not with the drivers, the team, the engineers or the tires,' said Ribeiro. 'It was the car.'

Above: The Kmart/Budweiser pit crew's well-drilled routine was thrown into confusion when Christian Fittipaldi's Swift suffered an air-jack failure which left the right-rear corner grounded, but the Brazilian fought back to take sixth place at the flag.

Left: Richie Hearn triggered the caution period that was to shape the race when his Ralphs/Food 4 Less Lola spun into the barriers after a tire deflated.

Right: It's thumbs-up for his new Reynard from Andre Ribeiro. Having said farewell to his troublesome Lola, the revitalized Brazilian could look forward to a competitive second half of the season.

Bryan Herta was powerless to resist
Alex Zanardi's charge, but third place
represented his best result of the season
to date with Bobby Rahal's Shell Reynard.

'I should have seen the board,' admitted Zanardi later. 'I didn't. I cannot blame anybody [but myself].'

Operating blithely on the 'follow the leader' premise, several other contenders – namely Tracy, Andretti, Mauricio Gugelmin, Dario Franchitti and Juan Fangio – also pulled onto pit lane. De Ferran, running second on the road, was not among them.

'I saw the sign,' said de Ferran, 'and to be honest I was amazed when Alex came in.'

De Ferran and the remainder of the field – save Blundell, whose crew figured it was too early to complete the distance with just one more pit stop – waited one more lap before taking on fuel and fresh tires. Accordingly, they fell into line behind Zanardi and company, although, to their credit, the CART officials quickly issued instructions for the transgressors to fall back in line behind those who had followed the correct procedure.

The resultant shuffling of positions ensured that the caution period was extended by a couple of laps, during which the Target/Chip Ganassi crew shrewdly called Zanardi into the pits one more time for a splash of methanol. The decision was to prove crucial. Sure, the additional stop dropped him almost to the back of the pack, but while the other leaders were

obliged to conserve fuel in order to reach the finish with only one more pit stop, Zanardi was able to run flat-out with the mixture on full-rich.

The extra few laps of caution also scuppered Blundell's plans. If the race had been restarted immediately following the usual clean-up, the Motorola car might have been able to complete the race with one fewer pit stop, which *could* have proved decisive. It was not to be. After relinquishing the lead immediately after the restart and making his pit stop under green-flag conditions, the Englishman played catch-up for the remainder of the afternoon.

De Ferran took off into the lead when the race was restarted with 32 laps completed, but Zanardi's troubles weren't over. This time he was assessed a 'drive-through' penalty for violating the blend line rule while exiting the pits after his initial visit. By the time he rejoined, Zanardi was well adrift of the main pack in 22nd position.

De Ferran soon established a slim lead ahead of Fittipaldi, who remained within a second or so and never allowed his countryman to relax.

Jimmy Vasser outbraked Herta into Turn One at the restart, while behind them Scott Pruett (Brahma Reynard-Ford) made a better exit from the hairpin to usurp Greg Moore (Player's

Reynard-Mercedes) prior to Turn Three. As usual, the Burke Lakefront Airport was providing plenty of exciting action for the record-sized crowd.

Herta repassed Vasser with a neat, incisive maneuver into Turn One on lap 41, and over the next eight laps he gradually halved a 4.7-second deficit to Fittipaldi – only for all his hard work to be nullified once again by a slower car, this time the Panasonic/Duskin Reynard-Toyota of Hiro Matsushita.

On lap 58, de Ferran pulled onto pit lane for his second routine stop. Most of the remainder of the field followed suit next time around, although both Fittipaldi and Herta waited until lap 60 before taking on service. Cruelly, Fittipaldi's excellent drive was neutered by an air-jack failure which cost him almost half a minute.

Zanardi actually led a couple of laps before stopping on lap 62, and his torrid pace allowed him to exit the pits in fifth behind de Ferran, Blundell (who had yet to make his final stop), Herta and Moore.

On lap 68, Moore's solid run ended prematurely due to a rare engine failure. Shortly afterward, fellow title contender Andretti also fell by the wayside due to an electrical problem.

Zanardi was now in third, some six seconds behind Herta, who in turn was

almost 10 seconds behind de Ferran. The margins diminished rapidly as the top duo both were having to conserve fuel. Herta also was hindered by fading brakes.

'I drove as hard as I could to keep him behind me,' said Herta, who went on to secure a solid third, 'but it was hopeless. I was having to over-drive the car and finally I slid wide on one corner, which allowed him to get a run on me.'

Zanardi moved into second with a dozen laps remaining, then reduced the deficit to de Ferran at the astonishing rate of a second per lap.

'I could see him making ground on me,' said de Ferran. 'I was pushing hard but I was really on a fuel economy run. I had to run leaner and leaner just to get to the end.'

Zanardi finally slipped through under braking for Turn One on lap 85, his magnificent recovery drive complete. The remaining handful of laps proved to be no problem at all.

'There are no words to express my happiness,' said Zanardi, who celebrated his stunning success with a series of tire-smoking donuts in front of the pits. 'All credit to my engineer, Mo Nunn, who gave me a perfect car right at the start of the weekend. I got the most out of the car that it had to offer, drove 120 percent the whole way. It's a very good feeling.'

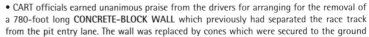

CLEVELAND SNIPPETS

• Marlboro Team Penske duo **AL UNSER JR.** and **PAUL TRACY** struggled throughout practice and qualifying but found their Mercedes-powered cars noticeably improved after some extensive changes prior to the final warmup. Tracy's progress was hindered by the penalty for pitting while the pits were closed, but Unser took advantage of excellent strategy *(right)* to earn a confidence-boosting fourth.

• **CHRISTIAN FITTIPALDI**'s preparations for the race were interrupted by a heavy crash during a test at Road America, caused by a front suspension pushrod failure. The Brazilian, who was fortunate not to suffer any additional injury to his broken right leg, drove impressively all weekend. He fell to 12th after a mishap in the pits but charged back to sixth at the finish.

• **MARK BLUNDELL** was fast all weekend in his Motorola Reynard-Mercedes, but lost all chance of a good result due to his team's chosen pit strategy: 'That's the way the cookie crumbles,' said the Englishman, who passed Patrick Carpentier, Parker Johnstone and Dario Franchitti within the final three laps to finish ninth.

• CART officials earned unanimous praise from the drivers for arranging for the removal of a 780-foot long **CONCRETE-BLOCK WALL** which previously had separated the race track from the pit entry lane. The wall was replaced by cones which were secured to the ground and offered the additional benefit of improved sight lines for spectators. The work was carried out in time for the Sunday morning warmup after some safety concerns had been voiced during the regular drivers' meeting on Saturday afternoon.

• **GUALTER SALLES** equaled his previous best qualifying position, 12th, with Davis Racing's Indusval Reynard-Ford and looked to be on course for a points-paying finish until hindered by a broken clutch.

• The engineers from **LOLA CARS** provided a whole host of revisions for their difficult T97/00 chassis, but to no avail. 'It's like having a $10 phone bill and searching under your cushions to pay the bill with pennies,' said a disappointed Richie Hearn. 'It might be too little too late. Every morning I keep waking up hoping, hoping.'

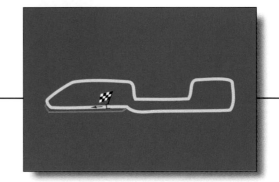

PPG CART WORLD SERIES • ROUND 10
MEDIC DRUG GRAND PRIX OF CLEVELAND

BURKE LAKEFRONT AIRPORT,
CLEVELAND, OHIO

JULY 13, 90 laps – 189.540 miles

Place	Driver (Nat.)	No.	Team Sponsors Car-Engine	Tires	Q Speed	Q Time	Q Pos.	Laps	Time/Status	Ave. (mph)	Pts.
1	Alex Zanardi (I)	4	Target/Chip Ganassi Racing Reynard 97I-Honda	FS	133.048	56.984s	1	90	1h 41m 40.661s	111.848	22
2	Gil de Ferran (BR)	5	Walker Valvoline/Cummins Reynard 97I-Honda	GY	131.822	57.514s	2	90	1h 41m 41.942s	111.824	16
3	Bryan Herta (USA)	8	Team Rahal Shell Reynard 97I-Ford XD	GY	131.163	57.803s	7	90	1h 41m 58.626s	111.519	14
4	Al Unser Jr. (USA)	2	Marlboro Team Penske Penske PC26-Mercedes	GY	129.352	58.612s	18	90	1h 42m 05.176s	111.400	12
5	Bobby Rahal (USA)	7	Team Rahal Miller Lite Reynard 97I-Ford XD	GY	130.774	57.975s	9	90	1h 42m 08.080s	111.347	10
6	Christian Fittipaldi (BR)	11	Newman/Haas Kmart/Budweiser Swift 007.i-Ford XD	GY	131.251	57.764s	5	90	1h 42m 15.453s	111.213	8
7	Paul Tracy (CDN)	3	Marlboro Team Penske Penske PC26-Mercedes	GY	130.760	57.981s	10	90	1h 42m 23.949s	111.060	6
8	Scott Pruett (USA)	20	Patrick Brahma Sports Team Reynard 97I-Ford XD	FS	130.125	58.264s	16	90	1h 42m 29.835s	110.953	5
9	Mark Blundell (GB)	18	PacWest Racing Group Motorola Reynard 97I-Mercedes	FS	131.767	57.538s	3	90	1h 42m 30.058s	110.949	4
10	Parker Johnstone (USA)	27	Team KOOL Green Reynard 97I-Honda	FS	130.033	58.305s	17	90	1h 42m 30.805s	110.936	3
11	*Dario Franchitti (GB)	9	Hogan Motor Leasing Reynard 97I-Mercedes	FS	130.548	58.075s	11	90	1h 42m 31.709s	110.919	2
12	*Patrick Carpentier (CDN)	16	Bettenhausen Alumax Aluminum Reynard 97I-Mercedes	GY	129.156	58.701s	19	90	1h 42m 32.061s	110.913	1
13	Jimmy Vasser (USA)	1	Target/Chip Ganassi Racing Reynard 97I-Honda	FS	130.174	58.242s	15	90	1h 42m 33.300s	110.891	
14	Andre Ribeiro (BR)	31	Tasman Motorsports LCI/Marlboro Reynard 97I-Honda	FS	130.896	57.921s	8	90	1h 42m 33.942s	110.879	
15	Mauricio Gugelmin (BR)	17	PacWest Racing Group Hollywood Reynard 97I-Mercedes	FS	131.190	57.791s	6	90	1h 42m 34.802s	110.864	
16	Raul Boesel (BR)	40	Patrick Brahma Sports Team Reynard 97I-Ford XD	FS	130.297	58.187s	14	90	1h 42m 35.810s	110.846	
17	Adrian Fernandez (MEX)	32	Tasman Tecate Beer/Quaker State Oil Lola T97/00-Honda	FS	125.694	1m 00.318s	25	89	Running		
18	Michel Jourdain Jr. (MEX)	19	Payton/Coyne Herdez/Viva Mexico! Reynard 97I-Ford XD	FS	128.014	59.225s	20	88	Running		
19	*Gualter Salles (BR)	77	Davis Racing Indusval/Marlboro Reynard 97I-Ford XD	GY	130.394	58.144s	12	88	Running		
20	Hiro Matsushita (J)	24	Arciero-Wells Panasonic/Duskin Reynard 97I-Toyota RV8B	FS	123.949	1m 01.167s	26	86	Running		
21	Juan Fangio II (RA)	36	All American Racers Castrol/Jockey Reynard 97I-Toyota RV8B	GY	126.880	59.754s	23	85	Engine		
22	*Arnd Meier (D)	64	Project Indy Hasseroder Pils/J.A.G. Lola T97/00-Ford XD	GY	123.394	1m 01.442s	27	78	Running		
23	Michael Andretti (USA)	6	Newman/Haas Kmart/Texaco Havoline Swift 007.i-Ford XD	GY	131.541	57.637s	4	74	Engine		
24	Greg Moore (CDN)	99	Forsythe Player's Ltd./Indeck Reynard 97I-Mercedes	FS	130.369	58.155s	13	67	Engine		
25	P.J. Jones (USA)	98	All American Racers Castrol/Jockey Reynard 97I-Toyota RV8B	GY	126.955	59.719s	21	42	Transmission		
26	*Charles Nearburg (USA)	34	Payton/Coyne Nearburg Exploration Lola T97/00-Ford XD	FS	119.916	1m 03.224s	28	34	Handling		
27	Max Papis (I)	25	Arciero-Wells Racing MCI Reynard 97I-Toyota RV8B	FS	126.899	59.745s	22	22	Engine		
28	Richie Hearn (USA)	21	Della Penna Ralphs/Food 4 Less Lola T97/00-Ford XD	GY	126.013	1m 00.165s	24	20	Tire/accident		

* denotes Rookie driver

Caution flags: Laps 21–31, accident/Hearn. **Total:** one for 11 laps.

Lap leaders: Alex Zanardi, 1–22 (22 laps); Gil de Ferran, 23 (1 lap); Mark Blundell, 24–32 (9 laps); de Ferran, 33–57 (25 laps); Christian Fittipaldi, 58–59 (2 laps); Zanardi, 60–61 (2 laps); de Ferran, 62–84 (23 laps); Zanardi, 85–90 (6 laps). **Totals:** de Ferran, 49 laps; Zanardi, 30 laps; Blundell, 9 laps; Fittipaldi, 2 laps.

Fastest race lap: Alex Zanardi, 58.666s, 129.233 mph on lap 82.

Championship positions: 1 Tracy, 106; **2** Moore, 95; **3** de Ferran, 94; **4** Andretti, 91; **5** Zanardi, 90; **6** Pruett, 71; **7** Vasser, 69; **8** Boesel, 61; **9** Gugelmin, 56; **10** Unser Jr., 49; **11** Herta, 45; **12** Blundell, 35; **13** Rahal, 34; **14** Johnstone, 29; **15** Carpentier, 27; **16** Fittipaldi, 20; **17** Moreno, 13; **18** Ribeiro and Fernandez, 12; **20** Franchitti, 7; **21** Hearn, 6; **22** Fangio, 3; **23** Papis, 2; **24** Salles, Danner and Jourdain, 1.

Ω OMEGA
OFFICIAL TIMEKEEPER OF CART

TORONTO

1 – BLUNDELL

2 – ZANARDI

3 – RIBEIRO

PPG CART WORLD SERIES • ROUND 11

Controlling the race from the front, Mark Blundell resisted intense pressure from Alex Zanardi to record his second win in three starts with the Motorola Reynard.

Overleaf: Andre Ribeiro confirmed that he had put his troubled start to the season behind him with an impressive third place at the wheel of his new Reynard-Honda.

Michael C. Brown

I T'S amazing how much difference a win can make. Mark Blundell had struggled to find any kind of a rhythm during the first half of the season. He was consistently outpaced by PacWest teammate Mauricio Gugelmin. But then came an inspired drive to victory in Portland. Suddenly it was as if a weight had been lifted from his shoulders. The Englishman was competitive throughout the subsequent race weekend in Cleveland – even though the final results didn't reflect that fact due to a bungled pit stop strategy – and was fast from the get-go in Toronto.

Blundell was beaten to the pole by fellow Briton Dario Franchitti, showing sensational form with Carl Hogan's similar Reynard-Mercedes, but the Scotsman was tipped into a spin at the first corner by an uncharacteristically over-zealous Bobby Rahal. Blundell inherited the lead and effectively controlled the remainder of the afternoon.

This time there was no need for a dramatic rear-guard action. Blundell took advantage of two excellent pit stops by Butch Winkle's crew and led all but two laps en route to his second victory with Bruce McCaw's Motorola Reynard-Mercedes.

'I would have to say that was one of my best [ever] races,' declared Blundell. 'We started on the front row, led from the beginning, made no mistakes, and stayed there to the very end. The team did a fantastic job in the pits. It was a great day.'

Not so for Franchitti. The 24-year-old rookie began the race in a confident frame of mind after heading the timing charts through most of the morning warmup session. Unfortunately, his hopes were dashed at the very first corner when Rahal, starting from row two, poked the nose of his Miller Lite Reynard-Ford down the inside line. Rahal jumped hard on the brakes as he strove to avoid contact, but too late. His left-front wheel clipped the right-rear of Franchitti's Hogan Motor Leasing Reynard – not heavily, but enough to send the pole-winner into a lazy spin.

'I got a good start and Dario left an opening on the inside,' claimed Rahal. 'I think he saw Mark on the outside and didn't see me up next to him on the inside. I think I surprised him and he turned in and I tried not to hit him. But I couldn't avoid him. I feel bad because I don't like to race that way. I like Dario and he's a very good driver. I don't think he knew the turn was wide enough for both of us.'

Franchitti was rather more succinct: 'I believed I had a clear line there and Bobby caught me and we went for a spin.'

Amazingly, there was no massive pile-up. Blundell somehow squeezed between Franchitti and the outside wall as Rahal snuck through on the inside. The remainder of the drivers displayed remarkable presence of mind as they awaited space for a clear passage. The only other car significantly delayed was Christian Fittipaldi's Kmart/Budweiser Swift-Ford, which required a push-start by the CART safety crew.

The order at the end of the first lap saw Blundell ahead of Rahal, Scott Pruett, Andre Ribeiro and Greg Moore, all of whom snuck through on the low side. Michael Andretti performed a miraculous avoidance maneuver on the outside to emerge in sixth, fortunate to lose only a couple of places. Next were Raul Boesel, Alex Zanardi, who was briefly trapped behind Andretti, then Jimmy Vasser and Paul Tracy, who made significant progress after starting 15th and 14th respectively.

Inside the first dozen laps, only one driver among the top 12 improved his position substantially: Zanardi. The Italian breezed by Boesel and Andretti on successive laps after the green flag, then trailed Moore for only one more

QUALIFYING

Michael Andretti's Kmart/Texaco Havoline Swift 007.i-Ford/Cosworth was the pace-setter on the opening day of practice and qualifying, followed by Mark Blundell. But perhaps even more impressive was the performance of Dario Franchitti, who claimed third on the provisional grid with Carl Hogan's unsponsored Reynard-Mercedes despite losing valuable track time due to a gearbox problem in the first session.

'I'm surprised, to be honest,' said the Scotsman. 'We had some power-understeer in the slow corners and some oversteer coming off the turns, but we worked around it. I had to adjust my driving style a bit.'

On Saturday, Franchitti worked some more on the chassis and lowered his time by almost 1.5 seconds during final qualifying.

'I knew the car was improving all the way through the session and I was trying not to worry about what everyone else was doing,' he said. 'It's one of the first times I've actually felt a big improvement in the car between the start of qualifying and the end with the couple of adjustments that we did make. I just went out there with a clear mind and went for it. It was a good lap.'

Good enough, in fact, to secure his first CART pole in only his 11th attempt.

Fellow Briton Blundell also produced his best ever qualifying effort, second in the PacWest Racing Group's similar Motorola Reynard-Mercedes, which differed from the pole-winner only insofar as it was equipped with the softer primary compound tires rather than the more durable optionals preferred by Franchitti and the majority of the Firestone teams.

Bobby Rahal, who always seems to run especially well in Canada, set the third fastest time in his Miller Lite/Team Rahal Reynard-Ford. A disappointed Andretti wound up fourth on the grid, hindered in the morning practice by a blown engine and unable to find a clear lap in qualifying. Ominously, these were the only Goodyear representatives to qualify among the top 10.

'I really wanted this pole bad,' said Andretti, who, amazingly, had not won a $10,000 Marlboro Pole Award since Long Beach in 1995. 'You only have a two-lap window while the tires are at their peak and I didn't get to take advantage of that window.'

Fast learner

DARIO Franchitti was virtually unknown in North America prior to signing for Carl Hogan at the beginning of the season. But his credentials were impeccable. An accomplished kart racer in his teens, Franchitti won the British Formula Vauxhall Junior Championship in 1991 and added the senior Vauxhall title two years later, driving for Paul Stewart Racing. The Scotsman with an Italian heritage – hence his name – continued his progression in Formula 3, then was selected to join the factory Mercedes Junior Team, finishing a strong third in the FIA International Touring Car Championship.

When the ITC was canceled at the end of the '96 season, Franchitti was left without a regular ride. Nevertheless, he remained under the wing of Mercedes, whose motorsports boss, Norbert Haug, had recommended teammate Jan Magnussen to substitute for the injured Emerson Fittipaldi in several PPG Cup races for Hogan Penske Racing. Magnussen, of course, subsequently opted to join the fledgling Stewart Grand Prix operation, and when Hogan decided to strike out on his own, Haug lost no time in arranging a meeting between Hogan and Franchitti.

The pair struck up an immediate rapport. Time was short, allowing for virtually no testing prior to the start of the season, but Franchitti immediately impressed the team with his professionalism, his general demeanor and, above all, his speed.

The first race at Homestead provided a difficult baptism.

Franchitti had never before raced on an oval

and hadn't competed in an open-wheel car for two years. His inexperience caught him out when he crashed while attempting to make room for the race leader. Still, he progressed in leaps and bounds, leading strongly in only his sixth race, at Gateway, before the transmission let him down and ultimately claiming his first pole in only his 11th attempt.

'I've been lucky because I'm driving very, very competitive equipment and that always helps,' he said with characteristic modesty. 'It was the same in ITC. It is a big change from driving an ITC car to one of these, but because it's all happened so fast, you don't tend to worry about that sort of thing – you just need to worry about getting to the top of the time sheets.'

After achieving that objective, Franchitti learned one more aspect about working with the ebullient Hogan: 'I'd been warned about his bear-hugs,' smiled Franchitti, 'and I was a bit worried. I knew it was going to hurt but I didn't notice it too much. It was a good thrill for the whole team.'

circuit before outbraking the Canadian impressively on the outside line at the end of Lakeshore Boulevard. Next time around he usurped Ribeiro at the same location, this time on the inside. Pruett was his next victim, succumbing to an incisive pass into Turn One.

Zanardi lost no time in minimizing the 1.8 second gap to Rahal, then took advantage of a slight slip by the veteran to pounce cleanly past under braking for Turn Five. Now only Blundell remained ahead of the charging #4 Target Reynard-Honda.

At the opposite end of the field, Franchitti also was displaying his talents. After restarting 27th, he stormed to 14th by lap 17. Excellent pit work by Shad Huntley's crew enabled Franchitti to vault up to 11th by lap 37, but with Al Unser's Penske next in his sights, the young Scot slightly misjudged his line at the Turn Three hairpin and clipped the inside wall. It was enough to send his car caroming into the cement on the exit of the corner.

'It was my fault and I apologize to the team,' said a chastened Franchitti.

'Our day is going to come,' proclaimed Hogan team manager Peter

Scott. 'The kid is unbelievable. I was really confident, if we had gotten a yellow, we all would have bunched up and I think he could have won the race.'

If he could have caught Blundell . . . who continued to lead strongly. Zanardi had made rapid progress through to second place but he was unable to make any impression on Blundell, who, indeed, extended his advantage from 1.3 seconds on lap 22, when he had some trouble finding a way past Arnd Meier, to a little over four seconds on lap 29. There the margin settled, with Rahal staying reasonably close for a half-dozen laps or so until his Goodyear tires began to lose their edge. By the time Rahal pulled onto pit lane for his first scheduled stop, on lap 32, he had fallen some six seconds behind the two leaders.

Blundell and Zanardi stopped together on lap 34. Moore and Boesel remained out for one and two laps more respectively before making for the pits. The status quo remained, at least so far as the top two positions were concerned. Excellent work in the pits by Steve Ragan's crew, however, catapulted Ribeiro's LCI/Marlboro Rey-

nard-Honda to third place, and gradually the Brazilian began to reel in the similar Reynard-Honda of Zanardi. Andretti also was running well, his Swift apparently making better use of the Goodyear tires than any of the other chassis.

Blundell survived a scare on lap 54 when he encountered a problem down-shifting at the end of Lakeshore Boulevard, causing him to slide wide at the apex of Turn Three. Fortunately, there was no recurrence of the difficulty, and after seeing Zanardi close almost onto his gearbox, the Englishman put his head down and began to turn a series of fastest laps in the mid-60-second range. Zanardi also increased his pace, but not by enough to prevent the margin from stretching out once again to 1.5 seconds. Then came another challenge for Blundell in the form of Parker Johnstone, whose Team KOOL Green Reynard-Honda was running 14th and in grave danger of going a lap down.

Johnstone later claimed not to have held up the race leader. Nevertheless, Blundell's lap times rose into the high 61-second bracket for six laps before

he was able to find a way past. By which time Zanardi once again was hard on his heels.

At the completion of lap 69, Zanardi made his second pit stop, on schedule. Everything ran smoothly. Moore, however, had not yet stopped for service, and unfortunately he arrived at the apex of Turn One at precisely the same moment as Zanardi, who was on fresh, cold tires. Zanardi, rather than allow Moore clear passage, attempted to race him into the turn. Predictably, the Target Reynard did not have anything like the adhesion Zanardi had become accustomed to – and in an instant he slid just wide enough to clip Moore's right-rear wheel, sending the Player's car heavily into the outside wall. Moore was understandably irate after being robbed of the opportunity to score valuable PPG Cup points. Zanardi, who steadfastly refused to accept any blame for the incident, was fortunate to suffer no damage to his car.

Blundell made his final pit stop during the ensuing caution period and was permitted a modicum of breathing space due to the fact three slower cars were positioned between himself and the fired-up Zanardi prior to the restart. Zanardi soon put that situation to rights, and when Blundell was held up while lapping Hiro Matsushita less than five laps from the finish, the stage was set for a thrilling fight to the wire.

'It's nerve-wracking when you are in front, leading the race,' said Blundell. 'You don't want to make a mess of it, but on the other hand, Alex was still pushing.'

'Mark drove a very good race,' praised Zanardi after moving within three points of PPG Cup leader Paul Tracy, who finished a distant 10th in his Marlboro Penske-Mercedes after surviving a minor skirmish with the wall in the early stages. 'I caught him, but on this kind of track, when you get behind another car you lose a bit of downforce and it's very difficult to overtake. And at the end he made no mistakes.'

The final podium position was claimed by Ribeiro, who lost a position to Andretti during the second round of pit stops but quickly redressed the balance.

'To be competitive and finish on the podium is incredible,' said Ribeiro. 'We sat in this car for the first time two weeks ago. We didn't have any real information on the car, so the team did a fantastic job. Now we are back at the front and able to fight.'

Andretti also was content with fourth, especially since he was hindered by the lack of first gear in the closing stages.

TORONTO SNIPPETS

Photos: Michael C. Brown

• PPG Cup points leader **PAUL TRACY** *(left)*, born and raised in Toronto, was not a happy camper after qualifying a distant 14th in his Marlboro Penske-Mercedes: 'Today was a huge disappointment for me. We're really struggling with the Marlboro car and both Al [Unser] and I have physically exhausted ourselves just trying to drive the car. The car was great on the ovals but we just can't get the grip level on the road courses.'

• A new underwing, developed following some tests in the Williams wind tunnel, was the tweak of the week from **LOLA CARS**, but once again there was no quantum leap forward for Adrian Fernandez or Richie Hearn. Lola also was in the news due to the formation of a group comprising engineers Roger Tyler, Chris Saunders, Ben Bowlby and Duncan MacRobbie, plus accountant Chris Reeder and sales director Peter Spruce, who had combined forces to attempt a management buy-out of the financially troubled British company.

• Race winner **MARK BLUNDELL** diplomatically refused to name names when he was asked about the behavior of some slower drivers who cost him time during the race: 'I really am disappointed with a couple of people. They should know better. It's very frustrating when people don't look in their mirrors and even worse when they don't heed the blue flags.'

• Franchitti and Blundell ensured the first **ALL-BRITISH FRONT ROW** for an Indy car race since Jackie Stewart and Graham Hill achieved the feat in a non-championship event at Fuji Speedway in Japan in 1966.

• **GIL DE FERRAN** experienced one of his worst weekends of the season. He never found a good balance for his Valvoline/Cummins Reynard-Honda during practice and qualifying, and while overnight changes made a dramatic improvement for the final warmup, de Ferran lost five laps fairly early on due to a sticking throttle. Fading brakes finally caused him to park the car after 40 laps: 'These things happen, unfortunately,' commented the Brazilian.

• A weekend total of **164,406 SPECTATORS** attended the 12th annual Molson Indy Toronto, an increase of 8.5 percent over the previous record set in 1996.

PPG CART WORLD SERIES • ROUND 11
MOLSON INDY TORONTO

EXHIBITION PLACE,
TORONTO, ONTARIO, CANADA

JULY 20, 95 laps – 163.495 miles

Place	Driver (Nat.)	No.	Team Sponsors Car-Engine	Tires	Q Speed	Q Time	Q Pos.	Laps	Time/Status	Ave. (mph)	Pts.
1	Mark Blundell (GB)	18	PacWest Racing Group Motorola Reynard 97I-Mercedes	FS	105.142	58.926s	2	95	1h 45m 43.936s	92.779	21
2	Alex Zanardi (I)	4	Target/Chip Ganassi Racing Reynard 97I-Honda	FS	104.498	59.289s	6	95	1h 45m 44.595s	92.769	16
3	Andre Ribeiro (BR)	31	Tasman Motorsports LCI/Marlboro Reynard 97I-Honda	FS	104.488	59.295s	7	95	1h 45m 55.810s	92.605	14
4	Michael Andretti (USA)	6	Newman/Haas Kmart/Texaco Havoline Swift 007.i-Ford XD	GY	104.797	59.120s	4	95	1h 45m 57.033s	92.588	12
5	Scott Pruett (USA)	20	Patrick Brahma Sports Team Reynard 97I-Ford XD	FS	104.572	59.247s	5	95	1h 46m 09.872s	92.401	10
6	Mauricio Gugelmin (BR)	17	PacWest Racing Group Hollywood Reynard 97I-Mercedes	FS	104.172	59.475s	10	95	1h 46m 10.367s	92.394	8
7	Jimmy Vasser (USA)	1	Target/Chip Ganassi Racing Reynard 97I-Honda	FS	103.374	59.934s	15	95	1h 46m 15.666s	92.317	6
8	Raul Boesel (BR)	40	Patrick Brahma Sports Team Reynard 97I-Ford XD	FS	104.393	59.349s	8	95	1h 46m 18.575s	92.275	5
9	Bobby Rahal (USA)	7	Team Rahal Miller Lite Reynard 97I-Ford XD	GY	104.921	59.050s	3	95	1h 46m 20.073s	92.253	4
10	Paul Tracy (CDN)	3	Marlboro Team Penske Penske PC26-Mercedes	GY	103.451	58.889s	14	95	1h 46m 25.206s	92.179	3
11	Christian Fittipaldi (BR)	11	Newman/Haas Kmart/Budweiser Swift 007.i-Ford XD	GY	103.850	59.659s	13	94	Running		2
12	Parker Johnstone (USA)	27	Team KOOL Green Reynard 97I-Honda	FS	102.546	1m 00.418s	19	94	Running		1
13	Michel Jourdain Jr. (MEX)	19	Payton/Coyne Herdez/Viva Mexico! Reynard 97I-Ford XD	FS	102.821	1m 00.256s	18	94	Running		
14	Adrian Fernandez (MEX)	32	Tasman Tecate Beer/Quaker State Oil Lola T97/00-Honda	FS	101.386	1m 01.109s	22	94	Running		
15	Max Papis (I)	25	Arciero-Wells Racing MCI Reynard 97I-Toyota RV8B	FS	101.338	1m 01.138s	23	93	Running		
16	*Patrick Carpentier (CDN)	16	Bettenhausen Alumax Aluminum Reynard 97I-Mercedes	GY	101.587	1m 00.988s	21	93	Running		
17	Bryan Herta (USA)	8	Team Rahal Shell Reynard 97I-Ford XD	GY	103.880	59.642s	12	92	Running		
18	*Gualter Salles (BR)	77	Davis Racing Indusval/Marlboro Reynard 97I-Ford XD	GY	103.258	1m 00.001s	16	92	Running		
19	Juan Fangio II (RA)	36	All American Racers Castrol/Jockey Reynard 97I-Toyota RV8B	GY	99.744	1m 02.115s	25	91	Running		
20	Al Unser Jr. (USA)	2	Marlboro Team Penske Penske PC26-Mercedes	GY	102.895	1m 00.213s	17	91	Running		
21	P.J. Jones (USA)	98	All American Racers Castrol/Jockey Reynard 97I-Toyota RV8B	GY	101.980	1m 00.753s	20	89	Out of fuel		
22	Hiro Matsushita (J)	24	Arciero-Wells Panasonic/Duskin Reynard 97I-Toyota RV8B	FS	96.386	1m 04.279s	27	89	Running		
23	Greg Moore (CDN)	99	Forsythe Player's Ltd./Indeck Reynard 97I-Mercedes	FS	104.261	59.424s	9	69	Accident		
24	*Arnd Meier (D)	64	Project Indy Hasseroder Pils/J.A.G. Lola T97/00-Ford XD	GY	99.499	1m 02.268s	26	62	Fuel pressure		
25	Gil de Ferran (BR)	5	Walker Valvoline/Cummins Reynard 97I-Honda	GY	104.014	59.565s	11	40	Brakes		
26	*Dario Franchitti (GB)	9	Hogan Motor Leasing Reynard 97I-Mercedes	FS	105.694	58.618s	1	39	Accident		1
27	Richie Hearn (USA)	21	Della Penna Ralphs/Food 4 Less Lola T97/00-Ford XD	GY	100.550	1m 01.617s	24	23	Transmission		
28	Dennis Vitolo (USA)	34	Payton/Coyne Racing Lola T97/00-Ford XD	FS	95.604	1m 04.805s	28	19	Handling		

* denotes Rookie driver

Caution flags: Lap 1, accident/Franchitti and Fittipaldi; laps 70–77, accident/Moore. **Total:** two for 9 laps.

Lap leaders: Mark Blundell, 1–33 (33 laps); Greg Moore, 34 (1 lap); Raul Boesel, 35 (1 lap); Blundell, 36–95 (60 laps). **Totals:** Blundell, 93 laps; Moore, 1 lap; Boesel, 1 lap.

Fastest race lap: Mark Blundell, 59.185s, 104.682 mph on lap 92.

Championship positions: 1 Tracy, 109; **2** Zanardi, 106; **3** Andretti, 103; **4** Moore, 95; **5** de Ferran, 94; **6** Pruett, 81; **7** Vasser, 75; **8** Boesel, 66; **9** Gugelmin, 64; **10** Blundell, 56; **11** Unser Jr., 49; **12** Herta, 45; **13** Rahal, 38; **14** Johnstone, 30; **15** Carpentier, 27; **16** Ribeiro, 26; **17** Fittipaldi, 22; **18** Moreno, 13; **19** Fernandez, 12; **20** Franchitti, 8; **21** Hearn, 6; **22** Fangio, 3; **23** Papis, 2; **24** Salles, Danner and Jourdain, 1.

Ω
OMEGA
OFFICIAL TIMEKEEPER OF CART

U.S. 500

QUALIFYING

Scott Pruett and locally based veteran team owner Pat Patrick have experienced every kind of emotion in recent years at Michigan Speedway. In 1995 there was unadulterated joy as Pruett passed Al Unser Jr. on the final lap to secure a long-overdue maiden CART victory. Last year there was abject disappointment as Pruett was forced out after only three laps of the inaugural U.S. 500 due to engine failure. His return for the Marlboro 500 was equally disappointing due to another breakage soon after passing Andre Ribeiro for the lead in the closing stages.

Twelve months on, Pruett gained some recompense by securing the pole with a magnificent qualifying lap at 233.857 mph. Afterward he paid tribute to Ford and Cosworth for overcoming the problems which had plagued his challenge for the 1996 PPG Cup title: 'Ford has made a huge step forward. That's why we're on top. They've done their homework.'

So had the Brahma Sports team, which displayed its potential from the commencement of practice on Friday as Pruett's new-for-'97 teammate Raul Boesel set the pace in the opening session. Boesel eventually qualified third on the two-by-two grid, sandwiching the Hollywood/PacWest Reynard-Mercedes of Mauricio Gugelmin, who had been fastest during the earlier Saturday morning practice with an amazing lap at 236.453 mph.

'I'm disappointed I didn't get the pole but it's not the end of the world,' said Gugelmin. 'The important thing is we have a fast and consistent car for the race. My qualifying laps were as fast as the car would go today, so I'm very happy in that respect. You do the best job you can and sometimes somebody goes a bit quicker. We had the car trimmed out as far as it would go.'

Jimmy Vasser, the defending pole-winner and champion of the U.S. 500, was fastest of the Honda contingent, fourth in Chip Ganassi's #1 Target Reynard 97I, followed by the similar KOOL car of Parker Johnstone, who was delighted with his best qualifying performance of the season. Bobby Rahal was next, quickest of those running Goodyear tires in the Miller Lite Reynard-Ford.

'We had a bit of understeer,' said the veteran, 'but the car was pretty good. You have to have a comfortable car for 500 miles.'

Zanardi capitalizes on others' misfortune

THIRD time proved a charm for Alex Zanardi, who had led strongly in each of his first two starts on the high banks at Michigan Speedway during an impressive rookie season but failed to finish either race. But the victory did not come easily. After making a hash of his first pit stop and falling all the way to 21st position by courtesy of a drive-through penalty for running over an air hose, Zanardi next had to overcome a handling problem.

'I had a terrible push early on, and then at the end of the run the car was going loose,' he recounted. 'So I was in big doubt because I didn't know what to do [in terms of making adjustments to the car].'

By lap 54, Zanardi was in grave danger of being lapped by the flying Andre Ribeiro: 'I couldn't even come close to the speed Ribeiro was running. I was obviously a bit concerned.'

Then came his first slice of good fortune when Parker Johnstone's accident ensured a full-course caution, enabling him to regain the lost ground and make some changes to the car during his next pit stop. As the race progressed, Zanardi made additional adjustments from within the cockpit.

'I was able to balance the car from an aerodynamic point of view,' he said, 'and then it was perfect.'

Zanardi took full advantage as he worked his way steadily forward, grasping the lead for the first time on lap 119. Scott Pruett emerged as his closest challenger as the race entered its final 150 miles, but after the American crashed heavily in Turn Two, Zanardi's lead was never again seriously threatened.

'I'm human, sometimes I make mistakes,' he said, 'but today I think I did a [heck] of a job and I'm very happy.'

The victory moved Zanardi into the lead of the PPG Cup standings for the first time, by a margin of 127–121 over fourth-place finisher Paul Tracy. But that, he said, was of little consequence: 'Obviously, the championship is very important and it's something I would very much like to win, but there are a lot of factors which can work against us. Sure enough, I'm very confident, but I think we must concentrate on every single event and get the most out of it. It's too early [to think of the championship]. The other guys are very strong. Anything can happen.'

ALEX Zanardi was ecstatic after claiming victory in an attrition-filled U.S. 500 at Michigan Speedway. Justifiably so. The 30-year-old Italian's third win of the season represented his first triumph on an oval and vaulted him ahead of Paul Tracy into the lead of the PPG Cup standings. It also helped silence his critics: 'There are some people, who maybe don't like me, that said I would never win a 500-mile race because I wasn't smart enough,' claimed Zanardi. 'I'm very happy because I was able to prove them wrong.'

The driver of Chip Ganassi's Target Reynard-Honda did make one mistake, during his first scheduled pit stop, but thereafter he drove flawlessly, taking the lead for the first time just before halfway and effectively controlling the latter stages.

'You always need to be lucky to win a 500-mile race,' added Zanardi, 'there's no doubt about that. But I was taking care of my equipment.'

Reliability, indeed, proved to be the key to success. Of the nine different drivers who led at one stage or another, only three were among the slim group of 11 survivors at the completion of 250 laps.

First to show out in front – appropriately after starting from the pole – was Scott Pruett. Defending race and series champion Jimmy Vasser briefly looked to the outside line in Turns One and Two but thought better of it and promptly lost a couple of positions as he tucked back in line. Pruett and fellow front row qualifier Mauricio Gugelmin meanwhile battled side by side into Turn Three, with Pruett taking the preferred line and the lead at the completion of lap one. But not for long. Gugelmin almost immediately ducked out of the draft and sling-shotted past Pruett's Brahma Reynard-Ford, there to remain for the opening 35 laps before the first round of scheduled pit stops was triggered by a full-course caution for debris on the track.

Andre Ribeiro, who had stopped during an earlier caution to replace a punctured tire, assumed the lead ahead of Michael Andretti, who had risen impressively from 19th on the grid to third inside the first 60 miles. Next were Gugelmin, the two Brahma cars of Pruett and Raul Boesel, and top rookie Patrick Carpentier's Alumax Reynard-Mercedes. Among those to suffer problems were Parker Johnstone, who had run strongly among the top five, Zanardi, Tracy and Dennis Vitolo, all of whom were adjudged to have violated pit lane procedures.

'I realized I was going too fast and

then I realized I was heading for [teammate] Jimmy [Vasser]'s pit box,' related Zanardi sheepishly. 'That was a terrible mistake which could have cost me the race.'

Instead it cost him merely a drive-through penalty. Ditto the other violators.

Ribeiro set off briskly at the restart, quickly establishing a four-second margin over Andretti, who was content to bide his time. Johnstone resumed a lap down to Ribeiro after serving his penalty. Shortly afterward the Team KOOL Green Reynard-Honda suddenly veered off line and slammed into the Turn Two wall. Johnstone's crash ensured another full-course caution and the next round of pit stops. The timing was perfect for Ribeiro, who in any case was within a couple of laps of requiring service. But as the Brazilian began to slow down and make his way toward the pits, his LCI Reynard-Honda suffered a broken transmission.

Shortly afterward, countryman Gugelmin also encountered a problem. In his case it was a faulty spark box. The PacWest team replaced the offending item and sent Gugelmin on his way, albeit five laps down to the leaders. Another potential victory had gone by the boards. Gugelmin, though, soldiered on gamely, taking advantage of the long list of retirements to finish sixth. He also served notice of what might have been by setting the fastest lap of the day at 232.581 mph.

Pruett and Boesel led the way after electing not to stop during the caution. Andretti resumed in third. At this stage the Kmart/Texaco Havoline Swift-Ford/Cosworth was the fastest car on the track, and by lap 76, following a brief tussle with Pruett, Andretti had taken over the lead. His glory, too, was short-lived. Three laps later, Andretti was coasting toward his pit, transmission broken.

'The car was flawless, perfect,' said a distraught Andretti after posting his eighth consecutive DNF at Michigan Speedway. 'This is a real heart-breaker. I wanted to win this one. We could probably have lapped the field by the end of the race. The car was that good. We should have come away leading the points but now we're going to come away with nothing.'

Fellow title contender Greg Moore also suffered mechanical problems, retiring inside the first 20 laps. Vasser was another to be victimized by gearbox woes.

Dario Franchitti took over the point in his Hogan Motor Leasing Reynard-Mercedes and led strongly until giving best to Bobby Rahal on lap 94. He was

Opposite: A day to relish for some of the minnows. The high rate of attrition gave several of the less fancied runners a welcome opportunity to score PPG Cup points. Dennis Vitolo, Max Papis, Hiro Matsushita, Gualter Salles, Juan Fangio II and Arnd Meier filled places seven through 12.

Bottom right: Mark Blundell battles for position with Bryan Herta. The Englishman maintained his recent good form with a hard-earned second place.

Despite picking up fourth-place points, Paul Tracy lost the PPG Cup championship lead after another frustrating weekend with the Marlboro Penske-Mercedes.

unconcerned. There was still a long way to go. But not, sadly, for Franchitti, who was out after 101 laps due to yet another broken gearbox. Boesel suffered a similar problem less than 40 miles later. The field was thinning fast.

Rahal continued to lead until making his next pit stop, under green, on lap 119. Zanardi, having moved up steadily since his earlier indiscretion, took over the lead for a couple of laps before following Rahal onto pit road. His stop was slightly quicker than Rahal's, and by the time they were both up to speed, Zanardi had gained the upper hand.

A few laps later, the next drama in this eventful afternoon unfolded as Rahal attempted to follow Zanardi around the lapped car of Vitolo between Turns One and Two. He didn't quite make it, sliding high and then slamming into the wall.

'I was trying to pass Vitolo and I went to the outside to go around him,' related Rahal after clambering, uninjured, from his wrecked Miller Lite Reynard. 'But he just kept putting me higher and higher on the track and I hit the marbles. I knew I was going to hit a ton. It's a testament to these cars that I could walk away from a crash like that.'

Patrick Carpentier, who had moved quietly up to third in Tony Bettenhausen's Alumax Reynard-Mercedes, became the eighth different leader when Zanardi elected to make a precautionary tire change following Rahal's crash. But this wasn't to be the young French-Canadian's day either, forced out by an engine failure after 144 laps.

'I just shut it off when I lost power going down the backstretch,' related Carpentier. 'But I can tell you I had the best car out there today. I was flat out, the car worked really well in traffic, the engine was strong and we had

great pit stops. Even though we didn't get the results we wanted, this was a great weekend for us.'

Pruett regained the lead, followed at the 150-lap mark by Tracy, who was running unobtrusively but well for Roger Penske.

Zanardi, Mark Blundell (Motorola Reynard-Mercedes) and Bryan Herta (Shell Reynard-Ford) remained in close attendance, with Gil de Ferran's Valvoline/Cummins Reynard-Honda also on the lead lap.

Zanardi, though, was on the move. Three laps later he was in the lead, and slowly he began to stretch his advantage. By lap 174, following another round of green-flag pit stops, Zanardi still led from Tracy, Blundell, Pruett and de Ferran. Herta was now one lap off the pace after stalling his engine as he attempted to 'baby' his Reynard's transmission.

On the very next lap, Pruett hit the wall in Turn Two in what appeared to be a virtual carbon copy of the earlier incidents which sidelined Johnstone and Rahal. Exit one more contender.

'I don't know what happened,' said Pruett. 'I was cruising along in sixth gear, not taking any chances, waiting for the end to make a move, and then between Turn One and Two the nose just washed out. I thought I caught it but just ran out of room.'

The sixth caution of the day turned out to be the last. The final stages, indeed, were largely uneventful as Zanardi proceeded toward the checkered flag. Blundell was forced to conserve fuel in the closing stages, having made his final pit stop on lap 211. The Briton also was hindered by a tad too much understeer. He was content with second.

'I'm very pleased to have achieved my best finish on an oval,' said Blundell, 'and for it to come on a demanding superspeedway like Michigan makes it even sweeter. Our car was pretty uncomfortable at the start of the race, especially in traffic, but together with the crew I was able to achieve a decent balance. It's a real challenge to adapt the car to the conditions of the day, and when you do it successfully, it's a very good feeling.'

Zanardi also could attest to that, although afterward he maintained a keen sense of perspective: 'When you win a race like this, you cannot say you are the best of the best. A lot of people, including my teammate, Jimmy Vasser, were doing a good job and had to retire for various reasons. Target/Chip Ganassi Racing gave me a very good car, a reliable car, and I was able to finish.'

Aerodynamic changes achieve their objective

As part of their continuing efforts to minimize the escalation in speeds, especially on the superspeedways, CART officials mandated the use of so-called 'tunnel blockers' at Michigan Speedway. The blockers took the form of wedge-shaped inserts, fitted to the rearmost end of the underbody venturi tunnels, and were intended to restrict the amount of downforce – and therefore grip – generated by the cars through the corners.

Reynard chief designer Malcolm Oastler confirmed the effectiveness of the inserts, which, according to wind-tunnel data, resulted in a 25 percent decrease in downforce at 200 mph.

Nevertheless, several drivers had expressed concern after experiencing a drastic lack of rear-end adhesion during tests leading up to the U.S. 500.

'It's OK when you're running on your own,' declared Mauricio Gugelmin, 'but when you have other cars around you the thing becomes virtually undrivable.'

There was some talk of removing the blockers, although following a meeting the previous weekend in Toronto, such speculation was dismissed as impractical.

'We may or may not have reached the right decision in terms of the

best way of slowing down the cars,' said Bettenhausen Motorsports Technical Director Tom Brown, 'but at this stage it's just too late to take any other route. We've known about these rules for several months; the chassis manufacturers have developed the cars in the wind tunnels and decided upon what they think are the appropriate specifications; and the teams have come up with their own setups. It would be stupid to throw all that out of the window just a few days before the race.'

Curiously, the drivers' fears proved unfounded, as two days of practice and qualifying passed with not so much as a spin.

'I can't explain it,' said Gugelmin on Friday. 'When I tested here it was terrible. I literally felt like there was a snake under my car. I had a headache for a week thinking about it! But now, I have to say, it feels OK. Actually, today, I've been dealing with a push, which is a comfortable way of driving around here.'

'[Running] by myself, I haven't noticed any difference,' added Bobby Rahal. 'In traffic, I don't want to say it's insecure, but you can't just run right up underneath somebody. I think the changes will have the desired effect.'

Indeed, while there were three major crashes during the race, none was attributed to the rule changes.

MICHIGAN SNIPPETS

• Dennis Vitolo, Max Papis, Gualter Salles and Arnd Meier all took advantage of the high attrition to claim career-best finishes. **MICHEL JOURDAIN Jr.** *(below)* also ran impressively, rising as high as sixth, just three laps down, before his Herdez/Viva Mexico! Reynard suffered a broken transmission.

• Davis Racing crew member **SANDRO MAURO** was fortunate to escape serious injury when he was inadvertently clipped by Parker Johnstone as the Team KOOL Green Reynard exited its pit stall following an early stop. Mauro bravely returned to tire-changing duties after a visit to the CART Medical Center, although subsequent X-rays revealed four broken bones in his right foot.

• Johnstone's eventful day wasn't over. He later **CRASHED MASSIVELY** in Turn Two and was treated for a cut to his head after a suspension component pierced his helmet. After paying tribute to the CART regulations and the structural integrity of his Reynard chassis, an understandably emotional Johnstone told ABC Sports pit reporter Jack Arute: 'I think if it wasn't for the Bell helmet I wore, I wouldn't be standing here talking to you right now.'

• The rash of **TRANSMISSION PROBLEMS** suffered by the Reynard teams later was traced to a combination of excessive heat build-up (due to the sustained high speeds) and insufficient tolerances within the selector mechanism.

• Erstwhile PPG Cup points leader **PAUL TRACY** experienced a traumatic day which included a malfunctioning telemetry system, a broken radio and a handling imbalance in the waning stages. 'The car was good during the early part of the race,' said Tracy. 'Unfortunately, we developed a big push during the last segment. It's too bad because we were hoping for a podium finish but we really hung in there and were able to score some good points.'

• Of the 11 finishers, Hiro Matsushita spent the least amount of time on pit lane. **BRAD FILBEY**'s crew completed six routine stops in a total elapsed time of 210.052 seconds.

U.S. 500
PRESENTED BY TOYOTA

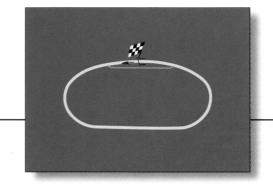

MICHIGAN SPEEDWAY,
BROOKLYN, MICHIGAN

JULY 27, 250 laps – 500.000 miles

Place	Driver (Nat.)	No.	Team Sponsors Car-Engine	Tires	Q Speed	Q Time	Q Pos.	Laps	Time/Status	Ave. (mph)	Pts.
1	Alex Zanardi (I)	4	Target/Chip Ganassi Racing Reynard 97I-Honda	FS	230.947	31.176s	7	250	2h 59m 35.579s	167.044	21
2	Mark Blundell (GB)	18	PacWest Racing Group Motorola Reynard 97I-Mercedes	FS	229.358	31.392s	11	250	3h 00m 07.316s	166.554	16
3	Gil de Ferran (BR)	5	Walker Valvoline/Cummins Reynard 97I-Honda	GY	229.548	31.366s	10	249	Running		14
4	Paul Tracy (CDN)	3	Marlboro Team Penske Penske PC26-Mercedes	GY	228.122	31.562s	18	249	Running		12
5	Bryan Herta (USA)	8	Team Rahal Shell Reynard 97I-Ford XD	GY	230.194	31.278s	8	248	Running		10
6	Mauricio Gugelmin (BR)	17	PacWest Racing Group Hollywood Reynard 97I-Mercedes	FS	233.493	30.836s	2	242	Running		8
7	Dennis Vitolo (USA)	34	Payton/Coyne Racing Lola T97/00-Ford XD	FS	218.652	32.929s	27	242	Running		6
8	Max Papis (I)	25	Arciero-Wells Racing MCI Reynard 97I-Toyota RV8B	FS	222.188	32.405s	23	241	Running		5
9	Hiro Matsushita (J)	24	Arciero-Wells Panasonic/Duskin Reynard 97I-Toyota RV8B	FS	221.089	32.566s	26	241	Running		4
10	*Gualter Salles (BR)	77	Davis Racing Indusval/Marlboro Reynard 97I-Ford XD	GY	227.913	31.591s	20	240	Running		3
11	Juan Fangio II (RA)	36	All American Racers Castrol/Jockey Reynard 97I-Toyota RV8B	GY	221.273	32.539s	25	226	Transmission		2
12	*Arnd Meier (D)	64	Project Indy Hasseroder Pils/J.A.G. Lola T97/00-Ford XD	GY	no speed	no time	28	224	Running		1
13	Michel Jourdain Jr. (MEX)	19	Payton/Coyne Herdez/Viva Mexico! Reynard 97I-Ford XD	FS	228.521	31.507s	17	182	Transmission		
14	Scott Pruett (USA)	20	Patrick Brahma Sports Team Reynard 97I-Ford XD	FS	233.857	30.788s	1	174	Accident		1
15	*Patrick Carpentier (CDN)	16	Bettenhausen Alumax Aluminum Reynard 97I-Mercedes	GY	229.336	31.395s	12	144	Engine		
16	Christian Fittipaldi (BR)	11	Newman/Haas Kmart/Budweiser Swift 007.i-Ford XD	GY	228.797	31.469s	14	128	Lost wheel		
17	Bobby Rahal (USA)	7	Team Rahal Miller Lite Reynard 97I-Ford XD	GY	230.991	31.170s	6	126	Accident		
18	Raul Boesel (BR)	40	Patrick Brahma Sports Team Reynard 97I-Ford XD	FS	232.769	30.932s	3	120	Transmission		
19	*Dario Franchitti (GB)	9	Hogan Motor Leasing Reynard 97I-Mercedes	FS	229.321	31.397s	13	101	Transmission		
20	Al Unser Jr. (USA)	2	Marlboro Team Penske Penske PC26-Mercedes	GY	228.680	31.485s	16	97	Engine		
21	Michael Andretti (USA)	6	Newman/Haas Kmart/Texaco Havoline Swift 007.i-Ford XD	GY	227.935	31.588s	19	79	Transmission		
22	Richie Hearn (USA)	21	Della Penna Ralphs/Food 4 Less Lola T97/00-Ford XD	GY	222.573	32.349s	22	60	Turbo control		
23	Andre Ribeiro (BR)	31	Tasman Motorsports LCI/Marlboro Reynard 97I-Honda	FS	229.936	31.313s	9	57	Transmission		
24	Jimmy Vasser (USA)	1	Target/Chip Ganassi Racing Reynard 97I-Honda	FS	232.506	30.967s	4	57	Transmission		
25	Parker Johnstone (USA)	27	Team KOOL Green Reynard 97I-Honda	FS	232.161	31.013s	5	53	Accident		
26	Adrian Fernandez (MEX)	32	Tasman Tecate Beer/Quaker State Oil Lola T97/00-Honda	FS	228.680	31.485s	15	46	Engine		
27	Greg Moore (CDN)	99	Forsythe Player's Ltd./Indeck Reynard 97I-Mercedes	FS	227.762	31.612s	21	19	Engine		
28	P.J. Jones (USA)	98	All American Racers Castrol/Jockey Reynard 97I-Toyota RV8B	GY	221.613	32.489s	24	11	Engine		

* denotes Rookie driver

Caution flags: Laps 11–20, blown engine/Jones; laps 33–39, debris; laps 54–64, accident/Johnstone; laps 79–84, oil/Andretti; laps 126–138, accident/Rahal; laps 175–182, accident/Pruett. **Total:** six for 55 laps.

Lap leaders: Scott Pruett, 1 (1 lap); Mauricio Gugelmin, 2–35 (34 laps); Andre Ribeiro, 36–56 (21 laps); Pruett, 57–75 (19 laps); Michael Andretti, 76–78 (3 laps); Pruett, 79–81 (3 laps); Dario Franchitti, 82–93 (12 laps); Bobby Rahal, 94–118 (25 laps); Alex Zanardi, 119–129 (11 laps); Patrick Carpentier, 130–143 (14 laps); Pruett, 144–152 (9 laps); Zanardi, 153–214 (62 laps); Gil de Ferran, 215–219 (5 laps); Zanardi, 220–250 (31 laps). **Totals:** Zanardi, 104 laps; Gugelmin, 34 laps; Pruett, 32 laps; Rahal, 25 laps; Ribeiro, 21 laps; Carpentier, 14 laps; Franchitti, 12 laps; de Ferran, 5 laps; Andretti, 3 laps.

Fastest race lap: Mauricio Gugelmin, 30.957s, 232.581 mph on lap 71.

Championship positions: 1 Zanardi, 127; 2 Tracy, 121; 3 de Ferran, 108; 4 Andretti, 103; 5 Moore, 95; 6 Pruett, 82; 7 Vasser, 75; 8 Blundell and Gugelmin, 72; 10 Boesel, 66; 11 Herta, 55; 12 Unser Jr., 49; 13 Rahal, 38; 14 Johnstone, 30; 15 Carpentier, 27; 16 Ribeiro, 26; 17 Fittipaldi, 22; 18 Moreno, 13; 19 Fernandez, 12; 20 Franchitti, 8; 21 Papis, 7; 22 Vitolo and Hearn, 6; 24 Fangio, 5; 25 Matsushita and Salles, 4; 27 Danner, Jourdain and Meier, 1.

Michael C. Brown

MID-OHIO

1 – ZANARDI

2 – MOORE

3 – RAHAL

Bryan Herta took full advantage of his pole position to seize the lead at the start ahead of Alex Zanardi and Greg Moore, with Gil de Ferran, Dario Franchitti and the rest of the field in pursuit. However, his hopes of scoring his maiden CART victory were to be dashed by a massive tire failure on lap 19.

QUALIFYING

The battle for the pole boiled down to a fascinating duel between Bryan Herta and Alex Zanardi. Both were equipped with Reynard chassis, of course, but while Herta's Team Rahal entry boasted a Ford/Cosworth engine and Goodyear tires, Zanardi's Target/Chip Ganassi #4 machine relied upon Honda horsepower and Firestones. There seemed to be little to choose between the two combinations.

Zanardi claimed first blood by setting fastest time in the Friday morning practice, but Herta redressed the balance when it mattered, fastest in provisional qualifying by just 0.026s.

'It's a nice feeling,' said Herta, who had set the scene by posting the fastest lap ever seen at Mid-Ohio during an open CART test in June. 'This is a hometown track for us because the team is based an hour away in Columbus. It's great for the local fans and also for many of the team members who don't travel to all the races because they and their families come along and it's kind of like a family picnic.'

Herta ensured there was plenty to celebrate on Saturday afternoon too. Surprisingly, very few of the top contenders managed to improve upon their best times from Friday. Even so, Herta again set the pace with a superb 1m 06.308s – fractionally slower than his previous best – on his final lap. Zanardi remained second on the grid ahead of the Player's Reynard-Mercedes of Greg Moore.

'I think we're in good shape for the race,' declared Herta, despite some concerns about the longevity of his softer-compound Goodyear Eagles. 'I think I might have a small advantage because these guys [Zanardi and Moore] are fighting for the championship and they have to think about that. Frankly, I have less to lose and more to gain than them so I think that is an advantage.'

Zanardi's Firestone tires were markedly more consistent than Herta's Goodyears, as evidenced by a string of 66-second laps by the PPG Cup points leader: 'It would have been good for the ego to go to bed with the pole in our pocket,' he said with a smile. 'Let's hope we can put that right tomorrow.'

Moore, who encountered a broken suspension during the final session, also was confident: 'I think maybe Alex will be a little conservative in the race because he has a good points lead. I don't care. I want to win this race.'

Gil de Ferran also was right on the pace – and equally hungry for a victory – as were Dario Franchitti and Mauricio Gugelmin.

B RYAN Herta was the only driver to seriously threaten Alex Zanardi's superiority during the Miller 200. Herta, who lives less than an hour away from the Mid-Ohio Sports Car Course in New Albany, a suburb of Columbus, qualified sensationally on the pole with Team Rahal's Shell Reynard-Ford/Cosworth and led confidently from the start. After just 18 laps, however, Herta's hopes of a long-overdue maiden CART victory were cruelly dashed when his left-rear Goodyear tire literally exploded just before the braking area for Turn Two.

'I'm delighted that we got the pole position and led the race for as long as we did,' said Herta, 'but I just wish it could have gone on a little longer. I feel bad for the team because they gave me a great car. Everything was going according to plan. I pulled away a little at the start and then took it easy to save my tires. I knew Alex would get close but I didn't think he could pass me.'

Zanardi, indeed, was content to play follow-my-leader in the early laps, running conservatively in his Target Reynard-Honda. He felt confident that Herta's Goodyear tires would prove inferior to his own Firestone rubber, which had displayed superior wear and consistency during practice and qualifying. Nevertheless, the Italian remained concerned about the proximity of Greg Moore's Player's Reynard-Mercedes in third place.

'We were expecting to see Bryan in some trouble with his tires,' revealed Zanardi. 'My plan was to wait a little

Unable to match the pace of race winner Alex Zanardi, Greg Moore *(right)* took a richly merited second place after another impressively mature display at the wheel of Jerry Forsythe's Player's Reynard.

Below right: The ever-consistent Gil de Ferran recovered to take sixth place at the flag after an embarrassing spin in pit lane had ended his chances of a podium finish.

bit, not take any chances, and let Bryan cook his tires so that I would be able to overtake him easily. But I had to change my strategy because Greg was in my mirrors. He is young and very talented.'

The top three continued to run in close company – and in nose-to-tail formation – until the fateful lap 19.

'As I went into Turn Five on the previous lap, I could feel the car move a little bit,' said Herta, 'and in Turn One it did it again. Then, on the next straightaway, it went "boom!" '

Herta did a masterful job of maintaining control of his car.

Damage, however, was extensive. Even the gearbox casing was cracked as a result of the flailing tire carcass. And with shreds of rubber littering the track, the officials were left with little option but to order a full-course caution.

Zanardi, who had taken over the lead, took the opportunity to make a pit stop on lap 20. He was followed by Moore and Gil de Ferran, whose Valvoline/Cummins Reynard-Honda, on Goodyears, had been holding steady in fourth place, three seconds behind the leading trio. De Ferran, however, lost his chance of a top finish after he glanced in his mirrors as he accelerated out of his pit box, saw Moore bearing down on him, and promptly lost control.

'I was just trying to avoid a collision in the pits and I ended up spinning,' said de Ferran, who rejoined at the tail of the field. 'Sometimes these things happen. We were both lucky that it wasn't worse.'

Jimmy Vasser also encountered a problem when the right-rear wheel nut became jammed on his Target Reynard-Honda. The unfortunate Vasser was obliged to make an additional pit stop, relegating him to 21st, behind de Ferran.

The other leading positions remained unchanged as Zanardi resumed ahead of Moore, Dario Franchitti, once more driving splendidly in Carl Hogan's Reynard-Mercedes, and Christian Fittipaldi, who again out-qualified Newman/Haas team leader Michael Andretti. Ahead of them all, though, was Mauricio Gugelmin, who had eschewed the opportunity to make a pit stop.

'I couldn't believe the others could make it to the finish with only one more stop,' declared Gugelmin's race engineer, Andy Brown. 'No way could we make it. We weren't even prepared to make a stop.'

The Hollywood Reynard-Mercedes duly led the field when the race was restarted after 23 laps. Gugelmin took advantage of his hot tires and low fuel load to extend his advantage to almost

four seconds before pulling into the pits for routine service on lap 29. But he fell to the back of the pack and was unable to make up the deficit.

'I drove flat-out all day but all I came up with was a seventh place,' said a frustrated Gugelmin.

Zanardi inherited the lead and never looked back. Moore held station some four seconds or so behind through the middle stages of the 83-lap contest, while Franchitti, who was unable to match their pace, remained ahead of Fittipaldi until the Brazilian pulled off with a broken gearbox after 41 laps.

'In racing those things happen, but I hope that one day things go my way,' said the disappointed Fittipaldi. 'It would have been hard to win today but we definitely had enough for a podium finish. We just need a little luck.'

Bobby Rahal took over in fourth, the veteran's Miller Lite Reynard-Ford now first among the Goodyear class, followed by the two Brahma Reynard-Fords of Scott Pruett and Raul Boesel. Michel Jourdain Jr. also was running superbly, especially given his relative lack of experience. The young Mexican easily held off the attentions of Andre Ribeiro's LCI/Marlboro Reynard-Honda until throwing away all the good work by stalling the engine during his second pit stop. Jourdain rejoined at the tail of the lead lap, whereupon he gained rapidly on Ribeiro before spinning off at the Esses.

'Michel was looking good for a potential fourth- or fifth-place finish,' said team co-owner Dale Coyne. 'Unfortunately, he made two small mistakes which are part of the learning process.'

The second round of pit stops was otherwise uneventful, save for Rahal briefly stalling his engine and falling behind Pruett. Zanardi, meanwhile, had extended his lead over Moore to around 12 seconds. The gap remained stable for the next dozen laps as Zanardi was content to circulate in the mid-1m 09s range. Suddenly, however, on lap 65, the Italian raised the tempo dramatically.

'That's when we took a bit of a gamble,' related Zanardi.

'We decided to go back to full-rich [on the fuel mixture]. We tried to pull out a big enough gap so we could make another pit stop, and we were lucky enough that everything worked.'

Moore's team, by contrast, opted to conserve fuel with the intention of reaching the finish without stopping a third time.

Turning the fastest laps of the race, Zanardi stretched his lead to almost half a minute by lap 70, when Jourdain's

Photos: Michael C. Brown

Chassis switch helps Jourdain's education

TO many people, Michel Jourdain Jr. was a revelation at Mid-Ohio. The Mexican, still a month shy of his 21st birthday, qualified a fine 14th, ahead of such luminaries as Paul Tracy, Bobby Rahal, Andre Ribeiro and Al Unser Jr. He then ran as high as seventh with Payton/Coyne Racing's Herdez Competition/Viva Mexico! Reynard-Ford/Cosworth before stalling at a pit stop and then compounding his error with a spin.

Jourdain, however, had showed steady improvement ever since exchanging his difficult Lola T97/00 chassis for a Reynard 97I in mid-season. He equaled his previous best qualifying effort, 22nd, the very first time he sat in

the ex-Team Rahal Reynard – at Portland in June – then posted a personal best in each subsequent outing at Cleveland (20th), Toronto (18th) and Michigan (17th).

'The car's much easier to drive and easier to feel what it's doing,' said Jourdain, whose previous experience amounted to a solitary season of Mexican Formula 2 and a mixture of CART and IRL events with uncompetitive equipment in '96. 'In the Lola sometimes I was as much as three seconds a lap slower and I didn't know where I was going to improve. The car felt OK, but it just wouldn't go faster.'

Jourdain's progress has been aided by a fruitful partnership with race engineer Dave Morgan. The Englishman had been drafted across from the team's other car due to the change of chassis, since Jourdain's previous cohort, Mike Wright, had been on loan from Lola Cars. Morgan, like Wright before him, was impressed with his young charge: 'He doesn't have much experience,' said Morgan, 'but he listens well and he wants to learn.'

Sure enough, Jourdain, 19th in the first practice on Friday, clipped almost two full seconds from his previous best in provisional qualifying: 'We made several changes and the car showed good improvements,' he reported.

He was brought down to earth by a couple of spins on Saturday morning, both of which resulted in red-flag stoppages, while in the afternoon his hopes of rising higher up the grid were thwarted by another interruption shortly after he had switched onto a fresh set of tires. Nevertheless, with the Saturday times generally a little slower than the previous day, Jourdain's position within the top half of the field was assured.

Miserable weekend for Penske

MARLBORO Team Penske, winners of four straight races at the scenic and challenging Mid-Ohio Sports Car Course between 1992 and 1995, never came close to displaying that kind of form. Indeed, for the second time in as many races, both Paul Tracy and Al Unser Jr. languished among the lower half of the field.

'My Marlboro car's balance is like a knife-edge,' said Unser after qualifying a dismal 18th, three places behind Tracy. 'It either falls off on one side [push] or the other [loose]. Our continual problem is that we just can't get the car working through the corners.'

The team appeared to make progress prior to the Sunday morning warmup, both drivers feeling the car to be improved, but the race began disastrously as erstwhile championship leader Tracy was eliminated following an incident on the opening lap.

'When we were coming up over the hill going into Turn Seven, Michael [Andretti] got together with someone, I think it was Pruett, and spun out,' related Tracy. 'Everyone just came to a stop and it was a big scramble with nowhere to go. Parker [Johnstone] moved over to avoid the incident and we came together. Unfortunately, it broke the right-front suspension and ended our day.'

Unser managed to escape that drama, moving up four positions on the opening lap. Shortly afterward, he was an innocent victim when Mark Blundell's Motorola Reynard-Mercedes encountered an engine problem just as Unser was contemplating a passing attempt.

'I was trying to get underneath him when he suddenly slowed and I wound up climbing over his left-rear tire,' said Unser, who resumed after a pit stop to change a puncture, then made use of a typically brisk pit stop to climb as high as 12th before succumbing to a lack of engine coolant.

'There was sidepod damage from the collision and we developed a water leak which we realized when the temperatures started to climb,' explained Unser. Exit Penske #2.

In all, it was a weekend to forget.

Bottom: Bobby Rahal's third place confirmed his team's growing competitiveness but offered scant consolation for the bitter disappointment of Bryan Herta's sudden exit while leading the race.

---

spin ensured only the second (and last) full-course caution of the afternoon. Zanardi was able to duck into the pits for a quick splash of methanol without relinquishing the lead.

The caution allowed Moore a little more leeway but he was still unable to challenge Zanardi in the closing stages: 'I was having to conserve fuel desperately,' said Moore. 'I think if we'd had enough fuel we might have been able to catch Alex but it's tough to say. Maybe we should have gone full-rich and run a three-stop strategy? Hindsight's a beautiful thing.'

Franchitti, Pruett, Andretti and Ribeiro all opted to make an additional pit stop, relegating them to the tail end of the lead lap. Ribeiro also earned himself a penalty for speeding in the pit lane, while the luckless Franchitti was obliged to make yet another pit stop after the telemetry suggested he still would not have enough fuel to reach the finish. The young Scot wound up a totally unrepresentative 11th, and it came as no consolation when subsequent investigation revealed the fuel information to have been utterly false.

Rahal took advantage of the situation – and of his own car's excellent fuel economy – to gain his first podium finish of the season on his home track.

'Our plan was to make just two pit stops, so we made extremely good mileage,' said a delighted Rahal, who also made the right decision by choosing the more durable of the two Goodyear tires. 'We knew we might have a chance with the harder tire. They were consistent, and as we made changes to the car and the tire pressures, we got quicker and quicker.'

Boesel was never especially fast but he, too, drove a smart, consistent race. He was rewarded with a fourth-place finish.

'We pitted during the early yellow and then ran the fuel very conservatively,' said Boesel. 'The strategy and the pit stops were the difference for me today.'

Close behind at the finish were Vasser and de Ferran, both of whom had carved impressively through the pack following their earlier delays. Vasser took advantage of a moment's hesitation by de Ferran to gain one more position in the Esses, then held off a determined challenge from the Brazilian to maintain fifth.

Teammate Zanardi, meanwhile, underlined his claim to a second successive PPG Cup title for Target/Chip Ganassi Racing by speeding to victory number four. And while he was elated at his latest success, Zanardi admitted to a feeling of relief when Herta's fine early charge came to a premature end: 'Bryan was doing a beautiful job until his tire exploded,' praised the series leader. 'That was a little unexpected but it was welcome. I know it's not very sporting, but when you're fighting for the lead, you take every help you can get!'

Photos: Michael C. Brown

MID-OHIO SNIPPETS

• GIL DE FERRAN's eventful weekend included a spin in Turn 11 on Saturday morning which ended with his Valvoline/Cummins Reynard-Honda perched ignominiously atop the tire barrier. 'It seemed like a normal lap and then I braked and the car snapped sideways and I couldn't catch it,' said the Brazilian. Fortunately, the car sustained minimal damage which Dan Miller's crew was able to repair in time for final qualifying.

• CART President Andrew Craig confirmed that Tim Allen, star of the hit ABC television show 'Home Improvement' and an avid motor racing fan (as well as an occasional competitor), would join Rock 'n Roll Hall of Fame member 'Smokey' Robinson in presenting the PPG CART World Series END-OF-SEASON AWARDS BANQUET at the Century Plaza Hotel in Los Angeles.

• Arciero-Wells Racing confirmed it would offer a test drive in its MCI Reynard-Toyota to the winner of the KOOL TOYOTA ATLANTIC CHAMPIONSHIP. Current PPG Cup series Rookie of the Year points leader Patrick Carpentier enjoyed a similar arrangement in '96, using the experience to excellent effect by earning a ride with Bettenhausen Motorsports/Team Alumax.

• The BARBER DODGE PRO SERIES unveiled a brand-new Reynard-built chassis to replace the current fleet of Mondiale-built cars in '98. The impressive Reynard 98E featured an Indy car-style state-of-the-art composite chassis and a six-speed sequential Hewland gearbox mated to a 3.2-liter production-based V6 engine from the Dodge Intrepid.

• GUALTER SALLES (below) ran solidly inside the top 10 for Davis Racing until being ousted, for the third race running, by an electrical problem – this time caused by the wiring loom chaffing through beneath a shroud within the cockpit area.

• After BRYAN HERTA lost his chance of victory, mentor Bobby Rahal valiantly upheld his team's honor with a strong drive to third place. 'His day will come,' said Rahal of his protege. 'Today does nothing but confirm that he can win races. Sitting on pole and leading the race was good for Bryan and the team. It was good for us emotionally.'

• CHARLES NEARBURG returned to Payton/Coyne Racing for his second PPG Cup appearance, this time equipped with a Reynard 97I purchased from Davis Racing. The Formula Atlantic veteran qualified ahead of both Arnd Meier and Hiro Matsushita before suffering a massive clutch failure in the warmup. Doug Myers and the crew worked hard to fit a replacement, only for the car to be stranded on the grid by a broken throttle cable. Tough luck.

PPG CART WORLD SERIES • ROUND 13
MILLER 200

MID-OHIO SPORTS CAR COURSE, LEXINGTON, OHIO

AUGUST 10, 83 laps – 187.414 miles

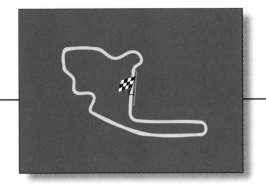

Place	Driver (Nat.)	No.	Team Sponsors Car-Engine	Tires	Q Speed	Q Time	Q Pos.	Laps	Time/Status	Ave. (mph)	Pts.
1	Alex Zanardi (I)	4	Target/Chip Ganassi Racing Reynard 97I-Honda	FS	122.601	1m 06.303s	2	83	1h 41m 16.682s	110.456	21
2	Greg Moore (CDN)	99	Forsythe Player's Ltd./Indeck Reynard 97I-Mercedes	FS	122.287	1m 06.473s	3	83	1h 41m 21.553s	110.367	16
3	Bobby Rahal (USA)	7	Team Rahal Miller Lite Reynard 97I-Ford XD	GY	120.559	1m 07.426s	16	83	1h 41m 23.320s	110.335	14
4	Raul Boesel (BR)	40	Patrick Brahma Sports Team Reynard 97I-Ford XD	FS	121.334	1m 06.995s	11	83	1h 41m 29.719s	110.219	12
5	Jimmy Vasser (USA)	1	Target/Chip Ganassi Racing Reynard 97I-Honda	FS	121.585	1m 06.857s	9	83	1h 41m 31.887s	110.180	10
6	Gil de Ferran (BR)	5	Walker Valvoline/Cummins Reynard 97I-Honda	GY	121.957	1m 06.653s	4	83	1h 41m 32.633s	110.167	8
7	Mauricio Gugelmin (BR)	17	PacWest Racing Group Hollywood Reynard 97I-Mercedes	FS	121.878	1m 06.696s	6	83	1h 41m 33.084s	110.159	6
8	Michael Andretti (USA)	6	Newman/Haas Kmart/Texaco Havoline Swift 007.i-Ford XD	GY	121.472	1m 06.919s	10	83	1h 41m 42.389s	109.991	5
9	Scott Pruett (USA)	20	Patrick Brahma Sports Team Reynard 97I-Ford XD	FS	121.827	1m 06.724s	7	83	1h 41m 43.573s	109.969	4
10	Andre Ribeiro (BR)	31	Tasman Motorsports LCI/Marlboro Reynard 97I-Honda	FS	120.400	1m 07.515s	17	83	1h 42m 01.164s	109.653	3
11	*Dario Franchitti (GB)	9	Hogan Motor Leasing Reynard 97I-Mercedes	FS	121.891	1m 06.689s	5	83	1h 42m 03.450s	109.612	2
12	Parker Johnstone (USA)	27	Team KOOL Green Reynard 97I-Honda	FS	121.324	1m 07.001s	12	82	Running		1
13	Richie Hearn (USA)	21	Della Penna Ralphs/Food 4 Less Lola T97/00-Ford XD	GY	119.374	1m 08.095s	22	82	Running		
14	Max Papis (I)	25	Arciero-Wells Racing MCI Reynard 97I-Toyota RV8B	FS	118.490	1m 08.603s	24	82	Running		
15	*Patrick Carpentier (CDN)	16	Bettenhausen Alumax Aluminum Reynard 97I-Mercedes	GY	119.156	1m 08.220s	23	82	Running		
16	*Arnd Meier (D)	64	Project Indy Hasseroder Pils/J.A.G. Lola T97/00-Ford XD	GY	115.175	1m 10.578s	27	81	Running		
17	P.J. Jones (USA)	98	All American Racers Castrol/Jockey Reynard 97I-Toyota RV8B	GY	119.434	1m 08.061s	20	80	Running		
18	Michel Jourdain Jr. (MEX)	19	Payton/Coyne Herdez/Viva Mexico! Reynard 97I-Ford XD	FS	120.679	1m 07.359s	14	80	Running		
19	Hiro Matsushita (J)	24	Arciero-Wells Panasonic/Duskin Reynard 97I-Toyota RV8B	FS	114.668	1m 10.890s	28	78	Running		
20	*Gualter Salles (BR)	77	Davis Racing Indusval/Marlboro Reynard 97I-Ford XD	GY	119.975	1m 07.754s	19	58	Electrical		
21	Christian Fittipaldi (BR)	11	Newman/Haas Kmart/Budweiser Swift 007.i-Ford XD	GY	121.778	1m 06.751s	8	41	Transmission		
22	Al Unser Jr. (USA)	2	Marlboro Team Penske Penske PC26-Mercedes	GY	120.243	1m 07.603s	18	37	Engine		
23	Adrian Fernandez (MEX)	32	Tasman Tecate Beer/Quaker State Oil Lola T97/00-Honda	FS	119.392	1m 08.085s	21	27	Engine		
24	Bryan Herta (USA)	8	Team Rahal Shell Reynard 97I-Ford XD	GY	122.649	1m 06.277s	1	18	Tire/suspension		1
25	Juan Fangio II (RA)	36	All American Racers Castrol/Jockey Reynard 97I-Toyota RV8B	GY	118.446	1m 08.629s	25	13	Engine		
26	Mark Blundell (GB)	18	PacWest Racing Group Motorola Reynard 97I-Mercedes	FS	120.901	1m 07.235s	13	6	Accident damage		
27	Paul Tracy (CDN)	3	Marlboro Team Penske Penske PC26-Mercedes	GY	120.652	1m 07.374s	15	1	Accident damage		
NS	*Charles Nearburg (USA)	34	Payton/Coyne Nearburg Exploration Reynard 97I-Ford XD	FS	115.609	1m 10.313s	26	–	Throttle cable		

* denotes Rookie driver

Caution flags: Laps 19–22, blown tire/Herta; laps 70–72, tow/Jourdain. **Total:** two for 7 laps.

Lap leaders: Bryan Herta, 1–18 (18 laps); Alex Zanardi, 19–20 (2 laps); Mauricio Gugelmin, 21–29 (9 laps); Zanardi, 30–83 (54 laps). **Totals:** Zanardi, 56 laps; Herta, 18 laps; Gugelmin, 9 laps.

Fastest race lap: Alex Zanardi, 1m 07.735s, 120.009 mph on lap 66 (record).

Championship positions: 1 Zanardi, 148; **2** Tracy, 121; **3** de Ferran, 116; **4** Moore, 111; **5** Andretti, 108; **6** Pruett, 86; **7** Vasser, 85; **8** Gugelmin and Boesel, 78; **10** Blundell, 72; **11** Herta, 56; **12** Rahal, 52; **13** Unser Jr., 49; **14** Johnstone, 31; **15** Ribeiro, 29; **16** Carpentier, 27; **17** Fittipaldi, 22; **18** Moreno, 13; **19** Fernandez, 12; **20** Franchitti, 10; **21** Papis, 7; **22** Vitolo and Hearn, 6; **24** Fangio, 5; **25** Matsushita and Salles, 4; **27** Danner, Jourdain and Meier, 1.

Ω OMEGA
OFFICIAL TIMEKEEPER OF CART

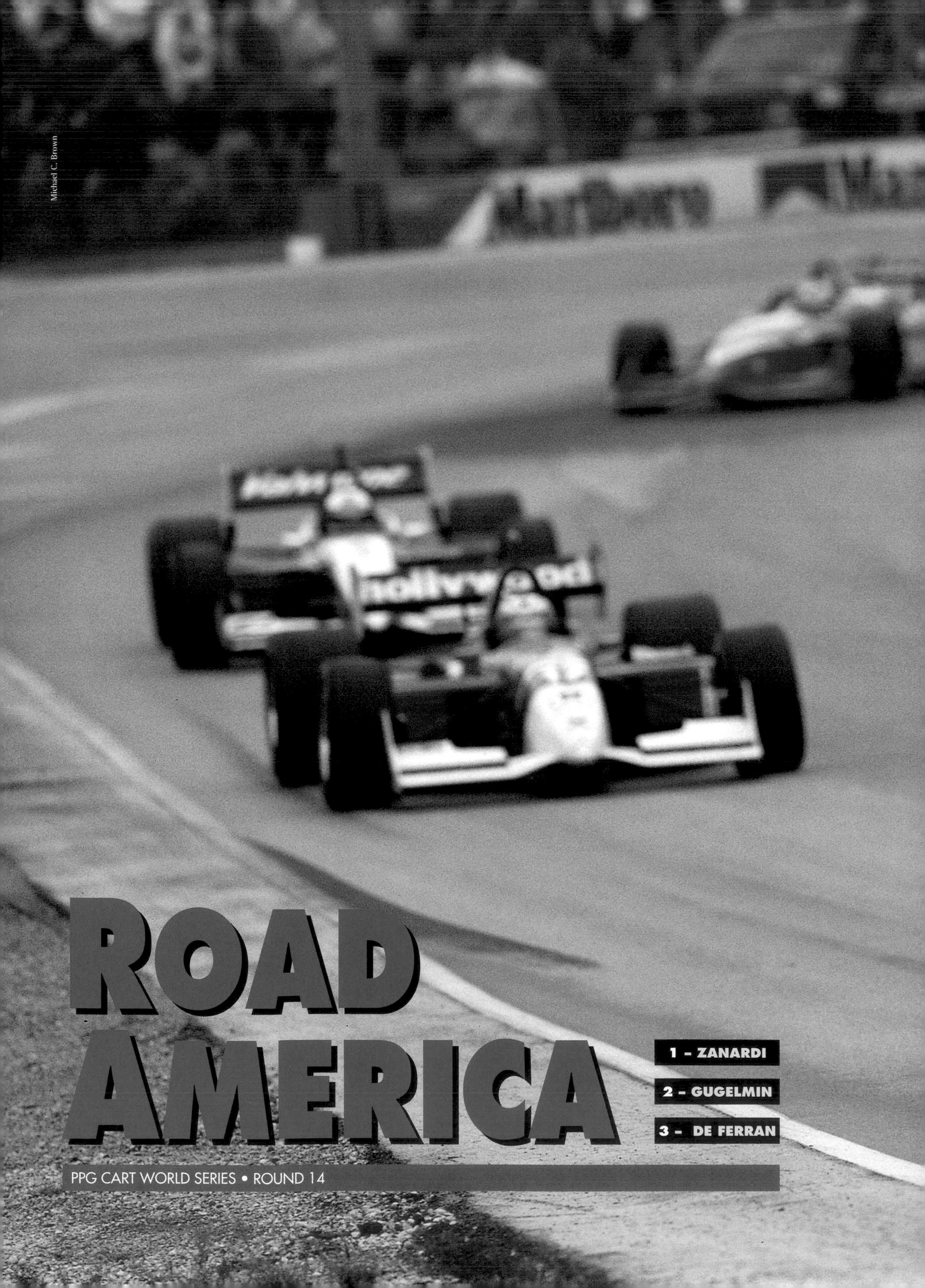

Michael C. Brown

ROAD AMERICA

1 - ZANARDI

2 - GUGELMIN

3 - DE FERRAN

PPG CART WORLD SERIES • ROUND 14

ALEX Zanardi was content to take a cautious approach in the wet opening stages of the 50-lap Texaco/Havoline 200. He survived a couple of slips in the treacherous conditions, but as the circuit began to dry, Zanardi continued his relentless march toward the PPG CART World Series title by taking his fifth victory of the season aboard Chip Ganassi's Target Reynard-Honda. A pair of perfectly coordinated pit stops by Rob Hill's crew also proved crucial as Zanardi made up a position on each occasion.

'I have to give credit to my boys,' said Zanardi. 'Many, many times they have basically put me in a position where I came in [to the pits] behind somebody and went out with a big advantage. Once again, today, they were unbelievable.'

Zanardi's gains in the pits came at the expense of the PacWest Racing Group, with Mauricio Gugelmin losing a position on the first round of pit stops and teammate Mark Blundell being beaten out during the final sequence. Blundell gave chase in the last stint, only to be thwarted by a blown engine with just over two laps remaining. Nevertheless, Bruce McCaw's team once again had made its presence felt.

'I'm disappointed for Mark because he was very strong,' said Gugelmin after finishing second for the fourth time in his CART career. 'It would have been a great result for the PacWest team to put both cars on the podium.'

The second pole of Gugelmin's career provided further proof of his competitiveness, although a torrential downpour meant he had to wait a couple of hours past the original start time before leading the 28-car field toward the green flag.

CART officials had wisely abandoned their attempt to commence the race on schedule, and even though the rain had ceased by the time the competitors reassembled on the front straightaway, the decision to order a single-file start on the soaking wet track represented another smart decision.

Gugelmin duly led the way into Turn One from Blundell, Zanardi, Dario Franchitti, Michael Andretti and Scott Pruett. Farther back, after equaling his career-best grid position, 12th, Gualter Salles lost control of his Indusval Reynard on the exit of the first turn. As the Brazilian gyrated toward the curb on the exit of the corner, Paul Tracy dodged to the inside in avoidance, only to see Salles gain just enough traction on the slippery asphalt to arrest the spin. His car virtually came to a halt in the middle of the road, leaving the luckless Tracy with nowhere to go. The Canadian's Penske promptly ran across the nose of Salles' car before caroming into the tire barrier and performing a lazy roll.

'I guess we just can't buy any luck these days,' said Tracy, who emerged unscathed but frustrated after being sidelined on the opening lap for the second race in a row. 'I had to go one way or the other and I chose the wrong way. I've been racing cars since I was seven and I've never been upside down before.'

After three laps behind the pace car, Gugelmin once again took off at the head of the pack. Soon, though, he came under increasing pressure from teammate Blundell.

'In the beginning the car was running well,' declared Gugelmin, 'but after seven or eight laps I started to lose traction. I just over-worked the tires. The car went very loose.'

Sure enough, on lap nine, Blundell made a better exit from Turn 14 and drew alongside Gugelmin as the PacWest pair drag-raced toward the start/finish line. The Englishman easily gained the lead prior to Turn One.

Franchitti also ran well in the early laps. The young Scot made light of the

Early in the race, Gil de Ferran leads a midfield crocodile including Bryan Herta, Raul Boesel, Greg Moore, Bobby Rahal and Jimmy Vasser. De Ferran kept his hopes of taking the PPG Cup alive with a third-place finish.

QUALIFYING

Changeable weather conditions plagued both days of practice and qualifying at Road America, and rain on Saturday afternoon ensured that times established on Friday would be used to determine the final grid positions. That spelled bad news for Raul Boesel. The Brazilian had headed the time sheets following the initial practice session on Friday morning, which began on a wet track, but was unable to set a representative time in the afternoon due to a blown engine in his Brahma Reynard-Ford.

Countryman Mauricio Gugelmin (below) stepped into the breach, despite the fact his progress in the first session had been hindered by electrical glitches in both of his Hollywood Reynards. Impressively, PacWest teammate Mark Blundell annexed the other front row position in his similar Motorola Reynard-Mercedes.

'We had two good days of testing here and we're starting from where we left off,' revealed Gugelmin, whose only problem came on Saturday morning when he was halted by a blown Mercedes engine. 'I'm happy for the team.'

Alex Zanardi's own earlier test session wasn't nearly so productive, cut short after the PPG Cup points leader spun off the road, but he bounced back to set the third fastest time in Chip Ganassi's Target Reynard-Honda.

Rookie Dario Franchitti continued his fine form, qualifying fourth in Carl Hogan's Reynard-Mercedes and looking especially fast through the very quick Carousel turn which leads onto the back straightaway. The young Scot made more progress with his car on Saturday morning, topping the charts for much of the session, before being halted by a broken gear linkage cable.

'It's a shame we didn't have a chance to go for the pole,' said Franchitti, 'but it's so close that instead of moving up to the front row, we might just as easily have slipped back to the fifth row. So maybe [the weather] worked out in our favor.'

Michael Andretti, fastest of the Goodyear contingent, and Scott Pruett also were within a half-second of the pole time.

Michael C. Brown

Donuts all around

ALEX Zanardi was not especially well known in North America prior to joining Chip Ganassi's team at the start of the 1996 season, but since then he has carved quite a reputation for himself. Initially the reaction from the fans was entirely positive. After all, he burst on the scene in impressive style, winning Rookie of the Year honors and all but dominating the second half of his rookie campaign. In the final race at Laguna Seca, however, Zanardi ruffled more than a few feathers with his controversial last-lap pass of Bryan Herta.

The popular Californian had overtaken Zanardi earlier in the race and seemed headed for a well-deserved maiden victory until Zanardi lunged down the inside line under braking for the infamous Corkscrew Turn. If Herta had turned in, as usual – or if he had not glanced in his mirrors at the last moment and spied Zanardi aiming directly at his left-hand sidepod – the pair would have crashed. Plain and simple. Herta, however, did see Zanardi's desperate bid for glory, and in a split-second act of self-preservation, he elected to leave room for the Target Reynard, which promptly slid directly across the front of his own car's nose, brakes locked, before running off the road on the opposite side of the track. Zanardi, expertly, regained control just in time to head off Herta's attempt to regain the position. And went on to win the race.

That singular maneuver galvanized the racing community like no other. Some fans revered Zanardi for his audacity and determination to seek nothing less than victory; others loathed him for what they perceived as a reckless disregard for safety.

Zanardi himself steadfastly denied any wrong-doing. So far as he was concerned, Herta left the door open and should have expected the unexpected.

Since then Zanardi has redeemed himself, at least to some degree, by virtue of his trademark, crowd-pleasing, tire-burning 'donuts' which followed his victories at Long Beach, Cleveland and, now, Road America.

'The fans waited here in the cold and the wet for so long, and were so loyal, that I just had to do something for them,' said Zanardi, a gleam in his eye. 'I wanted to show them how much I appreciated the fact they all stayed to watch the race.'

And just to complete the picture, Zanardi's jubilant crew 'toasted' him in Victory Lane, fresh donuts in hand.

tricky conditions by ousting Zanardi on lap five and quickly homing in on the PacWest duo. Andretti followed in fourth, best-placed among those running Goodyear tires, which, as at Portland, were not as fast as the Firestones until a dry line began to emerge and the pace gradually quickened.

Race leader Blundell completed lap 13 in 2m 06.640s, faster by 10 seconds than in the earlier stages. Andretti, meanwhile, after passing Zanardi and pulling away by as much as four seconds, found himself under renewed pressure from the #4 Target car. The time was ripe, he decided, for a change to slick tires.

Andretti resumed in 16th after his pit visit but managed not even one complete lap before losing control under braking for Canada Corner and spinning ignominiously into the gravel trap.

'I don't regret making the decision [to change tires],' said Andretti. 'I do regret making the mistake. I just

locked the rear brakes. I tried to save it but I couldn't. I blew it.'

Andretti's miscue signalled the first round of pit stops as well as the demise of Franchitti, who, curiously, failed to notice the crossed yellow flags as he exited the pits and promptly crashed on the exit of Turn One as he attempted to pass race leader Blundell. Team owner Carl Hogan was not amused.

All except Bryan Herta took the opportunity to make their first pit stops and change onto dry-weather tires. Herta, by contrast, elected to stay out on wet tires, seeking to pull away at the restart and wait until the track was a little drier before changing to slicks. Crucially, too, with the remainder of the field having stopped on lap 15, Herta hoped to be able to reach the finish with one fewer pit stop.

It was an interesting strategy. But the rash of cautions which followed, interrupting the flow of the middle stages, did not work in his favor. As

Confirming his wet-weather prowess, Christian Fittipaldi scythed his way through the field to claim fourth place after a mistake in qualifying had left him in a lowly grid position.

Michael C. Brown

Herta pulled away briskly following the restart on lap 19, in his wake were various minor incidents, one of which saw Adrian Fernandez spin luridly across the grass in Turn Eight following contact with close buddy P.J. Jones. Curiously, it was deemed worthy of another full-course caution, despite the fact the Mexican's Tecate/Quaker State Lola-Honda was quickly refired and sent on its way.

Herta took the opportunity to make his first pit stop and resumed at the back of the pack. He never really featured thereafter. Indeed, he was hindered by fading brakes which caused him to spin out of ninth place on the final lap.

Blundell regained the lead, pursued by Zanardi, who had moved ahead of Gugelmin during the pit stops. Next was Gil de Ferran, although Andre Ribeiro rocketed into contention at the following restart before running wide both in Turn One and Turn Three. The errors bounced Ribeiro's LCI/Marlboro Reynard back to 10th behind Pruett, Christian Fittipaldi, Greg Moore, Raul Boesel and Bobby Rahal.

Other brief cautions were necessary after Hiro Matsushita removed a wheel from his Reynard-Toyota in Turn 14, and then when Ribeiro, having repassed Boesel, was clobbered from behind by his countryman, who had lost control of his Brahma Reynard under braking for Turn One. Exit both stage left. Jimmy Vasser and Parker Johnstone also made contact in Turn Five. Each blamed the other. Vasser rejoined at the

Fittipaldi redeems himself after practice error

CHRISTIAN Fittipaldi endured another weekend of mixed fortunes. He started a lowly 18th after sliding off the road during the only dry qualifying session on Friday, but provided one of the highlights of the Texaco/Havoline 200 as he fought his way through to a fine fourth at the checkered flag.

The 26-year-old Brazilian, already acknowledged as one of the most accomplished wet-weather racers, began to move forward immediately, taking advantage of the first-corner melee between Gualter Salles and Paul Tracy, then passing Al Unser Jr., Parker Johnstone, Jimmy Vasser and Bobby Rahal inside the first dozen laps. Raul Boesel, Greg Moore and Scott Pruett also fell victim as the track continued to dry. Along the way, Fittipaldi had to contend with a persistent electrical glitch which prevented him from utilizing the full-throttle gear-shift system on his Kmart/Budweiser Swift-Ford/Cosworth 007.i.

Usually, during each up-shift, an electrical sensor detects the movement of the lever in the driver's hand and momentarily cuts the throttle just long enough for the selector mechanism within the gearbox to engage the required gear. The entire process is completed within a few milliseconds and does not require the driver to lift his foot from the throttle. Except that for most of the race, the system was malfunctioning.

'We were down about 30 horsepower,' estimated Fittipaldi. 'I had to lift off the throttle every time in order to shift because the gear wouldn't go in because the engine wouldn't cut out. That forced me to lose a lot of time.'

Nevertheless, Fittipaldi closed on Gil de Ferran in the waning stages and moved up to fourth when Mark Blundell's engine blew a couple of laps from the finish.

'The car was so good,' declared Fittipaldi. 'We definitely had a top-three car today. If I hadn't screwed up on Friday and spun, we would have started higher and definitely had a podium.'

back of the pack while Johnstone retired with damaged suspension.

The action at the front wasn't quite so fraught, although Gugelmin made an excellent restart on lap 27, moving briefly ahead of Zanardi for second place before Turn One. A lap later, Zanardi redressed the balance by slipping through neatly under braking for Turn Five.

Blundell and Zanardi soon began to edge clear of Gugelmin. De Ferran followed in fourth ahead of Fittipaldi, Pruett, Rahal and Moore, who were embroiled in a tight battle until the Canadian attempted to pass Rahal, appropriately, at Canada Corner. Moore slithered through on the inside but was traveling too fast for the track conditions, which remained

especially damp underneath the trees. The Player's Reynard spun into the gravel in a virtual mirror image of Andretti's earlier lapse.

'I'm disappointed to finish the race that way,' said a chastened Moore. 'It was my mistake.'

The incident triggered both the final full-course caution of the day, on lap 35, and the second round of pit stops. Once again, Zanardi was assisted magnificently by his crew as he emerged from the pits ahead of Blundell.

The two leaders quickly pulled away at the restart. Their lap times gradually approached qualifying pace as the track continued to dry, and even after Zanardi turned the fastest lap of the race on lap 47, edging out to a two-second advantage, Blundell never gave up the chase. Sadly, next time around, Blundell's hopes evaporated when his Motorola Reynard-Mercedes coasted to a halt on the back straightaway, engine blown. A relieved Zanardi was able to ease off and coast home to victory.

'Sometimes you need a little bit of luck,' said Zanardi, who had slid wide on a couple of occasions without relinquishing the lead. 'I made more than one mistake and got away with it.'

Gugelmin inherited second place, well clear of a spirited tussle between de Ferran, Fittipaldi, Pruett and Rahal.

'I had a car that was miles too stiff for the conditions,' noted Gugelmin, 'but overall I'm very happy. We're not going to stop working hard to get that first win.'

ROAD AMERICA SNIPPETS

• Elkhart Lake's Road America circuit has been gradually upgraded over recent years. A NEW GRANDSTAND overlooking Canada Corner had been installed during the off-season, while future plans, unveiled during the weekend by Road America's president, Jim Haynes, include the construction of a new Snap-On bridge to provide easier access to the inside of the demanding Carousel turn.

• 'It feels like a win for us,' said team owner John Della Penna following RICHIE HEARN's career-best equaling ninth-place finish. Added Hearn *(right)*, who has struggled all season long with his Ralphs/Food 4 Less Lola: 'The car was actually well balanced. I was having fun out there for a change.'

• PacWest duo MAURICIO GUGELMIN and MARK BLUNDELL ensured the first sweep of the front row for a single team since Target/Chip Ganassi Racing achieved the feat at Mid-Ohio in 1996.

• GUALTER SALLES had an eventful race. In addition to his opening lap spin, caused when he attempted to leave room for Jimmy Vasser, the Brazilian rookie was involved in another couple of incidents. He kept going, however, and served notice of his potential by setting ninth fastest lap of the race with Gerald Davis' Indusval Reynard-Ford.

• The inherent dangers of the extremely fast four-mile road course were exemplified by two separate ACCIDENTS. The first occurred during practice when Patrick Carpentier's Reynard came perilously close to vaulting the cement wall prior to Canada Corner. (Greg Moore experienced an almost identical accident in '96.) Then, on raceday, Arnd Meier spun at Turn 14, slid across the grass and was launched over the top of the somewhat antiquated two-layer Armco guardrail. The car came to rest within a few feet of the spectators. Fortunately, no one was injured in either incident.

• PPG Cup drivers Jimmy Vasser and Bryan Herta, CART President Andrew Craig and team owners Steve Horne, Barry Green and Bruce McCaw were among an illustrious panel of judges who selected two young American drivers, Buddy Rice and Matt Sielsky, as winners of the prestigious VALVOLINE TEAM USA SCHOLARSHIP.

• GIL DE FERRAN's fifth podium finish in seven races enabled him to move into second place in the PPG Cup standings, albeit 38 points adrift of runaway leader Alex Zanardi.

Michael C. Brown

PPG CART WORLD SERIES • ROUND 14
THE CHICAGO TRIBUNE PRESENTS
THE TEXACO/HAVOLINE 200

ROAD AMERICA,
ELKHART LAKE, WISCONSIN

AUGUST 17, 50 laps – 202.400 miles

Place	Driver (Nat.)	No.	Team Sponsors Car-Engine	Tires	Q Speed	Q Time	Q Pos.	Laps	Time/Status	Ave. (mph)	Pts.
1	Alex Zanardi (I)	4	Target/Chip Ganassi Racing Reynard 97I-Honda	FS	142.110	1m 42.546s	3	50	1h 57m 54.544s	102.995	20
2	Mauricio Gugelmin (BR)	17	PacWest Racing Group Hollywood Reynard 97I-Mercedes	FS	142.342	1m 42.379s	1	50	1h 58m 00.692s	102.905	17
3	Gil de Ferran (BR)	5	Walker Valvoline/Cummins Reynard 97I-Honda	GY	141.264	1m 43.160s	7	50	1h 58m 05.292s	102.838	14
4	Christian Fittipaldi (BR)	11	Newman/Haas Kmart/Budweiser Swift 007.i-Ford XD	GY	139.226	1m 44.670s	18	50	1h 58m 06.373s	102.823	12
5	Scott Pruett (USA)	20	Patrick Brahma Sports Team Reynard 97I-Ford XD	FS	141.763	1m 42.797s	6	50	1h 58m 07.573s	102.805	10
6	Bobby Rahal (USA)	7	Team Rahal Miller Lite Reynard 97I-Ford XD	GY	140.780	1m 43.568s	11	50	1h 58m 09.273s	102.781	8
7	Al Unser Jr. (USA)	2	Marlboro Team Penske Penske PC26-Mercedes	GY	140.358	1m 43.826s	14	50	1h 58m 29.487s	102.488	6
8	Jimmy Vasser (USA)	1	Target/Chip Ganassi Racing Reynard 97I-Honda	FS	140.649	1m 43.611s	13	50	1h 58m 34.120s	102.422	5
9	Richie Hearn (USA)	21	Della Penna Ralphs/Food 4 Less Lola T97/00-Ford XD	GY	136.324	1m 46.898s	24	50	1h 59m 04.125s	101.991	4
10	Juan Fangio II (RA)	36	All American Racers Castrol/Jockey Reynard 97I-Toyota RV8B	GY	137.444	1m 46.027s	21	50	1h 59m 13.001s	101.865	3
11	Bryan Herta (USA)	8	Team Rahal Shell Reynard 97I-Ford XD	GY	141.182	1m 43.220s	8	49	Off course/brakes		2
12	Adrian Fernandez (MEX)	32	Tasman Tecate Beer/Quaker State Oil Lola T97/00-Honda	FS	137.423	1m 46.043s	22	49	Running		1
13	*Gualter Salles (BR)	77	Davis Racing Indusval/Marlboro Reynard 97I-Ford XD	GY	140.706	1m 43.569s	12	49	Running		
14	P.J. Jones (USA)	98	All American Racers Castrol/Jockey Reynard 97I-Toyota RV8B	GY	136.166	1m 47.022s	25	49	Running		
15	Max Papis (I)	25	Arciero-Wells Racing MCI Reynard 97I-Toyota RV8B	FS	137.127	1m 46.272s	23	48	Running		
16	Mark Blundell (GB)	18	PacWest Racing Group Motorola Reynard 97I-Mercedes	FS	142.242	1m 42.451s	2	47	Engine		1
17	*Charles Nearburg (USA)	34	Payton/Coyne Nearburg Exploration Reynard 97I-Ford XD	FS	no speed	no time	28	45	Running		
18	Greg Moore (CDN)	99	Forsythe Player's Ltd./Indeck Reynard 97I-Mercedes	FS	140.737	1m 43.546s	10	33	Off course		
19	*Arnd Meier (D)	64	Project Indy Hasseroder Pils/J.A.G. Lola T97/00-Ford XD	GY	131.777	1m 50.587s	26	33	Accident		
20	Michel Jourdain Jr. (MEX)	19	Payton/Coyne Herdez/Viva Mexico! Reynard 97I-Ford XD	FS	138.996	1m 44.843s	19	29	Accident		
21	Raul Boesel (BR)	40	Patrick Brahma Sports Team Reynard 97I-Ford XD	FS	140.865	1m 43.452s	9	24	Accident		
22	Andre Ribeiro (BR)	31	Tasman Motorsports LCI/Marlboro Reynard 97I-Honda	FS	139.827	1m 44.220s	16	24	Accident		
23	Parker Johnstone (USA)	27	Team KOOL Green Reynard 97I-Honda	FS	139.435	1m 44.513s	17	23	Accident		
24	Hiro Matsushita (J)	24	Arciero-Wells Panasonic/Duskin Reynard 97I-Toyota RV8B	FS	129.536	1m 52.500s	27	19	Accident		
25	*Dario Franchitti (GB)	9	Hogan Motor Leasing Reynard 97I-Mercedes	FS	141.912	1m 42.689s	4	15	Accident		
26	Michael Andretti (USA)	6	Newman/Haas Kmart/Texaco Havoline Swift 007.i-Ford XD	GY	141.766	1m 42.795s	5	13	Off course		
27	*Patrick Carpentier (CDN)	16	Bettenhausen Alumax Aluminum Reynard 97I-Mercedes	GY	138.548	1m 45.182s	20	2	Transmission		
28	Paul Tracy (CDN)	3	Marlboro Team Penske Penske PC26-Mercedes	GY	140.096	1m 44.020s	15	0	Accident		

* denotes Rookie driver

Caution flags: Laps 1–2, accident/Salles and Tracy; laps 14–17, spin/Andretti; lap 19, tow/Salles and Fernandez; laps 20–22, accident/Matsushita and Jones; laps 25–26, accident/Ribeiro and Boesel; lap 35, spin/Moore. **Total:** six for 13 laps.

Lap leaders: Mauricio Gugelmin, 1–8 (8 laps); Mark Blundell, 9–15 (7 laps); Bryan Herta, 16–19 (4 laps); Blundell, 20–35 (16 laps); Alex Zanardi, 36–50 (15 laps). **Totals:** Blundell, 23 laps; Zanardi, 15 laps; Gugelmin, 8 laps; Herta, 4 laps.

Fastest race lap: Alex Zanardi, 1m 43.672s, 140.566 mph on lap 47.

Championship positions: **1** Zanardi, 168; **2** de Ferran, 130; **3** Tracy, 121; **4** Moore, 111; **5** Andretti, 108; **6** Pruett, 96; **7** Gugelmin, 95; **8** Vasser, 90; **9** Boesel, 78; **10** Blundell, 73; **11** Rahal, 60; **12** Herta, 58; **13** Unser Jr., 55; **14** Fittipaldi, 34; **15** Johnstone, 31; **16** Ribeiro, 29; **17** Carpentier, 27; **18** Moreno and Fernandez, 13; **20** Hearn and Franchitti, 10; **22** Fangio, 8; **23** Papis, 7; **24** Vitolo, 6; **25** Matsushita and Salles, 4; **27** Danner, Jourdain and Meier, 1.

Ω OMEGA
OFFICIAL TIMEKEEPER OF CART

VANCOUVER

1 - GUGELMIN

2 - VASSER

3 - DE FERRAN

Michael C. Brown

Having been right on the pace all season, Mauricio Gugelmin finally scored his first CART win after a typically polished display at the wheel of the Hollywood Reynard-Mercedes.

Overleaf: Al Unser Jr. leads Parker Johnstone through the tight Turn Three hairpin on his way to a hard-fought fifth place. The tortuous Concord Pacific Place circuit is to be extensively revised in 1998, creating additional overtaking opportunities and reducing the track's notorious bumps.

A COUPLE of hours after confirming his loyalty to the PacWest Racing Group at least through the end of the 1999 season, Mauricio Gugelmin emerged from an exciting Molson Indy Vancouver with a long-overdue and extremely popular maiden CART victory.

'Today was our day,' said the 34-year-old Brazilian. 'We kept working hard and never gave up. In this series, if everything isn't 100 percent, you don't stand a chance of winning. The team gave me a fast car and I was able to keep my head, keep my concentration and get my first win. It feels great.'

Gugelmin, as usual, was among the fastest contenders all weekend with

Bruce McCaw's Hollywood Reynard-Mercedes. Nevertheless, in the early stages, after qualifying fifth, Gugelmin had to be content to bide his time.

Alex Zanardi, instead, was the pacesetter. The PPG Cup points leader had qualified solidly on the pole with his familiar Target Reynard-Honda, and under a cloudless blue sky, in front of a virtual sell-out crowd, he quickly stretched out a comfortable lead over Bobby Rahal's Miller Lite Reynard-Ford. By lap 15, the #4 Target car was already four seconds clear, in a class of its own. Next time around, though, Zanardi appeared to miss his braking point for the Turn Three hairpin, sliding straight on into the escape road.

'I don't know why, but we had a problem with the brakes,' explained Zanardi. 'Sometimes the pedal would just go down completely.'

He then compounded the problem by stalling the engine as he waited for a break in the traffic in order to rejoin. Zanardi was lucky in that the CART Safety Team was almost immediately on hand to push him on his way. Even so, he fell all the way to 23rd before he could rejoin.

Rahal inherited the lead but wasn't afforded the luxury of being able to enjoy the experience, because while one of the Target cars had vanished from his sights, the other, driven by defending PPG Cup champion Jimmy Vasser, loomed large in his mirrors.

'I tried to run a conservative pace to save the tires since we were on the softer optionals,' related Rahal. 'But we lost grip and Jimmy was able to close in on me.'

So, too, did Gugelmin and Michael Andretti's Kmart/Texaco Havoline Swift-Ford, which once again appeared to utilize its Goodyear tires rather better than the Reynards. The top four were in nose-to-tail formation by lap 25, at which point Bryan Herta, running fifth in Team Rahal's Shell Reynard-Ford, decided it was time to switch to the harder-compound Goodyears. The Mid-Ohio pole-winner rejoined 17th after his pit stop.

Teammate Rahal was by now circulating at least 1.5 seconds slower than in the earlier stages, and on lap 26 he was unable to prevent Vasser from slipping down the inside under braking for Turn 10 in a neatly judged maneuver. Rahal fell back three more places over the course of the next handful of laps before bringing the Miller Lite car onto pit lane for service. Sadly, another strong performance by the veteran ended shortly afterward with a blown engine.

'It was a much shorter day than we

QUALIFYING

Mauricio Gugelmin's Hollywood Reynard-Mercedes was the pacesetter during the two morning practice sessions, but on each day during the afternoon half-hour periods of qualifying it was Alex Zanardi's Target Reynard-Honda which led the way.

'The best way to stay out of trouble is to start at the front,' announced Zanardi (somewhat ironically given the events of the following afternoon), who moved almost within reach of the PPG Cup title after securing his fourth pole of the season. 'Obviously, we're going to try to win the race, because the car is running well, but first of all we want to finish.

'I'm very happy and very proud. I'm very happy, too, to see my teammate, Jimmy Vasser, up there with me, and I hope we can have a good race.'

Vasser, indeed, qualified third in the sister Target car, equaling his best effort from earlier in the season at Surfers Paradise.

'We've changed our philosophy for this weekend in terms of our starting setup,' said Vasser. 'We've been out to lunch during the first day at the last five or six races, so we've always been playing catch-up. Now we've gone back to basics in terms of our setups and it seems to be working.'

Bobby Rahal was the meat in the Target/Chip Ganassi sandwich, achieving his first front row start since Vancouver in 1993 and ensuring his seventh top-three start in the popular event's eight-year history.

'With the exception of 1994, when we had the Honda engine, we've never been outside the top three in qualifying,' noted Rahal. 'I'm thrilled for our team. We've been very competitive the last six races or so. We'll make a few changes, but boy, I feel real good about the car right now.'

Michael Andretti, fourth, was equally happy with his Kmart/Texaco Havoline Swift-Ford/Cosworth, although he, like Rahal, felt his Goodyear tires were no match for the Firestones: 'I know the way the car feels and I think we should be a little further up the grid.'

Gugelmin, hindered slightly by a braking imbalance, had to make do with fifth: 'The problem is the bumps. You have to run the car soft, but then the aerodynamics are not so consistent. If you run stiff, your eyeballs are bouncing all over the place.'

Allsport USA

Big day for 'Big Mo'

MAURICIO 'Big Mo' Gugelmin had been oh-so close to a maiden CART victory on numerous occasions, only to fall short for a variety of reasons. But in the Molson Indy Vancouver, the popular Brazilian parlayed a thoroughly professional performance into a well-judged and richly deserved triumph. 'I feel like I shook a 40-pound monkey off my back,' said a relieved Gugelmin, who had finished second on four occasions during his previous 66 starts in CART competition – including twice earlier in the '97 season.

Gugelmin, like his close friend Ayrton Senna, who went on to win three Formula 1 World Championships before tragically losing his life at Imola in 1994, began his racing career in karts. He followed in the footsteps of Senna by moving to England in 1982 and claiming championships in Formula Ford, Formula Ford 2000 and Formula 3. His sights, too, were set on Formula 1, although after contesting 74 races with a variety of mediocre teams, he looked instead to a future in the PPG CART World Series.

Gugelmin found the blend of a friendly atmosphere and intense competition entirely to his satisfaction, and after an initial 'trial' of three races with Dick Simon Racing in 1993, followed by a season with Target/Chip Ganassi Racing, he signed a long-term contract with Hollywood cigarettes and the emerging PacWest Racing Group in 1995.

'Mo has been a big part of moving the team forward,' said PacWest principal Bruce McCaw. 'I'm really proud of the whole organization. We've built strong relationships with Mercedes-Benz and Firestone and we've shown we can challenge for wins on a regular basis.'

'The team is really the key,' echoed Gugelmin after claiming his first professional victory in more than 10 years (a Formula 3000 event at Silverstone in 1987, to be precise). 'I'm so pleased for my guys and especially for Bruce McCaw. He's the guy who put this team together and he deserves the credit. Mark [Blundell] got the first win and today was my turn.

'The hardest thing has been all the people asking when you're going to win the first one, but that's not going to happen anymore.'

185

Michael C. Brown

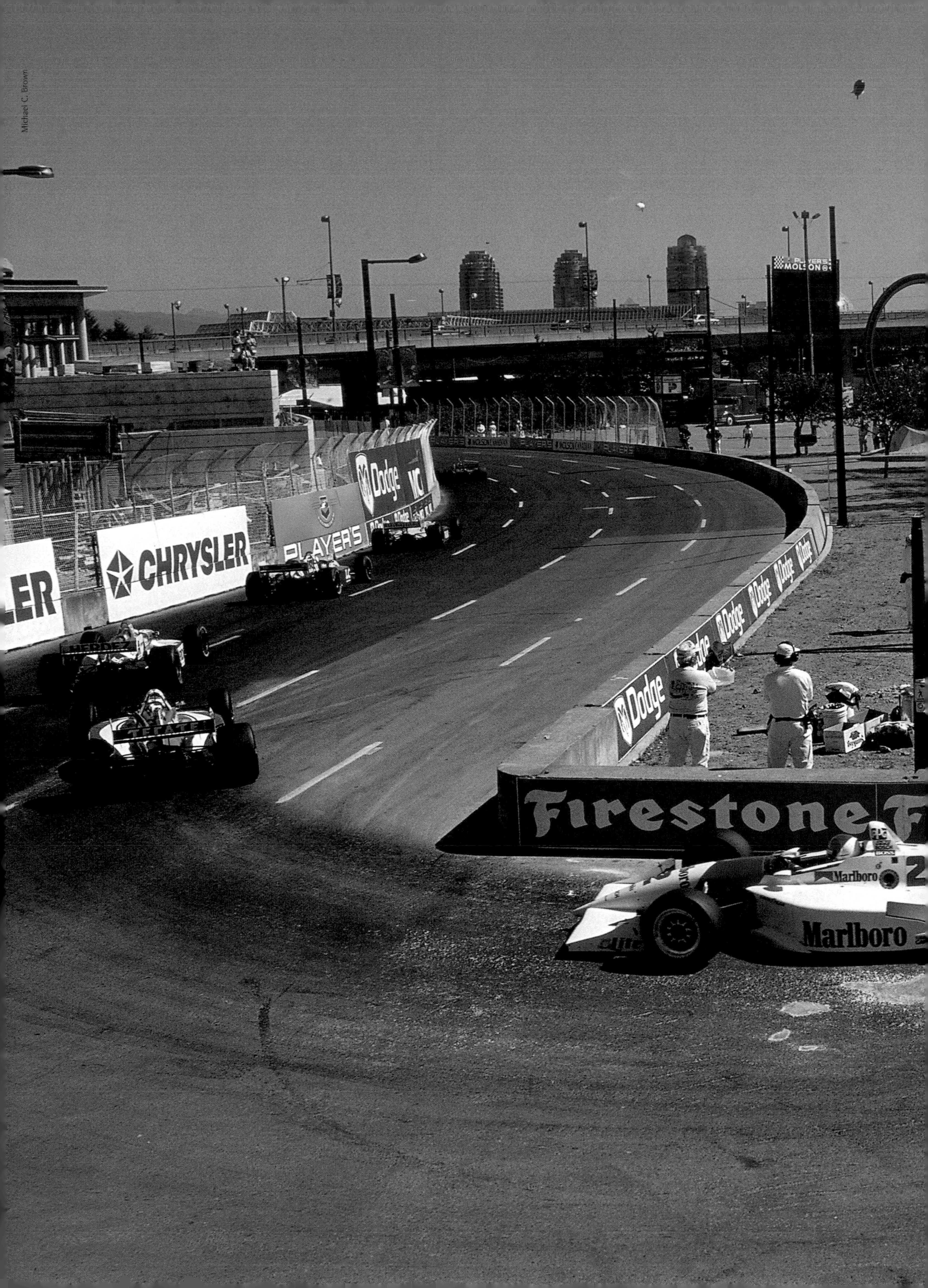

Photos: Michael C. Brown

Bryan Herta *(left)* was leading the race when he was pushed into a tire wall by his old sparring partner, Alex Zanardi, who was trying to unlap himself. An irate Herta was later highly outspoken in his criticism of the Italian's forceful driving.

wanted,' summarized the three-time PPG Cup champion.

Vasser extended his lead over Gugelmin to almost four seconds before making his first pit stop, on schedule, after 36 laps. He relinquished the advantage for only a couple of laps before the Brazilian also pulled onto pit lane. Vasser duly regained the lead, although he was already being hindered by a gearshift problem which forced him to abandon the usual full-throttle technique. He found himself trapped behind Al Unser Jr.'s Marlboro Penske-Mercedes following the pit stops, then exacerbated his predicament by clipping one of the omnipresent concrete walls.

'Al was trying hard not to go a lap down and I just tapped the wall,' reported Vasser. 'I bent a toe-link and the car was really funky after that.'

A couple of mid-race cautions served to erase his advantage over Gugelmin, but Vasser continued to hold the upper hand. Andretti remained close behind, while Zanardi, incredibly, had charged his way back up to fourth place by lap 65. Gil de Ferran, again running well in the Valvoline/Cummins Reynard-Honda, had become Zanardi's most recent victim.

'I looked in my mirror before Turn Two [a very fast right-hand sweeper leading toward the hairpin] and thought he was far enough behind me,' related de Ferran, 'and I braked as usual into Turn Three, peeked in my mirror, and saw this red thing coming at me at a million miles an hour. I

simply couldn't turn into the corner if I wanted to avoid both of us going home early. I had to wait, wait, wait and he almost took me into the tires.'

Five laps later, Zanardi overtook Andretti with a similarly incisive maneuver. The pass threw even the experienced American off his stride. On the very next lap, Andretti nudged the wall in Turn Seven, breaking his Swift's left-front suspension.

'I was just driving too hard,' admitted Andretti, for whom retirement spelled the end of his already slim hopes of claiming a second PPG Cup title. 'My tires were going off real bad. I was trying to keep up with the Firestone guys and I just made a mistake.'

Zanardi continued his remarkable drive by passing Gugelmin in the same location on lap 72. Gugelmin, however, took advantage of Zanardi's slight loss of momentum on the exit of the corner to reclaim his position. At last, someone was able to stem the tide. It was the first sign of resistance all day. This time it was Zanardi's turn to be caught by surprise. On the very next lap he braked too deep into Turn Seven and was fortunate not to make contact with the tire wall.

Zanardi resumed a couple of seconds in arrears of Gugelmin, whereupon, for a few minutes, the focus of attention switched onto pit lane. It was time for the second round of pit stops. Vasser was first in, on lap 74. The race leader was stationary for just over 14 seconds. Gugelmin followed him in a lap later. Crucially, he was on his way

after a mere 12.1 seconds, enabling him to emerge ahead of the #1 Target car. The balance of power had shifted. Zanardi, too, lost a little time, resuming behind Unser, who still required one more pit stop.

Out in front, meanwhile, was Herta, who also had stopped out of sequence after being involved in an earlier skirmish with Christian Fittipaldi's Swift.

Zanardi soon barged his way past Unser and began to close rapidly on teammate Vasser . . . only to slide straight on again in Turn Three. For the second time, Zanardi stalled the engine. He pleaded desperately with the CART Safety Team for a push-start, and on this occasion lost almost exactly a lap before rejoining the fray.

But did he give up? Not a bit of it! Zanardi passed Gugelmin for a second time on lap 85, albeit not this time for position, and on the next lap, not content with clipping the rear of race leader Herta's car on the exit of the hairpin, he dived blithely for the inside into the ensuing chicane. Boom! Exit an enraged Herta stage right – into the tire wall.

'It's ridiculous,' fumed Herta. 'He is trying to unlap himself and uses the rest of the field as pinballs. He thinks he can run into people and nothing will be said.'

Zanardi, of course, saw the incident from a different perspective: 'I was inside of him. He tried to turn in but there was not enough room for two cars.'

After a brief full-course caution while Herta's car was removed from the tire wall – and sent on its way at

the tail end of the lead lap – Gugelmin was left alone in the lead, followed by Vasser and de Ferran. A suitably inspired Unser ran fourth after a quick splash-and-go fuel stop, although he was no match for the irrepressible Zanardi, who stormed through from ninth at the restart and muscled past Unser with seven laps remaining.

'It's incredible to me that we came back from the problems we had to finish in fourth place,' said Zanardi. (No kidding!) 'It's a shame because we had the speed to win the race, but I'm pretty happy. I would say, today, I drove one of the most aggressive races of my life on a day that maybe I should have driven conservatively. However, you have to adapt your driving to the situation you find yourself in.'

Third place for de Ferran was enough to retain an outside hope of beating Zanardi to the PPG Cup title, while Vasser was reasonably content after recording his best result of the season. The top step on the podium, however, was reserved for Gugelmin, who brought to an end a remarkable sequence which had seen only Unser and Andretti emerge victorious from the seven previous races in Vancouver.

'The team did a fabulous job,' praised Gugelmin, one of the true gentlemen in this sport. 'It's something we've worked so hard for. We've come so close so many times, you begin to wonder what's on top of you. It didn't feel like one black cloud, it felt like a whole monsoon was on top of me! But we've done it now and it feels great.'

Zanardi oversteps the mark

ALEX Zanardi's spectacular drive also included a couple of unscheduled trips into the escape road at Turn Three *(right)*. Afterward he attributed his off-course excursions to braking difficulties: 'Sometimes the pedal would just go down completely,' he claimed. 'We will have to take them apart to understand why.' Nevertheless, even after his second mishap, Zanardi continued to brake consistently deeper than his rivals. He also displayed what several drivers considered to be more than a fair degree of aggression.

'He basically pushed [Bryan Herta] into the wall,' said eventual winner Mauricio Gugelmin, who had a bird's eye view of the incident which took out the erstwhile race leader. 'From where I was looking from it was quite spectacular, but I don't think Bryan would be too pleased.'

He wasn't.

'He thinks he can barge through anywhere and everybody's going to get out of his way,' said Herta. 'He thinks he owns this series. It's not the kind of driving that befits a true champion.'

Gil de Ferran diplomatically declined to comment directly on Zanardi's tactics, although he did say: 'I'd rather see less of those kind of moves. Having said that, this is the type of track that breeds that kind of maneuver. I think a very tough disciplinary code has to be set by the stewards of CART, because it's the nature of a racing driver to push the limit up until the point where someone says, nope, you've got to stop. This is the nature of the game.'

Sure enough, a couple of hours after the race, CART Chief Steward Wally Dallenbach announced that Zanardi would be levied a $25,000 fine. In addition, Zanardi was placed on probation until the end of the season.

'He made a couple of mistakes and he was desperately trying to make up for them,' said Dallenbach. 'But the manner in which he did so was reckless, thoughtless and dangerous.

'It was a great race and this kind of race can provoke some of this action, but as far as the stewards were concerned it was an unnecessarily rough action that will not be tolerated.'

VANCOUVER SNIPPETS

• By leading the first 15 laps, **ALEX ZANARDI** raised his tally of laps led for the season to 338 (gained in 10 different races), finally eclipsing Paul Tracy's total of 336. Tracy, who led six of the first seven events, last ran out front at Gateway in May.

• The 1.703-mile track centered upon B.C. Place stadium has never been especially popular with the drivers due to its excessively **BUMPY SURFACE**. For 1998, however, an entirely new layout, utilizing the eastern end of the current track and extending south around False Creek, is expected to offer a substantial improvement while also providing more opportunities for overtaking.

• Tracy's miserable sequence of misfortune continued as his Marlboro Penske-Mercedes was involved in an accident on the opening lap for the third successive race. Fellow Canadian Greg Moore also fell by the wayside after clipping a wall and breaking the suspension on his Player's Reynard-Mercedes. Consequently, only Zanardi and Gil de Ferran retained a mathematical chance of winning the **PPG CUP TITLE** with two races remaining.

• Mauricio Gugelmin's victory moved Brazil to within two points of the United States (214 to 212) in the battle for the CART **NATIONS CUP**.

• **JOHN DELLA PENNA** confirmed the procurement of a Swift 007.i chassis for Richie Hearn at the final race of the season in Fontana. The team also has ordered new Swifts for 1998.

• Jim Hall, who retired at the conclusion of the 1996 season and sold the remnants of his team to **GERALD DAVIS**, stepped in to offer assistance to the financially strapped organization, which had been forced to watch from the sidelines on Friday and Saturday after being unable to meet the payment schedule for its Ford/Cosworth engines. Rookie Gualter Salles 'qualified' the car during the Sunday warmup but retired early after clipping a wall.

• **DARIO FRANCHITTI** was running sixth in his Hogan Motor Leasing Reynard-Mercedes until spearing into the Turn Seven tire barrier while attempting to pass Al Unser Jr. The incident cost him a valuable opportunity to make up ground on rookie points leader Patrick Carpentier, who was absent after breaking a collarbone in a bicycling accident. Roberto Moreno substituted for Carpentier in the Team Alumax Reynard.

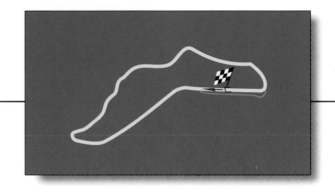

PPG CART WORLD SERIES • ROUND 15
MOLSON INDY VANCOUVER

CONCORD PACIFIC PLACE, VANCOUVER, B.C., CANADA

AUGUST 31, 100 laps – 170.300 miles

Place	Driver (Nat.)	No.	Team Sponsors Car-Engine	Tires	Q Speed	Q Time	Q Pos.	Laps	Time/Status	Ave. (mph)	Pts.
1	**Mauricio Gugelmin (BR)**	17	PacWest Racing Group Hollywood Reynard 97I-Mercedes	FS	112.481	54.505s	5	100	1h 47m 17.995s	95.228	20
2	**Jimmy Vasser (USA)**	1	Target/Chip Ganassi Racing Reynard 97I-Honda	FS	112.728	54.386s	3	100	1h 47m 20.867s	95.186	17
3	**Gil de Ferran (BR)**	5	Walker Valvoline/Cummins Reynard 97I-Honda	GY	112.382	54.553s	7	100	1h 47m 21.768s	95.173	14
4	**Alex Zanardi (I)**	4	Target/Chip Ganassi Racing Reynard 97I-Honda	FS	113.481	54.025s	1	100	1h 47m 25.733s	95.114	13
5	**Al Unser Jr. (USA)**	2	Marlboro Team Penske Penske PC26-Mercedes	GY	109.424	56.028s	22	100	1h 47m 34.433s	94.986	10
6	**Raul Boesel (BR)**	40	Patrick Brahma Sports Team Reynard 97I-Ford XD	FS	111.364	55.052s	12	100	1h 47m 41.155s	94.887	8
7	**Mark Blundell (GB)**	18	PacWest Racing Group Motorola Reynard 97I-Mercedes	FS	112.286	54.600s	8	100	1h 47m 48.411s	94.781	6
8	**Bryan Herta (USA)**	8	Team Rahal Shell Reynard 97I-Ford XD	GY	112.405	54.542s	6	100	1h 47m 48.462s	94.780	5
9	**Christian Fittipaldi (BR)**	11	Newman/Haas Kmart/Budweiser Swift 007.i-Ford XD	GY	111.230	55.118s	14	99	Accident		4
10	**Andre Ribeiro (BR)**	31	Tasman Motorsports LCI/Marlboro Reynard 97I-Honda	FS	111.287	55.090s	13	99	Running		3
11	**Parker Johnstone (USA)**	27	Team KOOL Green Reynard 97I-Honda	FS	110.197	55.635s	18	99	Running		2
12	**Juan Fangio II (RA)**	36	All American Racers Castrol/Jockey Reynard 97I-Toyota RV8B	GY	109.009	56.241s	24	98	Running		1
13	*Dario Franchitti (GB)	9	Hogan Motor Leasing Reynard 97I-Mercedes	FS	112.173	54.655s	10	95	Accident		
14	Hiro Matsushita (J)	24	Arciero-Wells Panasonic/Duskin Reynard 97I-Toyota RV8B	FS	104.786	58.508s	26	94	Running		
15	Roberto Moreno (BR)	16	Bettenhausen Alumax Aluminum Reynard 97I-Mercedes	GY	109.553	55.962s	20	80	Steering		
16	Michael Andretti (USA)	6	Newman/Haas Kmart/Texaco Havoline Swift 007.i-Ford XD	GY	112.659	54.419s	4	71	Accident damage		
17	Greg Moore (CDN)	99	Forsythe Player's Ltd./Indeck Reynard 97I-Mercedes	FS	112.257	54.614s	9	63	Accident damage		
18	Scott Pruett (USA)	20	Patrick Brahma Sports Team Reynard 97I-Ford XD	FS	111.978	54.750s	11	52	Accident		
19	Adrian Fernandez (MEX)	32	Tasman Tecate Beer/Quaker State Oil Lola T97/00-Honda	FS	110.834	55.315s	16	52	Accident		
20	Max Papis (I)	25	Arciero-Wells Racing MCI Reynard 97I-Toyota RV8B	FS	109.616	55.930s	19	52	Clutch		
21	Michel Jourdain Jr. (MEX)	19	Payton/Coyne Herdez/Viva Mexico! Reynard 97I-Ford XD	FS	111.099	55.183s	15	46	Accident		
22	Richie Hearn (USA)	21	Della Penna Ralphs/Food 4 Less Lola T97/00-Ford XD	GY	109.426	56.027s	21	44	Accident		
23	Christian Danner (D)	34	Payton/Coyne Racing Reynard 97I-Ford XD	FS	109.346	56.068s	23	41	Engine		
24	Bobby Rahal (USA)	7	Team Rahal Miller Lite Reynard 97I-Ford XD	GY	112.800	54.351s	2	34	Engine		
25	P.J. Jones (USA)	98	All American Racers Castrol/Jockey Reynard 97I-Toyota RV8B	GY	108.754	56.373s	25	19	Engine		
26	*Gualter Salles (BR)	77	Davis Racing Indusval/Marlboro Reynard 97I-Ford XD	GY	no speed	no time	28	19	Accident damage		
27	Dennis Vitolo (USA)	64	Project Indy SmithKline Beecham Lola T97/00-Ford XD	GY	98.003	1m 02.557s	27	1	Accident		
28	Paul Tracy (CDN)	3	Marlboro Team Penske Penske PC26-Mercedes	GY	110.395	55.535s	17	1	Accident		

* denotes Rookie driver

Caution flags: Laps 3–5, accident/Vitolo; laps 47–51, accident/Jourdain and Hearn; laps 53–56, accident/Pruett and Fernandez; laps 86–88, accident/Herta. **Total:** four for 15 laps.

Lap leaders: Alex Zanardi, 1–15 (15 laps); Bobby Rahal, 16–25 (10 laps); Jimmy Vasser, 26–35 (10 laps); Mauricio Gugelmin, 36–37 (2 laps); Vasser, 38–73 (36 laps); Gugelmin, 74–75 (2 laps); Gil de Ferran, 76 (1 lap); Bryan Herta, 77–86 (10 laps); Gugelmin, 87–100 (14 laps). **Totals:** Vasser, 46 laps; Gugelmin, 18 laps; Zanardi, 15 laps; Rahal, 10 laps; Herta, 10 laps; de Ferran, 1 lap.

Fastest race lap: Alex Zanardi, 55.136s, 111.194 mph on lap 82 (Record).

Championship positions: 1 Zanardi, 181; **2** de Ferran, 144; **3** Tracy, 121; **4** Gugelmin, 115; **5** Moore, 111; **6** Andretti, 108; **7** Vasser, 107; **8** Pruett, 96; **9** Boesel, 86; **10** Blundell, 79; **11** Unser Jr., 65; **12** Herta, 63; **13** Rahal, 60; **14** Fittipaldi, 38; **15** Johnstone, 33; **16** Ribeiro, 32; **17** Carpentier, 27; **18** Moreno and Fernandez, 13; **20** Hearn and Franchitti, 10; **22** Fangio, 9; **23** Papis, 7; **24** Vitolo, 6; **25** Matsushita and Salles, 4; **27** Danner, Jourdain and Meier, 1.

LAGUNA SECA

Michael C. Brown

It was the perfect result for Target/Chip Ganassi Racing, with 1996 PPG Cup champion Jimmy Vasser scoring his first win of the season and Alex Zanardi giving the team its second successive title with a third-place finish.

Below: Pole-sitter Bryan Herta led the race in the opening laps, chased by Zanardi, Pruett, Vasser, Blundell and Gugelmin. However, the Shell Reynard soon came under intense pressure as its Goodyear tires lost grip.

TARGET/Chip Ganassi Racing has developed an extraordinary affinity for Laguna Seca Raceway. In 1996, Alex Zanardi sped to a sensational victory on the central California road course while teammate Jimmy Vasser finished fourth to wrap up the coveted PPG Cup championship. Amazingly, 12 months later, in a race unencumbered by full-course cautions (the first in more than three years), their roles were reversed as Vasser secured the win and Zanardi guided his identical Target Reynard-Honda to a conservative third-place finish, enough to put the crown beyond the reach of Gil de Ferran.

'I think if we could choose how to finish this race, I, personally, would have picked this order,' said Zanardi. 'I'm just so happy for Jimmy because the boy's been through so many misfortunes [this year] and it's about time he got some luck and finally won a race. I'm absolutely delighted.'

'It's been real slim all year long,' concurred Vasser, who grew up within an hour's drive of Laguna Seca and whose boyhood love affair with the sport was kindled by regular visits to the race

track with his father. 'We were in a position to win a few races early on but certainly we didn't have the consistency that we had last year – and not even close to what Alex had. I know how Alex feels [as champion] and I'd much rather be in his spot but it's just great to get back in the winner's circle.'

Vasser's victory was the sixth of the season (and 15th all-time) for Target/Chip Ganassi Racing. It was also the 10th straight for Firestone, cementing its recently gained superiority over long-

time rivals Goodyear following a close tussle in the early part of the season. Nevertheless, while Firestone cars filled eight of the top nine grid positions, the one exception, Bryan Herta's Shell Reynard-Ford/Cosworth, was qualified sensationally on the pole by the gifted 27-year-old American.

Herta carried on the good work by taking the lead at the start. Zanardi had been unable to approach Herta's times during qualifying, but in race trim it was a different story as the pair quickly

established a clear advantage over Scott Pruett. The third-place Brahma Reynard-Ford, meanwhile, was under no real threat from Vasser, who, in common with several other front-runners, was content to run conservatively.

'We were running super-duper lean,' explained Vasser, 'to try to stretch our fuel window as wide as possible.'

The two PacWest Reynards of Mark Blundell and Mauricio Gugelmin filled out the top six, chased by Gil de Ferran in the second fastest Goodyear-shod car and Michel Jourdain Jr., who maintained his recent rise to prominence in Payton/Coyne Racing's Herdez/Viva Mexico! Reynard-Ford by edging clear of the next group of cars headed by Paul Tracy's Marlboro Penske-Mercedes.

By lap eight, the two leaders had stretched their margin over Pruett to 5.7 seconds; but there the gap stabilized. Before long it was apparent that Herta was in trouble. Whereas he had no trouble in lapping consistently in the 1m 11s during the early laps, by lap 18 he was circulating some four seconds per lap slower. His tires had deteriorated badly.

QUALIFYING

Bryan Herta has accumulated a remarkable record at Laguna Seca Raceway. The string began in 1991 when he won a Barber Saab Pro Series race at the Californian road course en route to the championship title. Next came a second-place finish and a victory during two years of Indy Lights. More recently, in three PPG Cup starts at Laguna he has qualified on the front row each time.

'I don't know what it is about this place but I always go well,' said Herta after claiming his second $10,000 Marlboro Pole Award of the season with Team Rahal's #8 Shell Reynard-Ford/Cosworth. 'Here, Mid-Ohio and Cleveland are all really fast, rhythm-type circuits, and for whatever reason they seem to suit my style. I can't really say why that is. If I could, I'd bottle it and take it everywhere else!'

But it wasn't all plain sailing. During qualifying on Friday, a blown engine forced Herta into his backup car, only for his session to be further blighted by a problem with the airjack. Then he ran out of fuel. Herta bounced back on Saturday, soon improving on Alex Zanardi's overnight best of 1m 08.339s and later putting the pole beyond reach with a magnificent new track record at 1m 07.895s.

To put the achievement in its proper perspective, Herta was the only Goodyear-contracted driver within the top eight; the next quickest, Gil de Ferran, was an amazing 1.060s adrift.

'The car felt very good,' said Herta. 'So far we haven't had any tire problems at all. The Goodyears seem to be quite consistent.

'It feels good to win the pole today,' he continued, 'but that is just the first part of our mission. We want the win too.'

Zanardi couldn't match Herta's pace, but he was ominously consistent, turning a series of 68-second laps. Scott Pruett also ran well, third in Pat Patrick's Brahma Reynard-Ford, followed by the PacWest pair, Mark Blundell and Mauricio Gugelmin, and the second Target car of Jimmy Vasser, who reckoned he could have improved if he hadn't encountered some traffic on his best lap.

One of the most impressive performances came from Michel Jourdain Jr., the young Mexican winding up a superb eighth in Payton/Coyne Racing's Herdez/Viva Mexico! Reynard-Ford.

Michael C. Brown

The magnificent Corkscrew is one of the most spectacular corners anywhere in the world. Jimmy Vasser launches his victorious Target Reynard-Honda down the celebrated switchback.

'The car felt good at the start and I opened up a lead early,' related Herta. 'But the tires went off so bad after 15 laps that I was driving my butt off to stay ahead of Alex.'

In the forefront of Zanardi's mind, however, was his desire to assure himself of the PPG Cup crown, which required merely a seventh-place finish. At the same time, Zanardi was all too aware of the fact that Herta was not his greatest fan following a pair of controversial incidents – in '96 at Laguna, where Zanardi barged past Herta on the final lap to claim a controversial victory; and at Vancouver merely a week earlier, when Zanardi had been placed on probation and fined $25,000 for blatantly pushing Herta into the wall.

'At the beginning my goal was not to get in front of him,' declared Zanardi. 'I could have taken second place today. And maybe if he would have won, it would make him a little bit less mad!

'It appeared clear that he was in big trouble and he was trying everything he had to hold the position. I thought he went a little bit over the line. I mean, he was moving over from the right to the left and the left to the right.'

Every time Zanardi tried to make a pass, Herta countered, employing his prerogative as the race leader to the full. It was a fascinating duel between two drivers who had evidently mastered the challenging 2.238-mile road circuit.

On lap 18, Zanardi was able to put the power down better than Herta on the exit of Turn Two, accelerating alongside on the short run toward Turn Three. But Herta wasn't beaten yet. He kept his nose parallel with Zanardi's rear wheels on the inside and braked deeper on the preferred line to reclaim the advantage. Two laps later, Zanardi saw a chance to out-brake Herta into Turn Five. The pass was clean . . . except that the championship leader carried too much speed into the corner and understeered wide on the exit. Herta once again was able to cling onto the lead.

By now Zanardi had rather more to worry about than just finding a way past Herta. The jockeying for position had allowed not only Pruett to close in, but the entire pursuing pack of Vasser, Blundell, Gugelmin and Jourdain, who had slid past de Ferran in Turn Two.

'All of a sudden, I saw all the other cars following me very, very close and I saw Pruett trying to squeeze his nose in, so I was in a very dangerous position,' recounted Zanardi. 'I had to make a decision, let everybody go, be safe, or otherwise try to get in front of him.'

Vasser wins . . . and spins

JIMMY Vasser has endured all manner of disappointments during an ultimately unsuccessful defense of his PPG Cup title. Nevertheless, following a fine drive to second place one week earlier in Vancouver, he was justifiably delighted after earning his first victory of the season for Target/Chip Ganassi Racing. He was pleased, too, when teammate – and new champion – Alex Zanardi offered his own congratulations on a job well done.

'Alex said he really wanted me to win the race today and it's a great thing to have a relationship like that within the team – and especially between the drivers,' noted Vasser. 'If I had to give up the championship to anybody, this is the guy I'd most like to give it up to. Alex is the best teammate I've ever had and I really, truly believe that he means what he says. He's not only a great teammate but a great friend, and I appreciate that.'

Ironically, the only hiccup encountered by Vasser during an otherwise flawless afternoon occurred on the cool-down lap. Zanardi had pulled alongside Vasser and the pair were sharing congratulatory waves as they descended the hill following the Corkscrew when, in a bizarre moment at Turn Nine, the two cars came into contact and Vasser was sent spinning.

'That was my fault,' claimed Zanardi. 'I was very happy and I was trying to drive with my knees. That's what I do in Italy when I'm playing with the radio and I thought I could do the same and wave both hands to congratulate Jimmy – but I couldn't!

'Actually,' he continued with a mischievous grin, 'we talked about what Jimmy could do when he won a race. I said why don't you do some donuts [referring to his own brand of tire-burning celebration which proved so popular with the crowds at Long Beach, Cleveland and Elkhart Lake]? He said, "No, no, the donuts are your trick, I want to do something a little different. Maybe I'll smash the car into the wall on the cool-down lap, what do you think?" So I thought I'd help him!'

He preferred the latter alternative. On lap 22, Zanardi bravely tried the outside line in Turn Two. It was never likely to work. Sure enough, a clash of wheels at the exit saw Zanardi's car jump briefly into the air and then slide off onto the dirt.

'I was still fighting hard,' said Herta. 'If we could have got a [full-course] yellow, we could have come in for a new set of tires and I could still have been leading. He tried to go 'round the outside and I had no tires left and I slid into him.'

Zanardi, wisely, chose not to exacer-bate the ill-feeling between the pair: 'He lost [control of] his car and there was no room left for me,' he said succinctly.

Pruett took advantage of the melee to slip gratefully into the lead. Herta continued in second, but only as far as Turn Six, where Vasser garnered the inside line. It was a clean pass. Herta stubbornly refused to give ground but succeeded only in running wide onto the dirt at the exit. In a flash, he was relegated to eighth: 'I don't blame Jimmy,' said Herta. 'It was just a racing incident.'

Herta gave up the unequal struggle a couple of laps later, diving into the pits for fresh tires. Unfortunately, these proved even worse, and it wasn't until his final stint that he was able to regain his earlier speed. By then he had fallen all the way to 12th, although a fine rear-guard action saw the Shell Reynard up to sixth at the end of what was ultimately a disappointing afternoon: 'I drove hard all day but the car wouldn't hook up,' said Herta.

Pruett continued to lead until making his first pit stop on lap 27. Vasser, though, by virtue of his conservative pace in the early stages, stayed out

one lap longer, then took advantage of excellent service by Grant Weaver's crew to emerge narrowly ahead of the Brahma Reynard. Vasser made the most of his opportunity and never relinquished the lead. Blundell jumped from fifth to second, thanks to a sensational second stop by Butch Winkle's crew, and chased hard in the closing laps, but Vasser was up to the challenge. He eventually took the checkered flag 0.543 seconds clear of the Englishman's Motorola Reynard-Mercedes.

'We changed our strategy in Van-couver and it's obviously paying off for us,' said a delighted Vasser. 'Hope-fully we'll be able to build on the momentum that we have established here late in the season and then come out swinging next year.'

Blundell was equally delighted: 'To be second today is an indication of our progress. Another podium result and a great day overall for PacWest.'

Truthfully, it might have been even better. Teammate Gugelmin was head-ed for a seemingly certain third, despite having to cope with fading brakes in the late stages, until a brake line failure on the final lap pitched him heavily into the tire wall in Turn Two – directly in front of a large group of Hollywood guests! Gugelmin was fortunate to emerge unscathed.

The luckless Pruett fared no better. He fell from second to fourth during the second round of pit stops and was running close behind Gugelmin when he was hit from behind by Andre Ribeiro in Turn Two with just five laps remaining. An angry Pruett was out, suspension broken. Ribeiro, mean-while, who had charged hard through-out the race after starting a lowly 10th

in his LCI/Marlboro Reynard-Honda, had to give best to Zanardi before the finish. De Ferran finished fifth, best among the Goodyear brigade, but it was not enough to prevent Zanardi from clinching the PPG Cup crown.

'The championship is just great,' said the Italian. 'The whole team has done a fantastic job this year. Every-body has worked very, very hard to provide the drivers with good cars and I think I may sound a little bit arrogant but I believe Chip is pretty lucky to have a couple of drivers like me and Jimmy!'

Andre Ribeiro once again shone in the LCI/Marlboro Reynard-Honda, charging through the field to take fourth place at the finish.

Rookie Salles reaps reward for team effort

SEVENTH place for Gualter Salles represented the best result of the season by a rookie driver – other than Patrick Carpentier's superb podium finish at Gateway International Raceway, of course. The result also moved the likeable 26-year-old Brazilian into a tie for second with Dario Franchitti in the battle for Rookie of the Year honors. Both trailed Carpentier by 17 points with just one race remaining.

Salles – and rookie team owner Gerald Davis – both displayed great fortitude during an oftentimes arduous initial campaign in the PPG Cup ranks. The program was only finalized shortly before the first race, and financial resources always were scarce. At the previous race, indeed, it took a vital injection of funding from Davis' former employer, Jim Hall, to keep the team afloat.

Back on an even keel, Davis Racing performed with characteristic aplomb throughout the weekend. Much of the team, including crew chief Alex Hering and race engineer Chuck Matthews, had operated, together, under Davis' guidance – and Hall's ownership – in 1996.

The continuity, allied to Salles' infectious enthusiasm, had served them well. Several times the #77 Indusval Reynard-Ford/Cosworth had displayed a good turn of speed, only to be thwarted by a variety of ailments. But at Laguna Seca, Salles maintained a solid pace, kept out of trouble, and moved steadily forward after starting 18th.

'We didn't have the fastest car but it was a very consistent car,' said Salles. 'We were able to run the same lap times at the end of a segment as we were at the beginning.'

Excellent pit stops also played a crucial role, with Salles picking up several positions during each routine service.

'It was a really good team effort,' summarized Salles. 'It was very important for us to finish the race. At Mid-Ohio we should have finished at least fifth, because I had made my last pit stop and I was running right behind Raul [Boesel], who finished fourth, before I had a problem. Sometimes you show promise but for some reason or another you don't fulfill your potential. But this time everything worked out fine, which was just what we needed.'

LAGUNA SECA SNIPPETS

• Mark Blundell's runner-up finish was enough to clinch the MANUFACTURERS CHAMPIONSHIP for Mercedes-Benz. Ironically, the Ilmor Engineering-developed IC108D failed to lead a lap for only the second time this season.

• PAYTON/COYNE TEAMMATES Michel Jourdain Jr. and Charles Nearburg form the book-ends of the generation gap within the PPG Cup series – and, coincidentally, both celebrated birthdays during the week prior to the Toyota Grand Prix of Monterey. Jourdain literally came of age on Tuesday, September 2, his 21st birthday, while Nearburg was 47 on Saturday, September 6.

• NEWMAN/HAAS RACING endured a dismal weekend with its pair of Swifts. Michael Andretti, uncharacteristically, crashed twice in Turn Four, while Christian Fittipaldi went off in precisely the same location on Saturday morning. 'The car's really a handful,' said Andretti. 'We just don't have the right setup. We're trying hard and pushing over the edge.'

• Former CART and Formula 1 champion EMERSON FITTIPALDI, rendered *hors de combat* by his crash at Michigan Speedway in '96, suffered another accident on the same day as the Laguna Seca race – in his native Brazil, where his ultra-light plane crashed into a swamp. Fittipaldi was lucky. He required surgery on a badly damaged vertebra but was expected to make a complete recovery.

• PATRICK CARPENTIER was cleared to race, just two weeks after sustaining a broken collarbone in a cycling accident, but realized on Saturday afternoon that he was not doing justice to Tony Bettenhausen's Alumax Reynard. 'Supersub' Roberto Moreno *(left)* once again stepped into the breach and drove impressively to a 10th-place finish.

• Rob Hill, crew chief for the PPG Cup-winning Target Reynard-Honda of Alex Zanardi, claimed the prestigious TOP WRENCH AWARD, presented by Snap-On Tools, during the Championship Association of Mechanics' annual prize-giving on Thursday evening. Other winners included Hogan Racing crew chief Shad Huntley (Jim McGee Preparation Award, presented by Earl's Performance Products) and Davis Racing's David Vaughn (A.J. Watson Award for Fabricator of the Year).

• Irish racer/businessman Martin Birrane emerged as a potential savior for LOLA CARS following the collapse of a proposed management buy-out. Birrane arrived at Laguna Seca on Saturday and expressed his intention of putting the financially crippled chassis manufacturer back on its feet.

Photos: Michael C. Brown

PPG CART WORLD SERIES • ROUND 16
TOYOTA GRAND PRIX OF MONTEREY FEATURING THE TEXACO/HAVOLINE 300

LAGUNA SECA RACEWAY,
MONTEREY, CALIFORNIA

SEPTEMBER 7, 83 laps – 185.754 miles

Place	Driver (Nat.)	No.	Team Sponsors Car-Engine	Tires	Q Speed	Q Time	Q Pos.	Laps	Time/Status	Ave. (mph)	Pts.
1	Jimmy Vasser (USA)	1	Target/Chip Ganassi Racing Reynard 97I-Honda	FS	117.021	1m 08.849s	6	83	1h 41m 38.813s	109.647	21
2	Mark Blundell (GB)	18	PacWest Racing Group Motorola Reynard 97I-Mercedes	FS	117.215	1m 08.735s	4	83	1h 41m 39.356s	109.637	16
3	Alex Zanardi (I)	4	Target/Chip Ganassi Racing Reynard 97I-Honda	FS	117.895	1m 08.339s	2	83	1h 41m 50.141s	109.443	14
4	Andre Ribeiro (BR)	31	Tasman Motorsports LCI/Marlboro Reynard 97I-Honda	FS	116.660	1m 09.062s	10	83	1h 42m 01.504s	109.240	12
5	Gil de Ferran (BR)	5	Walker Valvoline/Cummins Reynard 97I-Honda	GY	116.672	1m 09.055s	9	83	1h 42m 08.749s	109.111	10
6	Bryan Herta (USA)	8	Team Rahal Shell Reynard 97I-Ford XD	GY	118.666	1m 07.895s	1	83	1h 42m 32.993s	108.681	9
7	*Gualter Salles (BR)	77	Davis Racing Indusval/Marlboro Reynard 97I-Ford XD	GY	115.599	1m 09.696s	18	83	1h 42m 33.595s	108.671	6
8	Raul Boesel (BR)	40	Patrick Brahma Sports Team Reynard 97I-Ford XD	FS	116.119	1m 09.384s	15	83	1h 42m 54.010s	108.311	5
9	Mauricio Gugelmin (BR)	17	PacWest Racing Group Hollywood Reynard 97I-Mercedes	FS	117.157	1m 08.769s	5	82	Accident/brakes		4
10	Roberto Moreno (BR)	16	Bettenhausen Alumax Aluminum Reynard 97I-Mercedes	GY	111.522	1m 12.244s	26	82	Running		3
11	Al Unser Jr. (USA)	2	Marlboro Team Penske Penske PC26-Mercedes	GY	114.884	1m 10.130s	20	82	Running		2
12	Parker Johnstone (USA)	27	Team KOOL Green Reynard 97I-Honda	FS	115.659	1m 09.660s	17	81	Running		1
13	*Dario Franchitti (GB)	9	Hogan Motor Leasing Reynard 97I-Mercedes	FS	116.196	1m 09.338s	13	81	Running		
14	Max Papis (I)	25	Arciero-Wells Racing MCI Reynard 97I-Toyota RV8B	FS	115.049	1m 10.029s	19	81	Running		
15	Juan Fangio II (RA)	36	All American Racers Castrol/Jockey Reynard 97I-Toyota RV8B	GY	113.482	1m 10.996s	22	80	Running		
16	Scott Pruett (USA)	20	Patrick Brahma Sports Team Reynard 97I-Ford XD	FS	117.308	1m 08.681s	3	79	Accident damage		
17	P.J. Jones (USA)	98	All American Racers Castrol/Jockey Reynard 97I-Toyota RV8B	GY	113.452	1m 11.015s	23	78	Out of fuel		
18	*Charles Nearburg (USA)	34	Payton/Coyne Nearburg Exploration Reynard 97I-Ford XD	FS	110.372	1m 12.997s	27	78	Running		
19	Bobby Rahal (USA)	7	Team Rahal Miller Lite Reynard 97I-Ford XD	GY	115.682	1m 09.646s	16	76	Transmission		
20	Dennis Vitolo (USA)	64	Project Indy SmithKline Beecham Lola T97/00-Ford XD	GY	108.197	1m 14.464s	28	75	Running		
21	Christian Fittipaldi (BR)	11	Newman/Haas Kmart/Budweiser Swift 007.i-Ford XD	GY	116.461	1m 09.180s	11	71	Suspension		
22	Michel Jourdain Jr. (MEX)	19	Payton/Coyne Herdez/Viva Mexico! Reynard 97I-Ford XD	FS	116.743	1m 09.013s	8	69	Engine		
23	Adrian Fernandez (MEX)	32	Tasman Tecate Beer/Quaker State Oil Lola T97/00-Honda	FS	113.299	1m 11.111s	24	67	Brakes		
24	Greg Moore (CDN)	99	Forsythe Player's Ltd./Indeck Reynard 97I-Mercedes	FS	116.779	1m 08.992s	7	64	Engine		
25	Richie Hearn (USA)	21	Della Penna Ralphs/Food 4 Less Lola T97/00-Ford XD	GY	114.205	1m 10.547s	21	40	Transmission		
26	Paul Tracy (CDN)	3	Marlboro Team Penske Penske PC26-Mercedes	GY	116.228	1m 09.319s	12	23	Engine		
27	Michael Andretti (USA)	6	Newman/Haas Kmart/Texaco Havoline Swift 007.i-Ford XD	GY	116.181	1m 09.347s	14	12	Electrical		
28	Hiro Matsushita (J)	24	Arciero-Wells Panasonic/Duskin Reynard 97I-Toyota RV8B	FS	112.163	1m 11.831s	25	2	Oil leak		

* denotes Rookie driver

Caution flags: None.

Lap leaders: Bryan Herta, 1–21 (21 laps); Scott Pruett, 22–25 (4 laps); Jimmy Vasser, 26–83 (58 laps). **Totals:** Vasser, 58 laps; Herta, 21 laps; Pruett, 4 laps.

Fastest race lap: Mark Blundell, 1m 10.960s, 113.540 mph on lap 78.

Championship positions: 1 Zanardi, 195; **2** de Ferran, 154; **3** Vasser, 128; **4** Tracy, 121; **5** Gugelmin, 119; **6** Moore, 111; **7** Andretti, 108; **8** Pruett, 96; **9** Blundell, 95; **10** Boesel, 91; **11** Herta, 72; **12** Unser Jr., 67; **13** Rahal, 60; **14** Ribeiro, 44; **15** Fittipaldi, 38; **16** Johnstone, 34; **17** Carpentier, 27; **18** Moreno, 16; **19** Fernandez, 13; **20** Salles, Hearn and Franchitti, 10; **23** Fangio, 9; **24** Papis, 7; **25** Vitolo, 6; **26** Matsushita, 4; **27** Danner, Jourdain and Meier, 1.

OMEGA
OFFICIAL TIMEKEEPER OF CART

FONTANA

1 - BLUNDELL

2 - VASSER

3 - FERNANDEZ

QUALIFYING

After the remnants of Hurricane Nora had departed eastward, taking with it the rain which greeted the teams upon their arrival in the Los Angeles Basin, gradually clearing skies ensured near perfect weather conditions for the balance of the weekend. Official practice soon saw cars reaching above 230 mph, and by the end of the first session on Friday, Mauricio Gugelmin had set tongues a-wagging by posting a best of 240.150 mph. By Saturday morning he had raised the ante to a staggering 242.333 (30.142s) aboard his Hollywood Reynard-Mercedes.

A new qualifying procedure saw the cars take to the track in ascending order according to their practice speeds, which virtually guaranteed excitement as the fastest cars remained until last. Andre Ribeiro, third in line after encountering all manner of problems in practice, set the early standard at 235.717 mph. Nine cars later, Michel Jourdain Jr. was the first to eclipse Ribeiro's mark with a most impressive 236.603.

Raul Boesel and Greg Moore both came close but were unable to unseat the Mexican. Then came Bryan Herta, whose first lap

was good for only sixth fastest. Lap two, however, saw the Shell Reynard-Ford go 'P1' at 237.890.

'I'm real happy,' said Herta, 'because that's about as fast as we went in practice, with a tow, so it's good to go that fast on your own.'

Michael Andretti, Scott Pruett and Mark Blundell were unable to match Herta's speed, which set up an exciting climax with just Jimmy Vasser and Gugelmin left to run.

Vasser was the first to go. A huge cheer erupted from the grandstands as he sped across the start/finish line to complete lap one: 238.410 mph. Lap two saw even more speed from the Target Reynard-Honda: 239.222. But Gugelmin rose to the challenge. His final warmup lap took a mere 30.387s (240.379), which the Brazilian comfortably backed up with two more laps over 240.

'The car was just on rails,' said Gugelmin after turning the fastest qualifying lap ever, easily eclipsing both the CART standard set by Mario Andretti at Michigan Speedway in 1993 (234.275) and the IRL record set by Arie Luyendyk (237.498) at Indianapolis in 1996. The field average, incidentally, also set a new record at 233.192, bettering the previous mark of 228.082 at the U.S. 500.

Above: The breathtaking California Speedway, Roger Penske's magnificent new facility at Fontana, provided a spectacular setting for the season finale.

Right: The photographers get a taste of the champagne as Mark Blundell and Adrian Fernandez celebrate their success.

Photos: Michael C. Brown

A SPECTACULAR season of competition in the PPG CART World Series was brought to an appropriate conclusion at the Penske family's state-of-the-art California Speedway. Five drivers remained strongly in contention as the Marlboro 500 Presented by Toyota entered its last 100 miles, and the final margin of victory was a scant 0.847 seconds. Coincidentally, the same pair who had fought to the finish three weeks earlier on the altogether different Laguna Seca Raceway road course once again did battle on the two-mile, high-banked oval. This time, however, it was Mark Blundell's Motorola Reynard-Mercedes which emerged narrowly ahead of Jimmy Vasser's #1 Target Reynard-Honda.

'This feels so great to win the first [CART] race here,' said an elated Blundell after snaring his third victory of the season, 'and it also means our team won races on all of the different circuits, from superspeedways to road courses to street courses. This one is just fantastic.'

The thrilling finish came in stark contrast to the caution-filled early stages of the 500-mile season finale. The drama began even before the green flag, when the Toyota engine in Juan Fangio's Castrol/Jockey/AAR Reynard erupted into flames on the pace lap. It was not an auspicious beginning. The remaining 26 cars – already minus newly crowned PPG Cup champion Alex Zanardi and Rookie of the Year Patrick Carpentier, both of whom crashed heavily during practice and were unable to take part – trailed around behind the pace car for 10 laps while the oily mess was cleaned up. Then, just a couple of laps after the restart, Paul Tracy's miserable second half of the season ended abruptly when he spun and crashed in Turn Four.

'The car was loose from the start and I was just hanging back,' said the Canadian, who was bruised but otherwise uninjured. 'Midway through the corner I started sliding and the back end came around.'

Following another lengthy cleanup, Mauricio Gugelmin took off into the lead from the pole, chased by Vasser and third qualifier Bryan Herta, once again the top Goodyear exponent in Team Rahal's Shell Reynard-Ford. Early movers, however, included Michel Jourdain Jr., once again running well in Payton/Coyne's Herdez Reynard-Ford as he progressed from fifth to third, and Michael Andretti, who demoted the young Mexican on lap 25 and quickly set his sights on Vasser.

Andretti slipped into second place on lap 35, taking advantage of some slower traffic, and was hot on Gugelmin's tail when the yellow lights flashed on again on lap 40. Arnd Meier, already one lap down in Project Indy's Lola-Ford, became the latest victim in Turn Four, and as the young German's car spun around, veteran Arie Luyendyk, substituting for the absent Zanardi, was left with absolutely nowhere to go. The Dutchman's Target Reynard collected the hapless Meier, then slammed headlong into the wall. It was a massive impact. Luyendyk was knocked briefly unconscious but soon regained his senses and was alert enough to wave to the crowd as he was carried toward the waiting ambulance.

During the ensuing caution, Marlboro Team Penske's day ended when Al Unser Jr. pulled into the pits, his Penske-Mercedes trailing an ominous cloud of smoke due to a broken exhaust header.

Andretti took off into the lead at the restart, having slipped past Gugelmin during the first round of pit stops, while the racy Jourdain nipped briefly ahead of Vasser. Soon, though, Jourdain was slipping backward, his Firestone tires badly blistered inside just a handful of laps. It was to be a recurring theme for much of the afternoon.

'The tires got too hot,' declared Bridgestone/Firestone Director of Motorsports Al Speyer. 'It's difficult to hit the mark exactly right every time and we missed the mark a little today.'

Several other Firestone runners suffered an identical problem. Nevertheless, after examining the tires closely, the Firestone engineers were able to assure the teams it was a problem with the rubber compound rather than the construction. Simply, in the hot California sunshine – and with temperatures in pit lane reaching over 100 degrees – the tires were overheating. But they were not slowing down: 'There were a couple of problems but the track was very hot today,' said Blundell, who finished the race with a long line of blisters around the circumference of his right-rear Firehawk radial. 'Overall, the Firestone tires were still great, very consistent. They got us to the checkered flag and that's what counts.'

As Jourdain slipped down the order, his place was taken by Andre Ribeiro – also Firestone-shod, of course – in the Tasman team's LCI/Marlboro Reynard-Honda. The Brazilian had started only 11th but quickly worked his way forward.

On lap 84, Ribeiro drove past Gugelmin in Turn One, then almost immediately assumed the lead as Andretti pulled onto pit lane for routine

197

Zanardi and Carpentier ruled out after crashes

Newly crowned PPG CART World Series champion Alex Zanardi was unable to take part in the final race of the season after being involved in two devastating crashes during practice on Friday. The first incident came toward the end of the first session when Patrick Carpentier lost control of his Alumax Reynard-Mercedes in Turn Four and slammed backward into the outside wall. Zanardi was unable to avoid the wreckage and also took a heavy hit.

Carpentier, who was knocked briefly unconscious, spent a night in the hospital and was released the following morning. He did not start the race but still clinched Jim Trueman Rookie of the Year honors – the second time in five years that Tony Bettenhausen's team has secured the award.

Zanardi hopped out of his wrecked car unscathed and returned to the track later in the afternoon in his backup Target Reynard-Honda, only to lose control in a virtual mirror image of Carpentier's earlier crash. Once again, Zanardi emerged shaken but not physically injured. Later in the evening, however, Zanardi felt dizzy and was taken to the CART Medical Center. He was diagnosed as having suffered a mild concussion. After a further examination in the morning, he was denied medical clearance to drive.

As soon as team owner Chip Ganassi heard the news, he contacted Arie Luyendyk, who drove for the Target team in 1993 and had been contesting the Indy Racing League for the previous two years. The popular Dutchman arrived on Saturday afternoon and within 15 laps had posted a best time of 225 mph. He became more comfortable during the half-hour warmup on Sunday morning and worked his way up to 234.944 mph, fifth quickest in the session.

'It's not hard to pick it up,' said Luyendyk. 'The car's really good. It's just like riding a bicycle.'

Luyendyk (below), though, fared no better than Zanardi as he crashed heavily into the same Turn Four wall which had claimed Ganassi's other two cars on Friday. Fortunately, after a thorough checkup in the hospital, he was released later in the evening with a clean bill of health.

Left: Robby Gordon made a surprise return to the CART series in place of Dario Franchitti. His eighth-place finish represented the Hogan team's best result of a frustrating year.

Below left: The class of '97 gathers for an end-of-term photo. Sadly, the PPG Cup champion, Alex Zanardi, was unable to race following a crash during practice.

Patience rewarded. P.J. Jones *(bottom)* finally joined the list of points scorers with 10th place in Dan Gurney's Castrol/Jockey Reynard-Toyota.

Fernandez saves the best until last

ADRIAN Fernandez posted one of the single most impressive performances of the entire season as he guided Steve Horne's previously unloved Tecate/Quaker State Lola T97/00 to a superb third-place finish in the season finale.

'It was a great race, a great way to end the year,' said the delighted Mexican, who suffered through untold misery during the season, especially after Tasman teammate Andre Ribeiro took delivery of a new Reynard in midseason and immediately left Fernandez trailing in his wake. 'It was a very hard year for us mentally, but we worked hard all year and never gave up.'

Not surprisingly, Fernandez's confidence was at a low ebb prior to the final race of the season. Lola had continually produced new parts, each of which was supposed to improve the car's handling characteristics; but none had the desired effect. And here he was contemplating the conclusion of a dismal campaign – and certainly not relishing the prospect of turning laps in excess of 230 mph!

A new underbody, however, provided a remarkable transformation. And once Fernandez managed to convince himself of the revised car's totally new – and, at last, predictable – handling characteristics, he steadily moved forward after starting 14th.

'The car worked well all weekend,' said Fernandez, 'and the new undertray made it stable in traffic. This is the best surprise we could ever get. We have been coming to the tracks with a lot of new pieces and nothing seemed to work until now. The car wasn't super-fast but it was good in traffic.

'It has been very hard for the sponsors, and very hard for my career,' he continued. 'It's been very frustrating to be in the back, but this is a great result for us. It just shows that if you have the equipment, you can do the job. '

Bottom: The brake rotors of Bobby Rahal's Miller Lite Reynard-Ford glow as he cuts his speed from over 230 mph on his way to the pits for routine service.

service. Ribeiro, his car handling perfectly, stayed out for an additional four laps before making his second pit stop, then resumed with around a three-second advantage over the Kmart/Texaco Havoline Swift-Ford. Unfortunately, yet another strong run for Andretti ended less than 20 laps later due to a broken heat-exchanger.

'Just like Michigan, we had a car capable of winning,' related the disappointed Andretti, who parked his Swift rather than risk a blown engine as the temperatures began to climb dangerously. 'There was definitely more in the car than I was utilizing, but for 500-mile races you have to conserve the car.'

Greg Moore relinquished third position when he brought the Player's/Forsythe Reynard-Mercedes into the pits on lap 110 to change some blistered tires. Five laps later, the PacWest pair, Gugelmin and Blundell, also pulled onto pit lane. All three fell a lap behind the flying Ribeiro, who was having no such problems. And when the yellow lights flashed on for the fourth time, on lap 119, only three cars remained on the lead lap with Ribeiro. Two of them, Vasser and Gil de Ferran's Valvoline/Cummins Reynard-Honda – the highest-placed Goodyear car – were exactly where one would expect them to be, running solidly and consistently. The third car, though, was none other than Ribeiro's Tasman teammate Adrian Fernandez, who was driving a brilliant race

aboard his previously troublesome Tecate/Quaker State Lola.

Fernandez, indeed, had moved up quietly into second place, enjoying by far his best race of the season. Sadly, he, too, encountered tire problems shortly after the restart.

'The car started to get really loose and Steve [Horne] made a good call to bring me in,' related the Mexican. The unscheduled stop, on lap 149, relegated Fernandez to 10th. Nevertheless, he continued to charge hard and wound up a sensational third at the finish. 'To be able to finish like this, with the problems we have had, is really a great result for everyone.'

Gugelmin, Moore and Blundell continued to have problems, leaving Ribeiro to gradually pull away in the lead. By lap 191, only de Ferran remained on the lead lap. But then, 10 laps later, Ribeiro suddenly slowed as he crossed the start/finish line. He was out of fuel!

Ribeiro managed to coast around to his pit, but not without losing a great deal of time. He emerged from the pits in sixth, a lap behind the new leader, Gugelmin. And boy, was he mad! Ribeiro drove as hard as he could, anxiously trying to regain the lead lap, only to lose control on the exit of Turn Two.

'It is unfortunate because this should have been our race,' said Ribeiro after making relatively light contact with the inside retaining wall.

'We had a few obstacles but the car was really handling well.'

The final caution of the day set up an intriguing fight to the finish with six cars on the lead lap and just 36 laps remaining. De Ferran actually held the point, but his engine was fading fast and he fell to sixth at the finish.

Gugelmin blew past de Ferran at the restart and soon built a healthy advantage of four seconds over Moore. Gugelmin, though, suffered yet another blistered rear tire. On lap 232 he brought his Hollywood car onto pit lane one more time. The delay dropped him to a frustrated fourth at the end.

So Moore took over the point – until lap 240, when his Mercedes blew comprehensively going into Turn One. Vasser and Blundell, close behind, both lifted instinctively in expectation of one more full-course caution. But the signal never came. The track stayed green.

'From a driver's standpoint, in every situation like this I have ever been in, there has been a yellow,' said an aggrieved Vasser, who reacted fractionally after Blundell to the realization there was going to be no caution. '[Moore] blew big-time, there was flame all over. I slowed, downshifted two gears and Mark went by me.'

Sure enough, Blundell accelerated past Vasser into Turn Three. 'I just got the hammer down,' said Blundell. 'It's tough to go into Turn One committed without knowing if there was [fluid] down on the race track. But I did!'

Vasser chased for all he was worth in the remaining 10 laps as both leaders turned laps in excess of 234 mph. But 'Billy Bob' Blundell was not to be denied his first oval-track triumph: 'It was a great race,' he said. 'Jimmy faltered and we made the move and the rest is history.'

Photos: Michael C. Brown

FONTANA SNIPPETS

• OMEGA, the world-renowned Swiss watch company which was appointed official timekeeper of the PPG CART World Series at the start of the 1997 season, brings a state-of-the-art INFORMATION SYSTEM to every round of the series. Operated by a team of sports timing specialists, the OMEGA Timing and Scoring System provides race officials, teams, press and television with instantaneous information concerning on-track activities as well as statistical information about all aspects of the CART and Indy Lights series.

• Unofficial testing at California Speedway produced some impressive SPEEDS, led by Mauricio Gugelmin at better than 236 mph. Come race weekend, however, the speeds were even more sensational, primarily due to the fact that OMEGA's precise measurement of the track – taken midway across the racing surface – revealed a track length of 2.029 miles, slightly more than the presumed distance of two miles. Paradoxically, most of the cars' on-board data-gathering systems displayed a true lap distance of a fraction *under* two miles . . .

• At each race, the winner of the MARLBORO POLE AWARD earned a special key. Immediately following qualifying on Saturday afternoon at Fontana, all of the season's pole-sitters gathered to see whose key would match the ignition of a brand-new Mercedes-Benz E420 Sport. Bryan Herta was the popular winner.

• Alex Zanardi and Jimmy Vasser raised a total of $46,275 toward construction of Target House at ST. JUDE CHILDREN'S RESEARCH HOSPITAL in Memphis, Tenn., as part of a season-long charitable donation. Prior to qualifying, patients Heidi McKinney of Dalton, Ga., and Jason Hardy, of Arlington, Tenn., presented the drivers with two specially painted helmets *(as left)*, after winning a design competition.

• JUAN FANGIO II qualified at a more-than-respectable 231.262 mph in his Reynard-Toyota – faster, surprisingly, than the two Marlboro Penske-Mercedes of Paul Tracy and Al Unser Jr.

• The sale of the financially troubled LOLA CARS to Irish businessman/racer Martin Birrane was completed prior to the season finale. A double celebration was in order after Adrian Fernandez took the Tasman team's hitherto troublesome Tecate/Quaker State Lola T97/00-Honda to a magnificent third-place finish.

• Immediately after the race, both Team Rahal and Della Penna Motorsports revealed they would switch allegiance from GOODYEAR tires to FIRESTONE in 1998.

PPG CART WORLD SERIES • ROUND 17
MARLBORO 500
PRESENTED BY TOYOTA

CALIFORNIA SPEEDWAY, FONTANA, CALIFORNIA

SEPTEMBER 28, 250 laps – 507.250 miles

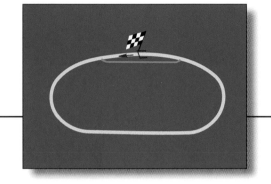

Place	Driver (Nat.)	No.	Team Sponsors Car-Engine	Tires	Q Speed	Q Time	Q Pos.	Laps	Time/Status	Ave. (mph)	Pts.
1	Mark Blundell (GB)	18	PacWest Racing Group Motorola Reynard 97I-Mercedes	FS	236.067	30.942s	8	250	3h 02m 42.620s	166.575	20
2	Jimmy Vasser (USA)	1	Target/Chip Ganassi Racing Reynard 97I-Honda	FS	239.222	30.534s	2	250	3h 02m 43.467s	166.562	16
3	Adrian Fernandez (MEX)	32	Tasman Tecate Beer/Quaker State Oil Lola T97/00-Honda	FS	234.680	31.125s	14	249	Running		14
4	Mauricio Gugelmin (BR)	17	PacWest Racing Group Hollywood Reynard 97I-Mercedes	FS	240.942	30.316s	1	249	Running		13
5	Bobby Rahal (USA)	7	Team Rahal Miller Lite Reynard 97I-Ford XD	GY	235.816	30.975s	10	249	Running		10
6	Gil de Ferran (BR)	5	Walker Valvoline/Cummins Reynard 97I-Honda	GY	235.360	31.035s	12	249	Running		8
7	Scott Pruett (USA)	20	Patrick Brahma Sports Team Reynard 97I-Ford XD	FS	236.810	30.845s	4	248	Running		6
8	Robby Gordon (USA)	9	Hogan Motor Leasing Reynard 97I-Mercedes	FS	235.034	31.078s	13	247	Running		5
9	Christian Fittipaldi (BR)	11	Newman/Haas Kmart/Budweiser Swift 007.i-Ford XD	GY	234.078	31.205s	16	247	Running		4
10	P.J. Jones (USA)	98	All American Racers Castrol/Jockey Reynard 97I-Toyota RV8B	GY	228.298	31.995s	21	244	Running		3
11	Parker Johnstone (USA)	27	Team KOOL Green Reynard 97I-Honda	FS	234.236	31.184s	15	243	Running		2
12	Max Papis (I)	25	Arciero-Wells Racing MCI Reynard 97I-Toyota RV8B	FS	no speed	no time	25	242	Running		1
13	Greg Moore (CDN)	99	Forsythe Player's Ltd./Indeck Reynard 97I-Mercedes	FS	236.297	30.912s	6	240	Engine		
14	*Gualter Salles (BR)	77	Davis Racing Indusval/Marlboro Reynard 97I-Ford XD	GY	no speed	no time	26	238	Running		
15	Richie Hearn (USA)	21	Della Penna Ralphs/Food 4 Less Lola T97/00-Ford XD	GY	224.861	32.484s	22	238	Running		
16	Dennis Vitolo (USA)	34	Payton/Coyne SmithKline Beecham Reynard 97I-Ford XD	FS	232.004	31.484s	17	231	Running		
17	Andre Ribeiro (BR)	31	Tasman Motorsports LCI/Marlboro Reynard 97I-Honda	FS	235.717	30.988s	11	207	Accident		
18	Michel Jourdain Jr. (MEX)	19	Payton/Coyne Herdez/Viva Mexico! Reynard 97I-Ford XD	FS	236.603	30.872s	5	195	Handling		
19	Michael Andretti (USA)	6	Newman/Haas Kmart/Texaco Havoline Swift 007.i-Ford XD	GY	236.289	30.913s	7	104	Overheating		
20	Raul Boesel (BR)	40	Patrick Brahma Sports Team Reynard 97I-Ford XD	FS	235.846	30.971s	9	83	Electrical		
21	Bryan Herta (USA)	8	Team Rahal Shell Reynard 97I-Ford XD	GY	237.890	30.705s	3	80	Engine		
22	Al Unser Jr. (USA)	2	Marlboro Team Penske Penske PC26-Mercedes	GY	229.980	31.761s	20	44	Exhaust		
23	Hiro Matsushita (J)	24	Arciero-Wells Panasonic/Duskin Reynard 97I-Toyota RV8B	FS	221.272	33.011s	23	40	Suspension		
24	Arie Luyendyk (NL)	4	Target/Chip Ganassi Racing Reynard 97I-Honda	FS	no speed	no time	27	39	Accident		
25	*Arnd Meier (D)	64	Project Indy JAG/Marcelo/Hawaiian Tropic Lola T97/00-Ford XD	GY	217.438	33.593s	24	38	Accident		
26	Paul Tracy (CDN)	3	Marlboro Team Penske Penske PC26-Mercedes	GY	230.401	31.703s	19	12	Accident		
NS	Juan Fangio II (RA)	36	All American Racers Castrol/Jockey Reynard 97I-Toyota RV8B	GY	231.262	31.585s	18	–	Engine		
NS	Alex Zanardi (I)	4	Target/Chip Ganassi Racing Reynard 97I-Honda	FS	no speed	no time	–	–	Accident in practice		
NS	*Patrick Carpentier (CDN)	16	Bettenhausen Alumax Aluminum Reynard 97I-Mercedes	GY	no speed	no time	–	–	Accident in practice		

* denotes Rookie driver

Caution flags: Laps 0–10, engine/Fangio; laps 13–21, accident/Tracy; laps 40–50, accident/Meier and Luyendyk; laps 119–124, debris; laps 209–213, accident/Ribeiro. **Total:** five for 41 laps.

Lap leaders: Mauricio Gugelmin, 1–43 (43 laps); Richie Hearn, 44–47 (4 laps); Michael Andretti, 48–83 (36 laps); Andre Ribeiro, 84–87 (4 laps); Jimmy Vasser, 88–89 (2 laps); Ribeiro, 90–161 (72 laps); Gil de Ferran, 162–163 (2 laps); Ribeiro, 164–201 (38 laps); de Ferran, 202–204 (3 laps); Gugelmin, 205–210 (6 laps); de Ferran, 211–214 (4 laps); Gugelmin, 215–231 (17 laps); Greg Moore, 232–239 (8 laps); Mark Blundell, 240–250 (11 laps). **Totals:** Ribeiro, 114 laps; Gugelmin, 66 laps; Andretti, 36 laps; Blundell, 11 laps; de Ferran, 9 laps; Moore, 8 laps; Hearn, 4 laps; Vasser, 2 laps.

Fastest race lap: Greg Moore, 30.900s, 236.388 mph on lap 83 (establishes record).

Final championship positions: 1 Zanardi, 195; **2** de Ferran, 162; **3** Vasser, 144; **4** Gugelmin, 132; **5** Tracy, 121; **6** Blundell, 115; **7** Moore, 111; **8** Andretti, 108; **9** Pruett, 102; **10** Boesel, 91; **11** Herta, 72; **12** Rahal, 70; **13** Unser Jr., 67; **14** Ribeiro, 45; **15** Fittipaldi, 42; **16** Johnstone, 36; **17** Carpentier and Fernandez, 27; **19** Moreno, 16; **20** Salles, Hearn and Franchitti, 10; **23** Fangio, 9; **24** Papis, 8; **25** Vitolo, 6; **26** Gordon, 5; **27** Matsushita, 4; **28** Jones, 3; **29** Danner, Jourdain and Meier, 1.

OMEGA
OFFICIAL TIMEKEEPER OF CART

dazzling LIGHTS

PPG-FIRESTONE INDY LIGHTS CHAMPIONSHIP REVIEW *by Jeremy Shaw*

THREE extraordinarily talented young Brazilian drivers took the PPG-Firestone Indy Lights Championship by storm in 1997. Any one of the trio would have made a worthy champion. In the final reckoning, however, Tony Kanaan *(above right)* emerged as top dog to ensure the third series title in only four attempts for Steve Horne's Tasman Motorsports Group. Teammate Helio Castro-Neves *(right)* finished a scant four points adrift, while Brian Stewart Racing's Cristiano da Matta was close behind in third place at the end of an intensely hard-fought 13-race championship.

The outcome, fittingly, remained undecided until the final lap of the final race at California Speedway. Only the Tasman twins were in a position to win the crown, with Kanaan having overcome a large deficit with just four races remaining to eke out an 11-point advantage prior to the decider. Both were well to the fore in the early stages of a spectacular event which saw the entire field jostling for position in one massive, drafting pack. On lap 33, however, Kanaan's car sustained a flat rear tire after making contact with Robby Unser coming off Turn Two.

Castro-Neves was in the lead as the caution lights flashed on, and he seemed to be in the catbird seat as Kanaan rejoined after a pit stop in 15th position – out of the points. Kanaan, though, fought up to 11th within a few laps, while Castro-Neves was jostled back to sixth as the battle for the lead continued to rage. The pendulum had swung back in favor of Kanaan.

When the race eventually finished under caution, due to another incident, Castro-Neves was in fourth place, Kanaan ninth. Those vital four points were enough.

'Life is full of surprises,' declared Kanaan in his heavily accented and rapidly improving English. 'Before

Trois-Rivieres, when I was 29 points behind Helio, I was thinking, "OK, the championship's gone, [but] I'm going to try to be as close as I can in the points to [finish] second;" and then life surprised me again, so it's a nice surprise.'

A veteran of karting and Italian Formula 3, the 22-year-old Sao Paulo native overcame a rocky start to his season brought about by a pinched nerve in his leg which prevented him from maximizing his potential during preseason testing. Wisely, Kanaan concentrated on picking up points in the early races. He first showed signs of his true competitiveness at Savannah, where he qualified on the front row, only to be forced out by a broken throttle spring. Then, following a disappointing 10th at Gateway, he recorded a sequence of seven consecutive podium results to overcome his teammate's points tally and set up the dramatic season finale.

Castro-Neves, meanwhile, began his year with three poles and two wins in the first four races. He fell to 16th in the Homestead opener after brushing the wall, and later in the season was involved in incidents both at Trois-Rivieres and Vancouver. His

impetuosity ultimately cost him the championship.

'My teammate Tony was pretty good, he was strong the whole season,' said Castro-Neves of his close friend and rival. 'I commit a lot of mistakes and from these mistakes I am learning. Of course, it's tough but it's OK, that's racing.'

Da Matta, too, was left to ponder what might have been. The 23-year-old put a disappointing year of Formula 3000 behind him by following countryman Gualter Salles to Brian Stewart Racing, and after a torrid start at Homestead, he soon began to make an impression. Indeed, da Matta finished second at Long Beach, then scored a brilliant victory on the Nazareth oval in only his third Indy Lights start. The street courses effectively put paid to da Matta's title hopes as he tangled with Robby Unser in Savannah, clipped a wall in Detroit, then, cruelly, ran out of fuel while running well in Toronto.

Still, da Matta easily claimed KOOL Rookie of the Year honors and will start the 1998 season as a heavy favorite for the title after signing with Tasman Motorsports.

Fourth in the final standings repre-

sented a disappointment for defending series champion David Empringham. The personable Canadian began his defense of the title in magnificent style, emerging from behind to win at Homestead, but thereafter things rarely seemed to go his way. He nevertheless displayed his qualities by rising from 25th on the grid (following a crash in practice) to ninth at Nazareth and from 14th to second at Milwaukee. So effective was Empringham in the four oval races, in fact, that he claimed the $10,000 Bosch Speedway Challenge (for the second year running) by a four-point margin over da Matta. A former two-time champion in Toyota Atlantic, Empringham once again proved he deserves a shot in the premier PPG Cup series.

Player's/Forsythe teammate Lee Bentham, also a graduate of Toyota Atlantic, displayed some promise, highlighted by a win at Gateway (his first-ever professional triumph), although the race was run under caution for much of the distance due to a persistent drizzle.

Sixth and seventh in the points were claimed by Team KOOL Green's Chris Simmons and Mark Hotchkis. The two Americans were curiously inconsistent but clearly talented. Both qualified on the pole and led races, but neither could make the breakthrough into Victory Circle.

Rookie Clint Mears, meanwhile, won twice for his family-run team. Yet another Toyota Atlantic grad, Mears was out-classed on the road and street courses – three times, indeed, he started dead last on the grid – but on the ovals he was awesome. No doubt, the extensive experience of his dad, three-time PPG Cup champion Rick Mears, proved invaluable. The younger Mears led from flag to flag at Milwaukee, and after winning the pole in Fontana, he fell as low as ninth but still came back to claim the victory.

Above: Running with his family team, Clint Mears shone on the ovals but struggled elsewhere.

Left: Tasman teammates Tony Kanaan and Helio Castro-Neves topped the points table at the end of a highly competitive season.

Below: Team KOOL Green drivers Naoki Hattori, Chris Simmons and Mark Hotchkis notched up three pole positions between them but failed to score a win.

Fourth place overall did little to advance the career of defending champion David Empringham (below), but Cristiano da Matta (bottom) is strongly tipped to take the title in 1998 after finishing third in '97.

1997 PPG-FIRESTONE INDY LIGHTS CHAMPIONSHIP

Final point standings after 13 races:

Pos.	Driver (Nat.), Sponsor(s)-Team	Pts.
1	Tony Kanaan (BR), Marlboro/Davene/Brahma/MTV-Tasman Motorsports Group	156
2	Helio Castro-Neves (BR), Marlboro/Kibon/Hudson/Brahma/MTV-Tasman Motorsports Group	152
3	Cristiano da Matta (BR), Medley Industria Farmaceutica/STP-Brian Stewart Racing	141
4	David Empringham (CDN), Player's/Indeck-Forsythe Racing	107
5	Lee Bentham (CDN), Player's/Indeck-Forsythe Racing	88
6	Chris Simmons (USA), KOOL/Klein Tools-Team KOOL Green	88
7	Mark Hotchkis (USA), KOOL/Klein Tools-Team KOOL Green	74
8	Clint Mears (USA), Penske Auto Centers/Mobil 1-Team Mears	53
9	Hideki Noda (J), Tenoras/Greddy-Indy Regency Racing	51
10	Airton Dare (BR), Banestado/STP-Brian Stewart Racing	51
11	Christophe Tinseau (F), Mi-Jack/E.S.I/Rose/City Bird-Conquest Racing	49
12	Fredrik Larsson (S), Marlboro-Stefan Johansson Motorsports	43
13	Luiz Garcia Jr. (BR), PetroBras-Dorricott Racing	38
14	Didier Andre (F), Playstation/Mack-Autosport Racing	35
15	Robby Unser (USA), Motorola/ADT Automotive-PacWest Racing Group	35
16	Naoki Hattori (J), KOOL/Klein Tools-Team KOOL Green	32
17	Geoff Boss (USA), Cross Pens/Omniglow Corporation/Aldila-Team Medlin	30
18	Sergio Paese (BR), Shopping Construcao Maringa-FRE/Primus Racing	27
19	David DeSilva (USA), DeSilva Gates/Men's Fitness/Exide-Lucas Place Motorsports	17
20	Oswaldo Negri Jr. (BR), Banco Sofisa-Genoa Racing	15

Note: All drivers ran identical Lola T97/20-Buick V6 cars on Firestone tires

Performance Chart

Driver	Wins	Poles	Fastest laps	Most laps led
Helio Castro-Neves	3	4	2	5
Cristiano da Matta	3	1	4	2
Tony Kanaan	2	3	–	2
Clint Mears	2	2	1	1
Hideki Noda	1	–	1	–
Lee Bentham	1	–	–	1
David Empringham	1	–	–	–
Chris Simmons	–	2	–	1
Mark Hotchkis	–	1	2	1
David DeSilva	–	–	1	–
Sergio Paese	–	–	1	–
Christophe Tinseau	–	–	1	–

Photos: Michael C. Brown

Hideki Noda not only became the seventh different race winner during what proved to be the most hotly contested season in Indy Lights history, he also was the first Japanese driver ever to win a CART-sanctioned event. The amiable 28-year-old made light of extremely difficult conditions at Portland and even passed Castro-Neves around the outside line en route to the checkered flag with Sal Incandela's Tenoras/Greddy/Indy Regency Racing Lola.

Teenaged Brazilian Airton Dare was the only driver to finish every one of the 13 races. The rookie had precious little experience prior to joining Brian Stewart's team, but he often showed a promising turn of speed during the races and completed all but three of the season's total of 628 laps. Next year he will join teammate da Matta in switching across to the Tasman team and most likely will be a man to watch.

The average grid size rose to a record 26 in 1997, four more than during the previous season, and the series reached a new level of competitiveness. Several fledgling teams joined the fray, most notably Conquest Racing, owned and run by 1991 series champion Eric Bachelart, and Stefan Johansson Motorsports, fielded by the former F1/CART racer who also kept his hand in by winning the 1997 Le Mans 24 Hours race with Joest Racing.

Conquest entered a car for Christophe Tinseau, winner of the final Formula 3000 race of the 1996 season at Hockenheim, and after a difficult beginning, the Frenchman began to make rapid progress in concert with newly hired race engineer Craig Perkins. Tinseau scored a best finish of third at Trois-Rivieres. Johansson's team was quick out of the box, although reigning Barber Dodge Pro Series champion Fredrik Larsson was involved in an inordinate number of accidents. The talented Swede finally fell out with his countryman – and mentor – and was shown the door after nine races.

Lucas Place Motorsports, a new combination formed by ex-Tasman crew member Chris Lucas and Ohio State University graduate Eric Place, showed best on the ovals. David DeSilva frequently failed to deliver in the races, however, and finally left the team. He was replaced for the final three events by Brian (grandson of '50s sports car legend Briggs) Cunningham, who led strongly in the finale at Fontana before crashing.

Luiz Garcia Jr. and Bob Dorricott Jr. (Dorricott Racing), Didier Andre (Autosport Racing), Robby Unser (PacWest Racing Group), Sergio Paese (FRE/Primus) and Geoff Boss (Team Medlin) also shone on occasion, but none on a consistent basis. In all, 35 drivers attempted to start at least one race, and with PPG Cup stalwart Bobby Rahal seeking to field yet another new team for up-and-coming young American Mike Borkowski, the Indy Lights series looks set for even further expansion in 1998.

Suddenly, your whole future flashes in front of you.

If you want a quick look at CART's future, check out the PPG-Firestone Indy Lights Championship today. More Indy Lights graduates raced and won in the 1997 PPG CART World Series than ever before. Paul Tracy and Greg Moore combined for five-straight wins while Bryan Herta won poles at Mid-Ohio and Laguna Seca. This trio of former Indy Lights champs anchored a full-time PPG Cup lineup of winners from CART's "Official Development Series" that also included Andre Ribeiro, Adrian Fernandez, PJ Jones, Juan Fangio II and Gualter Salles. That's more than a quarter of CART's 1997 starting field, and there's plenty more where they've come from. If you want to be part of CART's future today in the PPG-Firestone Indy Lights Championship, call Roger Bailey in the USA at (248) 528-3470

PPG Firestone INDY LIGHTS® CHAMPIONSHIP

barron's
TITLE

by Jeremy Shaw

Painted by CORBY Concepts

ALEX Barron was among a large and enthusiastic group of rookie drivers entering the KOOL/Toyota Atlantic Championship with high hopes at the beginning of the 1997 season. The young man from Vista, Calif. had accumulated impressive credentials during a long career in karting, but following one fairly mediocre season in Formula Ford 2000, during which he displayed some promise but achieved little in the way of tangible results, he was not expected to emerge as a serious threat for the title . . . not even after signing on with the crack Lynx Racing organization, which in 1996 thoroughly dominated the series with gifted French-Canadian Patrick Carpentier. But Barron, clearly, had not read the script.

His season began poorly, the Californian being sidelined by a broken transmission in the first race at Homestead and then losing time in the pits at Long Beach after tangling with pole-sitter Case Montgomery. Two races, then, and no points – but he bounced back sensationally on the tricky one-mile oval at Nazareth, where he qualified on the pole and led all the way.

'The key to that race was the fact I was able to go flat-out through Turns One and Two at the restarts and everyone else had to lift,' said Barron. 'The car was just perfect. I think it helped us that that track is almost like a road course, with the variety of corners and the elevation changes, and we had a good setup from the start.

'So far as the win was concerned, I always knew it would happen, but when it did, that gives you an extra boost of confidence because now you've actually done it. It always seems like your first win is the hardest.'

Barron carried on the good work by winning from the pole next time out on the Milwaukee Mile oval. He wasn't quite so convincing on the next two temporary circuits, starting fifth at Montreal and sixth at Cleveland, but each time he fought through to finish on the podium. The consistency served him admirably. And by the end of the season, three more victories at Mid-Ohio, Road America and Laguna Seca were enough to secure the 27-year-old Barron's position as a thoroughly deserving champion.

Six other drivers remained in contention through much of the season, although ultimately the man who pushed Barron hardest was his Lynx Racing Scholarship teammate, Memo Gidley. A graduate of karting, Formula Ford 2000 and the Barber Dodge Pro Series, Gidley also suffered one mechanical failure during the 12-race

season – in the final round at Laguna Seca, soon after he had taken the lead from Barron.

In the meantime, Gidley underscored his potential by winning both in Toronto, where he carved impressively through from sixth on the grid in a race peppered by full-course cautions, and in Vancouver, where he led convincingly from the pole. Gidley's

two north-of-the-border victories were enough to win the four-race Player's Challenge series by a margin of 67 points to 56 over Barron.

Third and fourth in the final points table went to Player's/Forsythe teammates Alexandre Tagliani and Bertrand Godin. The pair of French-Canadians each won on home soil, with Godin triumphing in front of a massive crowd

in Montreal for the Canadian Grand Prix and Tagliani securing the spoils in historic Trois-Rivieres. Series sophomore Tagliani also won the high-profile event at Long Beach, while Godin added another victory in front of the CART crowd in Cleveland.

Case Montgomery, by contrast, suffered a disastrous time. The experienced Californian began the year as

Alex Barron *(right)* claimed the title in convincing style after a disappointing start to the season. His main challenger was Lynx Racing teammate Memo Gidley *(bottom right)*, whose performances in the Canadian rounds of the series gave him victory in the Player's Challenge.

to Bill Fickling's P1 Racing Ralt RT41. Portuguese rookie Barbosa, a veteran of Formula 3 competition in Europe, claimed two seconds with RDS Motorsports, while Lazzaro never really gelled with veteran entrant Pierre Phillips and was unable to build upon a win and a second from the first two races in his Platinum Sound Ralt. Schroeder, meanwhile, after finishing runner-up to Carpentier in '96, was hoping to go one better this year after switching to a new team put together by CART team co-owner (with Frank Arciero) Cal Wells

III. But even with the vast engineering experience of Carroll Smith, the team never really got to grips with its Ralts. The only highlight from a dismal campaign for the New Jerseyan was a pole at Mid-Ohio.

Chuck West showed his speed with a couple of poles and a fastest lap, only for his skills to be masked by a series of misfortunes. Tony Ave, Bill Auberlen, Eric Lang, David Pook and Kenny Wilden also showed well during what was without question the most hotly contested season of Toyota Atlantic in many years.

1997 SCCA KOOL/TOYOTA ATLANTIC CHAMPIONSHIP

Final point standings after 12 races:

Pos.	Driver (Nat.), Sponsor(s)-Team Car	Pts.
1	Alex Barron (USA), Victory Circle/Red Line Oil-Lynx Racing Ralt RT41	178
2	Memo Gidley (USA), Lynx Racing Ralt RT41	136
3	Alexandre Tagliani (CDN), Player's/Indeck-Forsythe Racing Ralt RT40	123
4	Bertrand Godin (CDN), Player's/Indeck-Forsythe Racing Ralt RT40	121
5	Case Montgomery (USA), Microsoft/Wall Data-Sandy Dells Racing/Binder Racing	100
6	Steve Knapp (USA), Miller Milling/Manheim/ICG-P1 Racing Ralt RT41	99
7	Joao Barbosa (P), Agip/Toyota/Caetano-RDS Motorsport Ralt RT41	94
8	Anthony Lazzaro (USA), Platinum Sound/BG Products-Phillips Motorsports Ralt RT41	92
9	Jeret Schroeder (USA), MCI Racing-Precision Preparation Inc. Ralt RT41	70
10	Eric Lang (USA), LCI International/ACN-D&L Racing Ralt RT41	64

Performance Chart

Driver	Wins	Poles	Fastest Laps
Alex Barron	5	4	6
Alexandre Tagliani	2	2	2
Memo Gidley	2	1	1
Bertrand Godin	2	1	1
Anthony Lazzaro	1	–	–
Chuck West	–	2	1
Case Montgomery	–	1	–
Jeret Schroeder	–	1	–
Tony Ave	–	–	1

one of the hot favorites for honors, but nothing seemed to go his way. Even a change of teams failed to make any difference. Montgomery took a pair of podium finishes from the first three races (and the pole at Long Beach) with Sandy Dells Racing, and added another couple after switching to Cam Binder's operation. A victory, however, continued to elude him.

Steve Knapp, Joao Barbosa, Anthony Lazzaro and Jeret Schroeder also encountered more than their fair share of frustrations. Knapp, the 1996 FF2000 champion, began solidly with a trio of top-six finishes but didn't show his true potential until late in the season when he hooked up with race engineer (and cousin) Tom Knapp, who finally unlocked the key

RACING ROUND-UP

by Jeremy Shaw

Michael C. Brown

CHRYSLER'S commitment to an otherwise meagerly supported CART-sanctioned Super Touring Championship paid off handsomely in year two as gifted second-generation driver David Donohue *(above)* guided his factory-backed Dodge Stratus to an emphatic series victory. Donohue, whose late father, Mark, was a dominant force in North American road racing in the 1970s, employed a blend of pace and consistency – finishing all but one of the 18 races among the top five – and was able to wrap up the title with one round remaining at Laguna Seca.

'Our entire team has made a championship effort this year and they deserved a championship win,' said the 30-year-old Pennsylvanian, whose only real problems came in getting his PacWest Racing Group-entered Dodge away from the starting line.

'For some reason that's something I've had a problem with all year,' continued Donohue, who had plenty of practice after winning 10 poles. 'I had three or four good starts and the rest were really bad.'

The primary beneficiary from Donohue's largesse was Australian Neil Crompton, who won the opening two races of the season, at Long Beach, in Steve Horne's Tasman Motorsports Honda Accord and claimed four straight at the end of the year, three of them after Donohue had snared the pole. Crompton was the revelation of the year, although he created some ill feeling after punting both Donohue's Dodge and the Honda of America Racing Team Accord of Peter Cunningham off the road in Detroit. Crompton was promptly disqualified and then missed the next round at Portland due to budgetary constraints. Even so, he finished a mere two points behind Cunningham, who took four poles and four wins, in the final championship standings.

PacWest co-owner, manager and driver Dominic Dobson was generally out-paced by Donohue in the second Dodge, although he did win twice. Dobson also seemed to be a magnet for ill-fortune.

Defending champion Randy Pobst never really came to grips with his McLaren-built CEC/Antera BMW but did just enough to outpoint the enthusiastic and consistent Bob Schader, in a 1994 Mazda, for top Independent honors.

Barber Dodge Pro Series

As we closed for press, two races remained in the chase for Skip Barber's $100,000 'Career Enhancement' Award and the accompanying engine lease package for the 1998 PPG-Firestone Indy Lights Championship, worth an additional $50,000. Rino Mastronardi was in the catbird seat, the 26-year-old Italian having used his experience from 1996 to excellent effect by winning five of the first 10 races and establishing a 15-point cushion over fellow sophomore contender Derek Hill. The pair indulged in several entertaining battles, most notably at Road America where they exchanged the lead 10 times before Mastronardi *(below)* emerged victorious.

Both were tipped as potential stars of the future.

Iowan Chris Menninga made significant gains during the season, capped by winning the pole at Laguna Seca. Rhode Island's Andy Boss, younger brother of former series stalwart Geoff Boss, secured his first series victory at Mid-Ohio. Last year's Skip Barber Racing School 'Big Scholarship' winner Nicolas Rondet claimed a fine win at Minneapolis, marking himself as a clear favorite for Rookie of the Year honors. Tony Renna, Rocky Moran Jr. and a pair of Norwegians, Martin Stenshorne and Jarle Gasland, also showed good speed.

Michael C. Brown

1997 BARBER DODGE PRO SERIES
Point standings after 10 of 12 races:

1	Rino Mastronardi (I)	145
2	Derek John Hill (USA)	130
3	Chris Menninga (USA)	110
4	Andy Boss (USA)	109
5	Nicolas Rondet (F)	104
6	Rocky Moran Jr. (USA)	84

1997 CART NORTH AMERICAN SUPER TOURING CHAMPIONSHIP

Final point standings after 18 races:

Pos.	Driver (Nat.), Sponsor(s)-Team Car	Pts.
1	David Donohue (USA), Infinity/Silicon Graphics-PacWest Dodge Stratus	304
2	Peter Cunningham (USA), Red Line Oil-H.A.R.T. Honda Accord	282
3	Neil Crompton (AUS), Labatt Blue/LCI/McCormick Lines-Tasman Honda Accord	280
4	Dominic Dobson (USA), PPG-PacWest Dodge Stratus	230
5	Randy Pobst (USA), CEC/Antera-T.C. Kline Racing BMW 318i	188
6	Bob Schader (USA), Schader Motorsports Mazda 626	185
7	David Welch (USA), Red Auto Leasing-Fastech Racing Ford Mondeo	159
8	Darren Law (USA), INTRAX-Hartong Motorsports BMW 318i	157
9	Forrest Granlund (USA), Red Line Oil-H.A.R.T. BMW/Honda Accord	88
10	Ron Emmick (USA), Metalcraft Pontiac Sunbird/Schader Motorsports Mazda	37

Independents' Challenge:

1	Randy Pobst (USA), CEC/Antera-T.C. Kline Racing BMW 318i	188
2	Bob Schader (USA), Schader Motorsports Mazda 626	185
3	David Welch (USA), Red Auto Leasing-Fastech Racing Ford Mondeo	159

Michelin Cup – The Manufacturers' Championship:

1 Honda, 331; 2 Dodge, 305; 3 Toyota, 26.

Formula Ford 2000

The 1997 United States Formula Ford 2000 National Championship set a new standard for open competition as nine different drivers claimed victory in the first nine races! In fact, the tally might have reached 10 if Matt Sielsky hadn't made a slip on the final lap at Mid-Ohio, handing the win to eventual series champion Zak Morioka's John Hayes-prepped KFC of Brazil Van Diemen. Morioka, only 18 but in his third season of FF2000, made full use of his experience as he garnered top-four finishes from six of the final seven races to put the title beyond reach of 19-year-old Sielsky, who secured a season-high four poles in Dave Conti's Team KOOL Green Van Diemen.

Italian Andrea De Lorenzi was the only other two-time winner, displaying the capabilities of his country's Tatuus chassis. Other outstanding youngsters included Buddy Rice, Andy Lally and Jeff Shafer in the unique Nemesis design.

1997 UNITED STATES FORMULA FORD 2000 NATIONAL CHAMPIONSHIP

Final point standings after 12 races:

1	Zak Morioka (BR), Van Diemen	205	
2	Matt Sielsky (USA), Van Diemen	177	
3	Duncan Dayton (USA), Van Diemen	162	
4	Buddy Rice (USA), Van Diemen	153	
5	Andy Lally (USA), Van Diemen	147	
6	Ryan Hampton (USA), Van Diemen	133	

Mark Weber